INFANCY
IN AMERICA

An Encyclopedia

THE AMERICAN FAMILY

The six titles that make up **The American Family** offer a revitalizing new take on U.S. history, surveying current culture from the perspective of the family and incorporating insights from psychology, sociology, and medicine. Each two-volume, A-to-Z encyclopedia features its own advisory board, editorial slant, and apparatus, including illustrations, bibliography, and index.

Adolescence in America

EDITED BY Jacqueline V. Lerner, Boston College,
and Richard M. Lerner, Tufts University;
Jordan W. Finkelstein, Pennsylvania State University,
Advisory Editor

Boyhood in America

EDITED BY Priscilla Ferguson Clement, Pennsylvania
State University, Delaware County, and Jacqueline S. Reinier,
California State University, Sacramento

The Family in America

EDITED BY Joseph M. Hawes, University of Memphis,
and Elizabeth F. Shores, Little Rock, Arkansas

Girlhood in America

EDITED BY Miriam Forman-Brunell,
University of Missouri, Kansas City

Infancy in America

EDITED BY Alice Sterling Honig, Syracuse University;
Hiram E. Fitzgerald, Michigan State University;
and Holly E. Brophy-Herb, Michigan State University

Parenthood in America

Edited by Lawrence Balter, New York University

INFANCY IN AMERICA

An Encyclopedia

Volume 1
A–I

Alice Sterling Honig
Syracuse University

Hiram E. Fitzgerald
Michigan State University

Holly E. Brophy-Herb
Michigan State University

FOREWORD BY **Joy D. Osofsky, Ph.D.**
*Vice President, Zero to Three—National
Center for Infants, Toddlers, and Families*

A B C ⬤ C L I O
Santa Barbara, California
Denver, Colorado
Oxford, England

Library of Congress Cataloging-in-Publication Data
    Infancy in America : an encyclopedia / edited by Alice Sterling Honig,
Hiram E. Fitzgerald, and Holy E. Brophy-Herb.
      p.   cm. — (The American family)
    Includes bibliographical references and index.
    ISBN 1-57607-220-7 (hardcover : alk. paper); ISBN 1-57607-549-4 (e-book)
    1. Infants—United States—Encyclopedias.   1. Honig, Alice S.   II.
Fitzgerald, Hiram E.   III. Brophy-Herb, Holly.   IV. American family (Santa
Barbara, Calif.)
    HQ774.1528   2001
    305.232'0973'03—dc21

                                                            2001004691

06 05 04 03 02 01   10 9 8 7 6 5 4 3 2 1

ABC-CLIO, Inc.
130 Cremona Drive, P.O. Box 1911
Santa Barbara, California 93116-1911

This book is also available on the World Wide Web as an e-book. Visit
abc-clio.com for details.

This book is printed on acid-free paper ∞.
Manufactured in the United States of America

ABOUT THE EDITORS

Alice Sterling Honig is a pioneer in the training of infancy caregiving. She is professor emerita of child development at Syracuse University and consultant to numerous national programs for infants and toddlers.

Hiram E. Fitzgerald is University Distinguished Professor in the Department of Psychology, Michigan State University.

Holly E. Brophy-Herb is assistant professor in the Department of Family Ecology, Michigan State University.

CONTENTS

A-TO-Z LIST OF ENTRIES

VOLUME 1, A–I

A

Abortion
AB Problem
Accommodation
Acquired Immune Deficiency Syndrome (AIDS)
Action Schemes
Activity Level
Adaptability
Adaptation
Adaptive Behavior
Adjunctive Systems
Adolescent Parenting
Adoption
Affect
Affect Attunement
Affordance
Afterbirth
Age
Ages and Stages Questionnaires
Aggression
Alcohol Effects
Alcoholism
Alternative Birth
Altruism
American Sign Language
Amniocentesis
Amnion
Amniotic Fluid
Amygdala

Anaclitic Depression
Anal Stage
Analgesia
Analogy
Androgens
Anencephaly
Anesthetics
Anger
Anoxia
Anticipatory Grief
Anxiety
Apgar Scale
Apnea
Approach-Withdrawal
Art
Artificial Insemination
Assessment
Assessment, Evaluation, and Programming System
Assessment of Infant Caregivers
Assessment of Infant Environments
Assessment of the Preterm Infant Behavior Scale
Assimilation
Associationism
Associative Memory
Asthma
Attachment
Attention
Attention Deficit Disorder
Attention Span
Atypical Infant
Audiogram
Audition

VOLUME 2, J–Z

J

K

L

M

N

Contributors
and Their Entries

Although all authors listed on the title page deserve credit for the full volume, each was also responsible for specific sections. Of course, all errors in the final copy are the responsibility of the volume editors.

Jason B. Almerigi
Michigan State University
East Lansing, MI
   Neurobiology, Lateralization

Deborah Bailey
Michigan State University
East Lansing, MI
   Bathing, Grandparenthood, Parenting

Lauren R. Barton
Michigan State University
East Lansing, MI
   Bayley Scales, Exploratory Behavior,
   Perception, Sex Differences,
   Research Methods

Holly E. Brophy-Herb (volume editor)
Michigan State University
East Lansing, MI
   Alternative Birth, Birthplans,
   Cosleeping, Discipline, Doula,
   Emotion, Employed Mothers,
   Massage, Motor Development

Angela Casady
Michigan State University
East Lansing, MI
   Child Care: Choosing Quality, Early
   Intervention, Fertility Rates, School
   Readiness, Toys for Tots, Work and
   Family Policy

Hiram E. Fitzgerald (volume editor)
Michigan State University
East Lansing, MI
   Birth Defects, Circumcision, Cortisol,
   Learning, Memory, Midwifery,
   Pacification, Systems Theory,
   Theories of Development

Brooke Bartholomae Foulds
Michigan State University
East Lansing, MI
   Individuals with Disabilities
   Education Act

Julia Haddow
Michigan State University
East Lansing, MI
   Developmental Milestones, Songs

Lauren Julius Harris
Michigan State University
East Lansing, MI
    Lateralization, Neurobiology

Alice Sterling Honig (volume editor)
Syracuse University
Syracuse, NY
    Attachment, Home Visiting,
        Language, Lullabies

Anne M. Jarrett
Michigan State University
East Lansing, MI
    Audiology

Dorothy Elizabeth Jordon
Michigan State University
East Lansing, MI
    Children's Defense Fund, Failure to
        Thrive

Madeleine H. Lenski
Michigan State University
East Lansing, MI
    Prematurity

Heather Lewis
Michigan State University
East Lansing, MI
    Adoption, Crying, Feeding

Richard J. Lower
Michigan State University
East Lansing, MI
    Gay and Lesbian Parents

Chantel Laran Lumpkin
Western Michigan University
Kalamazoo, MI
    Caregiving, Cross-Cultural Research

Roni Arlene Mayzer
Michigan State University
East Lansing, MI
    Cognitive Development: Piaget

Cathleen Erin McGreal
Kalamazoo College
Kalamazoo, MI
    Infancy in Historical Context

Lorraine McKelvey
Michigan State University
East Lansing, MI
    Prenatal Development, Prevention

Marcel Montanez
Michigan State University
East Lansing, MI
    Family Composition, Motor
        Development

Eun Young Mun
Michigan State University
East Lansing, MI
    Behavioral Genetics, Temperament

Laura Lynn Nathans
Michigan State University
East Lansing, MI
    Home Visiting

Sonia Miner Salari
University of Utah
Salt Lake City, UT
    Intergenerational Day Care,
        Reproductive Technologies, Stem
        Cells, TANF

Lucy H. Seabrook
Westat, Inc.
Washington, DC
    Child Abuse, Maternal Deprivation

Nary Shinn
Michigan State University
East Lansing, MI
  Television

Ann Michele Stacks
Michigan State University
East Lansing, MI
  Adolescent Parenting, Case Worker,
    Divorce, Family Systems,
    Inclusiveness

Krista Marie Surowiec
Michigan State University
East Lansing, MI
  Facial Expressions, Modeling, Peer
    Relations, Rocking, Smiling and
    Laughter, Touch

Dawn Thomas
University of Illinois
Champaign, IL
  Individuals with Disabilities
    Education Act

Laurie Van Egeren
Michigan State University
East Lansing, MI
  Assessment, Autism, Coparenting,
    Mentally Ill Mothers

Deborah Weatherston
Wayne State University
Detroit, MI
  Infant-Parent Psychotherapy

Foreword

It is truly remarkable in 2001 that an "encyclopedia" is being published on infancy in America. A brief personal historical perspective is interesting to consider to place this volume in time and place. In 1974, while I was organizing a course on infancy at Temple University, it quickly became obvious that finding relevant readings for the course was going to require much library research, and either placing reserve articles for the students at the library or massive copying of articles. The relatively sparse amount of existing literature available with which to teach a course in infancy was so scattered and diverse that the professor could not identify a relevant book in the area to provide an overview and help the students (and professor) develop a perspective on the field. The literature on infancy tended to cross a number of different fields—developmental psychology and pediatrics being the most common. In 1979, in response to my own need for a resource book that would guide both teaching and research in the area, I edited the first edition of the *Handbook of Infant Development.* This was followed in 1986 by a second edition of this handbook as well as burgeoning academic, research, and clinical work in infancy. Several journals emerged focusing primarily on infancy. Other books, including texts, research volumes, and an

increasing amount of popular literature, were published. In the mid- to late 1980s and the 1990s, the field of infancy witnessed enormous growth in the more clinically oriented area of infant mental health, with an increasing focus on the social and emotional development of infants in addition to cognitive development. Publications in the field grew quickly, and many more papers and books reflected a clinical focus in addition to a research focus. In 2000, not one but two handbooks of infant mental health were published, one being a four-volume set. In addition, organizations formed and merged that were either membership groups (the World Association for Infant Mental Health, the International Association for Infant Studies) or those with a strong following such as Zero to Three/National Center for Infants, Toddlers and Families. All this is to say that we have seen an exponential growth in the field of infancy, now evidencing itself in the two volumes of *Infancy in America: An Encyclopedia.*

What is particularly interesting about these volumes is that the range of topics covered is very broad, reflecting the diversity and multidisciplinary nature of this field. At first glance, the reader would not necessarily have thought of all of these areas being represented as part of the infancy field. However, the many topics covered show how very much the field has grown. To provide some "food for thought" for the reader, consider some of the following topics in this A-to-Z list. Under the As, for example, are included such diverse topics as Accomodation, AIDS, Afterbirth, Alcoholism, Apgar, Approach Withdrawal, Art, and, not surprisingly, Attachment. Or consider the Ts, which include Tabula Rasa, Temper Tantrums, Temperament, Theories of Development, Touch, Training of Caregivers, Transition to Parenthood, and Twins. The editors have done a very good job of summarizing areas, such as attachment, that have been particularly important in infancy as reflected not only in their impact but also in the vast amount of research in the field. They have also covered areas that are crucial for more than an academic understanding of the field, such as child care, assessment, training, and organizations involved with the field of infancy that may be helpful to parents and professionals alike. Thus, these volumes reflect more than just another academically useful publication; they will also prove to be very helpful for parents.

A word about the editors. Alice Sterling Honig and Hiram E. Fitzgerald are two pioneers in the infancy field. Dr. Honig, with her collaborators, Dr. Bettye Caldwell and Dr. Ron Lally, was involved in developing and evaluating one of the very first infant care centers in the country in the 1960s, with a vision for group care for our youngest children that few had 30 years ago. Their experiment was successful—the follow-up data from their program shows even today some of the most remarkable results of good group care for high risk infants. Dr. Fitzgerald, in addition to his extraordinary academic contributions, was instrumental in start-

ing one of the first organizations representing researchers and clinicians in the field of infancy, the International Association for Infant Mental Health. This organization has since merged with another, for which Dr. Fitzgerald serves as executive director (the World Association for Infant Mental Health), and he, with his considerable academic and administrative skill, continues in his role of influencing and guiding the field. Holly E. Brophy-Herb brings an intergenerational flavor to the volumes, as she received her Ph.D. under Dr. Honig and continues to build and share expertise in the infancy area, following in the fine tradition represented by these two senior leaders in this field.

The interested reader may ask, "Why an encyclopedia ?" when there have been a number of handbooks already written in this area (noted and referenced in this book) from either a general perspective, or covering specific topics of infancy such as infant mental health, attachment, parenting, etc. This encyclopedia is unique in providing the reader with something very different from previous publications. You can decide if you are interested in learning more about one particular event or behavior, such as temper tantrums. You can read the brief description offered in this volume about the area and follow up with the references provided to gain more infomation. The volumes offer another unique component in the appendixes. The first focuses on resources, so if parents or professionals are interested in learning about where they can find organizations or resources in their area they can look to Appendix A. If a parent is interested in learning more about lullabies or other popular songs for toddlers he or she can look to Appendix B. This approach may have particular appeal for readers who want mainly reference information.

In sum, *Infancy in America: An Encyclopedia* should be useful for parents, practiononers, and professionals alike. It is nicely organized to describe important topics and to help the reader find additional information. This volume is a fine credit to the editors and authors, who have been successful in compiling a comprehensive description of this diverse and very important field. After all, if we want our children to develop positively and learn to adapt to this complex world, then prevention, intervention, and support must start in infancy. This book will help many readers identify where to start.

Joy D. Osofsky, Ph. D.
Professor of Public Health and
Psychiatry, Louisiana State University
Health Sciences Center, New Orleans
Director, Harris Center for Infant
Mental Health, LSUHSC, New Orleans
Vice President, Zero to Three/
National Center for Infants,
Toddlers, and Families

PREFACE

The span of human history that includes the conception that infancy is a special period in human development is surprisingly short. It is only within the past 300 years that infancy has been thought of as a significant period in its own right, and it is decidedly more recent that the events of infancy have been considered to be crucial for setting the tone for future development. Thus, the fact that an encyclopedia on infancy has not been published would very likely be inconceivable to parents, professors, and professionals; one wonders today why such a volume has not already been written.

This volume reflects the extraordinary disciplinary, theoretical, and methodological diversity that characterizes the scientific and clinical study of infants, their caregivers, and their caregiving environments. Why such an encyclopedia? No age period in human development has received the attention given to infancy during the past 100 years. The results of this attention have had a disproportionate impact on developmental sciences, leading to a far deeper understanding of the basic processes that regulate development than currently is known about older age periods. Moreover, recent attention given to brain development has generated unprecedented public awareness of the importance of infancy and early childhood. An encyclopedia of infancy capital-izes on this current campaign to heighten public awareness of the importance of infancy and early childhood by providing a resource that details the concepts and findings related to infancy, the critical issues in the field, and some of the individuals who helped to shape it.

The extraordinary attention given to scientific study of infants and young children over recent decades has a parallel in clinical studies and social policy. Clinical and policy issues related to infancy are tied respectively to the history and influence of psychoanalytic theory and to societal concerns for infants reared in nonoptimal environments involving poverty, poor nutrition, familial or neighborhood violence, poor parenting, and other factors. The breadth of factors contributing to risk naturally drew investigators from many disciplines and stimulated interdisciplinary collaborations at a level seldom seen in investigations focusing on older age periods. Scientists and clinicians from social work, nursing, nutrition, early childhood education, pediatrics, occupational and physical therapy, speech pathology, psychiatry, and psychology are all involved with clinical infant studies, preventive-intervention programs, and basic research with infants, toddlers, and their families.

Scientific, clinical, and cultural attention to the early years of life has also spawned a variety of professional and consumer organizations devoted to issues of infancy. Two prominent membership organizations are the International Society on Infant Studies (http://www.isisweb.org) and the World Association for Infant Mental Health (http://www.msu.edu/user/waimh). Each of these organizations sponsors its own scientific journal, *Infancy* in the former case, and the *Infant Mental Health Journal*, in the latter case. Zero to Three: The National Center for Infants, Toddlers, and Families provides training programs, generates clinical resource materials and advocates for policies that benefit infants and their families, and publishes *0 to 3*, a newsletter that serves as a journal for social policy, application, and clinical studies.

The zeitgeist, therefore, appears ripe for a volume that helps to translate the cumulative knowledge of infancy and early childhood to audiences that can benefit from the knowledge explosion, such as students, parents, and parents-to-be.

A

Abortion

The early termination of a pregnancy by the expulsion of the fetus from the uterus. Most abortions occur naturally and are referred to as "spontaneous." Accidents and infectious diseases are among the many factors that cause spontaneous abortions. Some abortions are referred to as "therapeutic" because they are performed to save the life or health of the pregnant woman.

AB Problem

The AB problem is a concept in Jean Piaget's theory of cognitive development. During stage 4 of the sensorimotor period of infancy, children understand that objects can exist even when out of sight but still have only a rudimentary understanding of logic. The fact that they sometimes use flawed reasoning is demonstrated by the AB problem: When an object is hidden at one location (A) but moved somewhere else (location B), the child will look for it in the original hiding place anyway—at A, not B.

Abusive Head Trauma

See Child Abuse and Neglect; Shaken Baby Syndrome

Accommodation

In Piagetian theory, "accommodation" refers to adaptive changes that are required when current cognitive structures are inadequate for processing new information. An infant cannot drink from a cup using his sucking scheme and, therefore, will have to learn to suppress that scheme and adopt new strategies in order to drink from a cup. Thus, in Piagetian theory accommodation is one of the important processes that facilitates the infant's transition from one cognitive stage to another.

> *See also* Assimilation; Cognitive Development; Piaget, Jean

Accreditation of Child Care

See Child-Care Accreditation

Acquired Immune Deficiency Syndrome (AIDS)

AIDS is a disease that affects the immune system and is caused by infection with the human immunodeficiency virus, or HIV. AIDS is found worldwide, reaching epidemic levels throughout sub-Saharan Africa. In infants, compared to adults, HIV infection progresses more rapidly to full AIDS.

> *See also* HIV

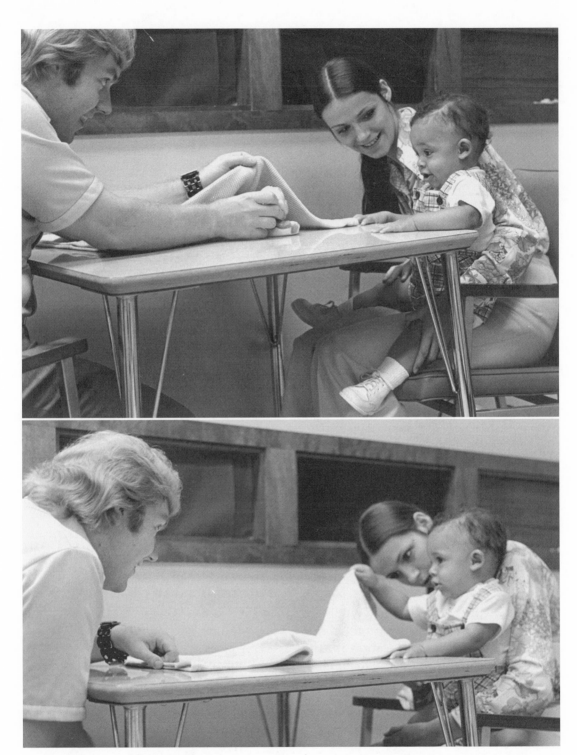

A demonstration of the AB problem. When an object is hidden at one location but moved somewhere else, the child will look for it in the original hiding place anyway. (Photograph courtesy Thomas Hagaman)

Action Schemes

The action scheme is a central concept in Jean Piaget's theory of cognitive development. During infancy, babies learn to put a series of basic actions that together create a more complex behavior. One example might be the way in which a baby grabs a favorite toy. To accomplish this task, the child must (1) reach out her arm, (2) open her hand, (3) grasp onto the toy, and (4) pull it toward herself. This is a planned pattern of movement designed to accomplish a goal.

See also Cognitive Development; Piaget, Jean

Activity Level

Activity level is the proportion of active periods to inactive ones. Some babies are always in motion, whereas others move very little during the day.

See also Temperament

Adaptability

Adaptability is a measure of easiness with which behavior can be changed in a desired direction in reaction to new stimuli.

See also Temperament

Adaptation

Through the process of adaptation, individuals change behavior in making appropriate responses to the demands of social and nonsocial environments. Because many theorists posit that human beings help to shape their own environments, adaptation is very much a process involving organism-environment transactions.

In Piagetian theory, adaptation involves two key processes—assimilation and accommodation—that continue throughout one's life span. Adaptation is the way that we reconcile our mental representation of reality against new information by actively exploring and interacting with the environment. When information can be fitted into our existing ways of thinking about things, we have assimilated the information into our existing mental representation. When we cannot assimilate new information into an existing mental representation, we must change the mental representation by accommodating to the novel information. The balance between these two processes accounts for changes in our adaptation to environmental events.

See also Accommodation; Assimilation; Cognitive Development; Piaget, Jean

Adaptive Behavior

Adaptive behaviors are behaviors that promote independent living, such as feeding and dressing oneself during early childhood; behaviors related to economic self-sufficiency during adulthood are also adaptive. From an evolutionary perspective, adaptive behaviors support survival in the organism's natural environment.

See also Adaptation

Adjunctive Systems

Systems that impact a primary system are said to be *adjunctive* to that system. Typically, the family is considered to be the primary system. In this case, adjunctive systems would include all systems to which individual members of the primary system are connected, such as the

A two-and-a-half-year-old boy dressing himself—putting his underpants on over his pants. (Elizabeth Crews)

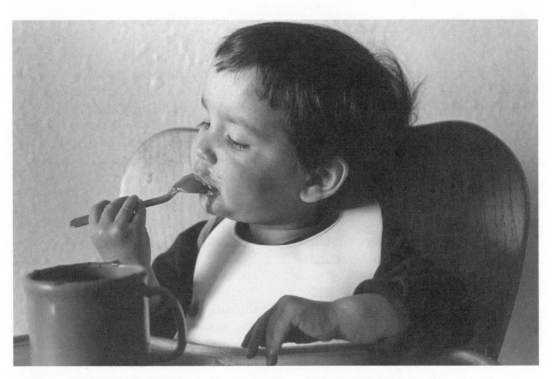

A fifteen-month-old feeding himself with a spoon. (Elizabeth Crews)

work environment, educational and religious institutions, as well as peer, social, and neighborhood groups.

See also Family Systems; Theories of Development

Adolescent Parenting

Any woman under the age of twenty who has given birth is an adolescent parent. Although societal factors such as the availability of birth control and the legalization of abortion have made adolescent parenting less likely, in the late 1990s the United States had the highest rate of adolescent births compared to other industrial nations such as England, Canada, Australia, Sweden, Germany, France, and Japan. Some factors have been associated with becoming a teen parent; these include, but are not limited to, a history of abuse, being raised by a single parent, and low educational goals. Becoming an adolescent parent has been shown to have many negative consequences for the adolescent, her child, and society. However, certain parent and child characteristics as well as societal factors contribute to positive outcomes associated with bearing a child before the age of twenty.

Rates of Adolescent Parenting

For a long period in the United States (almost three decades), the rate of births for fifteen- to nineteen-year-olds decreased. In 1955, for example, there were ninety births for every 1,000 girls in this age group; by 1989, this had decreased to fifty-eight births for every 1,000 girls. Since 1989, however, the birthrate for fifteen- to nineteen-year-olds has increased (from sixty-one births for every 1,000 females to about 100 by the late 1990s).

Several societal factors contributed to the 1955–1989 decline in birthrates for teens. First, during this time the birth-control pill became available. This made the chances of becoming pregnant less likely while allowing for sexual activity. Also, in 1973 abortion became constitutionally protected following the U.S. Supreme Court's ruling in the landmark *Roe v. Wade* case. Thereafter, many adolescents who became pregnant chose to end their pregnancy. For example, in 1974 29 percent of pregnant adolescents chose abortion; by 1985 this had risen to 42 percent, but it dropped to 30 percent by 1992.

Factors Associated with Becoming an Adolescent Parent

Some adolescents are more likely than others to become teen parents. Although adolescent mothers vary in terms of their economic backgrounds, level of education, family upbringing, and personalities, they are similar in many ways. As compared to adolescents without children, adolescent mothers are more likely to have low educational goals and to have low school achievement. Adolescent mothers are more likely to have been abused and to use drugs and alcohol. Furthermore, a majority of adolescent mothers were themselves born to teen mothers. Most adolescent parents are raised by a single parent in a household where the parent or parents have low levels of education. Adolescent parents also are more likely to have grown up in a household characterized by poverty and multiple problems such as death of a parent, substance abuse, and child maltreatment.

Outcomes of Teen Parenthood for Mothers

Becoming a parent has many positive and negative consequences for a person of any age, but adolescent parents often face special problems. One consequence for the adolescent parent is decreased likelihood of continuing education. Some adolescent mothers drop out of school before becoming pregnant; others drop out after becoming pregnant. Although adolescent mothers can of course graduate from high school or obtain a general equivalency diploma, they are less likely to go to college than peers who do not have children. As a result of lower levels of education, teen mothers can have difficulty finding employment to meet their financial needs. Low levels of education and employment increase the likelihood that an adolescent mother will live in poverty. And teen mothers are more likely to have more children than those who delay having a family; this further strains the already difficult economic situation of adolescent mothers.

Outcomes of Teen Parenthood for Children

The negative consequences of teen pregnancy also affect the child. Some of these are related more to social factors associated with adolescent parenting, such as poverty, than to the age of the parent. They begin before the child is even born. Adolescent mothers are less likely than older mothers to receive prenatal care and, therefore, are more likely to deliver premature or low-birth-weight babies. When adolescents do receive prenatal care, the infant often does not have health problems. Younger adolescents are more likely to have health problems during and after pregnancy, probably due to their own bodies' nutritional needs during adolescence. Adolescents are more likely than adults to have complications during pregnancy, including toxemia, anemia, urinary-tract infections, pro-

longed labor, premature delivery, and low-birth-weight infants. Low birthweight is sometimes associated with death, chronic respiratory problems, and cerebral palsy. Furthermore, children born to adolescent mothers are six times more likely to die from sudden infant death syndrome.

Children born to adolescents are at increased risk for cognitive developmental delays. Research has shown that children born to mothers who were younger than seventeen at the time of delivery were raised in a lower-quality home environment and were at a disadvantage as measured by cognitive development and academic achievement. These effects carry into the middle and high school years, and this includes lower educational attainment. For example, the younger an adolescent is at the time of her child's birth, the less likely that child is to finish high school. In addition, girls born to adolescent mothers are more likely to become teen mothers themselves. Children born to adolescent mothers are also more likely to be at risk for behavior problems. Children of adolescent parents have also been shown to have more emotional and behavioral problems in preschool and are more likely to abuse drugs and alcohol, show signs of anxiety, and suffer depression in adolescence. The possible reasons for this are that teen parents may lack the emotional and social support needed to parent; they may not provide a quality home environment; and they may not be emotionally available to their infants.

Consequences of Teen Parenthood for Society

Adolescent parenthood also has an effect on society. Because adolescent parents often have lower levels of education and, subsequently, decreased employment opportunities and few financial resources, many adolescent parents rely on government assistance to raise their children. Government subsidies such as Aid to Families with Dependent Children (AFDC), Medicaid, and Women, Infants, and Children help many teen parents provide food, shelter, and medical care for their children. Although exact figures on the costs of adolescent parenthood to society are difficult to determine, some estimates have been made. In 1989, for example, the welfare-related expenditures for all families whose first child was born to an adolescent mother was $21.55 billion. Included in this figure are AFDC, food stamps, and Medicaid expenditures. If the births of these children had been delayed until mothers were in their twenties, the United States would have saved an estimated $8.62 billion. The amount of money spent on programs that target some of the effects of teen parenting, such as special education and costs associated with juvenile delinquency, are impossible to know. Early prevention, intervention, and support programs can reduce these down-the-line costs.

Developmental Assets Related to Positive Outcomes

Clearly, then, negative consequences follow adolescent mothers and their children. Yet not all experience the consequences associated with adolescent parenting, and those who experience positive outcomes share some common characteristics. First, adolescent mothers' psychological well-being appears to be an important factor in more positive outcomes for teen mothers and their babies. Adolescent mothers who have relatively high self-esteem and a feeling that they have some control over their lives—

referred to as a "high internal locus of control"—have been shown to provide more supportive environments for children. For example, these mothers are more responsive to infant needs and vocalize more to their babies. Depressed adolescent mothers as a rule are less supportive, less involved, and less sensitive. Second, the teen mother's age is often related to the quality of parenting. Older adolescents are more likely to provide positive parenting. For example, they have been found to be more accepting, cooperative, accessible, and sensitive in their interactions with their twelve-month-old infants. This could be the result of maturity and an increased ability to place their infant's needs above their own. Finally, an adolescent's knowledge of child development is related to positive child outcomes. For instance, mothers who believe that talking to their children and letting them explore their environment is important are more likely to provide supportive home environments. Adolescents who understand that they have an important impact on their child's development are more likely to have positive interactions with their infants (for example, they smile at their infants more).

Although maternal characteristics are related to the outcomes of adolescent parenting, the child also plays a role. For example, adolescents may have a difficult time coping with infants who have difficult temperaments and require a great deal of care. Infants who cry a lot or suffer from complications associated with low birthweight, prematurity, or exposure to drugs and alcohol may be very difficult for an adolescent to parent. Premature infants are easily overstimulated, and infants exposed to drugs prenatally may have erratic sleep-wake cycles, may have a piercing cry, and may be difficult to comfort. Parenting an infant can be stressful even under the best of circumstances.

The environment in which the adolescent and child live also plays an important part in outcomes. An adolescent mother's family can provide emotional and instrumental support, and those who have a supportive family and/or partner are more likely to be competent parents. Adolescent mothers who live with their own mother and do not have major disagreements about childrearing are likely to benefit from the support they receive. These mothers are more likely to finish school and be employed. The involvement of the father has also been shown to impact child outcomes. Children whose fathers are involved in their lives have been found to have more positive cognitive and school outcomes.

See also Parenting; Parents

References and further reading

Alan Guttmacher Institute (website 2001). http://www.agi-usa.org.

Luster, Tom, and Holly Brophy-Herb. 2000. "Adolescent Mothers and Their Children." In J. D. Osofsky and H. E. Fitzgerald, eds., *The WAIMH Handbook of Infant Mental Health, Vol. 4: Infant Mental Health in Groups at High Risk.* New York: Wiley.

Luster, Tom, and Mary Mittelstaedt. 1993. "Adolescent Mothers." In T. Luster and L. Okagaki, eds., *Parenting: An Ecological Perspective.* Hillsdale, NJ: Lawrence Earlbaum, pp. 69–100.

Musick, Judith S. 1993. *Young, Poor, and Pregnant.* New Haven: Yale University Press.

National Perinatal Association (website 2001). http://www.nationalperinatal.org.

National Perinatal Information Center (website 2001). http://www.npic.org.

Shiono, P. H., and L. S. Quinn, 1994. "Epidemiology of Divorce." *Children and Divorce* 4(1): 15–28.

White, T. L., and E. Wethington. 1996. "Youth: Changing Beliefs and Behavior." In U. Bronfenbrenner et al., eds., *The State of Americans.* New York: Free Press, pp. 1–28.

Adoption

Adoption is a legal act granting legal family kinship membership to an individual. Adoption includes the transfer of parental rights and obligations from the family of origin to the adoptive family if parents are unable or unwilling to provide care.

The History of Adoption

Adoption is as old as recorded time. The ancient Greeks, Romans, Egyptians, and Babylonians all had adoption systems. The concept of adoption was not legally recognized in the United States until the 1850s, with the inception of the first adoption statutes. From colonial times to the 1850s, transfers of children to alternative parents occurred informally, without governing laws. Informal placements were often economically motivated. For example, farm families had a need for child labor. In addition, due to early industrial development, city dwellers were often unable to support or care for children. Transfers of children to other families were arranged by birth parents themselves or through charitable institutions. As the number of informal adoptions rose, and the inevitable abuse of the process occurred, the need for a formal process of adoption became greater. The early statutes did not resemble the laws today. For example, the lines between the adoptive and biological families were blurred.

The early laws defined the relationship between the adopted child and the adoptive parents but did not take into account the biological parents. As a result, adoptive families and biological families had no legal protection with respect to intrusions upon each other's lives following adoption. In the early twentieth century, statutes began to address the confidentiality of adoption information as to the public at large, but not between the par-

Parents being sworn in during adoption proceedings, with their nine-month-old adopted daughter. (Elizabeth Crews)

ties to an adoption. It was not until the 1930s that statutes were designed to preserve the exclusivity of the adoptive home. In the 1930s, 1940s, and 1950s, social workers began sealing birth and adoption records. Secrecy in adoption was thought to protect all parties to the adoption. Various social movements in the 1960s, 1970s, and 1980s changed these attitudes and, eventually, adoption legislation. The woman's liberation movement, the civil rights movement, the sexual revolution, and the adoptee's liberty movement all exacted change. Birth control, the legalization of abortion, the normalization of single parenthood, and step-/blended families also changed the adoption climate. During this time, birth parents and adult adoptees began to speak out about their experiences, rights, and needs.

Rates of Adoption
Domestic adoptions within the United States remain relatively stable, totaling around 50,000 per year, while intercountry adoptions (so-called foreign adoptions) have increased. For example, foreign adoptions increased from 4,323 in 1973 to 12,596 in 1997. The most prevalent countries of origin have been China and countries within the Russian Federation.

The demand to adopt children, particularly infant/toddlers, remains high. The

National Council for Adoption estimates that approximately 2 million individuals or couples seek information about adoption each year. Around 1 million of those wishing to adopt are infertile; the rest are so-called preferential adopters. Nearly 60 percent of current adoption seekers and planners prefer to adopt a child under the age of two.

Types of Adoption
There are three main adoption arrangements: traditional/closed, confidential/mediated/semi-open, and fully disclosed/open.

- *Traditional/closed adoption* is generally confidential, in that identifying information of participating parties is withheld. No social liaison among the families is anticipated. Requests for contact initiated under state laws with adoption agencies or the courts can be considered if both parties agree or register with a mutual-consent registry.
- *Confidential/mediated/semi-open adoptions* means that birth-family members and adoptive-family members can share information or request contact through an intermediary. On the basis of an informed decision, the parties can grant or withhold agreement to the request. Such information exchange or contact can be nonidentifying or, provided the parties are willing to waive their privacy, involve disclosure of identifying information and/or face-to-face meetings.
- *Fully disclosed/open adoption* means that names, addresses, and information are exchanged by the parties, generally in an initial face-to-face meeting. Ongoing contacts,

meetings, phone discussions, and/or letter exchanges are their own decision, but the implication is that liaison will continue.

Methods of Adoption
There are three main facilitators in adoption: private-agency adoption, public-agency adoption, and private/attorney adoption. In private-agency adoption, services and procedures vary, but the client is clearly the child. Some agencies encourage open adoption, whereas others practice more traditional adoption. Birth parents are often involved in the selection of the adoptive family, as well as the decisions regarding placement. Typically there is some communication between families, but most communication is arranged through the agency, which maintains confidentiality. Public-agency adoption is facilitated by public social-service agencies or other governmental agencies such as each state's Department of Economic Security (DES). Some districts will also directly handle the voluntary placements of newborns and young children when a family requests such services. In general, children adopted through DES have been in the foster-care system for some time. Lastly, private agencies and attorneys are beginning to work together to facilitate positive adoptions. In the past, agencies had specific requirements for prospective adoptive parents, including age, number of other children, length of marriage, stay-at-home parent, and so on. Private adoption developed as an alternative for those who did not meet all of these criteria. It also allows for more control in the selection process. Attorneys working in private practice provide access to most of the same services as adoption agencies, but they cannot pro-

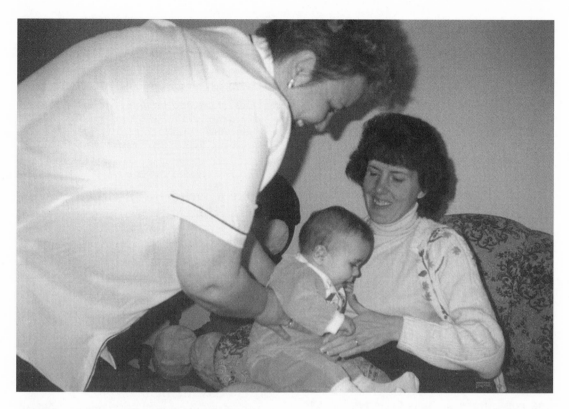

An infant begins what will be a long journey from a Russian orphanage to a midwestern American home. (Courtesy of Bradley T. Shaw)

vide counseling themselves. The major distinction between private and agency adoptions is the cost. Most agencies have a flat fee, whereas private adoption depends on the circumstances. Considerable cost can accrue if the birth mother doesn't have medical insurance or other protections. Today, private adoption generally has greater flexibility than many agency adoptions, in that it allows birth and adoptive parents to design a plan for how the adoption will proceed.

Laws and Common Practices
There is a multitude of laws surrounding adoption. A few key practices of importance governed by law are: home studies, voluntary termination of parental rights,

involuntary termination of parental rights, and nonidentifying information. Virtually every state requires some form of investigation into the suitability and fitness of the individuals seeking to adopt. The investigation usually involves a report referred to as a "home study." Generally, home studies are conducted prior to placement. Sometimes it follows placement but occurs prior to finalization of the adoption.

Of particular importance is the voluntary termination of parental rights, as parental consent is virtually a uniform requirement in all adoption statutes and is the most common method to attain voluntary termination of rights. Who is defined as a "parent," however, varies from state to state. The issue of paternity is controversial. Some states require the consent of the father for adoption, but others have passed legislation regarding uninvolved, unmarried fathers. According to current interpretations of the law, the rights of uninvolved, unmarried fathers correspond to the effort the father has made to establish a relationship with his child. A growing trend in state legislatures is the establishment of father registries, which usually require the father to file a paternity action within thirty days of the child's birth. This will result in the father's being notified of a pending adoption and grant him rights and responsibilities in what happens to the child.

In addition, there is the issue of involuntary termination of parental rights. The due process rights established in the U.S. Constitution require that severance of a parent's rights be supported by clear and convincing evidence. Generally, the involuntary termination of parental rights is an action of last resort. The following reasons can lead to the severance of parental rights: abandonment, abuse, neglect, mental illness, mental deficiency, chronic substance abuse, and felony conviction. Lastly, nonidentifying information is contained in a 1984 federal statute requiring that a health and genetic history concerning the biological parents be provided to prospective adoptive parents.

Costs of Adoption
Domestic adoptions on average cost between $15,000 and $20,000 for maternity home care, normal prenatal and hospital care for mother and child, pre-adoption foster care for baby, home study, counseling, and legal fees. Foreign adoptions range from $13,000 to $38,000 or more. Costs include home study, coun-

seling, legal fees, travel and related costs, translation/government fees, as well as fees to foreign and U.S. agencies.

> *See also* Family Composition
> ***References and further reading***
> National Council for Adoption. 1999.
> *Adoption Factbook III*. St. Paul,
> Minnesota: Park Press Quality Printing.

Adult Attachment Interview
See Attachment

Affect
"Affect" is a common synonym for "emotion."

> *See also* Affect Attunement; Basic Motives; Emotion

Affect Attunement
"Affect attunement" is a term coined by child psychiatrist Daniel Stern, in his book *The Interpersonal World of the Infant* (1985), to express parents' ability to share affective experiences or states with their infant. It can be viewed alternatively as mutual emotion sharing. Parents who are not able to share their infant's affective state (i.e., they cannot, so to speak, tune in with them) are thought to have difficulties interacting in the normal give-and-take with an infant.

> *See also* Affect

Affordance
In James J. Gibson's ecological theory of perception, "affordance" refers to things in the environment that we search for because they are useful. Affordances, therefore, are action possibilities that a given situation provides an individual.

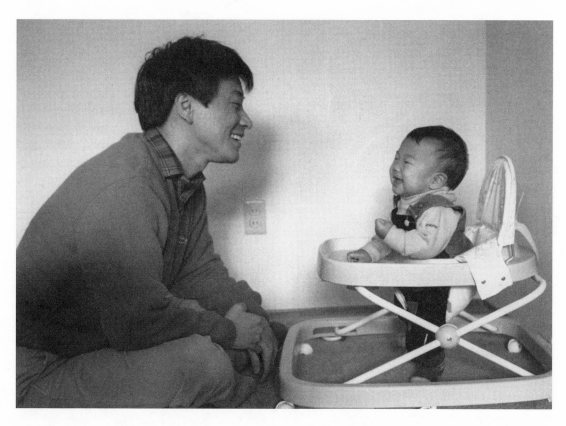

A father and eight-month-old son in social interaction. (Elizabeth Crews)

They relate the meaning of the perceptual experience that occurred to the infant's existing and future action possibilities. For example, a crawling infant/toddler quickly learns that a surface with visual cues, suggesting that there is depth, affords the possibility that the infant will fall if it crawls out over an edge. This is referred to as a "visual cliff." This information, then, is used by the infant to guide further action—that is, a decision not to crawl out over the edge. James and Eleanor Gibson were the first to develop the idea of affordance and the necessary coupling of sensation, perception, and motor movements throughout development.

See also Depth Perception; Perception

Afterbirth

Afterbirth is the detaching and expulsion of the placenta, umbilical cord, and other materials that follow the birth of a baby.

Age

As it pertains to development, age has three commonly used definitions. First, *chronological age* refers to the age of the child since birth. Second, *gestational age* indicates the age of the child (or fetus) since conception. Infants born prematurely often appear developmentally delayed when compared to full-term infants, and the child's gestational age, rather than chronological age, is often used as a measure, although there is

*A one-year-old at his birthday party.
(Elizabeth Crews)*

available every few months until age five years. At each assessment, parents complete thirty items regarding the child's ability to complete specific activities and tasks (e.g., "Does your child climb the rungs of a playground slide and slide down without any help?") and choose from the answers (e.g., "yes," "sometimes," and "not yet"). Parents are encouraged to try the activities with the infant to obtain an optimal response. Professionals then tally the parents' responses into scores for five developmental domains: communication, gross motor, fine motor, problem-solving, and personal-social. A Spanish-language version is also available.

See also Assessment

References and further reading
Bricker, D., and J. Squires, with others. 1999. *Ages and Stages Questionnaires: A Parent-Completed, Child-Monitoring System.* 2nd ed. Baltimore: Paul H. Brookes Publishing.

debate whether this is an appropriate tactic. Third, *developmental age* indicates the average age that a milestone or characteristic occurs regardless of the child's chronological age. For example, a cognitively delayed child may be five years old but have a developmental age of two; a four-year-old may have walking skills that are equivalent to a developmental age of eighteen months.

See also Developmental Models

Ages and Stages Questionnaires

A set of assessment instruments used with parents to screen children for developmental delay. Versions of the questionnaire begin from age four months and are

Aggression

Aggression is the infliction of harm on another person or an object. Some theorists require that the aggressive act be intentional, but others do not. The incidence of aggressive acts increases around age two, and gradually boys commit more physically aggressive acts than girls. Of the six types of aggression identified by Kenneth Moyer (predatory aggression, intermale aggression, fear-induced aggression, maternal aggression, irritable aggression, and sex-related aggression), irritable aggression accounts for most aggressive acts during the toddler and preschool years. Many years ago, social-learning theorists argued that there was a direct link between frustration and aggression; such a linkage would explain the origins of irritable aggression. When one toddler takes

Boys, three and four years of age, fighting over a shovel at preschool. (Elizabeth Crews)

another's truck, the frustrated toddler's solution is to try to take the truck back or to hit or push. Socialization involves teaching young children alternative strategies for dealing with such issues and to learn the nuances of turn-taking, sharing, and respect for others.

See also Child Abuse and Neglect; Emotion

Aid to Families with Dependent Children
See Temporary Assistance to Needy Families

Ainsworth, Mary
See Attachment

Alcohol Effects
This refers to the consequences of consuming alcohol. Applied to adults, this means the effects of alcohol consumption on driving, work performance, and antisocial behavior. In the case of infancy, however, the term refers more specifically to possible insults to the fetus that may surface later in development. Such effects do not show the symptoms of fetal alcohol syndrome. Fetal alcohol effects may be direct, as in the case of insult to the embryo or fetus, or they may be indirect, as outcomes of being reared by an alcohol-abusing or alcohol-dependent parent.

See also Alcoholism

Alcoholism
Mental health professionals use the term "alcoholism" to refer to alcohol-use disorders. According to the American Psychiatric Association's *Diagnostic and Statistical Manual IV*, there are two types of alcohol-use disorder: alcohol dependence and alcohol abuse. In both of these disorders, individuals may have difficulties at work, at home, in social situations, or when driving. Binge drinking is a form of alcohol abuse and is often seen among youths. When an individual develops tolerance, withdrawal, or compulsive behavior related to drinking, alcohol dependence is strongly implicated.

Alcoholism is the most common substance abuse today. Nearly 25 percent of all adult males in the United States met the criteria for an alcohol-use disorder sometime in life, and approximately 10 percent of the adult population currently meets the criteria. Children of alcoholics, compared to children with no family history of alcoholism, are six to ten times at greater risk for alcohol-use disorder, although nearly 70 percent do not develop alcohol abuse or dependence. Of the 7 million children under age eighteen who are exposed to alcohol, some 679,000 are less than two years of age.

Infants can be affected by parental alcohol abuse or dependence both before and after birth. Prenatal exposure can be direct, as when the pregnant women consumes alcoholic beverages, or it can be indirect, as when alcohol affects male sperm or leads to spousal abuse. Postnatal exposure can be direct, although consumption by children under five years of age is rare. Postnatal exposure primarily is indirect and involves being reared by parents who use alcohol and/or have an alcohol-use disorder.

Prenatal Exposure

In the 1970s, Ann Streissguth at the University of Washington played a significant role in focusing the attention of the public and the scientific community on the potential negative effects of prenatal exposure to alcohol. The fetus's developing brain and nervous system are especially vulnerable. Moreover, these effects are completely preventable. If the pregnant women does not consume alcohol, there cannot be alcohol-exposure effects. This simple and obvious fact provided the basis for one of the most massive public health campaigns in recent history, when warning labels were placed on all alcoholic beverages alerting consumers about the potential harmful effects of alcohol on the fetus.

Alcohol is a teratogen, a substance that can produce a congenital anomaly in the developing embryo and fetus. Alcohol consumed by a mother crosses the placenta and circulates in the bloodstream of the developing child. However, in addition to the direct teratogenic effects of alcohol, other factors must be taken into account when attempting to understand the relation between maternal alcohol consumption of its effects on the fetus. Coexisting medical or psychiatric disorders can increase the risk. Social problems, poverty, malnutrition, and use of other drugs, which often accompany the pregnancies of alcohol-using women, can also lead to increased risks for the fetus. The genetic susceptibility of mother and child to alcohol effects is another factor that may increase or decrease the risk for fetal damage in prenatal exposure. All these factors combined mean that there is no safe amount or safe time for pregnant women to consume alcohol.

Fetal Alcohol Syndrome. Fetal alcohol syndrome (FAS) refers to children who were exposed to alcohol prenatally who have growth deficiency, facial morphological abnormalities, and/or central nervous system deficits. It is the leading cause of mental retardation in the United States today. More specifically, a child diagnosed with FAS must have some symptoms in each of three categories: (1) growth deficiency in both the prenatal and postnatal periods; (2) abnormalities in facial and skull structure including small eye openings, alterations in nose and forehead structure, an absent or elongated groove between the upper lip and nose, a thin upper lip, a flattened midface, and underdevelopment of the upper or lower jaw; and (3) central nervous system deficits such as mental retardation and behavioral problems. FAS is easiest to diagnose between the ages of eight months and eight years because it is difficult to recognize the symptoms in newborns and because body changes at puberty make the physical features associated with FAS harder to recognize. Alcohol-related neurodevelopmental disorder (ARND), fetal alcohol effects (FAE), and possible fetal alcohol effects all describe characteristics in children who have some form of FAS.

Although overall rates of FAS might be underestimated due to difficulty in making a diagnosis, more recent estimates among the general population range from 3.3 to 9.7 cases per 10,000 live births. This relatively low rate again points to the importance of looking at factors beyond the direct teratogenic effects of alcohol.

A general behavioral picture of children with FAS reflects two key dimensions: difficulty regulating events in the environment, and poor cause-and-effect reasoning. For young children with FAS, impulsivity, hyperactivity, poor attention span, overfriendliness, and problems in social judgment are prominent. In school-age children, problems in self-regulation lead to problems in learning. Talking too much, rapid mood swings, and intrusive behaviors often continue through adolescence and into adulthood, leading to social isolation and loneliness.

FAS children often display delays and impairments in motor and speech development. More than 50 percent of FAS children have difficulties with sucking, show poor motor coordination, and show decreased muscle tone. As they grow, children with FAS often have learning deficits, frequent temper tantrums, difficulty making transitions from one activity to another, and have poor social skills. Older children with FAS exhibit higher rates of conduct disorder. They continue to demonstrate poor socialization and communication skills, as well a tendency to experience problems with alcohol and drug abuse, antisocial behavior, inappro-

priate sexual behavior, and other mental health problems.

Alcohol-Related Neurodevelopmental Disorder. ARND, also known as fetal alcohol effects, refers to prenatally exposed children who did not develop symptoms of fetal alcohol syndrome. Results of related research are not clear-cut. The amount of alcohol consumed, the timing of exposure, and lack of adequate control for confounding factors make it difficult to draw conclusions about this literature. Nevertheless, fetal alcohol effects have been reported.

Growth. Although physical deficiencies are not always found, there is evidence that children born to women with high alcohol consumption are shorter than other children, have reduced cranial circumference, and lower birthweights. However, findings also suggest that growth deficits are often not maintained as affected children grow older, especially in more advantaged rearing environments.

Motor Development. Some evidence suggests that both gross and fine motor skills are affected by prenatal alcohol exposure. Other studies have not found deficits in motor development as a function of prenatal alcohol exposure.

Cognitive Functioning. Although the evidence is not always consistent across studies, prenatal exposure to alcohol, even in low amounts, can lead to decreased cognitive functioning. Children exposed to only 1–1.5 ounces of alcohol per day have been shown to have IQ scores five to seven points lower than unexposed children. Other neuropsychological deficits have been found in prenatally exposed young children, including slower or less efficient information processing at age thirteen months and problems with memory, encoding, and overall mental processing at just under six years.

Postnatal Exposure

Children of alcoholics are at high risk for various types of behavior disorders. One or both parents are likely to have a history of childhood behavior problems, including illegal behavior, frequent arrests, chronic lying, relationship disturbances, failed relationships, depression, family violence, neuroticism, poor achievement and cognitive functioning, and low socioeconomic status.

In addition, children of alcoholics are themselves more likely to have problems such as hyperactivity, negative mood, problematic social relationships, deficits in cognitive functioning, higher levels of aggressive behavior, and more precocious acquisition of cognitive schemas about alcohol and other drugs.

Temperament and Alcoholism. Several studies have linked difficult temperament to heightened risk for the development of alcoholism and related psychopathology. Developmental models of psychopathology share much in common with risk aggregation models of the etiology of alcoholism. According to Robert Zucker of the University of Michigan, the risk aggregation model predicts that a hierarchical risk structure exists among children at high risk for alcoholism. This risk structures their genetic makeup, biological disposition, and rearing environment.

Incidents either increase or decrease the probability of stepping down the pathologic pathways that are characterized by early onset of behavior and alcohol problems and continued problems through adolescence and adulthood.

Autobiographical Memory and Affective Disorganization. The literature on alcoholism provides evidence that children of alcoholics, as young as three years of age, have constructed mental models about alcohol that include who uses it, where they use it, and how they behave under the influence. Preschool-age sons of alcoholic fathers are more likely to have cognitive models that include alcohol use as an attribute associated with adult male roles. In other words, three- to five-year-old sons of alcoholics already have a set of expectancies about when adult men drink and what they do when they drink. Cognitive psychologists call such memories "autobiographic" because they are derived from individual experience. Autobiographical memories are important because they are mental models that help us to organize new information about the events in our lives.

Thus, children of alcoholics as young as three years already have working models, or schemas, about familiar positive and negative events. Autobiographical memories are only partially based on experience, however, because they are constructed from experience and are influenced by exposure to others' constructions of experience, particularly those of parents. Charles Zeanah and his associates at Tulane University found that mothers who experienced high rates of serious spousal violence had disorganized attachment relationships with their toddlers. And whereas witnessing parental violence can elicit fear in young children about the well-being of a parent, it also provides the child with opportunities to code how fathers/husbands treat wives (or children), especially during drinking episodes. In short, the experience provides a context for constructing events, and events can provide a background for action at some future time (e.g., during adolescence and early adulthood).

Living in a family with an alcoholic parent presents many occasions to experience events related to drinking, parenting, and marital relationships. This linkage suggests a model of early autobiographical memory embeds expectancies into a family structure that includes emotional differentiation, self-regulation, interpersonal dynamics, socialization, as well as motivational forces involving beliefs, wants, and desires. This systems approach to the organization of the preschooler's autobiographical memory for alcohol use suggests that the child's schema is composed of at least four interdependent components: sensory-perceptual (sensory identification of substances, perceptual discrimination of substance); cognitive-motivational (attributions about appropriate users); emotional (self-regulatory and self-control processes, as well as interpersonal relationships); and social (socialization models, peer relationships, and dominance hierarchies/power).

See also Autobiographical Memory; Neurobiology; Systems Theory; Temperament; Teratogens

References and further reading
Fitzgerald, H. E., W. H. Davies, and R. A. Zucker. 2000. "Growing Up in an Alcoholic Family: Structuring Pathways for Risk Aggregation and Theory-Driven Intervention." In R. MacMahon and R. deV. Peters, eds. *30th Banff Conference on Behavior Science: Children of Disordered Parents*. Boston: Kluwer.
Fitzgerald, H. E., et al. 2000. "Prenatal and Postnatal Exposure to Parental Alcohol Use and Abuse." In J. D. Osofsky and H. E. Fitzgerald, eds., *WAIMH Handbook of Infant Mental Health, Vol. 4: Infant Mental Health in Groups at Risk*. New York: Wiley, pp. 123–160.
National Organization on Fetal Alcohol Syndrome (website 2001). http://www. nofas.org.
Streissguth, A. 1997. *Fetal Alcohol Syndrome: A Guide for Families and Communities*. Baltimore: Paul H. Brookes Publishing.
Substance Abuse and Mental Health Services Administration, National Clearinghouse for Alcohol and Drug Information (website 2001). http://www. health.org.
Zucker, R. A., et al. 2000. "The Clinical and Social Ecology of Childhood for Children of Alcoholics: Description of a Study and Implications for a Differentiated Social Policy." In H. E. Fitzgerald, B. M. Lester, and B. Zuckerman, eds., *Children of Addiction: Research, Health, and Policy Issues*. New York: Falmer Press.

Alternative Birth

Expectant parents have many options in their childbirth experience. Many choose *alternative birth experiences* in settings other than a traditional hospital labor and delivery unit. Most experts include the following as examples of alternative births: birth attended by a midwife, birth at home, birth in a birthing center; birth in a family-centered, homelike hospital setting with minimal medical intervention; and birth in a birthing pool (waterbirth).

The definition of "alternative" birth depends largely on cultural factors. For instance, in the United States home birth is considered an unusual and alternative birth choice, but in many European countries it is the norm. Trends in medical practice also influence perceptions of normal and alternative birth experiences. From a historical perspective, so-called alternative births were once the norm. For centuries women gave birth in the home attended by other women. Until the mid-1900s, home birthing was very common in the United States. With the dawning of the modern medical age, however, childbirth moved to the hospital, as it was viewed as a medical event rather than a normal and healthy event. The use of general anesthesia during childbirth became common, and infants were typically taken to the hospital nursery immediately after birth rather than being placed with their mothers. Fathers were not active participants in the birth process and, in fact, were rarely with their partners once labor began. Yet even when such practices were commonplace, some experts doubted the wisdom of modern medicine. For example, in the 1940s British physician Grantly Dick-Read advocated for childbirth education and provision of emotional support as techniques for reducing the fear and uncertainty surrounding childbirth. Dr. Dick-Read believed that fear contributed to the pain associated with childbirth. Likewise, he argued that laboring women, contrary to current medical practices, should not be left alone but rather should be in the presence of partners or other familiar people. The women's movement in the 1970s initiated a move toward increasing women's choices about labor and delivery. Women began to express dissatisfaction with hospital birth experiences, and they began to educate themselves about choices. In 1960, the International Childbirth Education Association was founded and continues to provide resources and information to expectant parents as well as training to childbirth educators. Perceptions of medical practices began to change in the late 1900s as well. Alternative birth was imbedded in a larger movement toward more holistic and family-friendly medical practices.

Birth Attended by a Midwife

A midwife is a trained professional who provides prenatal care to an expectant mother, delivers the baby, and provides postpartum care. Derived from an Anglo-Saxon word, "midwife" literally means "with women." Midwives vary in the kind and amount of training they have. The most highly trained midwives are certified nurse-midwives (CNMs). CNMs are trained both in nursing and midwifery care, and they are certified by the American College of Nurse-Midwives (ACNM). The ACNM is the professional association of CNMs and certified midwives. As of 1999, there were forty-seven ACNM-accredited nurse-midwifery education programs in the United States. The ACNM Certification Council, the accrediting division of the ACNM, is recognized by the U.S. Department of Education as an official accrediting agency for nurse-midwifery education programs.

Another organization, the Midwives Alliance of North America, was founded in 1982 to provide additional networking resources and establish competency guidelines. CNMs work in conjunction with a physician and are more likely to be part of the general health care system. A lay midwife, sometimes called a "direct service midwife," usually has little or no medical training and little formal training in midwifery care. Instead, the midwife apprentices under a more experienced midwife. Midwives provide care in homes, birthing centers, and hospitals according to state regulations. States, however, vary in their recognition of midwives and in regulations regarding where and to whom midwives may provide services. In many states, midwives are not recognized as professionals and not licensed to practice if they do not have medical training as a nurse or other health care professional.

Midwives tend to view birth as a very positive, family-oriented, normal event—an advantage for many mothers. Although a pregnant women can see several different doctors in a larger obstetrics practice and is unsure of which doctor will deliver her baby (it depends which doctor is on call), a midwife provides ongoing prenatal care. Over the course of the pregnancy, the mother and her family come to know and trust the midwife. Such a close working relationship can be a positive aspect of the birth experience. Midwives tend to be very supportive of birth plans and supportive of family involvement in the birth.

A 1998 study released by the National Center for Health Statistics and the Centers for Disease Control and Prevention reported excellent birth outcomes for infants and mothers attended by midwives. From a statistical point of view, rates of cesarean section, use of medication, and use of medically assisted births (via forceps or vacuuming) are lower for midwife-attended births. Likewise, midwives are often more likely to use techniques such as warm compresses on the perineum (the area between the vagina and the anus) and perineal massage to avoid a medical intervention such as an episiotomy (an incision made in the perineum to increase the width of the opening through which the baby will pass). Another difference between midwives and physicians is that midwives tend to stay with the laboring mother from the start of her labor (or from some point in early labor) to the immediate postpartum period. Physicians often have to care for many women at one time and, therefore, attend the final phases of the delivery, typically arriving as the mother prepares to push. Certainly physicians are monitoring the progress of the mother throughout the labor even if they are not physically present. Many women, however, like the continuity and continuous presence they find with a midwife. They feel

cared for and emotionally supported. Studies of women in labor show that when women feel they are emotionally supported (by a partner, doula, or midwife), they feel more positive about labor, perceive their labors as being less painful and more manageable, and may even have shorter labors. Although midwife care is not as common as conventional care by an obstetrician, more and more families are exploring this alternative service. For instance, the proportion of births utilizing midwifery services in 1989 was 3 percent but had grown to 6 percent by 1995.

Birth at Home
Giving birth at home can be a positive experience, as the home environment is typically the place in which the woman feels safest, most comfortable, and least inhibited. Most women feel at least somewhat anxious and fearful about the impending labor and delivery process, and traveling to and birthing in an unfamiliar hospital setting can be intimidating for some. Indeed, many who choose to give birth at home cite their comfort in and desire for familiar surroundings as a key reason. Mothers may also feel that they have a better chance of achieving their ideal birth at home. Even though a mother's choices might be outlined in a birth plan, being successful in having medical staff carry out the birth plan can be more challenging. Some women, dissatisfied with their hospital birth experiences, choose a home birth for a subsequent pregnancy. A nurse-midwife, midwife, or physician who provides medical care in the home as well as the hospital usually attends home births.

Despite the advantages of home birth, there are several pitfalls. Home births are generally not widely accepted in medical communities, and some physicians choose not to work with families seeking home birth. Many physicians have concerns about potential emergencies. Malpractice lawsuits are also a concern for many physicians. Midwifery care is therefore more common for home births, which are suitable only for healthy, normal, low-risk pregnancies. Risk factors such as maternal diabetes, high blood pressure, heart disease, premature or postmature labor, a breech-position baby, multiple pregnancy, history of hemorrhage, history of stillbirth, and active cases of sexually transmitted diseases generally rule out a home birth and necessitate a hospital birth. Even low-risk pregnancies, however, can be potentially problematic. Transporting the laboring mother to a hospital can be difficult, particularly if there is not a hospital close to the home. Emergencies such as a prolapsed cord, in which the umbilical cord emerges through the birth canal in advance of the baby, or maternal hemorrhage after birth, can be unexpected and carry very serious complications. Such conditions require immediate medical intervention.

Birth at a Birthing Center

Birthing centers, or alternative birthing centers, emerged in the 1970s in response to women's dissatisfaction with hospital births. For many, the birthing center is a compromise between home and hospital settings, offering the comforts of home with access to immediate medical care if needed. A birthing center is usually located near a hospital, and some hospitals are affiliated with birthing centers. Although birthing centers can provide the needed medical equipment and services to handle any emergency, they are designed to feel and look like a home setting. Birthing rooms might be decorated with domestic items such as pictures and

prints on the walls and cozy rocking chairs. Medical equipment is discreetly hidden in the room's furniture. Birthing centers tend to be flexible in following family birth plans and allow expectant mothers freedom in their labor and delivery experiences. Many mothers and families report that care is more personalized in a birthing center as compared to a conventional hospital setting. Many birthing centers are family-friendly, offering play areas for children as they await the birth of a sibling. Some expectant parents prefer that children be with them for parts of the labor and delivery. Birthing centers tend to be more able to accommodate such requests than hospitals.

Most birthing centers offer prenatal care as well. During the course of the pregnancy, families become familiar with the childbirth settings and staff. By the time of birth, most families feel comfortable at the birthing center. Prenatal screening also allows for identification of potential problems that may be encountered. Birthing centers tend to view the birth experience as a positive, normal, healthy event. Women and their families are encouraged to take an active role in their own prenatal care and in their birth experiences. Following the birth, mothers recover at the birthing center for twelve to twenty-four hours. Birthing centers also tend to be small. Certified nurse-midwives, obstetricians, family practitioners, and lay midwives might be on the staff. Studies also show that birthing centers offer a safe alternative to hospitals. As compared to a home birth, a birthing-center birth tends to be more accepted by the medical community, as well as many in the lay community.

Although birthing centers offer accessibility to medical intervention, low-risk births are better suited for such a facility.

Maternal risk factors, such as a cesarean section with a previous pregnancy, history of postpartum hemorrhage, chronic hypertension, drug addiction, as well as conditions associated with the pregnancy such as a multiple pregnancy, placenta prevaria (the placenta blocks the cervical opening), or premature birth, usually require a hospital setting. Many birthing centers have fairly strict guidelines for use relating to maternal and pregnancy risk factors. A final consideration is, of course, the availability of the birthing center. Despite the advantages, there are few if any birthing centers in most communities.

Birth in a Noninterventive Hospital Setting
Hospital births offer many advantages for families, primarily the safety and security of having a host of medical experts on hand to care for mother and baby. The first birthing room in a hospital opened its doors in 1969 in Connecticut. Since that time, many hospitals have made major improvements in the ways they provide labor and delivery care. Birthing units, often bearing names such as the Mother-Baby Center or the Family Birthing Center, reflect a more positive approach to birth as well as creature comforts. Birthing suites, a single place in which the mother labors, delivers, and recovers, are common in many hospitals, although the number of suites might be limited to just one or two. Some birthing suites feature whirlpools or birthing tubs. Most hospital rooms for laboring mothers at least have a shower. Although many hospitals do not having birthing suites, many do have facilities where the woman can labor, deliver, and recover in the same room. Conventional hospital settings required the mother to spend early labor in one room, delivery in

another room, and recover in yet another room—and then be transferred to a different room for additional postpartum recovery. Labor-delivery recovery rooms and labor-delivery postpartum rooms are a great improvement. Most hospitals encourage fathers to be active participants in the births of their children, and many facilities allow other people, if desired by the family, to be present for some or all of the birth. Rooming-in is becoming more common in hospitals across the country, and most hospitals have lactation consultants on staff who can provide support for mothers wishing to breastfeed.

Although home births and birthing-center experiences are limited to women with low-risk pregnancies, birth in a hospital's birthing unit is available to some women with high-risk pregnancies as well. Still, there are some medical conditions defined by hospitals requiring a more conventional approach to birth. Families may have a choice of hospitals in their communities. Visits to the hospital's labor and delivery area can help to identify the most positive environment for childbirth.

Laboring in a Birthing Pool and Waterbirths
A warm bath is relaxing for many women, and during labor it can be especially soothing. Many birthing centers and some hospitals have whirlpools or birthing pools/tubs available. Many experts believe that the water supports the woman's body in ways that a bed cannot. Many women prefer warm showers as well. Allowing the water to stream over the back and abdomen can be soothing during contractions.

Sometimes a laboring woman feels so comfortable in the water that she does not wish to leave. Some women laboring in a pool wish to birth the baby in the pool. This is known as a waterbirth and is a more dramatic example of an alternative birth choice. In a waterbirth, the baby is actually born into a birthing pool or tub. Waterbirths as an alternative approach first appeared in the Soviet Union in the 1960s under the guidance of Igor Charkovsky, sometimes known as the father of waterbirth. Advocates of waterbirth believe that the warm water in a birthing pool soothes the laboring woman, explaining that the water supports the woman's body in ways that a bed cannot. Some experts believe that the water supports the stretching and relaxation of the perineum, which is stretched as the baby emerges from the birth canal. If the perineum can stretch and relax, there is less chance of tearing and less need for an episiotomy. Likewise, they describe the warm water as simulating the intrauterine environment, thus making the baby's transition from the womb to the outside world easier. Critics of waterbirth say it poses a risk of drowning for the newborn. Supporters of waterbirth counter that the infant receives oxygen through the umbilical cord until it stops pulsating. They also explain that the infant is accustomed to a watery environment and will not try to breathe until he comes in contact with the air. They believe waterbirth poses little threat to the infant as long as the baby is brought to the surface of the water in the first minute or two after birth. However, waterbirth remains a less common alternative birth choice. Many physicians and other medical providers have concerns about the safety of a waterbirth for the mother as well as the baby. As with other alternative birth choices, women experiencing high-risk

pregnancies are usually not a good match for a waterbirth.

Choosing Alternative Birth Practices

Most women who choose an alternative birth practice have researched their choice carefully. They tend to be well-educated about childbirth and well-informed about their choices. For most healthy women in a low-risk pregnancy, a carefully planned alternative birth, attended by a qualified medical provider such as a physician or CNM, is usually safe. Women experiencing high-risk pregnancies have more limited choices. Still, high-risk mothers can apply the principles behind alternative birth, namely, informed choices, respectful practices, and family-centered facilities in more conventional settings.

Choosing alternative birth practices often has several benefits for mother and baby. The primary advantage for the mother is that she feels in control of her birth experience. This feeling often translates into less fear and anxiety. Perhaps due, in part, to this control and active participation in labor and delivery, use of pain relief medication is lower for women birthing in alternative settings. Likewise, there are lower rates of caesarian section surgeries and other medical interventions. When the mother can create her own environment, she often feels the climate is more emotionally supportive. Further, she is able to move about as she likes during labor and delivery. Some experts believe as well that babies benefit from alternative birthing practices. For instance, many infants show short-term effects from pain medication used by mothers during labor. Infants born under alternative practices may be less likely to experience side effects (such as increased drowsiness and a lack of alertness), as use of pain-relief medication is lower among mothers using alternative birth. The philosophy of alternative birthing practices not only emphasizes the emotional needs of the mother but also calls attention to those of the infant. Thus, babies are viewed as active participants in their own births. Mothers using alternative birthing practices often talk to their babies throughout the labor and delivery. Often, they pay special attention to the physical environment, such as dimming the lights as the baby emerges to lessen overstimulation the baby may experience.

Planning for Alternative Births
The first step in planning an alternative birth is to consider the available choices and determine the most desirable outcome. Parents should research options carefully, gathering information on the risks and benefits of each alternative. Keeping in mind their goals of an ideal birth, parents must weigh the characteristics of each option. Writing a birth plan can help parents organize their wishes and priorities. The next step is to identify a medical provider who will support the birth plan. Conversations with physicians and midwives can help parents determine which professional might be the best match. Midwives' associations and childbirth education groups can provide information to families electing alternative birth practices.

See also Doula; Midwifery

References and further reading
American College of Nurse-Midwives (website 2001). http://www.midwife.org.
Childbirth.org (website 2001). http://www.childbirth.org.
Jones, C. 1990. *Alternative Birth.* New York: Tarcher Press.
Kitzinger, S. 1991. *Homebirth.* New York: Dorling Kindersley.
————. 1996. *The Complete Book of Pregnancy and Childbirth.* New York: Knopft Press.
Korte, D., R. Scaer, and L. Baker. 1992. *A Good Birth, a Safe Birth: Choosing and Having the Childbirth You Want.* 3rd ed. Cambridge: Harvard Press.
Simkin, P., and L. Stewart. 1998. *NAPSAC Directory of Alternative Birth Services and Consumer Guide.* 13th ed. NAPSAC Intl.
Tew, M. 1995. *Safer Childbirth? A Critical History of Maternity Care.* Rev. ed. Oxford, UK: Oxford University Press.

Altruism

Altruism is a prosocial act carried out without the expectation for reward or compensation. An example might be when a neighbor or nonrelated adult saves a toddler from harm's way at personal risk.

See also Emotion; Prosocial Behavior

American Sign Language

American sign language (AMESLAN) is a language system that uses motor movements to represent symbols. Children as young as infants and toddlers can learn to communicate using AMESLAN. Just as spoken languages differ from one culture to another, so too do forms of sign language.

See also Language

Amniocentesis

Amniocentesis includes procedures whereby amniotic fluid is extracted from the amniotic sac (usually while monitoring the fetus by sonogram) in order to analyze cells for the presence of abnormalities or for gender identification of the developing fetus. Typically performed during the twelfth and sixteenth weeks of pregnancy, amniocentesis can lead to identification of chromosomal or metabolic disorders that occur because of genetic transmission or as a result of congenital anomalies.

See also Prenatal Care

Amnion
Amnion is a membrane containing fluid (the so-called bag of waters) that surrounds the fetus and protects it throughout prenatal development.

See also Prenatal Development

Amniotic Fluid
The salty solution that fills the amniotic sac and protects the embryo and fetus from mechanical injury.

See also Prenatal Development

Amygdala
The amygdala, one of the limbic structures, is located just anterior to the hippocampus in the forebrain. It plays an important role in emotional responsiveness, the experience of anxiety and fear, and memory for situations that evoke these feelings.

See also Neurobiology

Anaclitic Depression
The famous child psychiatrist René Spitz described a state of depression in infants and toddlers that occurred after prolonged separation from their mothers. Spitz detailed several symptoms associated with anaclitic depression, including weepiness, sleep disturbances, susceptibility to respiratory ailments, poor social responsiveness, and risk for developmental retardation. According to Spitz, infants

A depressed child at a child care center. (Elizabeth Crews)

develop anaclitic depression because of the loss of the love object (mother). Spitz's original work involved observations of institutionalized infants, and he suggested that if institutionalization persisted beyond about five months, hospitalism would develop and the infant would suffer severe emotional deprivation. A more contemporary infant psychiatrist, Antoine Guedeney, suggests that severe malnutrition also can lead to infant depression, although in this case depression would not necessarily involve loss of the love object.

See also Emotion

References and further reading
Guedeney, Antoine. 2000. "Infant Depression and Withdrawal: Clinical Assessment." In Joy D. Osofsky and Hiram E. Fitzgerald, eds. *WAIMH Handbook of Infant Mental Health, Vol. 4: Infant Mental Health in Groups at High Risk.* New York: Wiley, pp. 455–484.
Spitz, René A. 1965. *The First Year of Life.* New York: International Universities Press.

Anal Stage
The anal stage is the second stage of psychosexual development that typically occurs during the second and third year of postnatal life. According to Freudian theory, the child's psychosexual energy and the pleasure associated with it focus on the process of elimination.

See also Freud, Sigmund

Analgesia
Analgesia is a medication used during labor to reduce or eliminate the sensation of pain without inducing loss of consciousness. More generally, an analgesic would include any drug such as a tran-

quilizer, barbiturate, or narcotic that was used to reduce or eliminate pain.

See also Obstetrical Medications

Analogy
In evolutionary theory, "analogy" is the term used when similar selective pressures result in adaptations that show likeness from one species to the next but do not necessarily reflect common ancestry for that adaptation.

Androgens
Androgens are hormones that play a critical role in the biological differentiation of males. During early fetal development, the XY chromosomes influence the release of androgens such as testosterone that cause male genital organs to differentiate into the penis and scrotum. Low levels of androgens allow the female genital organs to continue their normal development.

See also Teratogens

Anencephaly
Anencephaly is a form of neural-tube deficit that involves the developing brain and spinal cord. The prevalence of neural-tube deficits is less than one per 1,000 live births. Anencephaly occurs when the upper end of the anterior neural tube fails to close. Neural tissue becomes exposed through the cranium. Most anencephalic infants survive only for a few days.

See also Genetic Disorders; Spina Bifida

Anesthetics
Anesthetic medication, given during labor, eliminates the sensation of pain

either by inducing a state of unconsciousness (various forms of gas) or by blocking the transmission of pain signals to the brain (spinal block, saddle block). Anesthetics typically are administered during the first stage of labor and/or during delivery to decrease or eliminate pain associated with childbirth.

See also Obstetrical Medications

Anger

Anger is one of the basic core emotions. Facial expressions that seem to express anger are present in the early months of life but seem to increase in frequency and intensity beginning at around four months of age. Anger may be expressed in several situations, such as when an interesting toy or stimulus is removed. The expression of anger becomes more deliberate and increases with age as infants gain the cognitive skills needed to act with intentionality in the world, value their actions, and understand the effects they have on the world. Once the infant recognizes that one can act on the environment and create interesting effects, the infant can respond with anger when an action is prohibited, a goal is blocked, and so on. An angry expression is usually characterized by lowered, knitted eyebrows, an open mouth angled downward, and open and intense eyes.

See also Emotion

Anoxia

Anoxia is the lack of oxygen during parturition (the birth process). It is a leading cause of neonatal morbidity and mortality.

Anticipatory Grief

Anticipatory grief is an emotional or affective state that develops in parents when they are separated from their prematurely born infant. Because of the premature infant's risk status, parents often anticipate that their baby will die. This may interfere with their subsequent ability to form strong emotional attachments with their infant.

Anxiety

Anxiety is an emotion related to the basic core emotion of fear. During infancy, anxiety is most often associated with stranger anxiety, which refers to the wariness and fear elicited when the infant is in contact with unfamiliar people, places, and things. Anxiety may produce a stress response in infants charac-

A one-and-a-half-year-old clinging to her mother. (Elizabeth Crews)

terized by crying and clinging to the care-giver/parent.

See also Emotion

Apgar Scale

The APGAR examination is a screening test for newborns that was developed in 1953 by anesthesiologist Virginia Apgar. The APGAR examination is administered one and/or five minutes after birth. It provides information about the newborn's physiological status on five dimensions: activity (muscle tone), pulse (heart rate), grimace (reflex irritability), appearance (color), and respiration (respiratory effort). Each indicator is rated on a three-point scale, with total scores ranging from 0 to 10. Scores in the 7–10 range generally are indicative of well-being, and scores in the

TABLE 1   Apgar scoring chart

	Rating		
Category	0	1	2
Activity (muscle tone)	Flaccid	Some flexion in extremities	Active motion
Pulse (heart rate)	None	Slow (below 100 beats per minute)	Over 100 beats per minute
Grimace (reflex irritability)	No response	Grimace	Strong cry
Appearance (color)	Blue, pale	Body pink; extremities blue	Completely pink
Respiration (respiratory effort	Absent	Slow	Good, crying

Source: Adapted from V. Apgar, "A Proposal for a New Method of Evaluation of the Newborn Infant," *Current Research in Anesthesia and Analgesia* 32 (1953): 260–267.

range of 0–6 are indicative of potential problems. Although low scores alert health care providers to possible complications, many newborns who score low at one or five minutes score in the acceptable range at ten to twenty minutes.

See also Assessment

Apnea

Apnea is the absence of breathing for periods of more than twenty seconds in the preterm infant and for periods of about fifteen seconds in the full-term infant. Although causal mechanisms have not been fully discovered, apnea in the preterm infant is thought to reflect aspects of the infant's immature respiratory system. A wide range of factors are linked to postpartum bouts of apnea. Infants with a sibling who experienced sudden infant death syndrome are at risk, as are infants with various neurological disorders.

See also Sudden Infant Death Syndrome

Approach-Withdrawal

Approach-withdrawal reflects individual differences in tendency toward a new object or person. Some babies easily accept new foods and toys and smile and babble at strangers, whereas others withdraw and/or cry upon first exposure.

See also Temperament

Art

Infants begin their attempts at artwork by making tiny marks on paper with a crayon or pencil held in a fisted hand by twelve months. Two-year-olds can scribble with long wavy strokes on a sheet of paper. Three-year-olds can make a round circle, although often the hand continues to create lines superimposed on one another, as the toddler may find it difficult to stop after producing just one circle. Three-year-olds can draw a straight line vertically and another horizontally. When asked to draw a person, children between three and four will often draw a circle (for a head) with two long lines coming straight down from the head. Sometimes the toddler adds tiny circles for eyes and a nose, but these may often be found at random places inside the circle head, rather than in normative positions. Early in the preschool years, children often show a surety of line and vivid use of colors in their drawings, but these signs of artistic vigor and creative use of color may disappear by early school years. Some children, talented in art, can make remarkable line drawings of a favorite character by four years of age. Many young preschoolers can draw stick figures to represent persons. They are able to draw a family picture when requested by a therapist, for example, who is trying to make custody assessments for a divorce case and wants to see whom the child includes among the stick-figure drawings, how close each family member is placed to another figure, and who may be omitted from the child's picture.

See also Songs and Sensory Development

Artificial Insemination
Artificial insemination is a procedure to induce pregnancy by introducing sperm into the vagina by a syringe rather than by sexual intercourse.

See also Fertilization

Assessment
Assessment is the process of obtaining information that can then be used to make responsible and informed decisions to assist the development of a child. Assessments are conducted for many reasons, including screening, diagnosis, program planning, and readiness and achievement testing. Because many different tests are available, with each targeting a specific domain of development and having a specific purpose, the examiner must clearly understand the function of the particular assessment for the individual child.

Screening is a process in which assessment is used to identify children experiencing or at risk for certain problems in health, cognition, physical development, or social skills. Three types of developmental risk provide a focus for the screening process: established risk, biological risk, and environmental risk. Established risk includes conditions that can be identified at birth or soon after that strongly predict developmental delay, such as genetic, neurological, cognitive, or physical impairments associated with Down syndrome, spina bifida, cerebral palsy, blindness, and limb deformities. Biological risk includes physical and medical traumas, such as extremely low birthweight, that occur during pregnancy, childbirth, or the newborn period that usually but not always cause developmental delay. Environmental risk conditions exist in the physical or family environment that may negatively affect the child's development, including exposure to lead paint, poor parenting skills, lack of access to medical care, unemployment, and parental drug abuse.

Screening may be conducted with large groups of children to determine who might be in need of more intensive assessment,

Warm interaction between a two-year-old and his caregiver. (Elizabeth Crews)

or it may be used with individuals referred by parents, caregivers, or teachers to evaluate specific areas that are especially problematic. By determining whether a child has a problem that may cause greater difficulty as he/she advances, early intervention can be implemented if necessary. Screening tests are designed to be a first step in the assessment process and are often brief. Ideally, they should meet two important requirements: sensitivity and specificity. Sensitivity indicates that the test is able to successfully identify at-risk infants, with a minimum of 80 percent of the children with problems receiving failing scores. Conversely, specificity indicates that the test accurately identifies children who are not at risk, with a minimum of 90 percent of the children without

problems passing the test. If the screening test is unable to meet these conditions, costly resources will be devoted to children who do not require services; more important, children in need of resources will be overlooked. However, during screening it is preferable to overclassify children in order to avoid missing children for whom services are necessary.

Diagnosis is the classification of the set of problems presented by the infant into a category that will enable intervention to be targeted effectively. Diagnostic categories enable professionals who specialize in different developmental areas to communicate more easily by providing a common language. A specific diagnosis, such as anxiety disorder, allows those who work with the child to have some understanding of the possible causes, the characteristic symptoms, and the potential outcomes. Diagnosis through assessment assists in the specification of treatment and may also qualify a family for access to special resources. The most commonly used diagnostic classification scheme for infants and young children is detailed in a manual published by Zero to Three: The National Center for Infants, Toddlers, and Families, entitled *Diagnostic Classification of Mental Health and Developmental Disorders of Infancy and Early Childhood* (1994). The manual provides specific guidelines for examiners to assist in determining whether a child meets the criteria for a particular diagnosis.

Program planning utilizes information regarding the child's strengths and weaknesses gathered during the assessment process to identify the problems that require remediation and to develop a problem-focused treatment approach. Optimally, a team consisting of professionals who specialize in the relevant developmental domains, such as psychology, physical health, language, motor skills, and nutrition, discusses the problem areas to address. In conjunction with the family, they determine what resources are available and work to overcome family factors that may impede successful implementation of the program, such as work schedules or lack of transportation. Assessment enables the program planning process to have distinct targets and specific goals and utilizes those areas in which the child is relatively skilled.

Readiness and achievement testing evaluates the child's knowledge and abilities in designated areas and is typically used with children entering or attending school. Readiness tests determine the extent to which a child is able to implement skills and retain an understanding

of concepts. For example, prior to entering kindergarten, a child might be administered a readiness test to determine whether he/she can count to ten and put on (but not tie) shoes. These tests are used to assess whether the child is reasonably prepared for a setting so that he/she will not be at a disadvantage. Achievement tests evaluate the extent of the child's knowledge and retention of school-based learning. A math test is an example of an achievement test.

Principles of Infant Assessment

Assessment methods have traditionally neglected to attend to unique aspects of the young child's development that affect the evaluation process. This has resulted in the exclusion of caregivers from the assessment process, lack of consideration of the effects of the testing context on the child, and misinformed expectations for developmental abilities. To address these problems, a work group assembled by Zero to Three developed a set of basic principles applied to the assessment of infants and young children:

1. Assessment must be based on an integrated developmental model. This principle highlights the need to consider the complex context within which children develop, including the physical, cognitive, and socioemotional characteristics intrinsic to the child, as well as the larger environment (e.g., family, community, culture) surrounding the child. Moreover, this approach emphasizes the need to focus on the child's optimal level of functioning rather than only determining the deficits. Because the child might function at a higher level in some contexts compared to others,

the child should be observed in a variety of settings to provide a more complete picture of his/her abilities.

2. Assessment involves multiple sources of information and multiple components. Evaluations should not be based on a single test. To best represent the diverse behavior that a child can exhibit over time and across situations, a variety of methods should be used that will provide different perspectives on his/her functioning. This includes the parents' perceptions of the child's abilities, developmental history, concerns, and techniques to support the child, observations of the child alone and interacting with the parents, and targeted assessments of specific areas of concern (e.g., language, hearing).

3. An assessment should follow a certain sequence. The following framework is suggested: (a) A link must be established with the parents by discussing their concerns, ascertaining their evaluations of the child's strengths and weaknesses, and identifying their goals; (b) the developmental history of the child should be obtained to determine what risk factors may have been present earlier in the child's life; (c) the child should be observed while playing with the primary caregiver(s); (d) the child should be observed while playing with a clinician; (e) assessment of specific areas that may be of concern should be conducted; and (f) the information from the various sources should be integrated within a developmental framework and discussed with the caregivers,

with a goal of implementing intervention if needed.

4. The child's relationships and interactions with his/her most trusted caregivers should form the foundation of an assessment. The child's optimal functioning is likely to occur in the context of interactions with a close caregiver. These interactions provide both a forum for assessing the child's abilities and the foundation for interventions, which will almost certainly require the caregiver's participation.

5. An understanding of sequences and timetables in typical development is essential as a framework for the interpretation of developmental differences among infants and toddlers. The period from birth to age three encompasses tremendous change in all domains of development, but individual children attain competencies at different rates. The examiner and team must have a thorough understanding not only of overall developmental milestones but also the range of ages that represents normal development for each milestone.

6. Assessment should emphasize attention to the child's level and pattern of organizing experience as well as attention to functional capacities. Functional capacities are cognitive and emotional characteristics that enable the child to function within the world, such as: (a) paying attention; (b) relating and engaging; (c) intentional participation in reciprocal interactions; (d) understanding the purposes and functions for sequences of behaviors; (e) symbolic understanding as opposed to requiring concrete

displays; and (f) putting together symbolic relationships. A child with well-developed functional capacities may, despite developmental delay or a physical handicap, be able to marshal his/her resources to function in a socially appropriate and adaptive manner.

7. The assessment process should identify the child's current competencies and strengths, as well as the competencies that will constitute developmental progression in a continuous growth model of development. This provides a context for the child's skills and enables the team to determine the age at which the abilities in question are typically demonstrated and the sequence of abilities that is likely to follow.

Additionally, Zero to Three has described several assessment practices that should be avoided: conducting assessment apart from the caregivers, allowing a strange examiner to assess the child without an extended familiarization period, assessing only easily measurable domains that have simple tests, and relying exclusively on formal tests that do not take into account the developmental level of infants and/or developmentally delayed individuals. These factors will inhibit the examiner's capacity to determine the infant's optimal level of functioning and provide a comprehensive portrait of the child's skills upon which to build.

Types of Assessment
As described in the Zero to Three guidelines, if one is to gain a comprehensive understanding of the infant's strengths and weaknesses, then assessment through multiple methods is recommended. Professionals in each developmental domain utilize tests that will provide specialized information for their area of expertise; for example, speech and language therapists may recommend a hearing test and physicians may request certain medical tests. Apart from these very specific tests, there are three general methods for evaluating infants: parent/caregiver reports, observations, and standardized tests.

Caregiver Reports. Information from the caregiver is critical. Caregivers can provide details of the child's developmental history, temperamental tendencies, home behavior, and functional skills. Furthermore, caregivers have the opportunity to observe the child for extended periods of time across a variety of situations and can thus suggest contextual influences that might help or exacerbate the child's behavior. Finally, it is usually parents who identify areas of concern and refer the child for assessment and treatment. The examiner's task is to obtain relevant information from the parents as effectively as possible.

Parents commonly give their perceptions of the child's functioning through interviews and questionnaires. An advantage of interviews is that the examiner can pursue in more detail aspects of the parent's report that might be especially crucial for diagnosis or intervention. In addition, interviews provide an excellent forum for establishing rapport with parents and establishing their role as a crucial part of the assessment and intervention team.

Interviews can be either unstructured or structured. In a unstructured interview, the examiner discusses parental concerns and asks questions that differ from family to family, depending on the problems presented by the individual child. In this type of interview, the examiner might ask how the child responds to strong sensory stimuli, whether he/she is interested in playing with other children, how the child makes his/her needs known to the parent, what a typical mealtime is like, and what activities are most enjoyable or difficult with the child. These open-ended questions encourage a flexible discussion in which the parents and examiner can focus on areas they perceive as most important and assist the examiner in forming an alliance with the parents. In a structured interview, a standard set of questions is asked of every parent in order to obtain specific information. One example of a structured interview is the Vineland Adaptive Behavior Scales, which compares parents' perceptions of the child's behavior with the behaviors of typically developing children of the same age.

Questionnaires. Questionnaires are another valuable assessment tool. They are a cost-effective method of gathering information because they do not require the direct participation of the examiner. This allows parents to complete them at home or in the office while the examiner works with the child. Questionnaire measures are usually targeted toward a specific domain of functioning such as self-care skills, word knowledge, motor skills, and aggressive behavior problems. Parents can be given several different questionnaires in order to capture a variety of information.

One issue in using parents in infant assessment relates to the accuracy of parent reports. Some have questioned whether parents have realistic views of

their child's behavior, especially children who present behavioral problems or developmental delays. Researchers examining this question have concluded that parents generally provide accurate information about their child's developmental abilities. Certain factors increase the likelihood that reports would be reliable. Parents are more consistent when questions focused on concrete, observable behaviors ("Can your child jump up and down using both feet?") rather than behaviors that require inference and judgment ("Does your child feel guilty when he/she does something wrong?"). In addition, structured interviews and questionnaires with clear instructions and specific guidelines provide better quality information than open-ended questions.

Observations. Observations are a crucial component of the assessment of young children, as infant/toddlers are not able to provide most information verbally. While observing the child, the examiner might note the child's gross and fine motor skills, language development, communication skills, impulse control, activity level, attention span, social responsiveness, problem-solving approaches, and overall mood. Observational assessment can take several different forms. The examiner may monitor the child's behavior during a formal observational process, structured or unstructured play, interaction with the caregivers or alone, or in the educational or child-care setting. Play-based assessment, such as the Transdisciplinary Play-Based Assessment, is an especially appropriate forum for several of these assessment approaches. In addition, observations can take the form of written descriptions, ratings on a specified scale, or tallies of individual behaviors observed, for example, every five seconds. Preferably, multiple observation sessions across a variety of settings should be conducted to obtain a comprehensive picture of the child's abilities and functioning.

Standardized Tests. Standardized tests assess domains of functioning in specified ways. For example, to evaluate cognitive development, the examiner might administer the mental scale of the Bayley Scales of Infant Development or the Fagan Test of Infant Intelligence; to assess sensorimotor development from the perspective of Piaget, he/she might administer the Ordinal Scales of Psychological Development. Each of these tests has different tasks intended to examine aspects of functioning believed to tap cognitive processing and to predict later mental development.

Test Characteristics. To be useful, questionnaires, structured observations, and standardized tests should have two properties: reliability and validity. Reliability is the extent to which the test is consistent. In other words, if we give the test today and give it again in a week or a month, do we get the same results? Validity is the extent to which the test measures what it is intended to measure. Do the questions ask about issues that concern us? Do the test scores relate to other measures of the behavior or characteristic? Do the test scores predict future outcomes? Reliable, valid tests enable us to have some confidence in our assessments so that we can plan interventions that are appropriate for the problems of the individual child.

See also Cognitive Development; Mental Development; Play-based Assessment; Q-sort;

References and further reading
Bergen, D. 1994. *Assessment Methods for Infants and Toddlers.* New York: Teachers College Press.
Blackman, J. A. 1995. *Identification and Assessment in Early Intervention.* Gaithersburg, MD: Aspen Publishers.
Meisels, Samuel J., and Emily Fenichel. 1996. *New Visions for the Developmental Assessment of Infants and Young Children.* Washington, DC: Zero to Three, National Center for Infants, Toddlers, and Families.

Assessment, Evaluation, and Programming System

The Assessment, Evaluation, and Programming System (AEPS) is an assessment tool used by specialists in child intervention to evaluate the abilities of young children who are at-risk or have disabilities. AEPS is designed to link assessment and intervention in order to comprehensively address the individual's needs. It is appropriate for children with mental ages between one month and three years. Initial assessment typically takes approximately two hours, and subsequent assessments to monitor the child's progress take much less. Individuals who conduct the evaluation must have a good understanding of early child development in order to properly score the AEPS. There are six domains: fine motor, gross motor, adaptive, cognitive, social-communication, and social. Information is intended for use with the interdisciplinary team to guide program planning and monitor progress. A supplementary set of materials is available to involve parent/caregivers during the evaluation process and to identify areas of concern to the family.

See also Assessment

References and further reading
Bricker, D., ed. 1993. *Assessment,
Evaluation, and Programming System
for Infants and Children, Vol. 1: AEPS
Measurement for Birth to Three Years.*
Baltimore: Paul H. Brookes Publishing.

Assessment of Infant Caregivers

The assessment of infant caregivers—an evaluation of caregiving skills and knowledge—is an integral part of quality infant caregiving and the professional development of caregivers. Assessment procedures are carried out for various reasons with different goals in mind. Whatever the goal, periodic assessments of caregivers and program practices are important to the provision of quality care for infants, toddlers, and families.

Goals of Assessment
Assessments of infant caregivers are generally carried out with one of two purposes in mind: either to support ongoing professional growth and development, or to identify or document a concern. The most positive goal is to incorporate ongoing assessments of caregivers as a part of general program assessment and quality improvement. From this perspective, assessment is not viewed as a threat by caregivers but as a part of the professional environment. With this goal in mind, program directors or other personnel carrying out the assessment build a relationship with the caregivers, and this relationship provides a safe context in which caregivers are encouraged to identify and to reflect upon their personal strengths and areas for growth. Such self-awareness is an important component in providing optimal infant/toddler child care.

Often, however, assessments of caregivers are carried out only when a prob-
lem is suspected. In such cases, assessment can be met with caution and suspicion by the caregiver, as the goal of assessment is to identify what is wrong with the caregiver's practices. The caregiver may believe, rightly so, that poor assessment results will lead to disciplinary actions or even to dismissal from employment.

Approaches to Caregiver Assessment
Regardless of the assessment goals, assessment practices can be carried out through informal or formal methods or a combination.

Informal Assessments. Informal assessments typically include the use of strategies such as self-evaluations or observational assessment by peers or the program director. Self-evaluations can help make caregivers aware of their own strengths and areas for growth in their work with infants and toddlers. Over time, self-awareness can improve the quality of care provided to children. Further, self-assessment can be an important part of program quality-improvement efforts. Similarly, observations by colleagues or by the program director, focusing on how infants and caregivers interact and how infants respond to caregivers, can provide a wealth of information about the caregiving quality. This information is useful to caregiver evaluations as well as overall program evaluations.

Formal Assessments. Checklists, rating scales, or observations by licensing consultants or program accreditors tend to be used in more formal assessments. Most checklists or rating scales include the following areas: caregiver-infant interactions, relationships with parents, the environment, toys, and materials, caregiving routines, cleanliness, and health and safety policies and procedures. Many times, environmental assessments, such as the Infant-Toddler Environmental Rating Scale, will include an assessment of a caregiver's skills and knowledge as part of an overall assessment of the child-care program. Similarly, accreditation assessments, such as those conducted by the National Academy of Early Childhood Programs, include an assessment of the caregiver as a component of program assessment. In terms of caregiver-infant interactions, information can be obtained about the ways in which the caregiver works to facilitate the infant's social and emotional development as well as cognitive, language, and physical development.

A comprehensive assessment consists of several components. Prior to using any assessment tool, the caregiver and program director should have had the opportunity to discuss the caregiver's roles, duties, and responsibilities as well as other employment goals and expectations. Such conversations ensure that the caregiver knows what is expected on the job. The next step in the assessment process is to gather assessment information through the use of observations or assessment tools. After collecting the information, the caregiver and the director should review and discuss the information collected. Based on the review of the information, new goals for job performance, as well as a plan for continued professional development, should be established.

See also Child-Care Accreditation

References and further reading
Best Practices Child and Family Assessment Protocol Pilot Project (website 2001). http://trc2.ucdavis.edu/cacredolo/bp/.
Dombro, A. L., L. J. Colker, and D. T. Dodge. 1998. *The Creative Curriculum for Infants and Toddlers.* Washington, DC: Teaching Strategies.
Greenman, J., and A. Stonehouse. 1996. *Primetimes: A Handbook for Excellence in Infant and Toddler Programs.* St. Paul, MN: Redleaf Press.
Honig, Alice S., and J. Ronald Lally. 1981. *Infant Caregiving: A Design for Training.* Syracuse: Syracuse University Press.

Assessment of Infant Environments

The process whereby environments are assessed, either by state representatives, accreditation representatives, program staff or administrators, or researchers. Assessments can be conducted for licensing or accreditation, for quality-improvement purposes, for self-evaluation, and for research purposes.

Assessment of the Preterm Infant Behavior Scale

The Assessment of the Preterm Infant Behavior Scale (APIB) is a sophisticated and detailed assessment tool developed by Heideliese Als to evaluate the developmental status of preterm infants. Based on the systemic principle of synaction, APIB owes its origins to the Brazelton Neonatal Behavioral Assessment Scale. The principle of synaction emphasizes the systemic and hierarchical nature of development and leads to assessment of the infant in each of five functional systems: physiological, motor organization, state organization, attentional/interactive, and self-regulation. The examiner also assesses the degree of integration among the functional systems.

See also Assessment

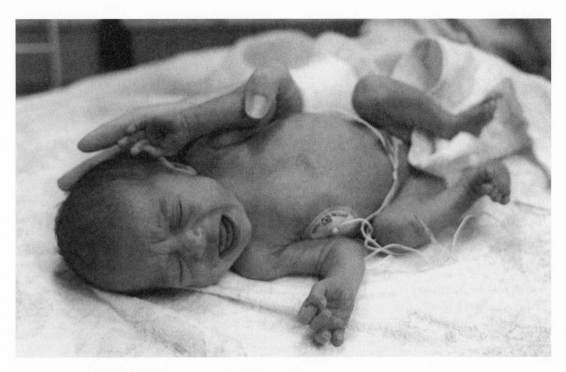

A premature infant in the hospital. (Elizabeth Crews)

References and further reading
Als, Heidelise, et al. 1982. "Toward a
    Research Instrument for the
    Assessment of Preterm Infants'
    Behavior (APIB)" and "Manual for the
    Assessment of the Preterm Infants'
    Behavior." In Hiram E. Fitzgerald, Barry
    M. Lester, and Barry Zuckerman, eds.
    *Theory and Research in Behavioral
    Pediatrics.* Vol. 1. New York: Plenum,
    pp. 35–64, 65–132.

Assimilation

In Piagetian theory, *assimilation* means
the adaptive changes that occur when the
infant uses his/her existing cognitive
structures to incorporate the demands of
the environment. An infant can assimilate a crayon into an existing scheme for
sucking but will have to accommodate to
learn how to drink from a cup. When the
toddler calls a brown cow swishing its
tail "doggie," he/she is assimilating the
cow into her existing schema or mental
representation of animals.

> *See also* Accommodation; Cognitive
> Development; Piaget, Jean

Associationism

Associationism is a theory of learning
that maintains that the contents of consciousness reflect the associative links
formed between ideas. Stimulus-stimulus
and stimulus-response associations are
thought to be especially important in
behaviorist explanations of learning. For
example, an associationist might argue
that infants exposed to two languages
during early development would learn the

cross-language word meanings through pair-associate learning. For example, infants and toddlers in Gaelic-speaking homes would learn these equivalences: *babai*—baby; *máthair*—mother, *athair*—father. Extensive study of language development suggests that associationist explanations for language learning cannot account for much of the rich complexity of information processing that regulates language acquisition.

See also Conditioning; Language; Learning

Associative Memory

The associative form of memory refers to the integration of two or more events (for example, associating a mother's face with her voice).

See also Memory

Asthma

Asthma is a breathing disorder and is the most common chronic health problem of childhood. Asthma attacks affect the child's ability to breathe; spasms of the air passages occur and they fill with mucus, resulting in coughing, wheezing, and shortness of breath. Although asthma occurs in concert with respiratory infections, attacks can also be caused by: stress; exposure to air pollutants, including cigarette smoke; animals, household dust, pollen, and molds; heavy exercise; and cold, rainy climatic conditions. There are various medications available to help children cope with asthma, but to date there is no cure. Although children with asthma can live normal, active lives, they are also always at risk for respiratory difficulties that can be life-threatening.

Attachment

The pioneer British psychiatrist John Bowlby, as well as the American innovator psychologist Mary Ainsworth, who captured the essence of attachment in her ingenious research, defined "attachment" as a long-lasting emotional bond revealed when a child seeks out and tries to stay close to a specific figure, especially when the child is under stress. Bowlby built on earlier Freudian theories that focused on the child's attachment to its mother as a learned secondary drive that developed because the mother satisfied the infant's oral needs. In contrast, Bowlby emphasized the importance of maternal attitude (warm, emotionally responsive) and the difficulties for the infant when separated from the mother. The baby's need for an attachment figure was just as fundamental as the need for nourishment.

Early attachment research focused on how infants and young children developed such a special relationship. Bowlby's idea was that attachment is a fundamentally important, biologically based aspect of human development, its function to furnish protection for the helpless infant.

Several kinds of biologically built-in baby behaviors, when activated, reveal the presence of a growing positive attachment. Some are signaling behaviors such as crying, calling, and reaching out to the special caregiver. Among self-propelled, executive behaviors are: approaching, seeking, climbing up on, clinging and grasping, or suckling on the special person.

Differential behaviors to the special caregiver occur when a baby will more frequently and more positively smile, call to, and follow after the attachment figure. There are other characteristics of the securely attached infant, including differ-

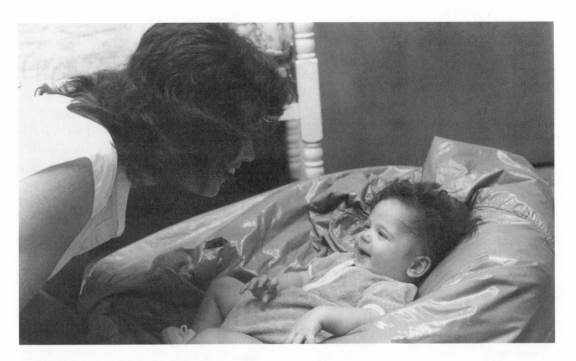

Bathing, feeding, and diaper changing provide the types of interactions that help infants to learn the dialogue of communication, emotion regulation, and emotional expressiveness. (Photograph courtesy of Timothy L. Ledesma)

ential referencing (i.e., looking toward the caregiver for reassurance signals) when fearful or scared; and differential ability to be soothed by the special attachment figure and to relax on the body of that special person so that the child can again set out to play, discover, and explore autonomously when the attachment figure is present and available.

No single behavior is an index of attachment. Attachment cannot be measured by any single infant behavior, such as crying when a caregiver leaves the room. Ainsworth, who worked initially with Bowlby in London, went on to study the development of attachment among African infants in Uganda. She carefully noted positive attachment behaviors, such as crying for, calling or reaching arms out to, smiling at, crawling toward, clinging

to, and climbing into the lap of the mother to receive comfort if tired or scared. Ainsworth also noted differential smiling and vocalizing more to the mother compared with a stranger. Mothers who could describe their infants in more detail had babies who were more securely attached. Yet attachment is not to be found in any single action or cluster of behaviors. For example, some infants who are not securely attached to a parent will still protest loudly if the parent leaves them alone with a stranger. Attachment is the emotional bond between the two persons and is a long-lasting relationship.

Attachment is always to a specific figure. Thus, a child may be securely attached to one parent or grandparent but not to the other. If the child loses the attachment figure who provides comfort and protection, he/she will grieve and become distressed. If the child is very young, life-long feelings of mourning and depression can occur after such a loss. Sometimes when a child is abandoned or neglected by a parent, then strong feelings of anger also occur along with anxious longing for the loved one's return. Selma Fraiberg called these mental representations "ghosts in the nursery." When such a child grows up and becomes a parent, then these ghosts can intrude into the new relationship and cause difficulties and disturbances, such as an inability to bond with or empathically care for the new infant.

Secure attachment is an intense loving relationship with a special other person. Both external and internal motivators galvanize children to demonstrate the kind of attachment they have developed with the primary caregiver. Attachment behaviors can be clearly seen when the infant is separated from the attachment figure, such as when a beloved parent leaves the room, or when a parent engrossed in watching a TV program ignores the infant who has taken a tumble and is demanding to be picked up. Attachment behaviors such as clinging may be activated when a usually cheerful infant, bewildered by frequent changes of hotel on a family vacation, becomes cranky and clingy with the caregiver. Not only external motivators but internal conditions as well arouse attachment behaviors. When a child is tired, sick, shivering from cold, or hurt and in pain, then he/she will try hard to reach the attachment figure to gain protection and reassurance. Once the baby gains physical closeness and absorbs comfort from the attachment figure, then the intensity of the activation of the attachment system will diminish. Indeed, a reassured baby may well slide off a par-

ent's lap and go over to explore toys across the room as long as the attachment figure is available and visible in the room. Such actions show that attachment is in balance with several other motivational systems. When there is strong fear (e.g., of the dark or a dog barking loudly) or wariness of a stranger who comes too close for the infant's comfort, then the attachment system will be activated. When the baby is well-fed and rested and the attachment figure is nearby, the baby may play independently and happily and ignore the nearby attachment figure. A variety of motivational control systems are in dynamic interaction with each other, as well as with the adult's caregiving system, in order to provide protection and safety for the young child.

For adults, the attachment, friendship/ affiliative, caregiving, and sexuality systems are interrelated. Parents play out their roles as attachment figures; they also have active roles in feeding, diapering, and bathing as well as in play, language communication, reading, and other caring/ teaching activities. But attachment is the first social behavioral system to develop. Bowlby highlighted four major functions of infant behavior: Seeking protection and care is in the service of the attachment system; avoiding potentially dangerous or frightening people or events is coordinated by the fear/wariness system; playful social interactions are coordinated by the affiliative system; and inquiry into unknown toys and environments is controlled by the exploratory system. For young children, then, attachment needs are shaped by continual transactions with caregivers and are always in dynamic interplay with exploration/curiosity and fear/wariness arousal.

The set goal of the attachment system is for the baby to feel secure. From intimate experiences with a caregiver during

A mother in Western Springs, Illinois, comforts her four-year-old daughter after a bad day. (Skjold Photographs)

the first year, the baby gradually builds up and constructs an internal picture—a working model of the attachment figure and of the self. This early, built-up model operates outside of consciousness.

Attachment, as a goal-corrected behavioral system, is flexible. Thus, the young child will devise different ways to bring the attachment figure close or to reach the attachment figure. If one method does not work, another will. For example, a toddler in a playpen may cry and lift up arms to be taken out and into the mother's arms. If those techniques do not work, the toddler, who is in early stages of toilet learning, may call out "Pee-pee!" in order to bring mama hurrying over to carry

him/her over to the potty, which he/she might promptly ignore. In this case, the infant used an ingenious, goal-corrected action (rather than familiar gambits that did not work) to achieve closeness with the attachment figure.

The attachment system is continually active. When babies feel secure, safe and deeply sure of availability of their attachment person(s), they move out to explore with vigor, absorbed in play. If they sense danger, become alarmed, or feel abandoned or threatened, their attachment needs surge, and they seek proximity to their beacon of safety, their special person who knows how to cope so well and will provide the surety and soothing they need. The internal working model of attachment involves the child's perception, cognition, attention mechanisms, memory, and fantasy cohesively organized. Increasingly, this model comes to shape the child's way of viewing others and colors the way in which the child grows to respond to social cues and to other peoples' actions and words.

Attachment builds slowly over the first years of life. The baby, gradually through innumerable tiny interactions with the caregiver(s), learns confidence in the availability of the attachment figure(s) in his/her life. By the second half of the first year, a child's behaviors become intensely focused upon one caregiver, and his/her behaviors become organized in response to the whereabouts and behaviors of the special attachment person. The mental models of self and of the relationship patterns with each caregiver become central components of personality.

Attachment, an internalized working model, serves as a guide for and interpreter of future emotions, perceptions, and behaviors across the life span and other relationships. Bowlby believed that attachment relationships play a crucial role in the development of later personality through the influence of these so-called working models. The critical component in intergenerational transmission is a person's notion of who his attachment figures are, where they may be found, and how they may be expected to respond. Similarly, in the working model of the self that anyone builds, a key feature is his/her notion of how acceptable or unacceptable the self is in the eyes of intimate attachment figures. The growing ability of the toddler and preschooler to integrate memories of experiences, thoughts, and feelings contributes to building the attachment representations.

These are "working" models because as children interact with others throughout life the internal models are possibly subject to modification. As Bowlby notes:

> When an individual is confident that an attachment figure will be available to him whenever he desires it, that person will be much less prone to either intense or chronic fear than will an individual who for any reason has no such confidence. Confidence in the availability of attachment figures, or a lack of it, is built up slowly during the years of immaturity—infancy, childhood, and adolescence—and whatever expectations are developed during those years tend to persist relatively unchanged throughout the rest of life. The varied expectation of the accessibility and responsiveness of attachment figures that individuals develop during the years of immaturity are tolerably accurate reflections of the experiences those individuals have actually had. (Bowlby, 1973, p. 235)

Attachment relationships, internally organized, operate at an unconscious level as dual templates. The baby learns about the caregivers' availability and nurturance in times of stress, and the baby also perceives his/her own worthiness and lovability. Consider a baby who has been neglected and/or abused. The baby grows up feeling unlovable and acts fearful as a child victim. When grown to adulthood, that person may also activate the internalized model for becoming in turn a rejecting/unloving and fearsome abuser. Thus, if the caregiving environment does not improve for the young child who is at risk for insecure attachment, then the internal working model has multiple representations and may be

Teaching young children to master personal skills encourages development of self-sufficiency and independence. (Photo courtesy of Paul Rochlen)

quite difficult to change without help from therapeutic personnel.

Bowlby discusses abnormal working models. For example, a young child who feels unloved can behave in ways to exasperate and stress a teacher or caregiver, until that adult responds sharply or with strong disapproval. Without realizing it, this child has arranged for circumstances that continue to confirm his/her unlovability. Another scenario that Bowlby discusses is when the child excludes from memory the inappropriate parent behaviors and claims that the parent was very loving. One little boy, being taken by ambulance to the hospital, explained to the attendant that his mother loved him a lot, but she had to burn his hand because "I was a bad boy."

Each attachment a baby forms is unique. A baby builds up a secure attachment with each separate person who cares for him/her. The baby responds to the adult's innumerable small daily gestures of care and degree of sensitive attunement as well as the synchrony in their interactions.

Attachment is relationship-specific, not infant-specific. The baby will form a secure attachment with a consistently emotionally available, caring person, tuned into distress signals and promptly meeting the baby's needs appropriately. Children need a special person or two the first years of life to develop a secure attachment. However, children securely attached both to mother and to father (when compared with children securely attached to just one parent) proved to be the most sociable, compliant, and friendly in response to overtures by a stranger dressed as a clown.

Researchers have confirmed the main tenets of attachment theory through decades of clinical, laboratory, and cross-cultural research. Many mental health pioneers, such as Erik Erikson, Sybil Escalona, Selma Fraiberg, Margaret Mahler and colleagues, and Donald Winnicott, carried out therapeutic intervention work with infants and families who lacked harmonious mutuality in their relationships. This work with families, and with very young children who suffered from mental health disturbances in parent-child emotional interactions, documented the difficulties we have now come to call "attachment" problems or "reactive attachment disorders."

Work with mothers delivering infants has pointed to the importance of a supportive nurturing person, called a "doula," for the mother during childbirth to increase the chance for initial positive bonding of mother and infant.

The Ainsworth Strange Situation Measure of Infant Attachment

After her work among the Uganda, Ainsworth moved to Baltimore and carried out in-depth studies of mother-infant interactions. She traced the relationship between infant attachments measured at about one year and prior, meticulously observed patterns of maternal behaviors with the infants in the home during the first year of life. To document this relationship, Ainsworth created the major method used to assess attachment today. This experimental procedure, called the Ainsworth Strange Situation, is used with young infants.

The Strange Situation measurement takes place over a twenty-minute period divided into three-minute episodes. In the first episode, mother and baby are introduced into a room with toys. Baby plays in the room with mother present. Then a stranger enters and mother leaves baby alone for three minutes with the stranger. Mother returns, and the stranger leaves. Reunion behaviors of the baby are carefully observed. Baby again plays in the room with mother present. Then she leaves and the baby is left alone for three minutes. This second departure of the mother is thus far more stressful in comparison with the first episode where mother left baby with the stranger. The stranger returns briefly, and then mother returns and the second reunion behaviors with mother are carefully noted and coded. The Strange Situation procedure can be used to measure an infant's relationship with any person, not just the mother, who is a salient attachment figure for the baby. Four major attachment patterns, with some subsets of each kind, have been revealed in research with the Strange Situation among infants twelve and eighteen months old.

The first pattern has been labeled secure attachment (B). During reunion, baby seeks contact (bodily or by smiles and greetings at a distance) and proximity to mother. Baby relaxes deeply on the attachment figure's body and accepts comfort and reassurance. Baby gains courage and energy to go back to constructive play. B babies use the caregiver as a secure base from which to explore the environment. Secure children express feelings and communicate even negative feelings openly with the caregiver. Secure babies trust the caregiver will be accessible and responsive if they need comfort, reassurance, care, or attention.

Mothers of B babies during home observations were more likely to hold babies in a tenderly careful way, enjoy close cuddles and playful affectionate interactions with baby, feed in tempo with infant needs and feeding styles, give babies floor freedom to play, interpret infant emotional signals sensitively, respond promptly, reliably, and appropriately to comfort infant distress, provide contingent pacing and judicious levels of stimulation in face-to-face interactions during routines and play, and help babies manage and cope with overwhelming or intense emotions.

From the Strange Situation, three patterns of insecure, anxious attachment have been identified: Avoidant (A) babies seem undisturbed by separation from mother and indifferent to her reentry. They ignore mother and do not ask for hugs or comfort. In contrast, at home they may be angry, demanding, and protest separation. These A babies rarely sink contentedly onto mother's body for comfort. Insecure/avoidant babies were rated years later by teachers as showing more behavior problems in a high-risk preschool group.

Mothers of A babies showed marked aversion to close bodily contact with baby. They tended to be unexpressive emotionally with their babies and more rigid and compulsive. More often than other mothers, they seemed overwhelmed by resentments, irritation, and anger, more rejecting, and more likely to express negative emotion. Also, these mothers were more likely to rebuff infant attempts to snuggle close or to obtain physical reassurance. They found it difficult to merge their styles into reciprocally satisfying interaction patterns. Very early, their babies begin to act more independent, as if they have already learned that they cannot expect to receive hugs or kisses. Thus A babies may develop anger and lack of trust in the

attachment figure, which will increase the child's risk for later social difficulties. The child may also be less compliant and cooperative and show increased aggressiveness or bullying of other children.

During the Strange Situation reunion, ambivalent/hesitating (C) babies approach mother obviously wanting to be comforted. Yet their reactions are ambivalent. The C baby turns away and cannot accept comfort. He/she may even hit at the mother or squirm to get down if she does pick him/her up. C babies show intense mixtures of anger and fear. They sometimes show inconsolable distress after separation. As toddlers, C babies show significantly more restricted exploration than secure toddlers. They have less imaginative symbolic play and significantly lower quality of play than secure infants. The child seems preoccupied with the mother, as if uncertain whether the caregiver is truly available when the infant needs adult protection or nurturance. Sometimes mothers of ambivalently attached babies are overcontrolling and overstimulating. They may ask questions while reading to the child yet never give the little one a chance to respond.

During earlier home observations, C babies' mothers picked up, held, and kissed the baby, but only when it suited their own tempos, needs, and wishes. Attuned to themselves more than to their babies, mothers of C infants provide inconsistent care. Intrusive and overcontrolling, these mothers sometimes try to dominate a play situation rather than follow the child's signals and leads.

At reunion, babies coded as dazed/disoriented/disorganized (D) seem to lack purposeful goals. They display contradictory behavior patterns, such as running toward mother for reunion, then interrupting the movement and looking

TABLE 1   Differences and similarities between securely attached and insecurely attached infants on later measures of social competence

Differences: Peer competence

Securely attached infants	*Insecurely attached infants*
Sympathetic to peers' distress	Spectator in social activities
Peer leader	Hesitant with other children
Other children seek his company	Hesitates to engage
Attracts attention	Socially withdrawn
Suggests activities	Withdraws from excitement
	A listener

Differences: Ego strength

Forcefully goes after what he wants	Uncurious about the new
Likes to learn new intellectual skills	Unaware, turned off, "spaced out"
Self-directed	

Similarities: Peer competence
Chracteristically unoccupied

Similarities: Ego strength
Does not persevere when goals are blocked
Suggestible
Becomes involved in whatever he does
Confidence in own ability
Sets goals that stretch abilities
Samples activities aimlessly, lacks goals
Indirect in asking for help

Source: Material adapted from L. A. Sroufe, "Attachment and the roots of competence." In *Human Nature,* Oct. 1978. Copyright © 1978 by Human Nature, Inc.

confused and not completing the goal of seeking proximity or comfort. Some show disordered temporal sequences, such as strongly avoiding the parent on reunion and then strongly seeking closeness. Babies coded as D constitute 2–10 percent of infants in white middle-class U.S. samples. Inquiry into their own attachment histories shows that mothers of D babies have suffered unusual trauma of separation from, or early loss of, their own parents. During the first years, high stability of Strange Situation classification has been reported for infants in white middle-class families.

The proportions of secure, avoidant, and ambivalent attachments vary depending on culture groups that have replicated the Ainsworth Strange Situation. In the United States, about two-thirds of babies are B (securely attached); 20 percent are A (avoidant); and about 10–15 percent are C (ambivalent/hesitating). In studies in Germany, Karen and Klaus Grossman and colleagues discovered varying frequencies for attachment classification of A, B, and C infants. In northern Germany, there was a far higher proportion of A babies than in U.S. samples (50 percent) both with mothers and fathers. Parents emphasized early independence more. Yet German A-type mothers were by far not as insensitive as Ainsworth's Baltimore A-type mothers; and B-type German mothers were not quite as sensitive as Baltimore B-type mothers. Years later in the preschool setting in the German research, when children were five years old, eighteen of twenty-four B children showed no behavior problems. In contrast, only two of eleven A children were free of aggression, hostility, or isolation. Thus, the expression of mothering for A, B, and C infants may not be quite the same in other cultures. Both in Japan and in Israel fewer babies were classified as A babies, but more anxious/ambivalent C babies were noted compared with the U.S. samples.

Infant Temperament and Attachment
Some theorists have postulated that attachment descriptions of infants can be more simply described by noting variations in biologically based infant temperament, or personality style. Babies have been described as usually fitting into one of three temperaments: easy/flexible; difficult/feisty; and slow-to-warm up/cautious. Specific infant temperament characteristics (measured as low, moderate, or high) that form these three clusters are: activity level; mood; approach or withdrawal to new persons/experiences; body regularity or rhythmicity (for voiding, feeding, and sleep patterns); threshold for distress/stress; intensity of response to distress; ability to adapt eventually to changes/stresses; task persistence; and attention span.

Clinicians have found that parents of difficult children are more stressed and their relationships with their children can be more problematical. Yet when mothers with irritable babies were highly focused upon and positively involved with their young babies, and they also received support from husbands or partners, then even though their infants had difficult temperaments those babies were just as likely to be securely attached to mother by one year of age.

Research has not found any inevitable correlation between irritable temperament and insecure attachment. In Holland, 100 highly irritable firstborn babies from poor families were randomly assigned with their mothers either to intervention or to a control group. Every three weeks, home visitors worked with the intervention group's mothers and focused on enhancing maternal sensitive responsiveness. Home visitors taught mothers how to observe their babies' cues, to adjust their behaviors to unique cues, and to select and carry out effective, appropriate responses. They encouraged mothers to imitate baby behaviors such as vocalizations while respecting infant gaze aversion by practicing adult nonintrusiveness. The importance of soothing a crying infant was highlighted and individualized for each mother. Playful interactions with toys were also promoted. All infants were videotaped in the Strange Situation at one year.

Intervention infants were more sociable, more able to soothe themselves, and they engaged in cognitively more sophisticated exploration than control babies. Significantly more intervention babies were securely attached to their mothers at one year. Thus, infant temperament style does not determine the security of infant attachment status.

Research has confirmed that other biological and medical factors or problems, such as deafness, prematurity, mental retardation, congenital illness, and cleft lip and/or palate conditions, also do not predict decreased probability of secure infant-mother attachment. The development of secure infant attachment depends more on maternal and family factors than on infant difficulties or personality.

Infant Attachment Classification and Early Childhood Behaviors
Longitudinal studies confirm the long-term consequences of early attachment. Ainsworth characterized maternal behaviors associated with secure and insecure

infant attachments as inducing either "virtuous" or "vicious" spirals of development. The more promptly that a mother picks up and comforts a distressed baby during the earliest months, the less a baby cries during the latter part of the first year. Contrast these findings with a commonly heard but untrue belief: "If you pick up a crying baby you will spoil him!" Infants classified as having anxious-insecure attachments are less compliant during toddlerhood with their mothers' requests, and the mother-child relationships are less harmonious than those between initially securely attached infants and their mothers.

Children who had been judged as having anxious/ambivalent attachment in infancy were significantly more dependent and helpless in preschool than children who had earlier been judged as secure infants. The insecure babies grew into preschoolers who were less confident and assertive and more likely to be exploited by peers who earlier were A babies. Five- to seven-year-olds who had been insecure/ambivalent in infancy have reported the most loneliness compared to children who had been securely attached during infancy.

Continuity of adaptation has been demonstrated from infancy into the early school years. Securely attached babies later in kindergarten showed more ego resiliency and ego control on Jack Block's ego measures. C babies showed emotional undercontrol; A babies showed emotional overcontrol. For toddlers, initial sociability with peers is greater for those who have been rated as securely attached in infancy. More antisocial behaviors occur among preschool children who have been classified as avoidantly attached in infancy. Preschool friendships are more concordant and positive for children earlier rated as securely attached. Higher social competence in school at six years of age has been associated with more secure attachment ratings in the first year of life.

Insecure avoidant A infants are often later characterized as bullies with peers in the preschool classroom. Insecure ambivalent C children in preschool sometimes behave as victims and have troubles with peer interactions. Social interactions were observed in a preschool classroom for children whose infancy Strange Situation classifications only the researchers knew about. The researchers also placed children who had been coded as A, B, or C in infancy to play in pairs. When A and C children played together, the C children experienced sarcasm, derision, and rejection by A peers. When two C children played together, they displayed immaturity and social ineptitude but not exploitation. C children were often isolated in the classroom. B children placed with other B children acted neither as victimizers nor victims.

These patterns emerged in just two to three play sessions. Classroom preschool teachers behaved differently with these youngsters, whose infancy attachment classifications they knew nothing about. Teachers gave more leeway for misbehavior and more nurturance to C children. Although these teachers were highly trained professionals, they did get angry sometimes—but only with A children. With the A children, teachers were highly controlling and had lower expectations for cooperative behavior. Teachers were least nurturing toward B children and had the highest expectations for compliance by B children.

Thus, infancy attachment status had a powerful effect later on preschool peer interactions as well as on teacher interactions even though the teachers were unaware of any infancy ratings for the children.

Secure attachment in early infancy has been related to later toddler competence in tool-solving problem situations. Babies who had been rated at twelve and eighteen months as secure, avoidant, or ambivalent were brought into the laboratory as older toddlers. First, the toddlers were given attractive play toys then soon after were asked to clean up. All the toddlers expressed strong negativism about having to stop playing with these new toys so soon. Next, the toddlers and their mothers were placed in a room with difficult tool-using tasks that were too hard for toddlers to solve by themselves. The children rated secure as infants now showed zestfulness in tackling the hard tasks (one involved a 6-foot lever that the toddler would need to work together with an adult in order to retrieve a treat) and were cooperative and compliant with maternal suggestions. In contrast, during the tool-using task, those who had been a year earlier classified as insecure infants now showed more of the following behaviors: opposition, crying, temper tantrums, lack of compliance with maternal suggestions, and lack of persistence in trying to solve the problems. Their mothers gave fewer helpful suggestions. This classic study illuminates the early linkages between attachment relationship in early infancy and later socioemotional and intellectual motivation to tackle difficult learning tasks during the preschool years.

Others studied early infancy attachment status in relation to later toddler competence. Optimally, mothers of secure babies were able to recruit the child's attention, communicate the nature of the goal of a game or toy, effec-tively reduce child frustration, avoid negative interruptions, avoid rejections or negation of child attempts at symbolic play, and show mutual pleasure and enjoyment during mother-toddler play.

Such adult interactions gave an advantage to secure infants, who were more readily able to take advantage of novel opportunities for exploration. Engrossed in learning tasks, acting positively motivated and purposeful, the secure young child could exploit more chances for learning and put more enthusiastic effort into those learning opportunities. Toddler attention span during structured task play was positively correlated with secure attachment to the mother. Anxious resistant toddlers showed much lower ratings on structured and unstructured tasks compared with secure infants or avoidant infants. Dazed/disoriented D infants operated at significantly lower levels of challenge compared with the A and B babies at thirteen months. A troubling finding was that maternal scaffolding for task mastery was only successful for securely attached babies. Such mother behaviors were not related to motivation or competence measures for the toddlers who had been insecurely attached to their mothers in infancy.

Differential Effects of Secure Attachment to Mother and Father
Although babies form attachments separately to each parent, research suggests that attachments to each parent may have differential effects on quality of adaptation. Attachment to the mother is significantly more predictive of a child's development beyond the infancy period. A review of the literature shows that fathers influence their infant's attachment, although they seem to be less influential than are mothers.

Paternal influences on infant attachment can be more indirect than direct. For example, if a young child has an alcoholic father, then the mother may become so worried about the lack of money for food or necessities and so fearful of rages from the father that she becomes too depressed to parent in a sensitive manner. As an indirect consequence, then, the father's behaviors result in an anxiously insecure infant-mother relationship.

German fathers of securely attached infants showed higher sensitivity in their playful challenges with their children at twenty-four months than fathers of insecurely attached infants. This sensitivity was highly stable over the first six years of life. The Grossmans suggest that child-father relationships can be more crucial for helping a child cope with environmental challenges. In contrast, attachment to the mother has usually been measured mostly by coping behaviors when the infant is under the stress of separation from the mother.

Infant-mother (compared to infant-father) attachment is a more salient predictor of later attachment ratings. The relationship between security of attachment to mother at one year and at six years is remarkably strong, whereas the relationship between security of attachment to father at eighteen months and at six years was considerably weaker, although positive.

Attachments to mother and father have differential predictive power for later child adjustment. For forty families whose children had received Strange Situation classifications at one year, the child's emotional openness and verbal fluency at six years were strongly related to security of attachment to the mother in infancy but unrelated to infant attachment scores with fathers. The six-year-olds were asked: "This little boy [girl's] parents are going away on vacation for two weeks. What's this little boy [girl] gonna do?" Children's constructive responses included calling on people to help or actively trying to persuade the parents not to go. These constructive responses correlated with the child's secure attachment to mother, but not at all with secure attachment to father.

When the six-year-olds were presented with a family photograph, secure children smiled, showed some interest, and put down the photo after a brief inspection. Those who had been insecurely attached (D babies) responded in disorganized ways to the photo.

Is Attachment Status Changeable?
Bowlby did not believe that early infant-mother interaction sets the pattern of an infant's attachment for all time. Other events during childhood can increase anxiety or increase the security of a relationship. He did believe that the kinds of psychological defenses that people use to cope with stresses will influence their adjustment. Thus, if anxiously attached persons use sublimation (pursuing knowledge and skills), altruism (actively caring for others), and humor, then adverse childhood experiences can be surmounted. Disturbances in adjustment are more likely when children use defense mechanisms such as self-hatred, projecting evil onto others, or overidealization of abusive parents.

Adolescents and adults can use reason and reflection as tools for change. They can think about and think through unpleasant earlier experiences and change initial models by their abstraction ability and their mental reconstruction of events. Teenage mothers who were better able to reflect on their own childhoods were mothering their own infants more effectively than adolescent mothers who received enriching home visits but did not demonstrate such reflectivity.

Among eighty-four high school seniors, although forty-nine were initially assessed as secure-attached at one year and thirty-five as insecure, by eighteen years of age 57 percent of the initially secure were adjusted and 43 percent maladjusted; 74 percent of the initially insecure were rated adjusted and 26 percent maladjusted. Life problems such as divorce or parental loss can change attachment outcomes. Adults who had anxious attachments in early childhood can reach out to make new friendships and participate in new relationships that bring personal and positive affirmation and disconfirm the negative messages about themselves that they received in the past. The role of marital conflict and external stressors as well as the effects of separations and losses after infancy need to be taken into account to give the domain of attachment a broader, more family systems–focused perspective.

Child Abuse in Relation to Attachment
Clinicians who work with abused children believe that attachment theory is central to understanding the causes and treatment of child abuse and neglect. Maltreating parents who have lived through severe emotional deprivation experiences themselves in the parent-child attachment process, and have been victimized by aggression in their own childhoods, tend to reenact these experiences when they become parents. The child is seen as the reincarnation of the parent as "bad self," for which he was punished when he was a child. This process prompts the parent toward identifying with his own punitive parent of the past. Then he/she can punish the child with a sense of full justification.

Maternal abuse has been explored as a function of the mothers' disruptions of attachment in early childhood. These mothers had not developed internal representations of intimate others as reliable and accessible. Physically abusive mothers reported significantly more "parentification" in their own childhood; that is, their own mothers had expected the children to be more nurturing and caring toward the parent. The abusive mothers reported more anxious childhood concerns for their own parents and had perceived themselves as more responsible for their parents' happiness compared with control families.

The abused babies became more insecurely attached over time: by eighteen months, 46 percent were classified as A, 23 percent B, and 31 percent C. In contrast, in the nonmaltreated group, the A, B, and C percentages respectively were 70, 67, and 26 percent. Thus, a greater proportion of maltreated infants is not securely attached. However, no clear pattern or relationship between maltreatment and quality of attachment has been found. Stability of attachment classification was higher for the nonmaltreated group (69 percent) than for the maltreated infants (41 percent) between twelve and eighteen months.

Abused toddlers do not typically respond with eye contact and positive gestures to friendly overtures from caregivers. They may sidle up to teachers rather than approaching the adults directly. When other children were hurt and cried, abused toddlers looked on with indifference or they reacted with anger toward distressed peers—even going over to smack a crying hurt child rather than showing empathy and concern.

Securely attached infants who have been maltreated tend to become insecure over time. Psychological unavailability of the caregiver strongly predicts insecure attachment as well as marked decrease in IQ over the first two years of life. When mothers were psychologically unavailable, then at twelve months 43 percent of infants, and at eighteen months 86 percent, were classified as avoidant in the Strange Situation; the rest were classified as C babies.

Day Care and Maternal Employment in Relation to Attachment

Maternal employment is difficult to assess in relation to attachment because of possible confounding variables, such as quality and amount of nonparental care or the timing of infant entrance into nonparental care by the employed parent. Some researchers find a slight risk of increase in insecure attachments, aggression, and noncompliance in infants whose mothers were employed full-time during the infant's first year of life. Others report no relationship between maternal work status and the quality of infants' attachment to their mothers as measured by the Strange Situation at twelve months.

Park and Honig noted both aggression (observed and teacher-reported) as well as positive social interactions among three groups of preschoolers. One group had been placed in full-time nonparental care in the first year of infancy, another during the second year, and the third group not until after thirty-six months. There was a slight increase in aggression among preschoolers who had been placed in full-time infancy care during the first year of life. But teachers also rated those preschoolers as higher in abstraction ability.

The largest and most comprehensive longitudinal research findings on attachment in relation to child-care effects are from the National Institute on Child Health and Human Development (NICHHD) child-care study, carried out in ten sites in the United States. At six, fifteen, twenty-four, and thirty-six months, 1,364 socially and racially diverse children were assessed after birth and followed to age six years, regardless of the type of child care they experienced naturally.

Positive caregiving and language stimulation contributed between 1.3 percent and 3.6 percent of the variance in early cognitive and language development. The higher the quality of provider-child interaction, the more positive the mother-child interactions, and the more sensitive and involved were the mothers over the first three years. The NICHHD study confirmed that the Ainsworth Strange Situation was valid for measuring attachment regardless of the kind of childrearing experiences (home or child-care provider) the children had.

The longer the time that infants and toddlers spent in group care, the fewer positive interactions with their mothers at six and fifteen months of age, and the less affection with their mothers at two and three years. However, family income, mother's vocabulary, home environment, and parental cognitive stimulation were more important than child-care quality in predicting cognitive and language advancements.

Children in center-based care made larger gains than those in family child-care homes. Children from ethnic minority groups were more likely to be cared for in settings that did not offer as many opportunities for messy play, reading books, and active explorations compared to children from other groups. Children reared in economically disadvantaged homes were more likely to be insecurely attached to their mothers. When mothers strongly endorsed statements supporting the possible benefits of maternal employment for children's development, their infants were more likely to be insecurely attached, and these mothers were also observed to be less sensitive and responsive. Their children were in poorer quality care at earlier ages and for more hours per week.

Infant day care per se (observed quality of care, amount of care, age of entry, and frequency of care starts) did not appear to be a risk factor for insecure attachment. Maternal sensitivity was significant: Mothers who were least sensitive and responsive had more infants classified A (16–19 percent), and fewer secure B (53–56 percent), compared with the most sensitive mothers (9–11 percent A, 12–14 percent D, 60–65 percent B). Dual-risk effects were found. The lowest proportion of secure attachment was noted when maternal sensitivity and child-care cruelty were both low. For children with less-sensitive mothers, attachment security proportions were higher if the children were in high-quality care than in low-quality care.

Gender and Attachment
Male infants have been found to be more vulnerable to deprivation of maternal affections. Over the first three months of life, mothers of girl babies spend more time talking with them and mothers of boy babies spend more time physically stimulating them by rocking, touching, and holding them. In the NICHHD study, at fifteen months boys received less responsive care than girls both in centers

and in child-care homes. Males may be more at risk for insecure attachments with their caregivers, whether in a center or a family child-care facility or at home. A trend has been noted for more boys than girls to have insecure attachments at twelve months with both mother and father when mothers are employed. A significantly higher proportion of insecure attachments to fathers in employed-mother families has been reported.

Poverty, Family Stress, and Attachment
Babies in stressed, low-income families show increased vulnerability for insecure attachment. This effect is even stronger when mothers enter employment early, before the infants are one year old. By late toddlerhood, during problem-solving tasks, there were no longer behavioral differences between children who had been assessed in infancy as initially secure or insecure.

In contrast, initially secure babies whose mothers returned to work later (between twelve and eighteen months) looked very different from initially insecure infants when faced with challenging tool-using problems and tasks. During these tasks, secure children in the late-work group were less likely to behave negatively, whine, act oppositional to maternal directives, ask for mother's help, display frustrations, and say no. The causes of such differences and how to ameliorate any negative effects of early return to full-time employment, particularly in stressed, low-income families, require further research. All the initially anxiously attached children showed more maladaptive behaviors as toddlers challenged by difficult tool problems.

Secure children in poor families where mothers did not return to work during infancy (the no-work group) were rated as more enthusiastic while engaged with the most difficult tool tasks, and these children were more persistent in trying to solve the tasks. They were more compliant and less negative, in significant contrast to the toddlers in the early-work group. Thus, for children at risk because of family poverty and stress, societal provision for and monitoring of high-quality care could be an urgent consideration. Yet of 400 day-care centers studied in the United States, most of the 5 million children received poor to mediocre care, with one in eight actually being located in a setting that jeopardized their basic health and safety needs.

Attachment Relationships with Teachers

Attachment to nonparental caregivers is currently being systematically assessed. Theoretically, preschool teachers may be expected to vary their behavior according to the maternal attachment history of the child, which gets carried into new relationships with nonparental caregivers. The emerging self is an inner organization of attitudes, expectations, and feelings built up from each child's history of emotional and behavioral exchanges and regulation with a special adult. There is some tendency for continuity in the inner organizing core because there is a likelihood that new relationships are formed in congruence with the earlier ones.

Teacher involvement and center quality affect infant attachment. Middle-class children nineteen to forty-two months old, and who had continuously been with their caregivers in group care for at least eight months, were observed in the Strange Situation carried out with the caregiver and also with a stranger in centers of high physical quality or low phys-

ical quality. High physical quality centers had varied and age-appropriate play equipment; attractive space differentiated according to activity areas; daily learning activities; parent-teacher conferences; child-sized furniture and facilities; display of children's work; and some individualization of activities and experiences. In addition, the teachers observed in each classroom were rated as high-involved or low-involved in positive interactions with children.

Children with high-involved caregivers contacted and interacted more with their teachers than with the stranger in the Strange Situation. They also had a higher level of exploration and movement in the caregiver's presence. Children with low-involved caregivers actually showed a preference for contacting the stranger. The effects of attachment to nonparental caregivers in child care seem to be mediated by the specific quality of the center as well as by the quality of involvement of the caregiver with the children.

Attachment to parents is independent of attachment to teacher. No relationship has been found between infant attachment scores with mother, with father, and with caregiver. In one study, about 10 percent of the children had insecure attachments to all three caregiving figures. Caregivers with whom infants developed a secure attachment seemed to be younger and more sensitive during free play than the caregivers with whom babies developed an insecure relationship advanced by stability of child care. Among infants from ten to thirty-eight months, assessed with the Attachment Q-Sort (see next section), ninety-one had secure attachments when they had been with the teacher for more than a year. Infants who had been for shorter time (five to eight months) or for medium amount of time (nine to twelve months) with teachers had 50 percent and 67 percent secure attachments, respectively.

Measuring Attachment Beyond Infancy: The Q-Sort Measure
For older toddlers or preschoolers, the Everett Water's Q-Sort is often used. The Q-Sort set consists of 100 items that assess the attachment, exploration, and related behavior of a young child in the home and other naturalistic settings. Items refer to specific behaviors rather than trait constructs. The contents of the item sets cover eight domains: the balance of attachment-exploration; response to comforting; emotional tone; social interactions; social perception; handling of objects; dependency; and endurance.

The Q-Sort items are each typed on a small card. The cards are sorted into piles from "very like" to "very unlike" the child by a caregiver or very knowledgeable professional who has observed the child extensively. For children (assessed by Q-Sort) who recently entered into day care, only short-term effects on exploratory behaviors and social interaction were found. No effects for child attachment to mother were found with items such as "child easily becomes angry at mother."

Age of toddler mediates stability of attachment to teacher. In a sample of children followed from infancy, the Q-Sort attachment ratings of preschoolers were used to measure preschooler-mother attachment. If the teacher changed before the children were thirty months old, then the Q-Sort ratings of child-teacher attachment were unstable. After thirty months, relationship quality with teachers tended to be stable regardless of whether or not the teacher changed. Infant twelve-month Strange Situation scores with the mother did not correlate with relationship with the teacher at four years. Neither was there any concordance for four-year-olds between attachment to mother and attachment to teacher.

The Water's Q-Sort was used with sixty-five middle-class infants (eleven to twenty months of age) in child care to assess the possible interactive effects of infant attachment with the mother as well as with the caregiver. When center quality was high, more intense caregiver play with babies occurred. Caregivers who had worked longest with babies were more positive about their relationship to the mothers. Caregivers who favorably rated (by Q-Sort) their relationships with mothers engaged in a higher intensity of play with babies, and the infant-caregiver attachment scores were higher. Infant attachment to the mother was lower when maternal anxiousness about separation was higher.

Preschoolers secure in infancy attachments have been rated as more socially competent. Four-year-olds played with their best friends, and Q-Sort scores of child-mother attachment were collected, and secure-secure pairs of preschoolers were more harmonious, less controlling, more responsive, and happier in their play together than secure-insecure pairs. Secure-secure dyads more often: negotiated a fair settlement on differences; negotiated peacefully with each other; complied with one another's requests and suggestions during play; endorsed their partners' preferences and attitudes; and shared secrets.

Measures of Adolescent or Adult Attachment
For adolescents and adults, the Adult Attachment Interview (AAI) developed by

Mary Main and colleagues is widely utilized. Inquiries in the AAI include: "Describe your relationship to your mother and father." "What did you do when you were upset in childhood?" "Did you ever feel rejected by your parents in childhood?" "Why do you think your parents behaved as they did?" These intimate questions reveal how aware an adult is about his/her own attachments in early childhood. How reflective is the adult? How forgiving or hating now? Does the adult overidealize parents? Adults are rated insecure if they are: defensive, overidealizing, nonreflective about their past in their families, have chaotic or poor childhood memories, repress memory for emotional episodes in their childhood, or remember negative episodes but with little feeling. In the AAI scoring system, patterns of responses considered to categorize an adult's state of mind with respect to attachment are: autonomous, dismissing, preoccupied, and unresolved.

Adults classified as autonomous are generally thoughtful, value attachment experiences and relationships, and freely examine the effects that past experiences have had on personal development. They provide balanced, noncontradictory descriptions of one or both parents as loving during childhood. Or if they have had unfortunate experiences such as neglect, abuse, rejection, or role reversal, they have come to forgive their parents for the maltreatments of the past. Despite difficult childhoods, autonomous adults are not defensive; neither do they idealize their parents. Indeed, they are quite reflective even while they express regret that in childhood they were not close to their parents.

Dismissing persons dismiss attachment experiences as unimportant for their own development and in raising their own children. Often they cannot remember early events, report contradictory stories, or give idealized descriptions of their early childhood. They reflect little on their experience. They either idealize or disparage their parents. Preoccupied persons are often enmeshed in their early experiences and family relationships, although they have trouble telling a coherent and clear story of their early childhood. Sometimes they are still dependent on their parents; some are intensely angry at parents; some want to please parents too much as adults. When classified as unresolved, adults seem confused and disoriented when discussing experiences of loss of a loved one or abusive experiences in their past.

Studies using the AAI and the Strange Situation show a 66–82 percent correspondence between patterns of maternal response to the AAI and their infants' patterns of response in the Strange Situation. In a meta-analysis (a study of the results of many studies) of associations between adult attachment representations and child parent attachment, one researcher confirmed the positive predictive validity of the AAI.

Adults who value attachment are more likely to have securely attached babies. In Germany, an attachment-valuing representation among mothers was associated with secure Strange Situation scores for the babies. Representations that devalued attachment were found among mothers for thirteen of fifteen insecurely attached infants. Those mothers who had securely organized representations of attachment were open and sympathetic in discussing attachment issues despite memories of problematic and unsupportive parents. Other mothers revealed memories of attachment figures who had been unsupportive, and these mothers strongly avoided thinking about attachment-related issues.

The AAI was used to interview ninety-six middle-class expectant mothers and their own mothers. The mothers were reinterviewed eleven months after birth. Babies were assessed with the Strange Situation at twelve months. There was a significant concordance between grandmother and mother AAI classifications and a 68 percent match between pregnancy AAI scores and infant Strange Situation scores. Maternal scores were stable from pregnancy until babies were one year.

When there were life changes over time, then insecure classifications were four times as likely as autonomous classifications. More grandmothers were classified as unresolved. Because they were older, they had possibly gone through more losses of significant attachment figures and been involved in more unresolved mourning. When only three AAI categories (leaving out unresolved) were used, then 65 percent of grandmother-mother-infant triads had corresponding attachment classifications in all three generations. Attachment classifications demonstrate consistent patterns of intergenerational transmission.

See also Emotion; Q-sort

References and further reading
Ainsworth, Mary, et al. 1987. *Patterns of Attachment: A Psychological Study of the Strange Situation.* Hillsdale, NJ: Lawrence Erlbaum Associates.
Bowlby, John. 1988. *A Secure Base: Clinical Applications of Attachment Theory.* London: Routledge.
Bretherton, Inge, and Everett Waters, eds. 1985. "Growing Points of Attachment Theory and Research." *Monographs of the Society for Research in Child Development* 50(1–2), Serial No. 209. Chicago: University of Chicago Press.
Steele, H., and Jude Cassidy, eds. 1999. "Internal Working Models Revisited."
Attachment and Human Development 1 (3) (Special Issue, December).
van den Boom, D. C. 1994. "The Influence of Temperament and Mothering on Attachment and Explorations: An Experimental Manipulation of Sensitive Responsiveness among Lower-Class Mothers with Irritable Infants." *Child Development* 65: 1457–1477.
Van Ijzendoorn, M. H. 1995. Adult Attachment Representation, Parental Responsiveness, and Infant Attachment: A Meta-analysis on the Predictive Validity of the Adult Attachment Interview. *Psychological Bulletin* 117: 387–403.

Attention

Attention is the process directing the individual toward stimulation in the environment in order to extract information contained in the objects or events surrounding the child. In a typically functioning infant, attention is selective—the baby does not respond to every stimulus in the environment. In the first few weeks of life, attention primarily involves the orienting response, and nearly any change in the stimulus environment elicits an orienting response, which prepares the individual for attention. Within two to three months there is a rapid increase in attention, and the infant begins to shift from reactive attention to more sustained attention. Habituation occurs when infants effectively "tune out" a stimulus or object that they have been exposed to repeatedly. Sometimes the infant's orienting response will completely cease; at other times the response will simply decrease in magnitude. The process of habituation allows individuals to focus their attention on novel or unfamiliar stimuli and to ignore stimuli that are unchanging.

See also Habituation; Orienting Response; Perception

Attention Deficit Disorder

Children with attention deficit disorder (now classified as attention deficit/hyperactivity disorder, or ADHD) represent the most frequent referral to mental health clinics nationwide. Males typically outnumber females on the order of 4:1–6:1. Children with ADHD have great difficulty self-regulating their attention, impulsivity, and activity. In fact, a case can be made for such children having difficulty controlling all aspects of self-regulatory functions. ADHD affects as much as 5 percent of the school-age population. Perhaps the common hypothesis is that difficult temperament in infancy is an early sign of ADHD. However, because many of the ADHD child's problems manifest most strongly in a structured school setting, many children do not present at mental health centers for diagnosis until after the preschool years. Treatment generally involves medication to help self-regulation and is combined with educational and parenting interventions.

See also Parenting

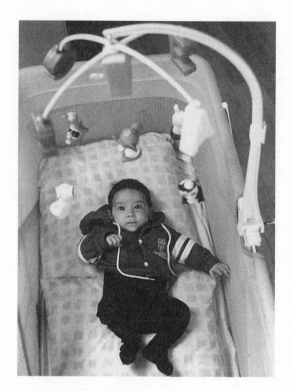

A ten-week-old baby studying a crib mobile. (Elizabeth Crews)

Attention Span

The attention span is the amount of time that an infant can focus attention without wavering. Early in infancy, attention span is very short, on the order of five seconds or less. Later in infancy, the infant's information-processing skills in combination with organization of the nervous system and cognitive/perceptual competencies expand the time that sustained processing can be maintained. Attention span is one of many important factors in the development of learning and memory.

Attention span is also a dimension of temperament. Some babies watch a mobile or play with a toy for a long time, whereas others lose interest immediately only after a few minutes no matter which toys are provided. For some babies with short attention span or high distractibility, few events are capable of sustaining their interest for long periods.

See also Habituation; Orienting Response; Temperament

Attunement
See Affect Attunement

Atypical Infant

Infants who deviate from some normal standard are referred to as "atypical."

Such infants might also be classified as high-risk infants, special-needs infants, or abnormal. Regardless of the label used, the underlying difference between them and typical infants always refers to some normal standard. That standard might be a height or weight growth chart, a developmental assessment tool, a characteristic facial morphology, or any other biological, psychological, or sociological characteristic against which the infant is compared. Often a standard such as two standard deviations below the normal mean (average) is used to designate atypicality. Regardless of the standard or the particular characteristic of interest, most norm-based standards for assessing deviance cause people to think of labels as describing individuals who are the same (homogenous) and are insensitive to the rich individual differences that occur within any label assigned to individuals (heterogeneous). For example, all boys are not the same; neither are all individuals with Down syndrome, or those who were born prematurely.

See also Trisomy

Audiogram

An audiogram is a graph depicting a person's response to various sounds. A person's response to low- to high-pitched sounds, at various levels of loudness, is recorded on the graph. Across the top of the audiogram, the frequencies of sound (different pitches) are listed. Looking up and down the side of the audiogram, the intensities of sound (loudness) are listed. The loudness or intensity of a sound is measured in decibels (dB). Decibels are used to express the level at which sound can be heard—the hearing level (HL). Threshold of hearing is the lowest level at

which an individual can correctly respond to the presences of sound 50 percent of the time. On a scale of dB HL, a whisper is about 10 dB HL, conversational speech about 60 dB HL, and a shout about 90 dB HL. When sound reaches 120 dB HL, it is uncomfortable for humans. Hearing impairments are measured using the dB HL scale. Impairments range from mild to profound. The degree of impairment does not necessarily tell about the effects of hearing loss. For example, a mild hearing loss is more detrimental to a child who is learning language. Children have no background with a language, and thus they are unaware of missed parts of speech that are not heard.

Hertz (Hz) is the technical term used in measuring pitch in vibrations or cycles per second. Pitch refers to how high or low tones. Audiograms can include information on speech reception and speech recognition ability.

Air and Bone Conduction

Most sounds are heard by individuals through the vibration of air particles as they reach the ear. Vibrations of objects cause displacement of air particles in waves that must travel through the outer, middle, and inner ear to be processed and perceived. When sound travels through the air and enters the outer ear, a person's ability to perceive sound is measured by air conduction. Sound travel through the ear can also be measured by bone conduction. Perception of sound by bone conduction occurs by means of a small oscillator placed on the bone behind the ear (mastoid) or on the forehead. When the oscillator vibrates, the skull is vibrated. Because the inner ear is surrounded by bone, the inner ear in vibrated, which causes fluid within the inner ear to vibrate in waves.

These sound waves can then stimulate the fine hair cells with the inner ear for hearing to be achieved.

Hearing Loss

The audiogram can allow one to quickly view the degree, configuration, and type of hearing loss in each ear. To interpret an audiogram, first look for the symbol key box on the audiogram. These symbols include the symbol for the right ear (circle or triangle) and the left ear (an X or box). Sometimes the right and left ear are also recorded by color (right: red; left: blue). Second, look for the arrangement of the symbols on the graph for the right ear (circles or triangles) and left ear (X or boxes). The placement of the symbols indicates the individual's threshold level (lowest level heard) at a particular intensity and frequency level. Intensity (loudness) level is displayed on the perpendicular scale. The degrees of hearing loss are measured in dB HL and are separated into mild (15–40 dB HL), moderate (41–55 dB HL), moderate-severe (56–70 dB HL), severe (71–90 dB HL), and profound (91+ dB HL).

Because children are learning language, mild hearing losses can effect a child's language development. A child with mild hearing loss can benefit from a hearing aid. They may need attention to vocabulary development. Preferential seating with adequate lighting and minimal noise is recommended. Lipreading instruction may be helpful as well as speech-language therapy.

Hearing-aid evaluations and training are recommended for moderate hearing loss. Preferential seating as well as use of FM trainers (an instrument with a transmitter worn by the teacher and a receiver worn by the student) are recommended. Speech-language therapy is recommended

with possible special class placement. Attention to vocabulary and reading is necessary. Lipreading instruction and speech conservations and correction may be needed.

Resource teacher or special class placement may be needed for moderate-severe hearing loss. Special help in language skills (vocabulary development, usage, reading, writing, grammar, etc.) is needed. Individual hearing aid and FM trainer are also needed. Lipreading instruction and speech conservations and correction may be needed.

For severe hearing loss, special programs, with emphasis on all language skills, concept development, lipreading, and speech are needed. Special supervision and supporting services are needed.

For profound hearing loss, full-time special programs for deaf children with emphasis on all language skills, concept development, lipreading, and speech are needed. Special supervision and supporting services are also needed. Oral verse manual communication should be considered.

The third step in interpreting an audiogram is to look at the configuration or shape of the symbols across the graph for each ear. Hearing loss can vary in the configuration (variations of degree of hearing loss over the pitch range). The three most common configurations include sloping, rising, and flat.

Sloping configurations show better hearing in the lower frequencies than in the higher frequencies. Sloping configurations mean the individual is able to hear low-frequency speech sound, like vowels, with hindered perception of high-frequency consonant sounds like /s/ and /f/. Because most noise is low-frequency, individuals can experience more difficulty perceiving speech while in the presence of noise.

Rising configurations show better hearing in the higher frequencies than in the lower frequencies. Rising configurations mean the individual is able to hear high-frequency speech sounds like consonants (/s/, /th/, /f/, /v/) with hindered perception of low-frequency sound like vowels.

Flat configurations show a similar loss of hearing in degrees across the frequency range. A flat configuration indicates difficulty across the frequency range.

Fourth, look at the combination of symbols for air and bone conduction for each ear to determine the type of hearing loss. Look for the right ear air conduction symbols (circle or triangle) and right bone conduction symbols (brackets /[/ and greater than />/). Look for the left ear air conduction symbols (X or boxes) and left bone conduction symbols (brackets /]/ and less than /</. Three main types of hearing loss exist: conductive, sensorineural, and mixed.

Conductive hearing loss requires air conduction symbols to be worse than 25 dB HL, bone conduction symbols to be better than 25 dB HL, and separation of air and bone conduction symbols of at least 10 dB. A conductive hearing loss indicates that there is difficulty in conducting sounds into the inner ear. Some common causes of conductive hearing loss include impacted wax, fluid in the middle ear, and damage to the eardrum or middle ear bones. Often conductive hearing losses can be corrected through medications or surgery. The individual's ability to hear sounds are affected only by loudness levels. Distortion of sounds is not as severely affected. Hearing aids are usually very helpful.

Sensorineural hearing loss requires air conduction symbols to be worse than 25 dB HL, bone conduction symbols to be worse than 25 dB HL, and separation of

air and bone conduction symbols within 10 dB. This type of hearing loss refers to problems in the inner ear and is usually considered to be permanent. Some causes of sensorineural hearing loss include congenital deformity, bacterial meningitis, progressive hereditary hearing loss, and noise-induced hearing loss. Most sensorineural hearing losses can not be corrected through medications or surgery. The individual's ability to hear sounds are affected by loudness levels and may also cause distortions of sounds. Hearing aids are very helpful, but limitations can be seen due to the damage in the inner ear that causes distortion.

Mixed hearing loss requires air conduction symbols to be worse than 25 dB HL, bone conduction symbols need to be worse than 25 dB HL, and separation of air and bone conduction symbols at least 10 dB. This is a combination of both conductive and sensorineural hearing losses. A combination of effects from conductive and sensorineural hearing losses (noted above) is possible.

The Speech Spectrum. On a audiogram, frequency (pitch) is displayed on the horizontal scale. Most speech sounds fall in the range of 300 to 3,000 Hz. Generally vowel sounds are in the lower frequencies and consonant sounds are in the higher frequencies. When looking at an audiogram, normal conversation speech sounds are generally 30–60 dB HL. Often the speech spectrum is displayed in a "speech banana." This depicts the shape of the variation of frequency and intensity levels for all the speech sounds.

The *puretone average* is a quick reference to the degree of hearing loss for speech. It is calculated by adding the threshold levels for 500, 1,000, and 2,000 Hz and dividing by three. This score is also used to confirm speech reception scores (at the lowest level, speech is perceived 50 percent of the time).

There are several approaches to the education of children with hearing loss. Many factors influence this choice for the parents. Parents of children with mild and moderate degrees of hearing loss will usually choose to educate their child through mainstreaming into a regular classroom. These children will often attend a regular class for most of the day and will use hearing aids and FM trainers.

See also Auditory System

Audition

Several types of hearing tests have been used over the years to evaluate a child's ability to hear, imperative to the development of spoken language. Depending on the age of the child, different audiometric tests are used to help determine the child's auditory ability. A child is never too young to test. Some people believe that a child born with hearing loss is totally deaf (all or nothing), but hearing loss can occur with different degrees, types, and configurations. The effects of hearing loss for an individual vary depending on these factors, and thus complete audiometric evaluation is necessary.

Audiometric Evaluation

Children from birth to five months of age are usually evaluated using objective test measures (auditory brainstem response, otoacoustic emissions, and acoustic immittance). When the child is able to maintain control of head and neck muscles (around five months), a combination of objective and behavioral tests (visual reinforcement audiometry, condition ori-

entation response) can be used. Children can become conditioned to use a version of adult testing procedures roughly at the age of two and a half (conditional play audiometry).

An infant's ability to respond to tones and his/her perception of speech are important. A child's detection (presence/absence), discrimination (same/different), identification (labeling), and comprehension (understanding meaning) of speech perception should be evaluated to determine the child's ability to use hearing for the understanding of speech.

Acoustic Immittance. This is a type of audiometric evaluation that can provide information on the presence or absence of middle ear pathologies. It is also used to help diagnose problems of the inner ear, auditory tube (the canal from the middle ear to the back of the throat that helps to equalize pressure in the middle ear), and facial nerve. During this test a small probe tip is placed in the ear, and an airtight seal is obtained. Air pressure is forced into the ear canal and then extracted from the ear canal. A change in air pressure in the ear canal causes a normally functioning eardrum (tympanic membrane) to move. This movement can be evaluated by examining the amount of sound that is either reflected or absorbed through the middle ear. This measurement is possible by measures of a small microphone and receiver that are housed within the equipment.

Response Tests. Audiometric evaluations can provide information on the type, degree, and configuration of hearing using an objective test in which electrodes are placed on the head (and sometimes the neck or shoulder). The electrodes record responses from the inner ear (cochlea), auditory nerve, and lower brainstem. When this test is used on an infant, the infant will need to lie quietly (often performed when the infant is asleep) while clicking sounds are presented to the ear. As the sounds enter the ear, the equipment can be adjusted to record responses from various intensity levels. Responses can also be recorded by manipulating the frequency range and through bone conduction (presenting the sound through a device that vibrates the skull instead of presenting the sound through earphones). The brainstem auditory evoked response test is the gold-standard test that is used to determine hearing status of an infant. The test can be performed within hours after birth.

Otoacoustic Emissions. This is a type of audiometric evaluation that can provide information on the function of the inner ear. It is an objective test in which a small probe is placed within the ear canal. The placement of the probe is important to help reduce environmental noise. This is important because the probe produces a sound that enters the ear canal, middle ear, and inner ear. In the normal functioning inner ear, thousands of tiny hair cells are stimulated by the presence of a sound. This stimulation not only causes electrical charges that are carried up to the brain but also produces an echo that can be measured. Most mechanical machines make a by-product sound due to the working movement of the machine. The echo that is recorded for otoacoustic emissions is thus a by-product sound by the working of the hair cells within the inner ear. In order for the echoes to be recorded, sounds must successfully travel through the ear canal, ear drum, middle ear, and inner ear, and then back in reverse order.

The discovery of otoacoustic emissions provided a cost-effective means to screen newborns' hearing. Many hospitals can use a combination of otoacoustic emissions and auditory brainstem response to effectively separate infants with and without hearing loss. Due to possible debris and unabsorbed tissue in the middle ear, rescreening may be needed.

Central Auditory Perception
The ability of the peripheral hearing system (outer, middle, and inner ear) to function normally does not always allow for "normal" perception of sounds. The electrical impulses from the inner ear must pass to the eighth nerve and synapse to many nerves before reaching higher auditory centers within the brain. It is possible for the electrical impulses and final auditory centers within the brain, as well as coordination of centers within the brain, to prevent sound from being processed and perceived normally. Individuals with central auditory perception disorders may have difficulty with persistence in listening, association of sounds, discriminating the signal from competing sounds, synthesis and integration of auditory information, attention, sequencing of auditory information, memory of auditory information, and more.

Central auditory perception ability is normally evaluated with a battery of tests. Because processing occurs on many levels, different levels need to be evaluated to determine the extent of person's ability to process sounds.

References and further reading
Colorado Infant Hearing Advisory Committee (website 2001). http://www.colorado.edu/slhs/mdnc/guidelines.html.

Auditory Perception
See Perception

Auditory System
The auditory system is one of the six sensory systems that extracts information from the external environment and transforms it into a neural form used by the brain. This transformation allows and contributes to the ability of the brain to perceive meaning associated with that sensation. Thus, the auditory system is crucial for awareness that stimulation is present in the environment; it is also crucial for babies in order to perceive which sound waves emanate from the same object and the implications of the characteristics of that sound. The other sensory systems include the visual, haptic, olfactory, gustatory, and vestibular systems.

See also Perception

Authoritarian Parenting
Diana Baumrind's classic research on parenting styles resulted in descriptions of three major styles: authoritarian, authoritative, and permissive. Authoritarian parenting is characterized by the use of limits and control, with expectations that children will comply with parental rules. Little attention is given to verbal give-and-take as an effective way to induce self-control. Children exposed to authoritarian parenting tend to have low social competence, although this is not necessarily the outcome for children who live in violent neighborhoods. In such circumstances, authoritarian parenting may "teach" children the adaptive skills necessary for survival.

See also Discipline; Parenting

Authoritative Parenting
Another type of parenting style described by Diana Baumrind. Authoritative parents tend to have children with good self-regulatory skills and strong social competence. Parents using this parenting style encourage their children to be independent but responsible. They use lots of verbal give-and-take to explain the rules of good conduct and are less punitive in their disciplinary practices than are authoritarian parents.

See also Discipline; Parenting

A mother having a serious chat with her nineteen-month-old daughter. (Elizabeth Crews)

Autism
Autism is a pervasive developmental disorder in which children have severe prob-

lems in communication and social interaction. Autism affects approximately one out of every 2,000 children, with boys five times more likely than girls to evidence autistic characteristics. At one time, people believed that autism resulted from poor parenting and a rejecting home environment; however, it is now recognized that autism is a neurological disorder thought to be triggered by biological or other factors. These causes are still under study but may include genetic disorders, rubella, and problems that occur during pregnancy and delivery that affect brain function. Most likely, autism is not one specific disorder but a variety of developmental disorders that have different causes but share similar impairments in language, cognition, and social interaction.

Because the symptoms of autism occur in different combinations and range from mild to severe, autism is considered a spectrum disorder, one that can be manifested in many ways. Thus, one child diagnosed with autism can appear distinct from another autistic child. However, individuals with autism typically share certain characteristics. Whereas some infants later diagnosed with autism are extremely fussy and attempt to avoid physical contact, many appear to develop normally until they reach twelve to thirty months. At this age, typically developing toddlers begin to acquire language and become more active participants in social interaction. In contrast, autistic toddlers are likely to have problems with communication, gaining language skills slowly or not at all. Some children learn to speak as well as their peers but have trouble expressing feelings and ideas, and other children communicate only with gestures.

Autistic children tend to withdraw socially and in particular exhibit problems in observing, interpreting, and offering social cues such as smiles, eye contact, and responding to their names. They are less likely to initiate spontaneous or pretend play and may instead focus on a single object, idea, or activity, repeating certain behaviors, such as rocking or pacing, over and over (called "stereotypy" or "perseveration"). In keeping with this reliance on ritualized behavior, autistic children often have difficulty coping with disruptions in routines, and emotional outbursts and self- or other-directed aggression are common. Autistic children may even experience sensory stimuli differently from those of typical developing children; for example, a particular color or texture might be perceived as physically painful. As many as 75 percent of autistic children are also mentally retarded; children who display autistic symptoms but whose intelligence test scores reach the average range may be diagnosed as having Asberger's syndrome. A small group of autistic children even qualify as gifted, although they must also cope with the problems that accompany autism.

Although some autistic individuals will be able to function independently in the community and get a job, marry, or attend college, there is no cure for autism, and most individuals will need some degree of supervision throughout their lives. However, autistic children can learn coping strategies and thereby lessen the effects of their disability. One of the most important factors in improving the prognosis for autistic children is early intervention. Numerous programs have been developed, typically beginning when the child is preschool-aged, that provide intensive intervention tailored to the child's particular strengths, interests, and limitations. Because of the variety of symptom combinations that can occur, a single type of program would be inadequate to address the needs of all autistic children. Therefore, the individualized nature of programs for autistic children is essential. Programs usually focus on behavior change, are highly structured, and include extensive collaboration between staff and parents. The Autism Society of America provides a network of community resources for families with an autistic child.

See also Neurological Impairments

References and further reading
Autism Society of America (website 2001).
http://www.autism-society.org.

Autobiographical Memory

Each individual's life experiences cumulate, and each of us can remember most of the events that characterize our life. These are memories about events, self-memories, self-biographies, or autobiographical memories. Several investigators have demonstrated a close link between language and autobiographical memory and the scripts that help us to code information about real-life events. Children at a family day-care center who are making turkeys to give to their parents for display on refrigerators and are told stories about Thanksgiving will learn a sequence of events (Pilgrims arrived, suffered hunger, contacted American Indians, learned about maize, feasted together in a day of thanks), will code these events into scripts or stories. These scripts become part of autobiographical memory.

It is important to note that autobiographical memory is a cognitive as well as social activity. The infant/toddler must actively encode the event. Rehearsing the event—telling parents what one did at the

day-care center, relating stories about Thanksgiving—and having parents retell it each Thanksgiving ("Remember the turkey you made for our refrigerator last year? What story did it tell?"), facilitate consolidation of the memory. Thus, autobiographical memory also is a social construction, especially built upon parental interactions that help to shape the key elements of the event to be remembered. Rehearsal and repetition are parenting strategies that reinforce event memory: "Tell Daddy what we did at the zoo today!" "Did we see a monkey?" "What did the monkey do?"

Researchers have demonstrated the origins of memory at least to the newborn period, and some claim that newborns even remember some events that occurred during prenatal development (e.g., memory of the mother's voice), but to date most investigators argue that autobiographical memory does not typically begin to become stable until the early preschool years.

See also Memory

References and further reading
Fitzgerald, H. E., et al. 2000. "Prenatal and Postnatal Exposure to Parental Alcohol Use and Abuse." In Joy D. Osofsky and Hiram E. Fitzgerald, eds. *WAIMH Handbook of Infant Mental Health, Vol. 4: Infant Mental Health in Groups at High Risk.* New York: Wiley, pp. 126–159.
Howe, M. L., and M. L. Courage. 1997. The Emergence and Early Development of Autobiographical Memory. *Psychological Review* 104: 499–523.

Autonomic Nervous System

The autonomic nervous system is part of the peripheral nervous system and regulates internal body functions such as blood pressure, body temperature, and digestion. It is composed of two subsystems, the sympathetic and the parasympathetic, that play reciprocal roles in the storage and expenditure of energy.

See also Neurobiology

Autonomy

Autonomy generally means freedom and self-sufficiency. In Erik Erikson's theory of psychosocial development, it is posed as the polar opposite of shame and doubt; it is timed to correspond with the anal period in Freudian theory. The toddler's resolution of the dialectic autonomy versus shame and doubt prepares him/her to address the next dialectic conflict in Erikson's stage theory of psychosocial development.

See also Erikson, Erik; Freud, Sigmund

Autosomal Disorders

"Autosomal" means "one soma," and it refers to congenital dysfunctions that require only a single mutant gene to become expressed in the phenotype.

See also Genetic Disorders

B

Babbling

When babies repeat consonants and vowels in alternating sequences (consonant-vowel reduplications), such as "bah-bah-bah-bah-bah" and "dah-dah-dah-dah-dah," they are babbling. Babbling frequently resembles repetitive sounds that acquire meaning in shortened form ("mama," "dada"), although not all babbles resemble meaningful utterances. Babbling emerges from cooing, the pleasant "oooooh" and "aaaaaaah" sounds that infants first make, usually around five months of age.

See also Language

Baby-Proficient Environment

This is an environment that is constructed in ways designed to facilitate

An eight-month-old boy "talking." (Elizabeth Crews)

the infant's successful exploration of it, thereby enhancing the infant's growth and development.

Baby Talk
See Language

Basic Emotions
Basic emotions are those that can be determined from physical cues, such as facial expressions. Basic emotions, which are sometimes called "discrete" emotions, include happiness, surprise, anger, sadness, and fear. Basic emotions are evident during early infancy. Some scientists believe basic emotions exist in the early weeks of life, whereas others believe that basic emotions emerge more gradually over the first year of life. With time and experience, the basic core emotions become differentiated, expanding the infant's repertoire of emotions. For example, the basic core emotion of joy expands to include related emotions such as happiness, contentment, and satisfaction. With the expansion of these companion emotions, toddlers and young children become better able to manage and respond to their feelings. While a seven-month-old expresses sadness at her parent's departure for work through crying, a three-year-old is able to express distress through whimpers or perhaps even verbalizations.

See also Basic Motives; Emotion

Basic Motives
According to infant researcher and child psychiatrist Robert N. Emde, there are five basic motives present in the new-

born infant that drive the infant toward ever-increasing competence: activity (exploratory behavior), self-regulation (physiological and behavioral states), social-fittedness (interpersonal interactions and relationships), affective monitoring (evaluating situations on the basis of pleasantness and/or wariness), and cognitive assimilation (seeking novelty and transforming it into the familiar).

See also Adaptation; Basic Emotions; Emotion

References and further reading
Emde, Robert N. 1996. "Thinking about Intervention and Improving Early Socioemotional Development: Recent Trends in Policy and Knowledge." *Zero to Three* 17(1): 11–16.

Bathing
Bathing as a part of personal hygiene is an essential ingredient to good health. Some

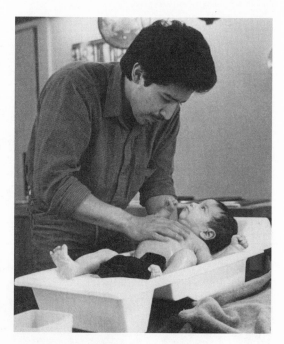

A father bathing his ten-week-old son. (Elizabeth Crews)

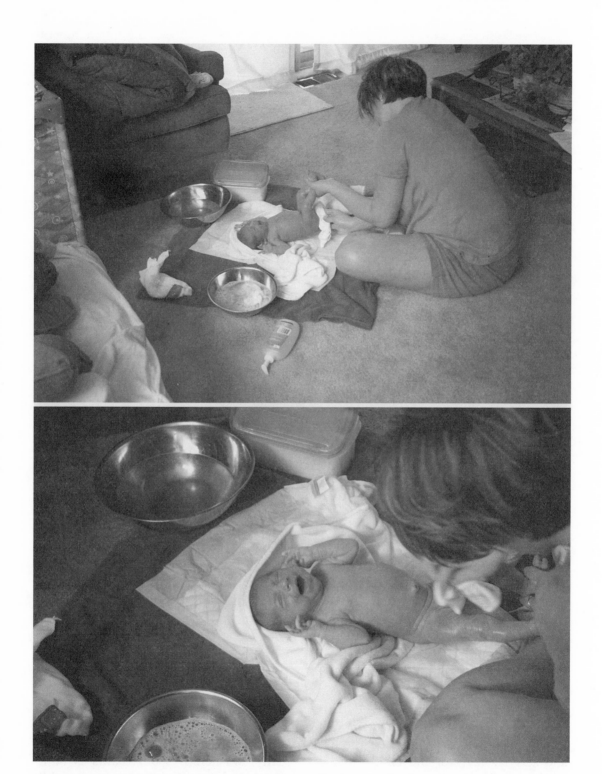

Washing a newborn infant is sometimes more easily done on the floor than in an infant tub. (Photos provided by Katherine Fitzgerald and Bradley Stevenson)

Older infants and toddlers often view bath time as fun time! (Top, courtesy of the Decker family; Bottom, courtesy of the Forbes family)

parents believe they must bathe their children everyday, but the frequency of bathing will vary depending on the age and activity level of the child. Infants need to bathe only once a week until they begin to crawl and get into messy activities. Even at this stage a bath once or twice a week with daily (or multiple daily) washcloth sponge-baths is sufficient. It is important to keep a child's face, hands, and bottom clean to maintain hygiene, contributing to good health. Older children can be bathed as needed following this general guideline.

Infant Bathing
Once the umbilical-cord stump has fallen off, an infant can be bathed in a specially designed tub that can be place inside of a kitchen sink or bathtub. Filled with two or three inches of warm water (about 90 degrees F), and using a mild soap, wash the infant either with your hand or a washcloth from top to bottom and from front to back. Wash the scalp with a wet soapy washcloth and cleanse the face with a moistened cotton ball. Rinse the baby thoroughly and dry with a large absorbent towel.

Separate from hygienic bathing is the concept of cobathing. With cobathing, parent and infant/toddler share the bath. Depending on the age of the child, cobathing activities can range from playful interactions of washing each other's backs to a relaxing soak in the tub. Cobathing is believed to reduce a new mother's stress. The skin-to-skin contact in the relaxing water can help mother and child bond and assist the new mom in nursing her baby. Cobathing is often suggested by breastfeeding organizations for mothers who are experiencing problems nursing their new babies.

Leboyer Childbirth Bathing
Frederick Leboyer believed that the traditional hospital delivery room created an inhumane experience for the infant's entrance into the world. The concepts in Leboyer's 1975 book *Birth Without Violence* challenged the harsh treatment of infants being held by their heels (to be shown to their mothers), immediately cutting the umbilical cord, putting infants under glaring lights, placing them on hard surfaces, and removing them from their mother to a nursery. Instead, Leboyer showed that babies could be brought into the world gently and as a result would respond to parents with vocalizations and eye contact rather than agonizing cries.

The Leboyer method of childbirth is based on the simple act of bathing the newborn in warm water immediately following the birth. Immersion into the water simulates the uterine environment from which the infant has just emerged. Soft light allows the infant's eyes to open while he/she is being gently cleansed in the warm water. This practice allows the infant to adjust to the new and strange environment and allows the parents an opportunity to begin the process of bonding with their newborn.

See also Alternative Birth; Attachment; Bonding

Bayley Scales of Infant Development

The Bayley Scales of Infant Development (BSID) assess the progress of an infant's or toddler's mental and motor development. During the course of development, children acquire a range of skills and abilities, from holding up their heads and reaching for objects to drawing shapes and naming objects. Scientists have long been interested in the order and timing of the development of these skills. Researchers like Mrytle McGraw, Mary Shirley, and Nancy Bayley carefully observed groups of children over time and noted what infants and toddlers could do at various ages. They learned that the order in which and ages at which abilities emerge are fairly predictable. For instance, children learn to crawl before they stand and stand before they walk. Although the timing of these events can vary among children, there is some consistency. So, most children learn to walk sometime between nine and fifteen months of age. However, some kids do not. These children show some delays relative to their same-age peers.

There are many reasons why developmental delays occur. For example, muscular disorders, other illnesses, and even lacking certain experiences (such as being permitted to move around one's own environment) might contribute to a delay in learning to walk. Being aware that there is a delay in development is the first step to understanding what factors might cause it and intervening to provide the best possible experiences or treatments to help the child learn important skills.

The BSID was created to help professionals decide if children are acquiring new abilities and whether or not they are learning these skills at about the same rate as other children. The BSID has three sections: a mental, a motor, and a behavior rating scale. The *mental scale* includes tasks designed to assess skills like memory, problem-solving, early number concepts, classifying items, and language and vocalization skills. The *motor scale* examines children's abilities to use big muscle groups (e.g., legs or other gross motor skills) and more precise muscle groups (e.g., fingers or other fine motor skills). It looks at the movements involved in actions like reaching, rolling, crawling, jumping, and scribbling. The *behavior rating* scale is the professional's observations of how the child responded to the test-taking situation. It includes

things like attention/arousal, engagement in the tasks and with people, how the child can be calmed, and how the child responds to switching between toys.

The BSID is used with infants anywhere from one to forty-two months old. To find out what a child can do, individuals present a series of games to the babies. They do things like dangle large rings on strings and watch to see if and how children reach for them, hide bunnies and see if and where kids look for them, show objects and listen to how children name them, and hand them a ball and watch how kids throw, bounce, or kick it. The games that are played and the skills professionals expect to see depend on the child's age. Developed by Nancy Bayley, the BSID describes the games to play as well as the abilities to look for at each of the different ages. The BSID's history goes back to the 1930s, but it underwent some major changes in 1993. At that time, Bayley tested 1,700 children in proportions consistent with racial/ethnic groups represented in the 1990 U.S. Census. The revised BSID also considers the educational level of parents, the geographic region, and the child's gender, all factors that might influence how a child develops. Bayley used the performance of kids in this representative sample to determine more accurately what responses are typical— that is, when children are given these specific games what should be expected of them at different ages. The care taken to decide these "norms" is one of the main reasons that the second edition of the instruments (BSID-II) is so widely used. The BSID-II is a leading instrument used to assess children's development for research purposes, to diagnose developmental delays, to plan intervention strategies, and to document changes in children's abilities over time.

See also Assessment; Developmental Delay; Early Intervention

References and further reading
Bayley, Nancy. 1993. *Bayley Scales of Infant Development.* 2nd ed. San Antonio, TX: The Psychological Corporation.

Bayley, Nancy
See Bayley Scales of Infant Development

Behavioral Assessment
Behavioral assessment is a general evaluation of the adaptive abilities of the individual, usually accomplished via the administration of a developmental examination.

Behavioral Genetics
Behavior genetics is a discipline that focuses on the role of genetic and hereditary influences on behavior and development. It addresses phenotypic differences among individuals in a population, ascribing phenotypic differences to genetic and environmental sources. The *phenotype* refers to the observable characteristics of an organism, both biological and behavioral. Individual differences found in physical appearances (e.g., height and weight), psychopathology (depression and schizophrenia), and social development (development of aggressive behaviors and friendship) are considered to be phenotypic differences, whereas the *genotype* is the basic genetic makeup of an individual, transmitted from parents to their offspring. Traditionally, behavioral genetics focused on how behavior can be explained by nature versus nurture. Some behavior

geneticists suggested that genetic effect sizes in human behavior exceed any other single source from environmental contributions and that environment gets too much credit, whereas in reality genetics counts most.

The concept of heritability (h^2) has been widely used as a quantitative measure for behavior genetics. It is defined as the proportion of phenotypic variance that can be accounted for by genetic differences among individuals. Although new approaches to estimate h^2 have recently developed, the traditional method of behavior genetics is to estimate h^2 from twins or siblings who were reared apart. The basic idea of h^2 starts from Gregor Mendel's laws of heredity. Monozygotic twins share the same genetic makeup, whereas dizygotic twins share half of and siblings share a quarter of what monozygotic twins share. If monozygotic twins are reared separately, then the differences between them are attributable solely to the variability in environment; if dizygotic twins are reared separately, then the differences between them are attributed to the differences in both heredity and environment. The typical steps to calculate the heritability estimate are as follows: (1) sample monozygotic and dizygotic twins who were reared separately; (2) compute correlations between pairs on a given trait of interest separately for two groups: monozygotic and dizygotic twin pairs; (3) subtract the differences in correlation coefficients between groups; and (4) multiply the difference by two. The final product of these four steps is the *heritability estimate,* expressed as follows:

$$h^2 = 2\,(r_{mz} - r_{dz})$$

where r_{mz} and r_{dz} are the intraclass correlations for a given trait tested between
pairs of monozygotic (mz) and dizygotic
(dz) twins. The constant of two is used
because of its assumption that dizygotic
twins share half of what monozygotic
twins share. If the correlation for monozygotic twins on a certain trait is .70 and the
correlation for dizygotic twins is .50 on
the same trait, then the heritability estimate is .40 (2 x (.70–.50) = .40).

This heritability estimation is based on
a set of assumptions. First, the genotypes
of parents are not correlated for the trait
studied. Second, the genetic influences on
the trait are additive. Third, shared environment is uncorrelated with genotype.
And fourth, identical twins do not share a
more trait-relevant environment than do
fraternal twins. However, in reality spouse
resemblance in a human phenotype exists.
A couple normally shares some behavioral
characteristics in common. For example,
spouses of alcoholic men are more likely
to also drink themselves. Thus, children of
alcoholic men are predisposed to more
than their fair share of genetic inheritance
due to the shared characteristics of drinking between father and mother. Furthermore, genetic influences are not likely
additive for complex traits, such as psychopathology, intelligence, and many
aspects of social development. Complex
traits normally involve interactions
between genetic traits. Besides, shared
environment is highly correlated with
genotype. In addition, identical twins
share more in common with their environment compared to fraternal twins or
siblings.

It should also be noted that the heritability estimate is a measure of individual differences in a population and is not
a measure of the relative importance of
genes and environment within an individ-

ual. First, the heritability estimate does
not say anything about the relative contribution of nature or nurture in a phenomenon of interest within an individual.
Second, the heritability measure describes
only the extent to which genetic inheritance contributes to observed differences
in developmental outcomes between individuals growing up in the same environment (i.e., a given population). It deals
only with individual differences within a
population and provides no information
about either similarities among individuals in a population or differences between
populations. Therefore, studies of behavior genetics should be carefully interpreted, and results from behavior genetics
should not be used as indicators of quan-
tified contributions of nature or nurture,
or genetic or environmental influences on
development.

See also Canalization; Genetic Counseling

References and further reading
Gottlieb, Gilbert. 1996. "A Systems View
    of Psychobiological Development." In
    D. Magnusson, ed., *The Lifespan
    Development of Individuals:
    Behavioral, Neurobiological, and
    Psychosocial Perspectives.* New York:
    Cambridge University Press, pp. 76–103.
Plomin, Robert, et al. 1997. *Behavioral
    Genetics.* 3rd Ed. New York: W. H.
    Freedman.

Behavioral Style

Individual differences in behavioral styles
represent a definition put forward by
Alexander Thomas and Stella Chess.
From their perspective, temperament is
conceptualized as the stylistic component
of behavior, which is different from motivation or abilities. They vigorously
emphasize that temperament is an independent attribute that cannot and should
not be treated as secondary to or deriva-

tive of other attributes such as personality or emotion.

See also Temperament

Bilingualism

An increasing number of American children are exposed to at least two languages during early development; hence, they are bilingual. As the population of the United States diversifies, the pool of bilingual children (roughly 7 million and counting) will increase. In California, Texas, and Florida the numbers of households in which English is not the parent's first language represent a significant percentage of the population, and in Washington, D.C., a preschool with fifty children could have nearly an equal number of languages represented in the children's collective family histories. Language diversity has always been characteristic of the United States, even before European colonialists arrived.

For a long time developmentalists and educators believed that dual-language learning was detrimental not only to language learning but also to cognitive functioning in general. During the last part of the twentieth century, however, investigators demonstrated that dual-language learning not only did not lead to deficits but often had a beneficial effect on language skills. Toddlers can have some early difficulties differentiating words and cross-words with languages, but by the preschool years bilingual children for

A mother helping her four-year-old with a project in a Spanish-English cooperative preschool. (Elizabeth Crews)

the most part have tied production to context (use Spanish at home and with Spanish-speaking friends, use English in school and with non–Spanish-speaking friends), and by elementary age they are generally proficient in both languages.

See also Language

Binaural Cues

Stimulation providing information about the auditory environment that requires two ears to process.

Biobehavioral Dysregulation

Biobehavioral dysregulation represents factors that affect the infant's ability to gain self-control of biobehavioral systems. For example, infants who fail to develop regulated body temperature, sleep-wake cycles, feeding cycles, bowel or bladder control, or activity levels are evidencing biobehavioral dysregulation. With older children, examples of biobehavioral dysregulation would include attention-deficit hyperactivity disorder, difficult temperament, oppositional behavior, and other types of externalizing and internalizing behaviors (depression, extreme shyness).

See also Temperament

Biobehavioral State

The *biobehavioral state* is the infant's overall level of arousal or functioning at any point in time, usually on a five- to seven-point scale ranging from deep sleep to screaming rage. Both biological as well as behavioral indicates of state are used. Biological indicates include tonic heart rate, respiration, galvanic skin response, and electrical activity of the brain. Behavioral indicates include body movement, visual alertness, and crying. Biobehavioral state is an important factor in all infant clinical and scientific work, because the infant's ability to respond to events in the environment will always be within the context of biobehavioral state. Even neurological evaluation of the infant must account for the accurate assessment of the infant's reflexes and overall responsivity to the environment.

See also Neurobiology

Biological Rhythms

Biological rhythms are any regular, repeating pattern of activity, ranging from the adult female menstrual cycle to more subtle rhythms, such as the release of adrenocorticosteroids into the blood stream. During prenatal development, such rhythms are linked to fetal movements. During the first few months of postnatal life, much of the infant's transition from biobehavioral disorganization to organization involves the development of rhythmic activities such as biobehavioral systems (release of growth hormones, organization of body temperature, heart rate, sleep stages, sleep-wake cycle, feeding times, and bowel and bladder control). Biological rhythms such as the sleep-wake cycle are referred to as "circadian," a term derived from the Latin words *circa* (around) and *dias* (day). Thus, circadian rhythms are about a day in length. Biological rhythms that exceed a day in length are referred to as "infradian" (e.g., the female menstrual cycle), and those that are less than a day are called "ultradian" (e.g., the rhythmic features of the heart rate, infant sucking, and infant crying).

FIGURE 1   Electroencephalogram (EEG) stages of sleep

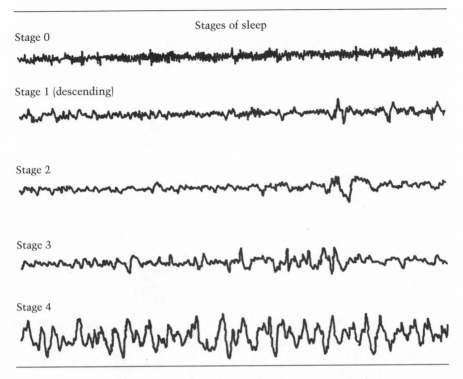

Stages of sleep

Stage 0

Stage 1 (descending)

Stage 2

Stage 3

Stage 4

Source: Adapted from W. B. Webb (1971). "Sleep behaviors as a biorhythm," in W. P. Colquhoun (ed.). *Biological rhythms and human performance*, pp. 149–177. New York: Academic Press.

When cycles repeat they are said to "oscillate," and the time for each oscillation to make a complete cycle is its "period." The number of cycles in a given time defines the *frequency* of the rhythm. Thus, one menstrual period is equal to one oscillation (from ovulation to menstruation), and within a year there are twelve to thirteen such oscillations (frequency).

Many rhythms synchronize to events in the environment, a process referred to as "entrainment." For most circadian rhythms, the key entraining stimulus is the light-dark cycle.

During infancy, rhythms that have captured much research attention include those associated with the sleep-wake cycle (and its links to growth-hormone production), feeding cycles (including sucking rhythms), and arousal states.

See also Behavioral Style; Biobehavioral Dysregulation; Crying; Pacification

Biological Vulnerability

Biological vulnerability refers to the degree in which the developing infant is detrimentally influenced by environmental or biological stressors. At the extreme, such stressors can lead to sustained damage to the infant (morbidity) or to death (mortality).

See also Genetic Disorders; Prematurity; Prenatal Development

Biomechanics

Biomechanics are the mechanics of biological, especially muscular, activity. Biomechanics is thought to play a key role in regulating the development of locomotion and motor skills, such as those involving reaching.

See also Fine Motor Skills; Gross Motor Skills; Motor Development; Reflexes

Birth

Roughly 270–280 days after conception, parturition (the birth process) begins for full-term infants. The mother may sense a decrease in overall fetal activity about one month before she eventually gives birth. The lower segment of the uterus drops, and the fetus moves so that its head is in a good position to lead the rest of the body through the birth canal. Sometimes labor symptoms are false. In such instances, the labor pains tend to be more irregular and do not change in intensity (as with real labor). In addition, the cervix does not dilate, and there rarely is spotting or discharge of blood during false labor. There are many indicators of true labor, including dilation of the cervix, contractions of the upper part of the uterus, abdominal pains, and backaches. Breathing properly and using relaxation exercises helps to increase the supply of oxygen to the muscles and can help to decrease the pain associated with labor and childbirth.

There are three phases to parturition. The first starts with the initial signs of

FIGURE 1   How the cervix opens

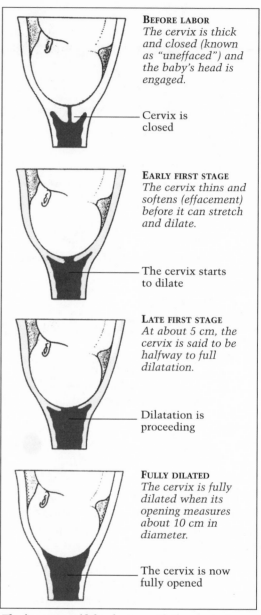

BEFORE LABOR
The cervix is thick and closed (known as "uneffaced") and the baby's head is engaged.

— Cervix is closed

EARLY FIRST STAGE
The cervix thins and softens (effacement) before it can stretch and dilate.

— The cervix starts to dilate

LATE FIRST STAGE
At about 5 cm, the cervix is said to be halfway to full dilatation.

— Dilatation is proceeding

FULLY DILATED
The cervix is fully dilated when its opening measures about 10 cm in diameter.

— The cervix is now fully opened

The first stage of labor begins with the onset of regular contractions. This causes the cervix to thin out, known as "effacement." Once the cervix has softened, the contractions cause the cervix to dilate progressively, so that the baby's head can pass through. Contractions draw the cervix up over the baby's head like a sleeve. (Reprinted from Pregnancy and birth: Your questions answered *with permission from DK Publishing, Inc. Copyright © 1997 Christoph Lees, Karina Reynolds, and Grainne McCartan. All rights reserved.)*

contractions and continues until full dilation of the cervix (about 10 centimeters). During this phase the amniotic sac can rupture as it is pushed toward the cervix. When the amniotic sac bursts, some women deliver relatively quickly, but others can show little dilation of the cervix for some time. In such instances, the obstetrician can elect to induce labor so that the danger of infection is minimized. The second phase of parturition spans the time from full dilation of the cervix to birth of the baby. During this phase, the lower part of the uterus expands and becomes nearly continuous with the fully dilated cervix and vagina to form the birth canal. The upper portion of the uterus continues to contract in order to help propel the fetus through the birth canal. The third phase covers the time from birth to expulsion of the placenta and membranes (the afterbirth). Uterine contractions also help to expel the afterbirth.

Presentation
Nearly 95 percent of all fetal positions during delivery are vertex. This means that they move through the birth canal headfirst, with the upper and back parts of the head leading the way. If the mother is delivering when lying on her back, this means that the baby would be born with its face toward the floor. However, the person assisting with the birth ordinarily rotates the baby shortly after the head appears (crowning). This rotation helps the fetus to move through the birth canal and, in fact, generally allows the obstetrician or midwife to present the mother and father with full frontal views of their newborn when he/she is delivered. Of course, in many cultures women are not lying on their backs when delivering. They might be upright, squatting, or lying on a vertical recline.

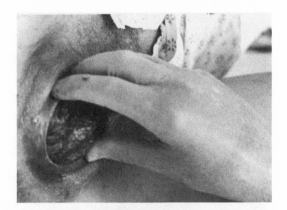

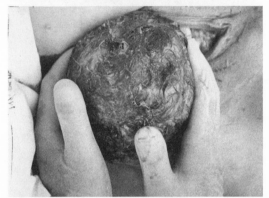

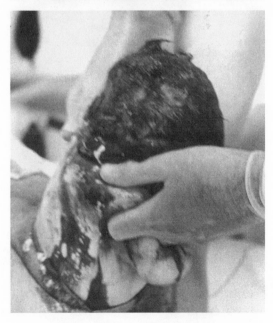

Normal vertex presentation of the full-term baby during the birthing process. (Courtesy of H. Vermeulen)

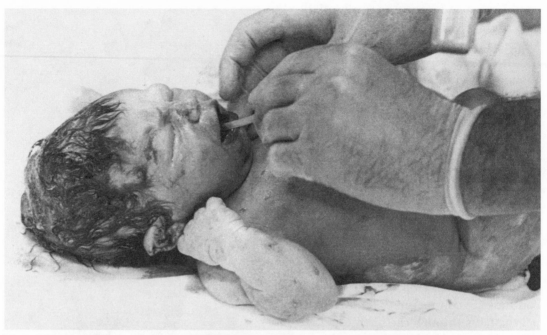

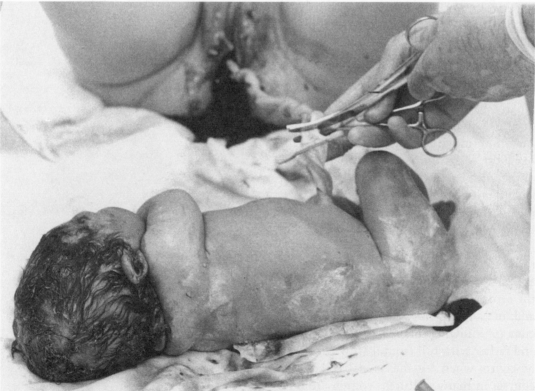

Following delivery, residual fluids are cleared from the infant's nose and mouth. The umbilical cord is cut and the infant is on her own for the first time in her life. (Courtesy of H. Vermeulen)

Whereas 95 percent of human birth presentations are in the vertex position, 5 percent involve fetal presentations that deviate from this position, referred to as "malpresentations." These include:

Brow: The head emerges first, but the upper front (brow) of the face leads.
Breech: A part of the pelvic extremity leads. In a full, or Frank, breech, the buttocks presents first and the legs are extended up toward the fetus's head. In a footling, or half breech, one leg emerges first. In a kneeling breech the knees present first.
Face: The head emerges first, but the full frontal face leads, rather than the upper and back of the head.
Transverse: The shoulder or upper arm leads, with the fetus lying across the uterus. This position puts the fetus especially at risk for oxygen deficit (anoxia) and/or damage to the head. Transverse presentations often involve cesarean delivery.
Compound: Two parts emerge simultaneously, for example, the hand and head.

Each of these malpresentations can take place through the birth canal, and each might involve assistance provided by an episiotomy, a surgical incision of the vulva that widens the opening for the fetus. However, any malpresentation poses dangers to both fetus and mother. In addition, some fetuses are simply too big to move through the birth canal, some are in danger of being exposed to a maternal infection, and some have a placenta that covers the cervical opening (placenta praevia). In these situations, delivery can be accomplished by cesarean section, which involves incising the abdominal and uterine walls and delivering the fetus.

In the United States, about 22–25 percent of all infants are born via cesarean section. Epidemiologists have identified several maternal characteristics that are predictive of cesarean section. Such characteristics include: high weight gain during pregnancy, pariety (first birth), marriage, short gestation, and multiple delivery. Although cesarean delivery has helped to reduce infant morbidity and mortality and has saved the lives of many women during delivery, it also comes with risks to both fetus and mother and is not, therefore, the preferred method of delivery in most circumstances.

See also Newborns; Prenatal Development

Birth Defects

Birth defects describe a range of problems related to birth outcomes, including genetic transmission (hemophilia), problems with cellular differentiation (Down syndrome), and environmental insults that occur prenatally (fetal alcohol syndrome). The social-emotional impact of birth defects is considerable for family members, as well as for the community in which that family resides. An interdisciplinary field, infant mental health, addresses the emotional and relationship consequences of birth defects for families. For most birth defects, the emotional consequences are lifelong, as families must adapt to the demands occasioned by the growth and development of their child. The economic costs of birth defects can be devastating to families and strain societal resources.

Birth defects generally are categorized in relation to the major biological systems affected. These are summarized as follows.

Neurological Malformations

Cerebral palsy is a variety of disorders linked to brain damage that may or may not involve motor or intellectual dysfunctions depending on the specific location of the damage, the networks impacted, and the degree of postnatal environmental intervention.

Spina bifida is caused by malformations affecting the vertebrae of the spinal cord resulting in a protrusion of the cord and nerve roots. The degree of dysfunction is linked to the site and degree of the malformation. Recently, attempts to correct spina bifida prenatally have been successful, although the long-term consequences of such corrective surgery have yet to be determined. Spina bifida generally affects motor performance but not intellectual competence.

Cardiovascular Malformations

Truncus arteriosus is a problem that leads to excessive blood flow to the lungs because the artery at the top of the heart is malformed. Infants with this malformation usually do not survive beyond the first year of life.

The *tetralogy of Fallot* refers to four heart defects that interfere with blood flow to the lungs, resulting in poor oxygenation. The problem usually arises during the first year of life and increases in severity through toddlerhood. The problem is correctable surgically with few long-term consequences.

Alimentary Tract Malformations

Cleft lip or palate is a split through the lip, the top of the mouth (hard palate), or the back of the mouth (soft palate) due to the failure of the oral structures to close during early prenatal life. All are correctable through surgical procedures but often present relationship difficulties for parents during the immediate postnatal period.

Chromosomal Malformations

Down syndrome, or trisomy 21, is associated with mental retardation, specific facial features, and congenital heart problems as well as other difficulties. If Down individuals survive to childhood, they are likely to have more or less normal life spans. The range of variation of mental retardation is considerably greater than once believed. The functional abilities of Down individuals therefore largely depend on the quality of their life experiences.

Other types of birth defects involve genitourinary, musculoskeletal, and abdominal problems. On a normal day in the United States some 10,700 babies are born; approximately 4 percent (about 420 infants) have an identifiable birth defect. Examples of the incidence of birth defects include the following: heart and circulation (1 in 115 births); cleft lip/palate (1 in 930 births); Down syndrome (one in 900 births); and fetal alcohol syndrome (one in 1,000 births). The March of Dimes has compiled a home-safety checklist in an effort to help prevent many birth defects. The most important recommendations are to maintain a smoke-free household, eliminate lead-based paint, check the house for molds, install carbon-monoxide detectors, check the basement for radon, have wells tested for nitrates, and avoid exposure to pesticides during pregnancy. It is important to remember that many birth defects have known causes, and prevention can minimize exposure of the fetus. A simple example will suffice: Fetal alcohol syndrome is completely preventable if one does not drink alcohol during pregnancy.

See also Prematurity; Prenatal Development

References and further reading
March of Dimes (website 2001). http://
www.modimes.org.

Birth Plan

A birth plan is a written document in which parents describe the environment, procedures, and processes they hope to experience during labor and delivery. Birth plans first gained popularity in the 1980s when childbirth educators and other advocates of choices in birth encouraged parents to discuss their preferences with physicians and midwives. There are two key advantages to writing a birth plan. First, the process of writing makes parents knowledgeable about the choices they have in labor and delivery care. Second, preparing a birth plan helps parents organize their options and set priorities. For instance, a parent may come to realize that freedom to move and walk during labor is most important. Another parent might describe her birth partner's active role in the labor and delivery experience as being most important. Written in a cooperative spirit, birth plans can be an excellent tool for parents and practitioners. A birth plan should result in increased communication between parents and their physicians, midwives, or other care providers.

Writing a Birth Plan
There are several resources one can use in preparing to write a birth plan. Many obstetrician practices provide sample birth plans or birth-planning forms to expectant parents. Widely available publications on pregnancy and birth usually include a discussion of birth plans and tips for preparing one. Likewise, there are many Internet resources providing infor-

mation on how to write a birth plan and offering sample birth plans. The content of a birth plan can be as brief or lengthy as parents choose. Generally, birth plans include preferences and requests related to: the involvement of birth partners or other supportive people during the birthing experience; the use of standard procedures in some hospitals such as enemas or standard use of IV or heparin/saline locks; the use of environmental props such as music; the use of whirlpools or the shower; procedures for fetal monitoring and internal exams; labor and delivery positions; pain relief; the use of medications to speed labor or delivery of the placenta; care for the newborn immediately after birth; circumcision; rooming-in options (in which the newborn sleeps in the room with the mother rather than in a nursery); and breastfeeding options.

Carrying Out a Birth Plan
Whether birth plans are carried out depends on the childbirth setting and the medical condition of the mother. Families choosing to have a birth experience in their home or in a birthing center are more likely to enjoy more flexibility. Still, many hospitals are supportive of birth plans as well. In preparing a birth plan, parents should gather information about the nonnegotiable policies and procedures of the facility as well as information about the flexible aspects of care. Hospitals may also have limited resources (e.g., only a few rooms in the labor and delivery area may have whirlpools). Although the use of a whirlpool might be outlined in a birth plan, whether or not that resource is available depends on timing and how many other families have requested to use whirlpools.

The medical history of the mother, the progress of the pregnancy, and the progress in labor and delivery all influence the degree to which medical staff can carry out birth plans. For instance, a mother with a history of chronic drug use during the pregnancy is likely to have a very different labor and delivery experience than a mother without such a history. Mothers who have high-risk pregnancies may be more prone to difficult labors, which may require more intensive medical intervention. For example, a mother who has experienced high blood pressure (hypertension) during her pregnancy will have to be monitored closely during her labor to ensure that both she and her baby are tolerating the labor and delivery. Many infants tolerate the intensity of labor and delivery very well, but problems can arise. A drop in the baby's heart rate, a breech position, and an especially long labor without significant progression in the labor are all valid reasons for medical intervention that may contravene procedures outlined in a birth plan. Parents should talk with physicians or midwives about potential emergency situations relative to the birth plan long before labor begins. Physicians, midwives, and nurses should work to support the birth wishes of parents, but their primary concern must be the health of mother and baby. Clear conversations between parents and their care providers regarding medical interventions are a necessary and important aspect of planning for any birth.

Making sure the birth partner is familiar with the birth plan is a good strategy. The birth partner can advocate for the mother's preferences when she is focused on her labor. Likewise a doula—a professional labor assistant—should be familiar with the birth plan so she/he can be supportive of parents' desired choices. Copies of the birth plan should be provided to the obstetricians' office, midwife, or other professionals in advance.

Most care providers will attach a copy of the birth plan to the mother's medical chart and forward a copy to the hospital's labor and delivery unit. However, bringing extra copies of the birth plan to the hospital or birth center is always a good strategy and helps busy labor and delivery care providers. Birth plans are designed to be flexible, and parents and care providers can revisit the content of the birth plan leading up to labor and delivery and even during labor itself.

See also Alternative Birth; Doula; Midwifery

References and further reading
Childbirth.org (website 2001). http://www.childbirth.org.
Doulas of North America (website 2001). http://www.dona.org.
Reynolds, K., C. Lees, and G. McCartan. 1997. *Pregnancy and Birth: Your Questions Answered.* NY: DK Publishing.

Birthmarks

Birthmarks are naturally occurring raised or discolored areas of the skin. Many newborns are born with birthmarks. Some birthmarks fade or disappear over time, and others are permanent. Generally, birthmarks pose more of a cosmetic concern than a health risk. On some occasions, medical intervention may be required. Common categories of birthmarks include: hemangiomas, pigmented nevus, cafe-au-lait spots, Mongolian spots, nervus simplex, and nevus flammeus.

Hemangiomas are birthmarks that occur when an area of the skin develops an abnormal blood supply. When this abnormal blood supply involves small blood vessels—the capillaries—the birthmark is commonly called a "strawberry," as the lesion is strawberry-colored. Strawberry marks can be evident at birth or appear shortly after birth. One out of every ten babies has this common birthmark. Strawberry birthmarks can be very small or very large, sometimes several inches or larger. Generally, strawberry birthmarks grow very quickly in the first six months of life and then slow in growth. They fade in color over time and disappear by the time a child is about ten years old. Because strawberry marks are noticeable on the face or other viewable areas, parents often inquire about treatment. Most physicians recommend allowing the birthmark to fade on its own unless there is a medical reason for treating it. For instance, if the birthmark appears over the mouth or nose, it may interfere with normal body functions and require treatment.

A second, more rare type of hemangioma is called a cavernous hemangioma. Only 1–2 percent of children have this type of birthmark, which results from an oversupply of blood from large blood vessels. Cavernous hemangiomas, often combined with a strawberry mark, are usually blue or bluish-red in color. They are generally larger than strawberry marks and grow quickly, although like strawberry marks they shrink and then fade. About 50 percent of the time, cavernous hemangiomas disappear by the age of five, and 95 percent of the time the birthmarks have disappeared by the time the child is ten or twelve years of age. Both strawberry marks and cavernous hemangiomas leave little or no residual discoloration, but both may leave slight scarring. The scarring can be treated by a dermatologist.

Pigmented nevus simply refers to a mole. Soft, brown moles can appear anywhere on the body, are generally harmless, and are permanent. Large moles, sometimes called congenital nevi, and those with hair growing in them have a higher risk of becoming cancerous. Physicians closely monitor changes in the shape and size of these moles and may recommend removing them. Congenital nevi can be so large as to cover an entire limb. Conditions this severe are extremely rare. A second type of mole is called an acquired nevi. Many people develop as many as thirty moles over their lives. Most acquired moles appear after the age of five, but children younger than five can develop moles. Most physicians advise monitoring any changes in size or appearance.

Cafe-au-lait spots, the color of cafe-au-lait, a coffee-milk beverage, are permanent birthmarks. Cafe-au-lait spots are flat areas of increased pigmentation in the skin. Sometimes cafe-au-lait spots are evident at birth, but they can also appear in the first few years of life. Multiple cafe-au lait spots, six or more, can be a symptom of a genetic disorder called neurofibromatosis and warrant a medical examination.

Mongolian spots, blue or gray in color, look very similar to bruises. Mongolian spots are most often associated with children of African American, Asian, Indian, and Mediterranean descent. They are usually evident at birth on the buttocks, back, legs, or shoulders. Mongolian spots look so much like bruises, parents may receive looks of disapproval from others who cannot distinguish the birthmarks from bruises, and sometimes they are even reported to the authorities for child abuse. These birthmarks generally fade in the first year of life, although in rare cases they can remain visible into adulthood.

Nevus simplex, often called a salmon patch or stork bite, are salmon-colored patches most often seen at birth on the face or the nape of the neck. These birthmarks become lighter during the first two years of life, often barely noticeable. Ninety-five percent fade completely over time.

Nevus flammeus, or portwine stains, are purplish-red in color and result from a malformation of small blood vessels. They are almost always present at birth and usually appear on the face or limbs. Although portwine stains fade, they are permanent birthmarks. As the blood vessels grow, the birthmark enlarges. Laser treatments can make the birthmarks less noticeable. Portwine stains usually do not present any health hazards, although in rare cases birthmarks found on the eyes and/or forehead can be a sign of abnormalities in brain structure and growth.

See also Newborns

References and further reading
Shelov, S. P., ed. 1998. *The American Academy of Pediatrics: Caring for Your Baby and Young Child.* New York: Bantam.

Biting

Biting is a common act among infant/toddlers. Biting usually occurs for one of two reasons. First, infant/toddlers explore their environments through their senses, and one common way to explore is by mouthing and chewing objects. Sometimes, out of curiosity, an infant/toddler will bite without any malice. Infants and toddlers also feel a developmental need to mouth, suck, and chew on objects (oral gratification). At times, infant/toddlers try to meet this need by biting another

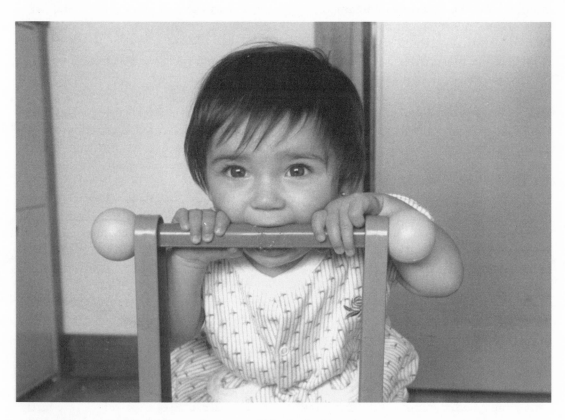

An eleven-month-old girl devouring a toy. (Elizabeth Crews)

child. The intent is not to hurt the other child; rather, the child is driven by the satisfaction gained from the act of biting. In fact, the infant/toddler may not realize that biting hurts. When infants are teething, they usually bite and chew on any object within reach. The gums are especially sensitive during teething, and the pressure on the gums that comes from biting feels good to the infant.

Second, infant/toddlers can bite out of frustration. Because infant/toddlers cannot always verbalize their wishes and needs, they often resort to physical means of expressing emotions. If an infant/toddler feels crowded, does not want to share a toy, feels threatened, wants a toy that another child has, and so on, the child could bite as a means to express emotion.

Caregivers and parents can employ several strategies to reduce or prevent biting. The strategy used depends on the motivation of the behavior. Thus, the first task is to understand why the child is biting. If the child is biting for oral gratification, the adult can provide plenty of rubbery, textured toys for chewing and mouthing. If the child is biting because he/she can find no other way to express feelings, the adult can work to label the feelings ("You look sad"), identify intentions ("You don't want Susie to touch your head"), and help the child to learn expression words ("You can say, 'No, Susie'"). Until infant/toddlers expand their verbal skills, teaching very young children some variation of sign language, sometimes called baby signs, can be helpful. Through the use of hand signs, infant/toddlers can express needs and wishes. This ability to communicate effectively reduces their frustration and is likely to reduce their need to bite.

See also Aggression; Language; Prosocial Behavior

References and further reading
Acredolo, L., and S. Goodwyn. 1996. *Baby Signs: How to Talk to Your Baby Before Your Baby Can Talk.* New York: NTC Publishing.
Gonzalez-Mena, J., and D. W. Eyer. 1997. *Infants, Toddlers and Caregivers.* 4th ed. Mountain View, CA: Mayfield.

Blindness

During infancy, many developmental milestones emerge in normal fashion for blind infants as they do for sighted infants; this is especially true for motor development and the major sequential steps involved in upright locomotion. Interestingly enough, even very young blind infants will "look" at their hands despite the fact that they cannot see them. This captures the essential problem for the blind infant: the inability to gain feedback about events in the environment through the visual system.

The distinguished social worker Selma Fraiberg and her colleagues were among the first to discover that if blind infants received feedback from the environment from other sensory modalities they could thrive in much the same way as sighted infants. Fraiberg taught parents how to relate to their blind infants using sound and touch as feedback stimulation. Her work with parents and blind infants generalized to a broad range of parent-infant relationship issues, and she is credited as one of the founders of the infant mental health movement.

Other investigators have designed instruments that provide echoes from objects in order to help the infant localize objects in space from auditory rather than visual information.

See also Perception

Bonding

Bonding generally describes the social-emotional relationship of the infant and its caregivers. In many respects, "bonding" is often used as a synonym for "attachment." Historically, however, the former was the term used by two pediatricians, Marshall Klaus and John Kennell, to describe what they believed was a critical event in the development of the mother-infant relationship. In a series of studies, Klaus and Kennel reported that during the first few hours after the birth of the baby conditions were optimal for mothers to develops a strong "bond" with their newborn infant; the quality of this bond had implications for subsequent development of attachment and social-emotional development. As a result of their studies, major changes in birthing practices occurred in hospitals all over the United States. Not only were fathers invited to be present during the birth of their infant; some hospitals developed birthing rooms in which most if not all members of the mother's family could be present. These and many other changes in delivery practices were beneficial outcomes of the work on bonding. Still, evidence to support the concept of bonding is mixed. Perhaps the best way to think of bonding is not as a fixed phenomenon of short-duration but as one in a series of experiences that facilitate the development of the mother-infant relationship.

See also Attachment

References and further reading
Klaus, Marshall H., and John H. Kennell. 1977. *Maternal-Infant Bonding.* St. Louis: Mosby.

Book-Reading

Reading to infant/toddlers is an excellent way to support language development. Some parents even begin reading to the

A grandfather reading to his eight-month-old grandson. (Courtesy of Heather Lewis)

Two toddlers enjoying books. (Courtesy of the Forbes family)

fetus in the womb, and others begin reading to infants in the first months of postnatal life. Reading to infants boosts language development in several ways. First, the act of reading exposes the baby to the sounds and rhythms of language. Second, the baby begins to hear new words, and over time exposure to new words builds the infant's vocabulary. Child-development experts know that children who were exposed to books and reading from an early age have larger vocabularies, learn to read earlier, and are generally better readers.

Reading with Infants and Toddlers
Because infant/toddlers learn best by actively exploring materials, visually exploring and mouthing books are common and appropriate behaviors. For this reason, books made of vinyl, cloth, or sturdy cardboard are best for infant/toddlers. These materials can be cleaned easily, are more durable, and are easier for infant/toddlers to handle. Books with large, simple pictures can be propped on the floor so even a young infant resting on his/her stomach can view the books. Older infant/toddlers like to hear favorite stories again and again. Labeling pictures in books is an enjoyable activity. Over time, toddlers can even fill in missing words in a short, repetitive story, an exercise that builds language and memory skills. Reading books together is an activity that builds many skills and nurtures a loving relationship between adult and child.

See also Language; Songs and Sensory Development

Bottle Tooth Decay

The baby's twenty primary teeth begin to emerge during the second quarter of the first year of postnatal life and continue to come in until approximately age three. For some infants the eruption of teeth is hardly noticed, but for others teething is a painful experience resulting in excessive crying and fussiness. During this period, bottle-fed infants are at risk for baby bottle tooth decay, caused by excessive exposure to sweetened foods (formula, fruit juices). Babies who are allowed to take a bottle to bed with them are especially at risk for subsequent tooth decay and gum problems. It is good dental practice to begin brushing teeth as early as possible, even if it is initially only a pretend game. Although the child eventually loses many of his/her first teeth, the practice of brushing teeth is important because it stimulates the gums.

See also Breastfeeding; Nutrition

Many parents choose bottle feeding over breast feeding because of the convenience it offers. Here, an aunt feeds her nephew with a bottle, allowing his parents time to attend to other matters. (Skjold Photographs)

Bottle-Feeding

Bottle-feeding is the practice of feeding an infant commercially prepared formula or breastmilk by using a bottle and nipple. Bottle-feeding formula is considered an alternative to breastfeeding. As with breastfeeding, bottle-feeding is a time for closeness and nurturing between parent/caregiver and infant.

Many parents who choose to bottle-feed cite reasons such as ease and convenience, ability to feed in public (many feel uncomfortable breastfeeding in public), greater father involvement in feedings, increased ability to "schedule" the baby, and being less tied to the baby for frequent nursings. Some women simply do not feel comfortable with the idea of a baby suckling at the breast, and still others are concerned that breastfeeding affects the appearance and size of their breasts. Some mothers and children are not successful in establishing a breastfeeding relationship, and therefore bottle-feeding breastmilk or formula is their alternative. As with breastfeeding, it is a personal decision whether or not to bottle-feed, based on lifestyle, values, and individual needs and circumstances.

Mechanics of Bottle-feeding

A four-ounce bottle is most often chosen for newborns and young infants until a larger bottle is needed. There are standard reusable bottles that require washing, and there are disposable bottles that use disposable liners. In addition, there are bottles that are angled to lessen swallowing

Maintaining sterile nipples and bottles is essential for the health of a baby. Be sure to wash both with hot, soapy water after each use as this father in Minnesota is doing. (Laura Dwight/Corbis)

Another argument in favor of bottle feeding over breast feeding is that it gives the father an opportunity to bond with the child as this father is doing with his two-year-old son. (David Hall/Corbis)

of air, bottles that have separate compartments for formula and water (for easy travel without fear of spoiling), and bottles with shelves to push out excess air.

Nipples can be rubber or silicone. There are three basic types: the expandable nubbin (designed to elongate during sucking), the standard bulb-type, and the orthodontic (a nipple designed to insert farther back into the mouth to allow a more natural milking action of the tongue). Through experimentation, parent and baby will discover which type is best. Minimizing air intake is important for the comfort of the baby. If the baby sputters or seems to choke during a feeding, the nipple hole might be too large. If the baby seems to be working hard and tires easily, or the baby's cheeks seem to cave in from sucking so vigorously, the nipple hole might be too small. This can be checked by tipping the bottle upside down without shaking. If milk flows instead of dripping, the hole is too large; if it doesn't drip at least one drop per second, then the hole is too small. The baby

will quit sucking from the bottle when he/she is full. A caregiver/parent should not force a baby to finish a bottle.

Caregivers should always wash their hands before preparing a bottle of formula. Bottles and nipples must be sterilized in boiling water before first use, and washed with hot, soapy water after each feeding. Following the directions on the box/can of formula exactly is essential. Formula in the refrigerator must be used within twenty-four hours (forty-eight hours maximum).

Formula
There are three types of formula: powdered, to which water is added; liquid concentrate, to be mixed half-and-half with water; and ready-to-feed liquid formula. The nutritional content of each is nearly the same, so choice is largely an economic and convenience issue. Powdered formulas are the least expensive but the most time-consuming to prepare. Ready-to-feed formula is the most expensive but most convenient to use, particularly

when traveling. Iron-fortified formula is recommended unless a doctor advises otherwise. Iron-fortified formulas contain the amount of iron recommended by the American Academy of Pediatrics and other organizations.

Babies may prefer one formula over another, and some experimentation may be required to find the most pleasing and digestible. Sometimes a baby is allergic or intolerant to a certain formula. The following signs could mean an infant is allergic: crying after most feedings, vomiting immediately after nearly every feeding, persistent diarrhea or constipation, colic, irritable behavior and/or frequent night waking, a red rash around the anus or on the face, and frequent colds and/or ear infections. If a baby persistently has one or more of these symptoms, a physician should be consulted.

Hypoallergenic soy formulas are sometimes suggested for babies who have an allergy to traditional cow's milk–based formulas, to babies who are lactose deficient, and to babies who have a rare disease in which they cannot metabolize lactose. A physician should always be consulted before switching to a soy formula.

Most babies prefer their formula warm, so it should be warmed by running warm tap water over the bottle for several minutes. The temperature can be tested by shaking a few drops onto the inner wrist. How much formula a baby requires varies and depends on weight, rate of growth, metabolism, body type, and appetite (which can change from day to day). Generally, from birth to six months the baby will require about 2–2.5 ounces of formula per pound per day. Many newborns take only an ounce or two at each feeding for about the first week. By one month most infants take about 3–4 ounces at each feeding, and from two to six months babies can take 4–6 ounces per feeding. Between six months and a year, the baby can take as much as 8 ounces per feeding.

Formula-fed infants are easier to schedule than breastfed babies. Formula is digested more slowly, so the interval between feedings is usually longer for bottle-fed babies. Parents must decide if they will feed their babies on demand (whenever they show signs of hunger such as fussing, crying, sucking fingers or fists, etc.) or at fixed intervals, usually about every three to four hours. A baby might be getting too little formula if he/she has slower than normal weight gain, decreased urine output, a loose, wrinkly appearance to the skin, and/or persistent crying. A baby might be getting too much formula if he/she experiences a lot of spitting up or vomiting immediately after a feeding, has colicky abdominal pain (pulls his/her legs up onto a tense abdomen) immediately after a feeding, or excessive weight gain.

Weaning

As in weaning from the breast, weaning is an individual decision that baby and parent will have to make together. Babies continue to have sucking needs until around two years of age or more, so a weaned baby may need other ways to meet his/her sucking needs such as a finger or thumb or pacifier.

See also Breastfeeding; Nutrition

References and further reading
American Academy of Pediatrics. 1998. *The Complete and Authoritative Guide: Caring For Your Baby and Your Child.* New York: Bantam.
Breastfeeding Support Network (website 2001). http://www.momsbags.com/index.html.
Huggins, K. 1990. *The Nursing Mother's Companion.* Boston: The Harvard Common Press.

La Leche League International. 1997. *The Womanly Art of Breastfeeding.* New York: Plume, Penguin Books.
———. (website 2001). http://www.lalecheleague.org.
Lactation Associates/National Alliance for Breastfeeding Advocacy (website 2001). http://members.aol.com/marshalact/lactationassociates.
Sears, W. and Martha Sears. 1993. *The Baby Book.* Boston: Little, Brown.
Small, M. 1998. *Our Babies, Ourselves: How Biology and Culture Shape the Way We Parent.* New York: Anchor Books.

Bowlby, John
See Attachment

Brain Damage
Brain damage is any physical change to brain matter that compromises functioning. It is most common in head trauma where the brain is damaged (e.g., insult by foreign object or substance, bleeding within the brain, loss of blood supply, excessive pressure caused by compression of the skull, shearing of white-matter tracts through concussion). Brain damage also occurs through the presence of toxic substances (e.g., carbon monoxide); tumors, which can destroy tissue directly or indirectly through pressure; nutrient deficiency, through the absence of one or more vitamins, minerals, or any other necessary nutrient; disease (e.g., herpes simplex); anoxia (oxygen deprivation); and vascular problems, including thrombosis, hemorrhage, and embolism. Some evidence suggests that severe emotional trauma and stress can damage the brain through the toxic effects of excessive quantities of glucocorticoids (a stress hormone). Stress particularly affects the hippocampus, which can effect a range of abilities, including memory and the ability to learn.

See also Neurobiology

Brain Development
The development of the brain begins with the formation of the embryonic disc approximately eighteen days following conception. It develops rapidly and is 25 percent of its adult size at birth and 90 percent of its adult size at five years of age.

See also Neurobiology
References and further reading
Families and Work Institute (website 2001). http://www.familiesandwork.org.
I Am Your Child Campaign (website 2001). http://iamyourchild.org.
The Ounce of Prevention Fund (website 2001). http://www.bcm.tmc.edu/civitas/links/ounce.html.

Brain Differentiation
Neurons initially lack specificity in their functioning. Through genetic instructions and a complex set of environmental and cell-cell interactions, a neuron gains specificity. Generally, the location and the nature of connections between a neuron and its target determine its function.

See also Neurobiology

Brain Function
Brain function is the physiological activity of the brain. Brain function underlies all behaviors, including sensation, movement, thinking, and regulation of the body.

See also Neurobiology

Brain Structure

Brain structure is the physical anatomy of the brain.

See also Neurobiology

Brain Waves

The activity of the brain recorded electronically by the use of noninvasive electrodes (sensors) placed on the scalp. Recordings of brain waves are known as electroencephalograms. Measuring the brain's electrical activity in this way is used to study auditory- and visual-information processing in nonverbal infants by observing visually evoked potentials or auditory-evoked potentials (characteristic brain waves from brain sites that are indicative of attentional processing). Other electrical activity of the brain can provide information about which part of the brain is involved in information processing, including whether the left, right, or both parts of the brain are activated.

Brazelton Neonatal Behavioral Assessment Scale

The Brazelton Neonatal Behavioral Assessment Scale (NBAS) was developed by T. Berry Brazelton and is one of the most frequently used tools to assess the developmental status of newborn infants. The NBAS is conducted with very young infants, usually on the third day after birth and again about a week later, to assess the responses that the infant has available in interacting with the environment. An important component of the NBAS is that the infant's score is based on his/her best performance rather than typical performance. The examiner is therefore encouraged to repeat tests later during the testing period if it appears the infant had not responded to the best of his/her ability earlier in the testing period. It is also recommended that the examiner rock, hold, and cuddle the infant as necessary to elicit the best responses available to the infant.

Many reflexive and temperamental behaviors, as well as the pattern of changes from one state to another as the examination progresses, are examined. "State" indicates the status of the infant's consciousness. For example, the NBAS identifies two sleep states (deep sleep and light sleep) and four awake states (drowsy, alert, excited, and crying). Items are designed to evaluate the manner in which the infant moves from one state to another. For example, the assessment begins when the infant is asleep. The examiner presents a stimulus, such as a light pinprick on the bottom of the foot, and observes how the infant responds and how rapidly he/she returns to the initial state.

The NBAS typically takes about thirty minutes to administer. A twenty-eight–item rating sheet has twenty-eight behavioral items, each on a nine-point scale, and eighteen elicited items, each on a four-point scale. Examples of behavioral items include cuddliness, irritability, alertness; examples of elicited items are response to light, a rattle, and a bell. Research indicates that higher scores on the NBAS are to some extent predictive of better performance on the Bayley Scales of Infant Development, a tool for assessing the developmental status of older infants. In addition, Brazelton provides several suggestions for using the NBAS to assist parents in becoming sensitive to their infant's behavioral signals.

See also Assessment; Bayley Scales of
Infant Development; Neurological
Assessment; Newborns; Self-Regulation

References and further reading
Brazelton, T. B. 1984. *Neonatal Behavioral
Assessment Scale.* Philadelphia:
Lippincott.

Brazelton, T. Berry

See Brazelton Neonatal Behavioral
Assessment Scale

Breastfeeding

In the 1800s, more than 95 percent of
infants born in the United States were
breastfed and were not weaned until two
to four years of age. Such practices are
common in nearly all cultures historically and with many cultures today. In
the United States, about half the infants
born are breastfed, for about four months.
The startling decline in breastfeeding
began in the early 1900s when modern-
ization (electricity, refrigeration, and
other such technological advances) led to
use of condensed and evaporated milks;
artificial infant feeding became big business. Formulas were promoted as better,
more modern, and healthier for babies.
Due to this marketing, and the thought of
convenience, mothers made bottle-feeding the norm. In the 1940s only 20–30
percent of babies in the United States
were breastfed. During the post–World
War II baby boom, breastfeeding became
unfashionable, out of date, and so uncom-
mon that women who chose to breastfeed
were considered odd. In the 1980s,
UNICEF and the World Health Organization, fueled by research on the benefits of
breastfeeding and anger at the formula
companies for marketing their formulas
to Third World countries, launched a

major campaign for a return to breastfeeding. Women again began to choose to
breastfeed. By the late 1990s, organizations such as the American Academy of
Pediatrics were encouraging breastfeeding for at least one year for all babies.

There are many factors that influence
the choice to breastfeed or not to breastfeed, including the challenges of working
and breastfeeding, wanting to involve the
father in feeding, fear of losing one's figure, and convenience. For example, the
mother might feel tied down because no
one else can feed her baby, or she may feel
isolated by having to find a private place
to nurse. Other obstacles to breastfeeding
in the United States include apathy and
misinformation among some physicians;
insufficient prenatal breastfeeding education; disruptive hospital policies (mother
and infant being separated right after
birth for infant tests); early hospital dis-
charges; lack of follow-up care and support for breastfeeding; lack of broad societal support; and media portrayal of
bottle-feeding as normal. Returning to
work is often cited as a primary reason
not to nurse.

The Family and Medical Leave Act,
however, provides up to a twelve-week
maternity leave, which has helped mothers establish a strong breastfeeding relationship. Before the Family Medical Leave
Act, women were expected to return to
work within a few weeks after giving
birth, which made breastfeeding difficult
to establish and sustain. Still, many
returning working women choose to stop
breastfeeding. Some companies are
attempting to encourage and support
breastfeeding, providing work breaks and
places to express breast milk, but most
provide no such accommodations. The
American Academy of Pediatrics issued a

TABLE 1   Some drugs excreted in breast milk

Alcohol	Corticosteroids
Amphetamines	e.g., coritsone, prednisone
Analgesics (nonnarcotic)	Cough suppressants
e.g., acetaminophen (Tylenol), aspirin	Diuretics
Anesthetics (inhalant)	Environmental chemicals
Antibiotics	e.g., DDT
e.g., penicillin, tetracycline	Ergot alkaloids
Anticancer	Expectorants
e.g., cyclophosphamide, methotrexate	Laxatives
Anticholinergics	Minerals, salts, metals
e.g., atropine, scopolamine	Muscle relaxants
Anticoagulants	e.g., curane, succinylcholine
e.g., warfarin	Narcotics
Anticonvulsants	e.g., ephedrine, pseudoephedrine
e.g., diphenylhydantoin (phenytoin),	Nasal decongestants
primidone	e.g., ephedrine, pseudoephedrine
Antidepressants	Nicotine
e.g., Elavil, Tofranil	Oral antidiabetics
Antihistamines	e.g., Orinase
Antiinfectives	Oral contraceptives
e.g., Flagyl	e.g., estrogens, progestogens
Antimalarials	Reserpine
e.g., pyrimethamine, quinine	Sedatives/hypnotics
Asthma preparations	e.g., bromides, chloral hydrate, diazepam
e.g., aminophylline	Thyroid and antithyroid drugs
Barbiturates	e.g., iodides, propylthiouracil
Caffein	Tranquilizers
Cardiac antiarryhymthia drugs	Vitamins
e.g., quinidine	

Source: Reprinted from Y. Brackbill. 1979. "Obstetrical medication and infant behavior," In *Handbook of Infant Development*, ed. J. D. Osofsky. New York: John Wiley & Sons, Inc., p. 90.

press release in March 1998 introducing the New Mother's Breastfeeding Promotion and Protection Act, which aims to encourage employers to better support breastfeeding mothers. Sufficient break times to express milk, pumping stations provided on-site, and efficient breast pumps are among the suggestions outlined in the act. Even when supportive policies are in place, attitudes about breastfeeding can be unwelcoming of nursing mothers.

Mechanics of Breastfeeding
As a baby suckles the breast, the nerve endings in the nipple are stimulated, which then send signals to the pituitary gland, directing it to continue to produce the hormone prolactin. The prolactin sig-

nals the alveoli (grapelike clusters of tiny, rounded sacs in which the milk is produced) to produce milk. As long as the breasts are suckled, they will continue to make milk. The suckling also causes the pituitary to release another important hormone, oxytocin. Oxytocin travels through the bloodstream to the breast, where it causes the cells lining the alveoli to contract, thereby squeezing the milk from the alveoli into the ducts. As the milk enters the ducts, the cells along the walls of the ducts also contract, sending the milk out to the milk pools beneath the areola. While prolactin makes the milk, oxytocin makes it available to the baby. This process of making the milk available to the baby is called the "let-down reflex" or the "milk ejec-

Milk production works on the principle of supply and demand. The more the infant suckles, the more milk the mother produces; conversely, the less the infant suckles, the less milk the mother produces. Baby and mother must work out the proper balance.

The first food for a breastfed newborn is a sticky clear or yellowish liquid called colostrum. This substance is produced by the mother's breasts before birth and for one to five days afterward. It is a unique compound of water, sugar, protein, fat-soluble vitamins, and minerals. Colostrum is the ideal first food for babies because it is easy to digest and contains disease-fighting antibodies. The main function of colostrum is to protect the newborn against infection and to provide important nutrients.

After the colostrum has run its course, true milk comes in. First is the transitional milk (from about six days to two weeks after birth), and then mature milk (from two weeks on). Human milk is made mostly of water, fat, carbohydrates, and proteins and contains antibodies and immunoglobins that help prevent disease and infection. The vitamins and minerals in the mother's diet will be reflected in her milk. Thus, a well-rounded diet will help ensure the healthiest balance of nutrients in the milk, as well as greater volume.

Milk composition varies at each feeding. The first milk of each feeding is the foremilk, which is thin, like skim milk. The later milk is called the hindmilk, much higher in fat and slightly higher in protein. The hindmilk is more filling to the baby and has greater nutritional value. In addition, the composition of breastmilk is very easy for the infant to digest and is therefore perfectly suited for the infant's immature digestive system.

FIGURE 1 Breastfeeding your baby
The Let-Down Process

As your baby sucks, several different hormones work together to produce milk and release it for feeding.

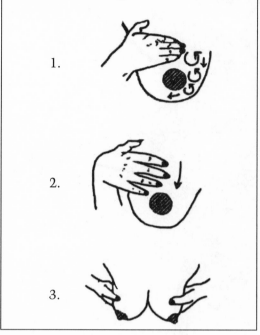

How to assist the Let-Down Process:
1. MASSAGE the milk producing cells and ducts. Start at the top of the breast. Press firmly into the chest wall. Move fingers in a circular motion on one spot on the skin.
2. STROKE the breast area from the top of the breast to the nipple with a light tickle-like stroke.
3. SHAKE the breast while leaning forward so that gravity will help the milk eject.
(Courtesy of the Lactation Institute)

---

tion reflex." In the early stages of lactation, it may take anywhere from several seconds' to several minutes' suckling to produce a let-down reflex. After lactation is established, some mothers find that simply hearing or thinking about the baby will result in a let-down response.

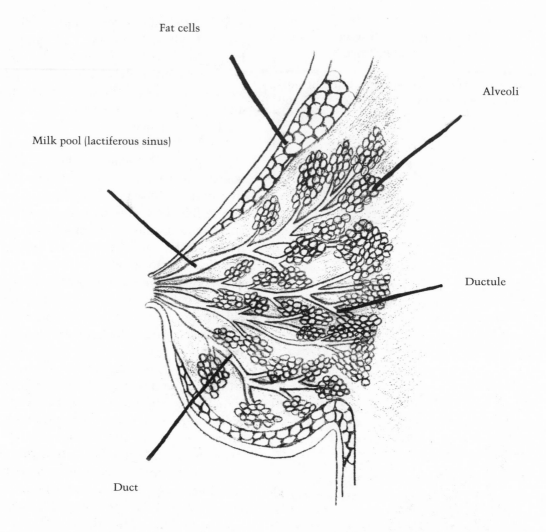

Fat cells

Alveoli

Milk pool (lactiferous sinus)

Ductule

Duct

Cross section of a lactating breast. (Pamela Wing)

The American Academy of Pediatrics recommends that a breastfed baby be fed on demand, each time he/she displays hunger cues such as fussing, crying, putting a fist in his/her mouth, or rooting toward a caregiver's chest. Babies should be expected to nurse often in the begin-ning, perhaps eight to twelve times in a twenty-four hour period. Because breast milk is digested more easily than formula, breastfed babies tend to eat more frequently than formula-fed infants. Breasts do not need to rest for any period of time to build up milk; it is produced constantly. Many new mothers worry that the baby may not be getting enough milk. This is rare. The baby is probably getting enough milk if he/she nurses at least eight times in a twenty-four hour period; can be heard swallowing; produces at least six to eight wet diapers in a twenty-four hour period after the fifth day; and passes seedy, yellow stools. Also, the mother's breasts should appear softened after nursing.

Benefits of Breastfeeding

Breastfeeding benefits baby and mother. First, breast milk is designed to meet the complete nutritional needs of the infant. For the first four to six months, it is the only food a baby needs. Even after other foods are introduced into the baby's diet, breast milk continues to supply essential fatty acids for proper digestion, as well as lactose for the proper growth of brain cells and the correct balance of amino acids (the building blocks of protein). In addition, breast milk has protective factors. Breast milk has high concentrations of white blood cells, which circulate inside the baby's intestines to combat harmful bacteria. Breast milk also contains immunoglobins, which are infection-fighting proteins. Because young infants have weak immune systems, the immunoglobins and antibodies are especially important to the infant's health. Antibodies are passed from mother to baby via breast milk. This defense system is continually updated. As germs in the mother's environment enter the mother's body, she produces antibodies that are, in turn, transmitted to the baby through breast milk.

Breastfeeding also helps prevent allergies by coating the intestinal lining, which prevents the passage of germs and allergens that could potentially cause allergies in the child. Tooth and jaw devel-

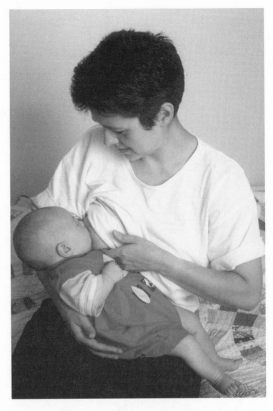

Many mothers prefer to breast feed their babies for many reasons. A mother nurses her hungry baby who is only two months old. (Laura Dwight/Corbis)

opment is also enhanced through breastfeeding. The breastfeeding baby has to use as much as sixty times more energy to get food compared to those drinking from a bottle. As the jaw muscles are exercised in suckling, their constant pulling encourages the growth of well-formed jaws and straight, healthy teeth. Babies can digest human milk more easily, and therefore it is more quickly assimilated into the body. In addition, diarrhea, constipation, and other intestinal upsets are much more infrequent in breastfed babies.

Because breast milk is tailor-made for each baby, it causes no gastrointestinal

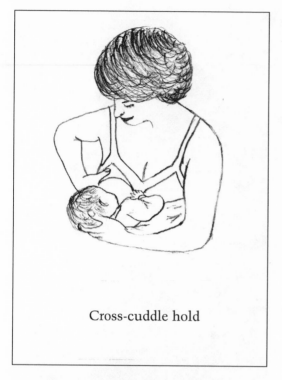

Cross-cuddle hold

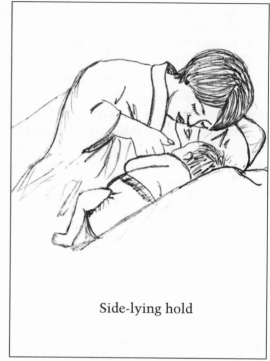

Side-lying hold

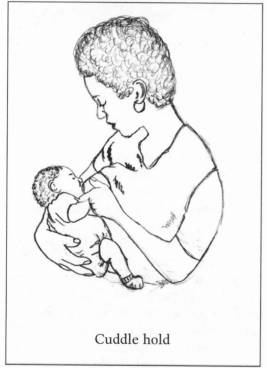

Cuddle hold

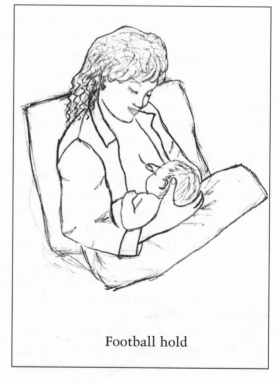

Football hold

Four illustrations of holding positions. (Pamela Wing)

irritation. Some studies suggest that breastfeeding may be protective against sudden infant death syndrome (SIDS). Some studies show lower SIDS deaths among breastfed infants. At this point it isn't clear if the milk itself, or the manner in which an infant breastfeeds, is the reason for this result. Breastfeeding may also aid in brain development. Some studies have shown that infants who are breastfed score significantly higher on IQ tests than formula-fed babies. Other studies have not shown a difference in intelligence scores. Finally, breast milk is a natural calming agent as well as a sleep inducer. The milk contains a sleep-inducing protein and the hormones oxytocin and prolactin, which have a calming effect on both mother and child.

Breast milk may also have positive health benefits later in life. There is evidence that adult conditions such as inflammatory bowel syndrome, juvenile diabetes, breast cancer, and malignant lymphoma occur more frequently among individuals who were formula-fed as infants. Chronic conditions such as asthma, allergies, and middle ear infections are more common in children and adults who were formula-fed. Scientists believe that breastfeeding itself does not prevent all of these problems but that the protective properties of breastmilk make an already susceptible infant less at risk or decrease the severity of the condition.

Breastfeeding benefits the mother in many ways as well. Prepregnancy weight and size are often reattained more quickly for breastfeeding mothers. Oxytocin released when nursing stimulates the contraction of the uterus, which helps it to stop postpartum bleeding and return to prepregnancy size. Breastfeeding also burns 50 to 1,000 extra calories per day. The release of prolactin when nursing acts as a calming agent for the mother. Many mothers report that breastfeeding provides a special time of emotional intimacy with their infants. Breastfeeding can also help space the birth of subsequent children. The mother who is exclusively breastfeeding may find that her menstrual periods are delayed for six months or more after her baby's birth. During this time, a mother will have very little chance of becoming pregnant. Breastfeeding is much cheaper and is more convenient than formula-feeding. Breast milk is free, is always ready and available, is always at the right temperature, and requires no sterilizing of bottles and nipples. Lastly, some studies have shown that mothers who breastfeed for even a few months are less likely to develop breast cancer, ovarian cancer, urinary-tract infections, and osteoporosis.

Feeding Positions
There are a variety of feeding styles or techniques in breastfeeding; mother and child must decide the best method. The first is the *cuddle hold*. In this position, the baby is held cradled in mother's arm, with his/her head lying in the crook of mother's elbow. Baby and mother are touching tummy to tummy, with baby's head facing and aligned with mother's breast. A pillow on mother's lap may help support the smaller newborn. Mother's forearm should support the baby's back while mother's hand holds the bottom or thigh. Next is the *cross-cuddle hold*. Just as in the cuddle hold, baby is positioned tummy to tummy, but baby is held with the opposite arm, so that mother's hand supports the back of his/her head. This allows mother to maneuver baby's head for proper positioning. In the *football hold*, the baby sits up at mother's side at about the level of her waist, so he/she is

facing mother. Mother supports baby's upper back with her arm, her hand holding baby's head at the level of her breast. Again, a pillow at mother's side may help position baby at the right level and offer comfort. The football hold is particularly helpful when mother has had a cesarean birth and needs to avoid placing baby on her abdomen, when mother needs more visibility in getting baby to latch on, if mother's breasts are large, if the baby is small (especially if premature), if baby needs extra guidance at the breast, or if nursing twins. Lastly comes the *side-lying position*. Mother and baby lie on their sides, tummy to tummy, as with the cuddle hold. Baby's head is in line with mother's breast. The side-lying position is helpful if mother has had a cesarean birth, if mother is uncomfortable sitting up, if the baby is sleepy and reluctant to begin nursing or stay awake very long, and if nursing at night.

Breastfeeding Problems
Sometimes mother and baby experience difficulties breastfeeding. First, the nursing pair can experience incorrect latch-on and, the mother sore maternal nipples. If the baby latches on incorrectly, sore, cracked nipples can result, with insufficient milk for the baby. Incorrect latch-on can occur when mother has overly engorged breasts, if she has flat, dimpled, or inverted nipples, or if baby is unable to take in the nipple and most of the areola (the dark circle surrounding the nipple). Often, baby needs some guidance in getting properly latched on, and mothers need extra support from a lactation consultant, nurse, or other experienced woman to learn proper latching. If a baby is properly latched on, then nipple soreness is much less likely to occur. Breastfeeding is a learned skill for many mothers and babies. Breastfeeding can be very difficult to establish in the first days and weeks after birth, and both can become frustrated and give up without support. Ideally, breastfeeding should begin in the first minutes after birth with the support of nurses, doctors, and/or a lactation consultant.

Rarely, a mother doesn't produce enough milk. There are signs of inadequate milk supply, as when baby is nursing six times or fewer in a twenty-four hour period after the third or fourth day after birth; the baby rarely swallows; the breasts do not soften after nursing; the baby is fussy or lethargic most of the time; the baby does not have good suction and has dimples in his/her cheeks or makes clicking noises; the baby is wetting fewer than six diapers in a twenty-four hour period; or the baby is not having bowel movements at least once a day. These are signs that the baby should be weighed and examined. If the baby has lost more that 10 percent of his/her birthweight, then parents and doctor may have to consider some form of supplementation.

Another potential problem is fatigue for the mother. Mothers can get overtired keeping up with frequent feedings, particularly in the beginning when nursing is frequent. The side-lying position can offer some rest while the baby nurses. Occasionally a baby under six months will suddenly refuse to nurse. This is called a "nursing strike" and may last for a few days but rarely means the baby is ready to wean (babies rarely decide to wean suddenly). Babies sometimes wean themselves gradually between eight and twelve months. Lastly, some mothers find it difficult to leave their babies for extended periods of time (often for work) and continue nursing. If away from her baby regularly for hours at a time, the mother must express milk (pumping milk manually or with a breast pump) and make sure the baby has enough milk for her long absences. The mother's commitment to breastfeeding and the supportiveness of her work environment are key factors in the decision to continue or discontinue breastfeeding.

Support Systems for Breastfeeding Mothers

La Leche League International is an organization that was formed to support breastfeeding mothers and their children. Founded in 1956, a time when breastfeeding was at a sharp decline and support was largely unavailable, Le Leche League was intended as a resource for mothers who wanted to breastfeed; it continues this important mission to this day. Monthly meetings occur at members' homes or at convenient public places and cover topics related to breastfeeding techniques and the support of breastfeeding. Mothers are encouraged to bring their nursing infants with them. Most Le Leche League groups have extensive lending libraries available to their members, as well as breastfeeding-aid products.

Weaning

Weaning is the process by which a suckling infant/toddler gives up breastfeeding for other sources of nutrition. Weaning is a personal decision, and when the baby, the mother, or both are ready to wean, then weaning gradually is in order. For example, the mother weaning her infant might begin to offer a cup of milk or juice in place of nursing. Over time, nursing is slowly replaced. A baby is fully weaned when he/she no longer nurses from the breast.

See also Bottle-Feeding; Nutrition

References and further reading
American Academy of Pediatrics. 1998. *The Complete and Authoritative Guide: Caring for Your Baby and Your Child.* New York: Bantam.
Huggins, K. 1990. *The Nursing Mother's Companion.* Boston: Harvard Common Press.
La Leche League International. 1997. *The Womanly Art of Breastfeeding.* New York: Plume, Penguin Books.
Sears, W. and Martha Sears. 1993. *The Baby Book.* Boston: Little, Brown.
Small, M. 1998. *Our Babies, Ourselves: How Biology and Culture Shape the Way We Parent.* New York: Anchor Books.

Breathing
See Apnea

Bruner, Jerome

In 1960, Jerome Bruner conceptualized learning theoretically as becoming more complex. The young child moves from using "enactive" to "iconic" to "symbolic" modes of learning. Thus, at first, infants learn by mouthing and manipulating three-dimensional materials and toys. By one year of age, babies also learn from two-dimensional, pictorial story materials. Toddlers and preschoolers learn from adults who use words as symbols for actions, feelings, items, and events. Bruner identified the important teaching task of adults as "scaffolding"—constantly and gradually increasing complexity while offering supports appropriate for the very young learner.

See also Language

C

Caldwell, Bettye

A leader in the early childhood education movement; with colleagues she developed the Home Observation of Maternal Environment scale, known as the HOME scale, which has been used extensively. HOME studies have included evaluation of the infant/toddler's home environment, as well as specific indicators of parent-child interaction when evaluating early child development.

Canalization

"Canalization" is a term coined by an embryologist to describe the process that keeps developing characteristics of the organism on a particular developmental pathway. As long as maintenance structures support the emergence of a particular outcome (development of an arm, upright locomotion, or self-regulation), then development will proceed along that pathway in a fairly uniform manner, suggesting continuity. Extreme environmental events are necessary to shift the organism from one developmental pathway to another. Such events can be an insult that occurs prenatally (and interferes with the pathway that ordinarily would result in arms), or an insult that occurs during the perinatal period (anoxia), or postnatally such that the organism must shift from one pathway to another as it adapts to

demands of its environment. The concept of canalization is bound to the concept of plasticity.

See also Behavioral Genetics; Plasticity

Capacitation

Although sperm are produced on demand, when they are released into the uterus they are not yet capable of fertilizing the ovum. Thousands of sperm die off before they enter the fallopian tube, yet even those that do enter must go through a process that changes the sperm so that it is capable of entering an ovum if it comes into contact with one. This process is referred to as "capacitation." The sperm is not the only active player in fertilization, of course. The ovum also regulates whether a sperm has the ability to enter it and complete fertilization.

See also Fertilization

Car Seats

Car seats are restraining devices designed for children ages birth to approximately nine years of age to afford protection when riding in automobiles. Car-seat designs vary depending on the age and weight of the child. Car seats are secured in place via the vehicle's seatbelt or are built into some newer vehicles. Freely retractable seat-belts (in which the belt pulls easily through the adjustment clip) can be used with car seats if a device known as a locking clip is used. The locking clip prevents the seatbelt from becoming too lose and compromising the security of the car seat. Most car seats are purchased with locking clips included. There are three major classes of car seats: infant car seats, convertible car seats, and booster seats.

Types of Car Seats
Infant car seats are designed to protect infants weighing approximately 5–20 pounds. Infant car seats are rear-facing, meaning that seated infants face the back of the vehicle. The safest placement is in the middle seat of the automobile's back-seat. The rear-facing position ensures more equal distribution of energy across the infant's body in the event of a head-on collision. Also, in the event of a side-impact collision, the infant seated in the middle of the car will not receive the full impact. Generally, rear-facing car seats should be used for the first year or until the infant is 20–22 pounds in weight and approximately 29–30 inches in length.

Convertible car seats are designed to be used with infants in the rear-facing position until the baby reaches a weight of 20–22 pounds and then in the forward-facing position for toddlers up to approximately 40 pounds. However, many convertible car seats now accommodate infant/toddlers in the rear-facing position up to 30 pounds. Most safety experts agree that adults should place infants and toddlers in the rear-facing position for as long as possible.

Beginning in 1999, all forward-facing car seats featured tether straps. The tether strap offers additional protection in the event of a crash because it allows for the

car seat to be anchored from the top to the automobile seat, in addition to the lapbelt through the underside of the car seat. The risk of injury is reduced because the tether strap reduces the degree to which the car seat will move forward during a car crash. Most automobiles manufactured after 2000 feature built-in anchors for tether straps as standard equipment. Tether anchors can be installed on cars manufactured prior to 2000, and most cars manufactured after 1989 have predrilled holes in which tether anchors can be installed. Most car-seat manufacturers offer tether straps that can be purchased separately.

Booster seats are designed for use with preschoolers and young children weighing 30–80 pounds. Many adults mistakenly assume that only infant/toddlers need to use safety seats. Seatbelts designed to fit adults, however, do not provide adequate protection for young children. Generally, children are eight or nine years old before they are big enough to be adequately secured using typical lap belts and shoulder belts. There are several kinds of booster seats: the high-back booster seat, the belt-positioning booster, and the shield booster. The high-back booster, appropriate for children 35–80 pounds, offers head and neck restraint, useful in automobiles without head restraints in the backseat. Most high-back boosters, which look like a bucket seat, have safety harnesses that, when detached, covert the booster seat into a belt-positioning model. This method uses the automobile's own lap belt and shoulder belt as its harness, which secures the child. Belt-positioning booster seats are appropriate for children weighing 40–80 pounds. When possible, both lap belts and shoulder belts should be used since lap belts alone offer less protection in the event of a car crash. The shield booster seat, appropriate for use with children weighing no more than approximately 40 pounds, does not offer head and neck support. Rather, the child sits in a low seat, and a padded shield is attached to the front of the booster seat with the shield resting against the child's chest. This type of booster seat can be used as a belt-positioning booster seat when the shield is not in use. The booster seat without the shield is appropriate for children weighing 40–80 pounds.

There are several types of safety harnesses available for infant seats, convertible seats, and booster seats, including the three-point harness, the five-point harness, the bar-shield, T-shield, or other shield. The three- and five-point harnesses each refer to the number of attachment points on the safety harness that secure the child. A three-point harness typically features clips, buckles, or other attachment devices at the child's chest and between the legs. A five-point harness features attachment points at the child's chest, with straps over each leg, which fasten into a clip anchored to a buckle between the legs. Most infant seats feature a three-point or a five-point harness. For infant seats, both the three- and five-point harnesses rate well in crash tests. Convertible seats use a five-point harness, bar-shield, or T-shield harness. A bar shield, usually padded and covered with fabric, lowers over the head and is snapped into a buckle and rests at chest level. A T-shield is a plastic shield that snaps to a buckle between the legs. In crash tests of convertible-seat models, the five-point harnesses offer the most protection. Most booster seats offer a five-point harness or shield of some sort.

Choosing Car Seats

In addition to choosing car seats based on age and weight of children, adults should purchase car seats that conform to all applicable U.S. Federal Motor Vehicle Safety Standards. Other important information includes crash-test performance ratings of car seats. Organizations such as Consumer Reports test dozens of car-seat models, rating each on crash-test protection. Similarly, the National Highway Traffic and Safety Administration offers free information on car-seat safety, including recalls. Consumers should be mindful of recalls and always register newly purchased car seats. If the car seat is registered with the manufacturer, the consumer will be alerted immediately in the event of a recall. Used car seats should never be used or purchased if the buyer does not know the history of the car seat. If the car seat has been involved in a crash, it may be damaged and unsafe to use.

Installing and Using Car Seats

Surveys of car-seat usage indicate that as many as 80 percent of car seats are not installed or used properly. Mistakes are sometimes made in positioning and securing the car seat and using the safety harness. Car seats always should be placed in the center of the backseat. Car seats placed in the front seat can be deadly, and car seats are not designed for use with front passenger air bags.

Second, the car seat should be tightly secured to the backseat using the seatbelts. Car seats should not move more than one inch in any direction once secured. When installing a car seat, the adult should maneuver the seatbelts through the appropriate slots and buckle the car seat into place. When tightening the seatbelt, the adult should press down on the car seat. A locking clip can be used to prevent seatbelts from loosening.

Infants, toddlers, and young children should be fitted snugly in the car seat.

Straps should not be tangled or knotted. When using three- and five-point harnesses, the chest clip should be maintained at armpit level. Generally, there should not be more than one finger's width between the child and the car-seat strap. Be sure to test buckles to ensure all straps are securely fastened.

See also Health and Safety

References and further reading
American Academy of Pediatrics (website 2001). http://www.aap.org.
National Highway Traffic and Safety Administration (website 2001). http://www.nhtsa.dot.gov.
National Kids Safety Campaign (website 2001). http://www.safekids.org.

Caregivers, Training of

Quality child care implies that caregivers and providers receive training specific to

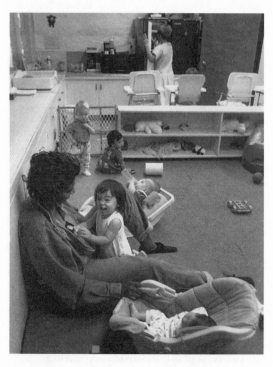

Caregiver and children at infant day care. (Elizabeth Crews)

the growth, development, and care of young children. The specific training required is dependent on the state's regulations and licensing requirements. Four well-established training programs are: Child Development Associate training, WestEd (Program for Infant Toddler Caregivers Training), Magda Gerber Educare Training, and Bank Street Training.

See also Caregiving; Child Care

Caregiving

Caregiving for infants and toddlers means care, supervision, and guidance from birth to age three. More specifically, it is defined as child care or childrearing. *Child care* is the care and attention given specifically to young children while their parents are employed. Child care raises several issues and concerns regarding quality, availability, accessibility, developmental appropriateness, cultural sensitivity, and readiness to learn. *Childrearing* means the cultural beliefs, rules, and practices that guide parents and society in caregiving.

Traditionally, parents are the biological or adopted mother and father of the child. In most cultures, parents are considered to be the child's primary caregivers and therefore are held responsible for providing the care, shelter, nourishment, and safety needed from birth to adulthood. Parents are also charged with the task of raising their children to be responsible, caring, and sociable human beings. In some cultures, others may be designated as the primary caregivers, responsible for the rearing and care of children. In the traditional Israeli communal society, known as the kibbutz, six-week-old infants are assigned to a bed in the infant house and to the care of a primary caregiver. The *metapelet,* or primary caregiver, is responsible for a group of three to four infants for twenty-one hours each day, from age six weeks until the children enter preschool. Parents visit daily with their children for about three hours in their own homes, after the workday. At about 7 P.M. the children are returned to their *metapelet* and assigned a bed in the infant house. In this communal society, each adult has an assigned role and job believed to be integral to the successful operation of the society. *Metapelet* are regarded as communal parents rather than traditional caregivers. As substitute parents, their assigned role is to provide care to and nurture young children, as well as to teach socialization skills, manners, play behavior, beliefs, and knowledge of the environment.

Traditional caregiving (provided by nonparents during the parents' workday) is more commonly referred to as "child care" or "day care." Nonparental caregivers are known as child caregivers, child-care providers or workers, domestic caregivers, educarers (providing both education and care), or teachers. Although some may also be known as day care workers, the term "day care" is used less often as more parents work nontraditional hours, thus requiring child-care services during evenings, overnight, and on weekends. This shift in employment trends has resulted in an increased need for odd-hour or round-the-clock child care. The shift has also resulted in the term "child care" being used as the more appropriate catch-all for all caregiving services provided to infant/toddlers in the absence of parents.

Child care is seen by some as a private concern involving the child, the parents, and the provider. Others see the influence of child care as impacting the current workforce and shaping generations of citi-

zens, making child care a public and national concern. According to the Children's Defense Fund *2000 Yearbook*, approximately 76 percent of children age birth to five years are placed in child care. Sixty percent are infants. Quality child care is thus a private and public issue, for it enables parents to work, secure in the knowledge that the care and well-being of their children are being provided for by capable and knowledgeable caregivers in safe and healthy environments. Each year, national child development organizations and parenting magazines release national and state-specific findings regarding child-care quality and use. Based on the assessments, quality child care consists of health and safety regulations; type and developmental appropriateness of provided care; availability of child care based on need; staff-to-child ratios; provider-parent relationships; teacher/provider training; and state policies that support the improvement and expansion of child care.

States with higher grades of child-care quality are most likely to report higher economies, safer neighborhoods, and better schools. Quality child care ensures that children are ready to learn and promotes neighborhood support of healthy and safe environments for children. Poor-quality child care jeopardizes the health, well-being, and development of children. Parents who have quality care are less likely to be distracted at work or to be absent from work. It is therefore important for parents to choose caregiving services that are affordable, accessible, appropriate to the needs of the child, supportive of the family's culture, and provided within a safe and healthy environment.

There are several caregiving options available to parents based on the caregiving setting, philosophy of care, and the parents' socioeconomic status. Parents

A working mother delivering her one-year-old son to a caregiver at a child-care center. (Elizabeth Crews)

can access child-care information for their community by calling the local 4C (Child Care Coordinating Council), resource and referral agency, or child-care network. They can provide a list of registered or licensed child-care providers in the area, as well as information on choosing the best child care for each child.

Types of Child care

Child-care settings include the child's home, the provider's home, and a child-care center. *In-home child care,* provided by nannies or au pairs, offers the most convenience for families; however, this option is also the most expensive. *Relative* (or *kin*) *caregiving* (i.e., by persons related to the child, such as grandparents,

older siblings, or others), can also provide care in the child's home while the parents work. *Family child care* is provided in the home of the caregiver. Family day care provides a home setting, individualized care in small groups, and flexible hours. The cost for families varies depending on the number of children in care and the ages of the children. *Center-based care* can be provided in a school, business, church, or hospital. The center setting is ideally designed to be developmentally appropriate to the ages and corresponding developmental stages of children. Child-care centers are licensed to care for more than twelve children. The actual number of children served is based on the ages of the children to be cared for, the adult-to-child ratios for the state of residence, the appropriate number of child-care staff, and the amount of space (including separate facilities). Child-care centers are open during predictable hours, and the program of care is typically more structured than in-home, relative, or family child care.

There are also child-care programs that are specific to developmental goals, such as child-development labs, as well as to special needs. *Respite care* is available and used mostly by parents of special-needs children. These programs are set up to provide short-term care for children, freeing parents for brief periods to run errands, go to the store or doctor, or simply take a break. Some programs set up to prevent parental child abuse have also been implemented as respite programs to aid parents when they are overstressed and therefore more likely to harm their children. There are also care programs that meet the specific needs of children with disabilities. Other programs include *before-school* and *after-school programs*, which provide care for children during the time when parents may need to travel to and from work. Parents typically choose child care based on their time needs, location of the caregiving setting, and financial capabilities.

Choosing Child Care
The Child Care Aware Action Campaign suggests that parents follow five steps when choosing quality child care: look, listen, count, ask, and be informed.

Look: Parents should visit several child-care homes or centers and make observations. Pay attention to first impressions. Notice if the setting appears safe. For example, if there are stairs, there should also be a gate across the stairwell to keep toddlers from falling or climbing up unaided. Also notice how the caregivers relate to the children, and how the children interact with each other. Pay attention to how toys, books, pictures, and furniture are arranged. Do children have ready access to toys and books, or must they wait for the caregiver to pass them out? Parents should pay attention to the lighting and colors. Is the setting bright and happy or dark and gloomy? Optimally, common play areas should be bright and happy, and nap areas should have calmer lighting and colors.

Listen: Child-care settings that are too quiet, except for during naptime, may indicate that there is not enough activity occurring to enrich the child's development. Places that are too noisy may indicate a lack of control. Notice if the children sound happy and involved. Pay attention to the caregiver's voice when she is talking with a child. Does she sound patient and cheerful? Also pay attention to background noises, like music, and the volume.

Count: Count the number of children and caregivers. The fewer children cared for by one primary caregiver, the more attention your child will receive. The recommended infant-to-caregiver ratio is 3:1–4:1. As children get older and more self-sufficient, the ratio increases. Parents may also request information from their state regarding the recommended ratios for the number of children and adults allowed in the caregiving space. Lack of space limits mobility and may increase tension among the infants and caregivers.

Ask: Don't hesitate to ask questions about caregivers' experience, training, and caregiving philosophy. Visiting different child-care facilities will usually prompt questions, from the mundane to the important, that involved parents should pose to caregivers and administrators.

Seek information: Conduct research into licensing, accreditation, and certification. Inquire about the other adults that may have contact with your child. Ask about emergency plans, substitute care, and sick-care policies. Ask about health policies and practices regarding handwashing, health screenings, and immunizations. Ask if there are restrictions placed on parental visits or calls.

Parents should be informed about efforts in their community and state to improve the quality of child care. Parents should also be aware of programs and activities available through local child-care agencies: 4C, resource and referral agencies, family resource centers, and child-care networks. Parents should also make an effort to stay informed on federal policies that impact child care, such as tax cuts, child health care, child-care subsidies, and the Family and Medical Leave Act.

When choosing child care, parents should plan to visit the selected settings two or three times before making a final choice. If possible, visit at least twice and at different times of the day, in order to get a better overview of the daily routines and activities. On the last visit, parents should bring their child along to see if the caregiver and setting would be a good match for the child's temperament.

Although it is not required in all states, many caregivers have specialized training in early childhood and licensing or registration as a child-care provider. Thus, they are much more than baby-sitters. Regardless of titles, however, child-care providers must show that they have the knowledge, ability, and resources to provide quality care to children placed in their care. Their philosophy of care supports the physical, emotional, mental, and social growth of the child, based on the child's age and stage of development. Developmentally appropriate programs promote responsive care, individual growth and development, self-identity, and self-confidence. Competent providers also support family involvement and have a relationship with parents and knowledge of parents' caregiving practices. As appropriate, efforts are made to integrate the parents' practices into the care of the child, providing consistency of care.

A primary concern is cost. Based on the Children's Defense Fund *2000 Yearbook*, full-time child-care costs can range from $4,000 to $10,000 per year per child. For some families, approximately one-fourth of income goes toward child care, and one out of three families with young children earns less than $25,000 per year. Still, wages paid to child-care workers are often surprisingly low. The average annual salary of a child-care worker is less than $15,000 per year. There are limited federal subsidies available to assist parents with the costs of licensed family day care or relative care, but only one in ten eligible children receives the financial support needed. The availability of quality child care is limited by lack of funding subsidies for child-care workers and working parents. Making less than a livable wage greatly reduces the number of trained child-care workers, the number of available child-care slots, and the ability for parents to work.

The need for quality caregiving continues to be great. Quality child care makes it possible for parents to work and contribute to society. Quality child care provides the early learning opportunities needed to help children become ready for school and sets the foundation for future life success. Quality child-care benefits parents, children, and society.

See also Caregivers, Training of; Child Care

References and further reading
Child Development Institute (website 2001). http://childdevelopmentinfo.com/development/.
Consumer Products Safety Commission (website 2001). http://www.cpsc.gov.
Early Head Start National Resource Center (website 2001). http://www.ehsnrc.org.
National Association for the Education of Young Children (website 2001). http://www.naeyc.org.
National Association for Family Child Care (for parents looking for an accredited home or providers seeking training) (website 2001). http://www.nafcc.org.
National Association of Child Care Resource and Referral Agencies (website 2001). http://www.naccrra.net.
National Child Care Information Center (website 2001). http://www.nccic.org.
National Head Start Association (website 2001). http://www.nhsa.org.
National Resource Center for Health and Safety in Child Care (website 2001). http://nrc.uchsc.edu.

Caregiving Competence

Child-care providers must be able to show that they have the knowledge, ability, and resources to provide quality care to children placed in their care. This is referred to as "caregiving competency," and the standards for competency are set by each state. The caregiver and caregiving setting must be able to provide at least a minimum quality of care for children. Credentials related to caregiving can emphasize specialized training in early childhood and care. However, in most states, specialized training is not a state requirement for most providers.

Competent caregivers have knowledge and understanding of the development of infants, toddlers, and young children. They understand and can relate to early childhood issues of security, exploration, and identity. This knowledge informs the design of the environment and activities that are developmentally appropriate to the ages and stages of infants and toddlers. Competent caregivers see themselves as facilitating learning for infant/toddlers through responsive care. Caregivers understand the importance of health and safety in the child-care setting and employ procedures to promote health and safety in all areas. Competent caregivers can relate to infant/toddlers in small groups and as unique individuals. Keeping groups small provides the opportunity for each child to receive more individualized attention; seven to eight infants or toddlers per every two adults is a good ratio. Small groups and consistency of caregiving help to promote feelings of security and trustworthy relationship-building.

Competent caregivers provide environments that ensure safety, promote health, provide comfort, maximize flexibility, encourage movement, and allow for choice. Routines regularly promote standard health and safety practices, such as handwashing and diaper-changing. Quality environments are also convenient for children and caregivers, providing appropriate spaces for movement, comfort, exploration, and storage. For example, books and toys for babies are placed at low levels, allowing toddlers to access them easily. Storage bins for adult use only are kept high and out of reach of toddlers.

Competent care also includes family involvement in the caregiving of the infant/toddler. Providers have a relationship with parents and knowledge of parents' caregiving practices. When possible and appropriate, efforts are made to integrate the parents' practices into the care

An elderly volunteer at a child-care center. (Elizabeth Crews)

of the child, providing a consistency of care between the home and caregiving setting.

> *See also* Caregivers, Training of; Caregiving; Child Care

Case Worker

A case worker is a person who usually works for a public social-service agency and oversees the care of individual clients. Many have studied social work, psychology, family relations, or related fields and tackle a variety of duties, including coordinating the type, timing, and duration of services that clients

receive. Case workers often determine eligibility for income-based services such as Aid to Families with Dependent Children, Medicaid, and Women Infants and Children. Having knowledge of available resources is another possible responsibility of a case worker. Clients are assigned a case worker when they apply for government services or are referred to child-protection agencies or the courts.

> *See also* Early Intervention

References and further reading
Woodside, Marianne, and Tricia McClam. 1998. *An Introduction to Human Services.* 3rd ed. Pacific Grove, CA: Brooks/Cole.

Catch-Up Growth Phenomenon

Height and body size are polygenetic characteristics, the expression of which is closely linked to environmental factors such as the quality and quantity of available food. However, the uterine environment also plays a role in body size. When a fetus develops in a small uterus, it will be smaller than it perhaps will be once it is free to express its genotypic potential. Similarly, a fetus in a large uterus will perhaps be a large baby—but eventually a small child. If a small baby has the potential to be a large person, postnatal growth may be faster than usual as the baby catches up. The large infant who is destined to be a smaller adult will "catch down" with a reduced growth rate. This catch-up growth phenomenon typically balances out by twelve to eighteen months of age.

See also Theories of Development

Categorical Perception

See Speech Perception

Cattell Intelligence Test

The Psyche Cattell Infant Intelligence Test is a psychometric test with items than can be used with infants from two to forty months. The standard deviation of this test was constructed to be identical to that of the Stanford-Binet (SB) Intelligence Scale, so that the Cattell could be used as a downward extension of the SB scale. At each monthly age, five items are provided for assessment. In addition, two extra items are provided, in case an infant rejects trying an item. This scale clearly defines what items belong to which month of age (or two-month age span for toddlers), so that the person testing the infant can hand a blank Cattell scale to parents who can follow along as items are administered. The procedure is to find a basal age at which all items are passed and a ceiling age at which the infant fails all items for that age category. Items passed are weighted so that the number of points achieved by an infant can be divided by the infant's age in months, and an IQ score can be computed, with a mean at 100 and a standard deviation of 15 points.

Items in the Cattell kit are made of wood, which may be easier for handling by infants who have cerebral palsy or other conditions that make plastic testing items, such as a pegboard, small cubes, or puzzle pieces, more difficult and slippery to hold.

Causality

Causality is an underlying concept in Jean Piaget's theory of cognitive development. Simply stated, it is the relationship between cause and effect—or action and consequence. In learning what consequences their actions have on the environment, babies come to understand their role in the world, the relationships between objects, and how things work.

Causality Toys

According to Jean Piaget's theory of cognitive development, children learn about the world by experimenting with objects and the environment and by observing cause-effect relationships. One way to encourage this kind of active learning is through the use of causality toys, which demonstrate that actions have consequences. For example, by kicking a mobile hanging over the crib (cause), infants can learn how to make the toy move in an entertaining way (effect) and realize that it is a product of their own doing.

Central Nervous System
The central nervous system is that part of the nervous system contained within the cranium and vertebrae and consists of the brain and spinal cord.

See also Neurobiology

Centration
Centration is the act of focusing on one aspect of a stimulus or problem and failing to incorporate other aspects. In one sense, it means focusing on one part while failing to see the whole, expressed in the common adage "failing to see the forest for the trees," which is characteristic of infants' early visual perceptual processing.

Cephalo-Caudal Direction of Development
One of the principles of organization that describes development that proceeds from top (cephalo) to bottom (caudal).

See also Motor Development

Cerebral Cortex
See Brain Development

Cerebral Palsy
A nonprogressive motor disorder caused by brain injury that begins in early infancy, involving at least one limb and resulting in uncoordinated motor movements. There are many forms of cerebral palsy, all of which involve motor dysfunction and most of which are evident by two years of age. Because of the complexity of etiologic factors, there currently is no accepted classification system for cerebral palsy. Although the incidence of mental retardation accompanying cerebral palsy is high, a full range of intellectual functioning is possible, including giftedness.

See also Neurobiology

Cervix
The opening part of the uterus, the cervix is capable of expanding during childbirth from its normal resting diameter of about 1 centimeter to about 10 centimeters during the final stage of delivery. Occasionally an embryo implants in the area of the cervix, causing a cervical pregnancy. Cervical pregnancies typically result in a spontaneous abortion of the embryo.

See also Birth; Fertilization

Cesarean Section
The surgical removal of the fetus from the mother by incising the abdominal and uterine walls. In the United States, 20–25 percent of all births are by cesarean section.

See also Birth

Child Abuse and Neglect
The term "child abuse" (or "child maltreatment") refers to the nonaccidental infliction of harm on a child. Child abuse can be committed by anyone who is responsible for the child's health or welfare, including parents, guardians, teachers, and others. There are four main types of maltreatment: physical abuse, sexual abuse, emotional abuse, and neglect. Although any of the forms of child mal-

Homeless newsboys sleep huddled in a corner outside the Mulberry Street Church in New York City, c. 1890. Photo by Jacob Riis. (Bettmann/Corbis)

treatment can be found separately, they often occur in combination.

Child abuse and neglect are defined in both federal and state legislation. Federal legislation provides the basic definitions by identifying a minimum set of acts or behaviors that characterize maltreatment. Each state then expands upon these federal guidelines. Because each state has slightly different definitions, it can be difficult to compare rates of child abuse across states. In addition, having different state laws means that what is legally punishable in one state might not be punishable in another.

The following definitions are summarized in the National Center on Child Abuse and Neglect (NCCAN) Clearing-house *1997 Factsheet.* The Child Abuse Prevention and Treatment Act (CAPTA), as amended and reauthorized in October 1996 (P.L. 104–235, sec. 111), provides the following definitions: A child is a person who has not attained the lesser of the age of eighteen, or except in cases of sexual abuse, the age specified by the child protection law of the State in which the child resides. Child abuse and neglect is, at a minimum any recent act or failure to act on the part of a parent/caregiver that results in death, serious physical or emotional harm, sexual abuse or exploitation, or an act or failure to act that presents an imminent risk of serious harm.

Child abuse and neglect, like most social problems, are complicated to explain, and many people disagree about why they occur. Most people agree, however, that child maltreatment is a symptom of difficulty coping with stress; and that risk factors are present at a variety of levels in the family, including the child, the parent, and the social and cultural systems that affect families.

Risk Factors for Child Abuse and Neglect

Many factors have been identified as clear risk markers for child abuse and neglect. Often a family will experience many risk factors at the same time, which increases the likelihood that maltreatment will occur.

Physical Abuse

Physical abuse is characterized by the infliction of physical injury as a result of punching, beating, kicking, biting, shaking, or otherwise harming a child. The parent/caregiver may not have intended to hurt the child: the injury may have resulted from overdiscipline or physical punishment. Although any of these injuries can occur accidentally when a child is at play, physical abuse should be suspected if the explanations do not fit the injury or if a pattern of frequency is apparent. If there are many injuries in various stages of healing, one should suspect that they did not all occur as a result of one accident.

Although it may be difficult to imagine that any person would intentionally inflict harm on a child, physical abuse is at times a result of inappropriate or excessive physical discipline. An angry caregiver or parent can be unaware of the magnitude of force with which he/she strikes the child. Below are listed several suggestions when you feel you may be losing control in a stressful caregiving

situation. After you make sure the child is in a safe place, try to calm down with the following tactics: Take time out; count to ten; take deep breaths; phone a friend; ask a neighbor to relieve you for a few minutes; look through a magazine or newspaper; listen to music; exercise; take a walk (after first making sure that children are not left without proper supervision); take a bath; write a letter; sit down and relax; lie down.

Physical abuse is the leading cause of serious head injury in infants. Shaken baby syndrome (SBS; also known as whiplash-shaken infant, shaken brain trauma, and pediatric traumatic brain injury), is a serious form of child abuse caused by vigorous shaking of an infant or young child by the arms, legs, chest, or shoulders. This is a severe form of head injury caused by the rebound of the baby's brain in its skull when shaken. A baby's head is large and heavy in proportion to its body. In addition, there is space between the brain and skull to allow for growth and development. Violent shaking is especially dangerous to infants and young children due to their undeveloped neck muscles and fragile brain and blood vessels. These delicate tissues are easily damaged by shaking, jerking, and jolting. The victims of SBS range in age from a few days to five years, with an average age of six to eight months.

Often there are no obvious outward signs of injury to a baby or young child's body, but there is injury inside, particularly in the head or behind the eyes. These injuries can include brain swelling and damage; subdural hemorrhage; mental retardation; developmental delays; blindness; hearing loss; paralysis; seizures; speech and learning difficulties; and death.

SBS is almost always caused by nonaccidental trauma (child abuse). The number-one reason a baby is shaken is because of inconsolable and incessant crying. Another common reason is toileting problems. Usually a caregiver is angry and shakes the baby to punish or quiet the child. In very rare instances this injury can be caused accidentally by actions such as tossing the baby in the air, playing too roughly, or jogging with a small baby in a backpack, when a caregiver does not realize how seriously this behavior can harm a child.

Although SBS is not limited to any special group of people, males tend to predominate as perpetrators, involved in 65–90 percent of shaken-baby cases. In the United States, adult males in their early twenties who are the baby's father or mother's boyfriend are typically the shaker. Females who injure babies by shaking them are more likely to be babysitters or child-care providers.

Immediate medical attention can help reduce the impact of shaking, but many children are still left with permanent damage. Although we don't know for sure, it is estimated that fewer than 10–15 percent of shaken babies recover completely. If the child survives, medical bills can be enormous, as the victim can require lifelong medical care for brain injuries such as mental retardation or cerebral palsy. The child might even require institutionalization or other long-term care.

Parent/caregivers can take several steps to comfort a crying baby. Anyone who takes care of a baby or small child should be reminded to never shake them, as there are nonviolent ways to stop baby from crying. Monotonous sounds such as running water or the sound of a vacuum cleaner can be comforting. Other strategies include: giving the baby a pacifier after checking to make sure he/she is not hungry or wet, swaddling the baby, and simply hugging and cuddling the infant gently. Very young infants can be carried around in a soft frontal carrier that holds the infant close to the caregiver's body.

Emotional Abuse
Also known as psychological abuse, emotional neglect, verbal abuse, and mental injury, emotional abuse includes acts or omissions by parents or caregivers that have caused, or could cause, serious behavioral, cognitive, emotional, or mental disorders. Patterns of this behavior include constant rejection of the child; terrorizing; refusal to provide basic nurturance; refusal to get help for a child's psychological problems; failure to provide the physical or mental stimulation that a child needs to grow; and exposing a child to corruption, including drug abuse and criminal behavior. Some parents/caregivers use extreme or bizarre forms of punishment, such as confining a child in a dark closet. Emotional abuse also includes less severe acts, such as habitual scapegoating, belittling, or rejecting treatment. Emotional abuse is almost always present when a child suffers from another form of abuse.

Emotional neglect includes such actions as marked inattention to the child's needs for affection, refusal of or failure to provide needed psychological care, spouse abuse in the child's presence, and permission of drug or alcohol use by the child. Parents who emotionally neglect their children can provide adequate physical care but do not provide adequate nurturing. In these families, the parents are detached and uninvolved with their children. Babies and toddlers might be left in their cribs for long periods of time, seldom talked to, cuddled, or hugged. The lack of love associated

A Kansas Highway Patrol trooper walks through the cutouts of children resting on the steps of the Kansas Statehouse Wednesday, April 7, 1999, in Topeka, Kansas, during a program to recognize April as Child Abuse Prevention Month. The steps were covered with cutouts of children for each of the 105 counties in the state and on the cutouts were the child abuse statistics for each county. (AP Photo/Topeka Capital-Journal, Chris Ochsner)

with emotional neglect can result in severe developmental problems.

An infant who is being severely deprived of basic emotional nurturance, even though physically well cared for, can fail to thrive and can eventually die. Less severe forms of early emotional deprivation can produce babies who grow into anxious and insecure children who are slow to develop or have low self-esteem.

Although the visible signs of emotional abuse can be difficult to detect, it leaves hidden scars that manifest in numerous behavioral ways. Although all parents can occasionally lose control and say hurtful things to their children, ignore them when attention needs were critical, or unintentionally scare them,

what is truly harmful is a chronic pattern of behavior.

What can you do when you feel that your behavior toward your child may be bordering on emotional abuse? The following suggestions are provided by the American Humane Association:

1. Never be afraid to apologize to your child. If you lose your temper and say something in anger that wasn't meant to be said, then apologize. Children need to know that adults can admit when they are wrong.
2. Don't call your child names or attach labeling behavior to the child. Do not use names ("stupid," "lazy") or disparaging phrases ("good for nothing," "you'll never

amount to anything," "if you could only be more like your brother," "you can never do anything right"); these tear down a child's self-esteem.

3. Address the behaviors that need correcting and use a time-out when the child misbehaves. Be sure to discuss the behavior that you are trying to change as the reason for the time-out and discuss your reasons with the child immediately after each time-out. Time-outs should be time-limited and never more than a few minutes.

4. Compliment your child when you see good behavior.

5. Learn to walk away from a situation when you feel that you are losing control. You can isolate yourself in another room for a few minutes (after first making sure that the child is safe), count to ten before you say anything, ask for help from another adult, or take a few deep breaths.

Sexual Abuse
Sexual abuse is the employment, use, persuasion, inducement, enticement, or coercion of any child to engage in, or assist any other person to engage in, any sexually explicit conduct or simulation of such conduct for the purposes of producing a visual depiction of such conduct. It includes all forms of rape, molestation, prostitution, or other form of sexual exploitation, including incest. In addition, sexual abuse includes fondling a child's genitals, intercourse, sodomy, exhibitionism, and commercial exploitation through the production of pornographic materials. Many experts believe that sexual abuse is the most underreported form of child maltreatment because of the

secrecy or conspiracy of silence that so often characterizes these cases.

Child Neglect
Child neglect is the most common form of child maltreatment in the United States. "Neglect" is defined as the failure of the child's parent/caregiver to provide the child with the basic necessities of life, when financially able to do so or when offered reasonable means to do so. The basic necessities include minimally adequate care in the areas of shelter, nutrition, health, supervision, education, affection, and protection. Neglect also includes failure to eliminate risk when a person is able to do so and has or should have knowledge of the risk. Child neglect occurs along a continuum from mild to severe, depending on the frequency, duration, and type of neglect, age of the child, potential consequences to the child's development, and the degree of danger to the child. Most children who suffer from neglect experience multiple types of neglect.

Physical neglect includes refusal of or delay in seeking health care, as well as abandonment, expulsion from the home, or refusal to allow a runaway to return home, and inadequate supervision. Severe physical neglect is generally associated with families who function poorly. Children in these severely neglecting families may not receive most of the basic necessities of life. Substandard housing is common; living areas can be littered with rotting food, garbage, and animal feces, with environmental hazards present and accessible. Classmates or teachers often complain of foul smells related to their lack of routine hygiene. Generally, these families have many children, not because the parents want children but because they fail to plan. These families are often headed by a single mother; however, when the parents do live together their behavior tends to be similar, and they often exacerbate one another's problems.

Families in which moderate physical neglect takes place are generally better off than the severe-neglect families. Although the children in moderately neglectful families can suffer from poor nutrition, often this is related to poverty and ignorance, not lack of caring. The family can be chaotic and disordered, but there is usually evidence that the caregiver is making an effort at parenting. Nutritional neglect is the failure to provide a diet of quality and nutritional balance that is developmentally appropriate. Sometimes babies are fed formula that is too watered down; children can be fed junk food without nutritional value or have to fend for themselves for food. The first effect of malnutrition will show in the child's being underweight. As malnutrition gets more serious, it also affects physical growth and, eventually, brain growth and development.

Health care or medical neglect is difficult to describe because of different opinions related to cultural background. Generally, a single omission in health care is unlikely to result in harm to the average child. However, specific patterns of health care omission, such as failure to immunize, could have harmful effects. In addition, there are times when failing to seek or comply with care for a single incidence can have a devastating effect, such as failure to professionally evaluate a severe head injury.

Parents characterized by severe health care neglect of their children are typically unable, unwilling, or inconsistent in assessing the severity of an illness or accident and thus sometimes seek emergency care only after the child's problem has advanced to the critical stage. They are often unable or unwilling to meet the needs of a child with a chronic condition. In contrast, in situations of moderate neglect, children will be taken to an emergency room for acute injuries or illnesses, but the parents will ignore chronic colds, defective vision, or dental needs. Parents considered moderately neglectful often demonstrate inconsistent and inadequate attempts to care for a child with a chronic condition.

Withholding of medically indicated treatment involves a failure to respond to the infant's life-threatening conditions by providing treatment, including appropriate nutrition, hydration, and medication, that in a physician's reasonable medical judgment will most likely ameliorate or correct such conditions. However, this does not include the failure to provide treatment to an infant when, in the physician's reasonable medical judgment, the infant is chronically and irreversibly comatose; the provision of such treatment would merely prolong dying; treatment would not be effective in ameliorating or correcting all of the infant's life-threatening conditions or otherwise would be futile in terms of survival of the infant; treatment would be virtually futile in terms of the survival of the infant; or the treatment itself under such circumstances would be inhumane.

Not all instances of health care noncompliance should be considered neglect. Well-intentioned parents may at times fail to comply with health care recommendations as a result of practical problems such as poor communication, a child's refusal to take a prescribed medication, transportation problems, and inability to pay for medication and appointments. There are also times when delay in seeking health care is simply an error in judgment. It is also important to acknowledge that parents can reasonably disagree with the recommendations of health care providers and seek additional professional opinions on treatment options.

One such situation involves the parents' decision to treat illnesses by spiritual means. Parents of some religious backgrounds feel that they are exerting constitutionally protected religious freedom when choosing spiritual treatment. The majority of states agree and have provided exemptions in their child abuse and neglect statutes for spiritual treatment. Courts, however, have not recognized spiritual treatment when a child's life is in danger or the child has died.

Abandonment and supervision neglect represent the two extremes of failure to supervise a child. Abandonment occurs when parents leave their child without arranging for appropriate supervision. Some infants, particularly those of drug-addicted mothers, can be abandoned immediately following birth. These infants become wards of the state and are placed in foster care, awaiting termination of parental rights so that they can be adopted. In supervision neglect, children are left for hours or days at a time. Supervision is often inadequate even when the parents are present, due to substance abuse, physical or mental illness, low intelligence, or immaturity. A child might also be left with an inadequate caregiver, such as a slightly older child or a person who is impaired, immature, or abusive. Supervision neglect depends on the child's age, developmental level, and length of time the child is left alone.

Educational neglect can include failure to comply with state requirements for school attendance or failure to provide an approved home-based school curriculum. This form of neglect also includes consistently allowing the child to avoid school without legitimate reasons, such as to care for siblings or to work. Educational neglect can also involve inattention to a child's special educational needs, such as failure to follow through with special interventions or programs recommended by the school.

Referrals and Reports
Instances of possible child maltreatment are referred to local child protective services (CPS) agencies, which are public-service organizations that receive and respond to reports of alleged maltreatment. CPS agencies decide whether to take further actions to protect a child.

In 1998, of the estimated 2.8 million referrals received, 34 percent were screened out and 66 percent were transferred for investigation or assessment. In 1997, more than half of all reports alleging maltreatment and referred for investigation came from professionals, including educators, law-enforcement and justice officials, social-service workers, and medical and mental health personnel. About 18 percent of reports were received from parents, other relatives of the child, or the victims themselves; 8.5 percent came from friends and neighbors, 12 percent from anonymous sources, and 8 percent from other sources. An estimated two-thirds of substantiated or indicated reports were from professional sources. The average annual workload of CPS investigation and assessment workers was 94 investigations. Slightly less than one-third of investigations (29.2 percent) resulted in a disposition of either substantiated or indicated child maltreatment. More than half (57.2 percent) resulted in a finding that child maltreatment was not substantiated. More than a tenth (13.6 percent) received another disposition.

"Prevalence" is defined as the number of people who have experienced at least one act of child abuse/neglect in their lifetime. "Incidence" refers to the number of child maltreatment cases that come to the attention of CPS agencies each year. Incidence, therefore, captures only reported cases of maltreatment. There are multiple sources of data that can be considered in estimating maltreatment incidence. These include self-report surveys, national incidence studies, and official reports. Using multiple sources of data is important, as indicated by the fact that national incidence studies have found that twice as many children were endangered as were actually harmed, and also that neglect is by far the most common form of maltreatment, debunking two previously held notions about child maltreatment.

Are Abuse and Neglect Increasing? The following data come mainly from the National Child Abuse and Neglect Data System (NCANDS) and the National Incidence Study (NIS) of Child Abuse and Neglect, both sponsored by the U.S. Department of Health and Human Services. The NCANDS annually collects and analyzes information on child maltreatment provided by state CPS agencies. NCANDS is funded by the National Center on Child Abuse and Neglect (NCCAN) of the Administration on Children, Youth, and Families at the U.S. Department of Health and Human Services. It is a voluntary national data collection and analysis program that combines both federal and state efforts.

In 1997, CPS agencies investigated an estimated 2 million reports that involved the alleged maltreatment of approxi-

mately 3 million children. Of these, just under 1 million (about 33 percent) were determined to be victims of substantiated abuse or neglect, meaning an allegation of maltreatment was confirmed according to the evidence required by state law or policy, or indicated abuse or neglect, meaning there is insufficient evidence to substantiate a case under state law or policy but there is reason to suspect that maltreatment has occurred or there is risk of future maltreatment.

Several studies have suggested that many more children suffer from maltreatment than are reported to CPS agencies. According to CPS reports, 13.9 children per 1,000 were victims of abuse or neglect; the NIS estimates that forty-two children per 1,000 were harmed or endangered by maltreatment.

The 1996 NIS reported a dramatic increase in maltreatment between 1986 (NIS-2) and 1993 (NIS-3). According to the NIS, the estimated number of children who experience harm from abuse and neglect increased 67 percent between the two studies (from 931,000 children to 1,553,800). This means that a child's risk of experiencing harm-causing abuse or neglect in 1993 was 1.5 times the child's risk in 1986. In particular, the estimated number of seriously injured children quadrupled from 141,700 in 1986 to 565,000 in 1993.

However, the number of victims of substantiated or indicated maltreatment decreased between 1996 and 1997, from slightly more than 1 million (1,030,751) to just under 1 million (984,000). The rate of maltreatment had been on the increase between 1990 and 1996, with an overall increase for that period of 18 percent. In addition, the 1998 rate of victimization was 12.9 per 1,000 children, a decrease from the 1997 rate of 13.9 per 1,000.

Neglect is the most common form of child maltreatment. Data for 1998 reveal the following numbers in CPS investigations: 53.5 percent neglect, 22.7 percent physical abuse, 11.5 percent sexual abuse, 6 percent emotional maltreatment, and 6 percent medical neglect; 25.3 percent of all victims suffered more than one type of maltreatment.

Child abuse and neglect affects children of all ages. Among children confirmed as victims by CPS agencies in 1997, more than half were seven years old or younger, and about 26 percent were younger than four years old. Approximately 22 percent of victims were children aged eight to eleven; another 25 percent were youth ages twelve to eighteen. A greater proportion of neglect and medical neglect victims were children younger than eight years, whereas a greater proportion of physical, sexual, and emotional abuse victims were children age eight or older. Children are consistently vulnerable to sexual abuse from age three on.

In 1997, approximately 52 percent of victims of maltreatment were female and 47 percent were male. Available data suggest that some differences exist in the types of maltreatment experienced by male and female children. Girls were sexually abused three times more often than boys were. Victims of emotional maltreatment also were somewhat more likely to be female (51 percent). Conversely, a slightly greater proportion of victims of other types of maltreatment were male, with males comprising approximately 51 percent of neglect victims and 52 percent of both physical abuse and medical neglect victims. Boys are at greater risk of serious injury.

Although children of families in all income levels suffer maltreatment, research suggests that family income is strongly related to incidence rates. In one study, children from families with annual incomes below $15,000 were more than twenty-five times more likely than children from families with annual incomes above $30,000 to have been harmed or endangered by abuse or neglect.

In 1998 victimization rates by race/ethnicity ranged from a low of 3.8 Asian/Pacific Islander victims per 1,000 children of the same race in the population to 20.7 African American victims per 1,000 children of the same race in the population. The victimization rate for American Indians/Alaska natives was 19.8, for Hispanics 10.6, and for Caucasians 8.5.

Based on data reported by CPS agencies in 1997, it is estimated that nationwide 1,196 children died as a result of abuse or neglect. Children age three and under accounted for more than 75 percent of these child fatalities. In reviewing the 1995–1997 child maltreatment fatalities (data from sixteen states), researchers found that 41 percent of children who died had prior or current contact with CPS agencies, with 44 percent of children dying from neglect, 51 percent from physical abuse, and 5 percent from multiple forms of maltreatment. These figures represent the lowest estimate of the problem, as not all child maltreatment fatalities are known to CPS.

A *perpetrator* of child abuse and/or neglect is a person who has maltreated a child, whether or not in a caregiving relationship to the child. In 1998, 60.4 percent of perpetrators were female. Female perpetrators were typically younger than their male counterparts, as reflected by the difference in their average ages (thirty-one versus thirty-four). More than four-fifths (87.1 percent) of all victims were maltreated by one or both parents. The most common pattern of maltreatment was a child neglected by a female parent with no other perpetrators identified (44.7 percent).

Victims of physical and sexual abuse, compared to victims of neglect and medical neglect, were more likely to be maltreated by a male parent acting alone. In cases of sexual abuse, more than half the victims (55.9 percent) were abused by male parents, male relatives, or other males.

In 1997, the majority of perpetrators of child maltreatment (75 percent) were parents, and another 10 percent were other relatives of the victim. People who were in other caregiving relationships to the victim (e.g., child-care providers, foster parents, and facility staff) accounted for only 2 percent of perpetrators. About 13 percent of all perpetrators were classified as noncaregivers or unknown (in many states, perpetrators of child maltreatment by definition must be in a caregiving role).

More than 80 percent of all perpetrators were under age forty. Overall, approximately 62 percent of perpetrators were female, although gender differed by type of maltreatment. An estimated three-quarters of sexual abuse cases were associated with male perpetrators; more than 70 percent of neglect and 80 percent of medical neglect were associated with female perpetrators. This is probably related to the fact that many more females than males serve as primary caregivers for children.

The Consequences of Child Abuse and Neglect

The experience of maltreatment is unique to each child depending on the type, intensity, and frequency of maltreatment, as well as characteristics of the child and parent. There is clear evidence that early maltreatment of a child has profound neuropsychological as well as behavioral impacts. Although short-term effects are related to suffering from the physical and mental cruelty of child abuse, long-term effects are many. These can include physical impairment, emotional disturbance, below-average IQ, delayed language development, behavioral problems, low self-esteem, refusal to attend school, separation anxiety disorders, and aggressive tendencies. Other consequences include an increased likelihood of future substance abuse, high-risk health behaviors, criminal activity, somatization, depressive and affective disorders, personality disorders, post-traumatic stress disorder, panic attacks, schizophrenia, and abuse of their own children and spouse. Recent research has shown that a loving, caring, and stimulating environment during the first three years of a child's life is important for proper brain development. This finding implies that children who receive maltreatment in these early years may actually have suboptimal brain development (*American Family Physician*, March 1999).

Sexual abuse is associated with an increase in many psychiatric disorders (including personality disorders, post-traumatic stress disorder, substance abuse, eating disorders, and depression), as well as sexually transmitted diseases and health problems. A 1995 National Institutes of Justice report indicated that children who were sexually abused were twenty-eight times more likely than a control group of nonabused children to be arrested for prostitution as an adult.

Child abuse and neglect result in social costs as well, including low-birth-weight babies, infant mortality, expensive medical treatment, special education costs, protective-service costs, foster-care costs, juvenile delinquency, adult criminality, psychological problems, lower occupational and educational achievement, and substance abuse.

The yearly costs of maltreatment that include medical care, family counseling, out-of-home care, and specialized education alone are estimated at approximately $500 million (U.S. General Accounting Office, 1991). According to a 1992 study sponsored by the National Institute of Justice, maltreatment in childhood increases the likelihood of arrest as a juvenile by 53 percent, as an adult by 38 percent, and for a violent crime by 38 percent. Being abused or neglected during childhood increases the likelihood of arrest for females by 77 percent. A 1999 study by the National Center on Addiction and Substance Abuse found that children of substance-abusing parents were almost three times more likely to be abused and more than four times more likely to be neglected than children of parents who are not substance abusers. Other studies estimated 50–80 percent of all child-abuse cases substantiated by CPS agencies involve some degree of substance abuse by the child's parents.

Lessening the Effects of Maltreatment
We now know that the effects of child maltreatment can be "buffered," or lessened, by several factors. One critical buffer appears to be the child's finding some adult who is loving or supportive. Additionally, resilient children can learn to "reframe" their past, that is, to look at their painful experiences in such a way that they do not blame themselves. Another buffer is the ability to break the isolation that characterizes the abusing family and to form relationships that help in crises.

According to the American Humane Association, many child-development and child-welfare professionals believe that spanking, hitting, or slapping is not effective as a form of discipline and is damaging to the self-respect and self-esteem of children. The practice of physically disciplining children, in the form of spanking, is widespread and has been practiced for generations. Two national surveys found that 90 percent of parents of three- and four-year-olds and 22 percent of parents of children under one year had hit their children. A 1997 study discovered that 44 percent of mothers reported spanking during the previous week, and they estimated spanking their child twice a week. Although these parents used physical discipline to reduce antisocial behavior, the opposite occurred in the long run: These children displayed an increased probability of aggression and other antisocial behavior.

The American Humane Association has compiled a list of reasons that parents give in using physical punishment. These include punishing "bad behavior" or because children "deserved" it, on the basis of perceived religious practices, within the context of an act of love, and for cultural practices within a particular community.

However, disciplining children with physical punishment does not facilitate learning; rather, physical punishment teaches children what not to do and fails to teach children what is expected of them. Using phrases like "I'm only doing this for your own good because I love you" or "This will hurt me as much as it hurts you" sends mixed messages to the child and may actually teach the child that people who love you hurt you, or the way that love is shown is by hitting.

Time-out, loss of privileges, allowing the child to experience natural non–life-threatening consequences for undesirable behaviors, and parental disappointment can be far more effective and consistent in teaching children how to reduce undesirable behavior while learning alternative appropriate actions.

See also Crying; Discipline; Domestic Violence; Early Intervention; Failure to Thrive; Ghosts in the Nursery; Infant-Parent Psychotherapy; Infant Mental Health

References and further reading
American Humane Association Children's Division (formerly the National Resource Center on Child Abuse and Neglect) (website 2001). http://www. americanhumane.org.
Kempe Children's Center (formerly the C. Henry Kempe National Center for the Prevention and Treatment of Child Abuse and Neglect) (website 2001). http://kempecenter.org.
National Center on Child Abuse and Neglect. National Clearinghouse on Child Abuse and Neglect Information (website 2001). http://www.calib.com/ nccanch.
National Committee to Prevent Child Abuse (website 2001). http://www. childabuse.org.
National Survivors of Childhood Abuse Program. Child Help National Child Abuse Hotline (website 2001). http:// www.childhelpusa.org.
NCCAN Prevention Program Database (website 2001). http://www.calib.com/ nccanch/database.
Parents United San Jose Chapter, Giaretto Institute (website 2001). http://www. localink.net/sjpu/.

Child Care: Choosing Quality

Choosing appropriate child care is a daunting task for first-time parents. Returning to work after a baby is born is a difficult transition for the parents as well as the child. Finding a special caregiver or child-care center can make this transition much easier.

In general, parents choosing to use child care outside of the home want to find the highest quality care that is available and affordable. However, many parents do not know what constitutes high-quality care. They might be impressed by the layout of the center or the personality of the director. They might not know how many adults are really needed to care for a certain number of children. Adult-to-child ratios vary according to the ages of children present. Parents may not be aware of the importance of staff training in early childhood education.

Child-Care Licensing
The United States does not have a uniform program of child-care licensing. Licensing falls under the jurisdiction of the states and is administered through a state department, such as health or human services. State licensing itself is an indicator of higher quality. Most centers are required to be licensed, but many family child-care homes operate without licenses. Even some centers, particularly cooperatives, preschools, hourly drop-off care, and church-operated child care, do not need state licenses in some states. In these cases, parents should be aware that local business licensing is not equivalent to state licensing. Although a few facilities that are not licensed by the state can be excellent, the quality is generally lower in unlicensed homes and centers.

Still, state licensing does not guarantee an optimal level of care. Many of the licensed centers in the United States simply provide custodial care. Children's physical needs are met in low-quality centers, but intellectual stimulation and social interactions are limited. When children are in low-quality care, their cognitive and social functioning is likely to be delayed unless parents are able to provide stimulating activities in other settings.

In family child-care homes, state licensing is more of an option. Thus, it tends to be a stronger indicator of quality. Research studies have shown that providers in licensed homes are more responsive to children in their care, spend more time talking and playing with them, and provide more activities. Only 13 percent of licensed homes are rated as poor-quality environments; 50 percent of unlicensed homes are considered to be poor quality. Licensed family child-care homes have a similar level of quality to that of licensed centers.

Quality Indicators
Several factors indicate quality in child care. Generally, accredited programs tend to offer high-quality programming. Accreditation is a citation of excellence above and beyond basic licensing requirements. Other quality indicators include staff training, low child-to-adult ratios, cognitive and social stimulation, and parental involvement.

> Checklist for Infant Child Care
> - Do the children seem busy and happy?
> - Is this a safe, inviting place for my infant to crawl and explore?
> - Are the providers responsive to infants needs?
> - Do children spend little time in high chairs or swings?
> - Are child-care providers sitting and playing with children on the floor?
> - Do child-care providers treat infant/toddlers with respect?
> - Do child-care providers talk more to the children than to each other?
> - Are children treated as individuals with their own preferences?
> - What types of toys are available?
>   Cloth or board books?
>   Washable stuffed animals and dolls?
>   Rattles, squeak toys, soft blocks?
>   Nesting toys, push, and pull toys?
>   Nonbreakable mirrors?

Staff Training
In both centers and family child-care homes, providers who take the time for continued training in early childhood education provide better care. Years of experience do not indicate quality, but continuing education does. Most states have requirements for training of directors and staff. One indicator of quality is the percentage of staff who have received their Child Development Associate (CDA) credential. Child-care providers who have obtained a CDA have attended several hours of outside training, passed an independent on-site evaluation of their competency, and completed oral and written examinations. When providers complete CDA training or other appropriate early childhood education, they are more likely to be warm and responsive to infants' needs.

> Questions to Ask When
> Looking for Child Care
> - What type of training does the staff have? It is desirable to have at least some training in child development.
> - How much employee turnover is there? It is desirable to have minimal staff turnover.
> - How do you feel about parents dropping in unannounced? Family-friendly policies and welcomed parental visits are positive signs of quality.
> - What are the views about good discipline strategies for older infants and

toddlers? Developmentally appropriate approaches should focus on positive guidance strategies designed to help children learn to function successfully in a social environment. Punitive strategies such as isolating the child or scolding the child are not the best choices.

- How will the staff help my child make the transition to child care? Responsive child-care providers will work with parents to develop a gradual transition to care. Common strategies include having the parent visit the center with the child, staying with the child for a period of time as the child adjusts, and working out predictable rituals for arriving at the center.

Low Child-to-Adult Ratios

Many states set ratios for infants and toddlers at a higher level than is optimal. Too many children and too few adults negate opportunities for high-quality, individual interactions between infants, toddlers, and their child-care providers. The National Association for the Education of Young Children requires one caregiver for every three infants in order for centers to meet accreditation standards. Because of these low ratios, many accredited centers lose money on infant care. As a result, it may be difficult to find an opening for infant care in high-quality centers, or the cost may be prohibitive. Some nonprofit centers or parent cooperatives provide very high quality care for a somewhat lower cost. One adult for every four infants is considered adequate, and a ratio of three infants to one caregiver is optimal. Group size for children under one should be no larger than eight

infants per two adults, and a group size of no more than six is most desirable.

Continuity of care is also an important feature of high-quality care. The interactions infants have with the special adults in their lives play an important role in how babies come to view themselves. When infants are treated in a sensitive and emotionally responsive manner, they come to view themselves as capable, valuable, and lovable individuals. Because infants spend so much time with child-care providers, those providers become very important to the healthy emotional development of infants. Sadly, the turnover rate in child care is extremely high, with 30–40 percent of child-care providers leaving their positions within any one-year period. Child-care programs with high turnover rates among staff are not as likely to promote feelings of security in children, particularly among infants.

Another aspect of continuous care has to do with primary caregiving assignments and prolonged contact between infants, toddlers, and their providers. *Primary caregiving* means than one adult takes primary responsibility for caring for a small group of infant/toddlers. The provider comes to know each baby's patterns, likes, dislikes, and cues, enabling her to provide the most sensitive and responsive care. After investing so much energy into building such intimate and trusting relationships with infants, many programs still transition infant/toddlers into new rooms at regular intervals. For instance, an infant might move to a young toddler room at age one. A better approach is to design a program that allows for child-care providers and infants and toddlers to stay together for as long as three years, if possible. This aspect of continuous care is sometimes called "looping." There are several ways to carry out a looping pattern. One approach is to have the child-care provider move with the infants/toddlers to another room as they age. A second approach is to keep the infants/toddlers in the same room with the child-care provider and continually alter the physical configuration of the classroom and the materials provided based on the changing ages and developmental needs of the group.

Cognitive and Social Stimulation
Centers and family child-care homes should encourage child-care providers to interact with children. Child-care providers should be down at the children's level, talking and playing with the infants. Infants love to have someone help them learn to roll over. Playing with rattles and balls encourages motor development and social skills. Infants need to be fed or cuddled at the instant they become hungry or feel insecure. Schedules, lines, and lengthy rules of behavior are inappropriate for very young children.

Parental Involvement
Good child-care centers and homes welcome parental involvement and feedback. There should be a regular parent-teacher conference time. Informal gatherings or parties for parents and their children can help families feel more comfortable with their child-care choice. Child-care providers should work together with families as partners in their children's care. Above all, child-care centers and homes should have an open-door policy, where parents are welcome to visit at any time.

Centers can be more expensive, and some parents worry about their children being in contact with so many other people. Young children in centers tend to get

sick more often initially; they may have higher immunity to diseases later on than children who stay at home. Even though infant child care is expensive, parents with lower income levels may be eligible for sliding fee scales at nonprofit centers. Government subsidies are available for all low-income parents at licensed child-care centers and homes.

Parents often prefer family child-care homes or on-site child care for their infants. When parents have a long commute, family child care may be preferable to on-site child care. In addition, the presence of one consistent caregiver provides a stable environment for young infants. The number of children present in the home is often limited to six. Only two infants under the age of one should be cared for by a single provider. As a result of these low ratios, children are less likely to catch contagious diseases. Parents should be aware that family child-care homes with higher ratios tend to provide better care. When providers only have one or two children in their home, they are less likely to be focused on the children. In addition, providers who are professionally committed to their business and who maintain memberships in their state or local family child-care associations tend to be more competent.

On-site child care is provided by some businesses, partly as a benefit to their employees. Working mothers are more easily able to continue nursing in these situations. In addition, parents enjoy spending their breaks and lunch hours with their young children. Businesses benefit by having a lower employee turnover. Yet these situations are not available or preferable for all parents.

Parents looking for child care should make their decision after visiting several settings. Spending more than a brief visit at each setting is necessary for an honest evaluation of the child-care environment. Parents should ask themselves several questions about each setting and make notes on indicators of quality, such as child-to-adult ratios and staff training.

After parents have made a preliminary decision, they should bring their child to visit the caregiver before the first day of child care. When children enter care, parents should drop in unannounced from time to time. Older infants who enter care for the first time often experience separation anxiety. An infant's crying when his parents leave is not a sign that parents have made the wrong choice. In fact, warnings that child care is detrimental to young children are unfounded by research. Child care can be a safe and a fun place for infants to grow and develop.

See also Caregivers, Training of; Caregiving

Child Study Movement

The child study movement, emerging from the work of psychologist G. Stanley Hall in the early twentieth century, embodied the growing notion that the development of very young children could be studied scientifically. This idea of studying children as a scholarly pursuit marked the birth of the field of child development. Hall's student, Arnold Gesell, advanced the child study movement and the science of child development by using systematic observations and methodical analyses of child behavior to learn how young children grow and develop. As part of the child study movement, the first preschools (play schools and nursery schools) developed. Moreover, nursery schools created as part of laboratory nurseries first became popular because of interest in child study. These university laboratory nurseries provided an environment in which early education practices could be modeled and in which research studies of child development could be carried out. Parent education also emerged as part of nursery schools, particularly in university-based laboratory schools, which focused on translating research findings into practical applications for parents. Further, parents were encouraged to come to nursery school with their young children in order to learn more about childrearing and child development.

See also Gesell, Arnold; Hall, G. Stanley

References and further reading
Roopnarine, J. L., and J. E. Johnson. 2000. *Approaches to Early Childhood Education.* 3rd ed. Upper Saddle River, NJ: Merrill.

Child-Care Accreditation

Child-care accreditation is a citation denoting that a child-care program has achieved a high standard of quality. Most states require that child-care centers, family child-care homes, and group day-care homes be licensed through a state regulatory system. Most licensing standards regulate basic health and safety practices, establishing a basic standard of quality below which programs cannot legally operate. Licensing is designed to provide a base level of quality to protect consumers. Accreditation standards, however, require accredited child-care programs to meet not only state licensing requirements but also additional standards related to adult-child interactions, curriculum, relationships with families, staff qualifications and professional development, administration, staffing, physical environment, health and safety, nutrition and food service, and program evaluation. In order to

A child-care center for toddlers and preschool-age children. (Courtesy of Alice Sterling Honig)

be accredited, the child-care program must be licensed by the state in which it operates and be in good standing.

Accrediting Organizations

In the United States, there are two organizations through which programs can seek accreditation. Child-care centers can apply for accreditation with the National Academy of Early Childhood Programs, the accrediting body of the National Association for the Education of Young Children. Accreditation criteria were adopted in 1984 and were revised in 1996. Family child-care homes and group child-care homes are accredited through the National Association for Family Child Care (NAFCC). The NAFCC was founded in 1982 and developed its first accreditation system in 1988. A new accreditation system was developed in 1998.

The Accreditation Process

The accreditation processes outlined by the National Academy of Early Childhood Programs and the National Association for Family Child Care are similar. Both accrediting organizations require programs to complete an application, conduct a thorough self-review process, and undergo an external review by observers from the accrediting organization. Next, all information is reviewed by the accrediting body and a decision is made as to whether or not the program meets accreditation standards. If the program meets the required standards, it is granted accreditation. If the program is denied accreditation, it can make the needed improvements and request another review. Accreditation through the National Academy of Early Childhood Programs and the National Association for Family Child

Care is awarded on a three-year cycle. Programs must be reviewed at the end of each cycle in order to renew the accreditation. The accreditation processes for child-care centers and family child-care homes are lengthy, requiring up to a year for completion. It can be costly as well. Fees for accreditation range from $400 to $1,000 depending on the type and size of the child-care program.

Accreditation and Program Quality
Accreditation generally results in higher-quality programs because each program must meet and maintain standards beyond basic licensing. Comparisons between nonaccredited and accredited programs show that accredited programs are rated as providing higher quality and as emphasizing the quality of adult-child interactions as well as the developmental appropriateness of specific activities for children.

Although the accreditation process is lengthy and costly, many caregivers and program administrators say that becoming accredited results not only in higher quality care for children but also has benefits for staff, such as increased professionalism, respect for the work and profession, and increased emphasis on professional development. Accreditation can also result in financial benefits for programs because accredited programs can choose to increase their fees.

Identifying Accredited Programs
After completing the accreditation process and receiving accreditation status, programs are eager to be recognized. Both the National Academy of Early Childhood Programs and the National Association for Family Child Care award accreditation certificates to programs that can be displayed in the building. These organizations also provide brochures describing the

benefits of accredited programs for distribution to current and prospective clients.

Also, both accrediting organizations maintain printed as well as electronic lists of accredited programs, and potential clients can request these lists. Local child-care referral agencies also maintain lists of accredited programs in their area.

See also Caregiving; Child Care: Choosing Quality; Family Day Care

References and further reading
National Association for the Education of Young Children. (1998). *Accreditation Criteria and Procedures of the National Association for the Education of Young Children*. Washington, DC: NAEYC.
——— (website 2001). http://www.naeyc.org.

Children's Defense Fund

The Children's Defense Fund (CDF) is a private nonprofit organization dedicated to advocacy and public education on issues vital to the welfare of America's children. CDF was founded in 1973 by Yale law graduate Marian Wright Edelman, who was the first African American woman admitted to the bar in Mississippi (1967), and who has been described as the country's preeminent child advocate. CDF has grown to include a budget in excess of $10 million, paid by foundations, corporation grants, and individual donors.

The mission of CDF is to "Leave No Child Behind" and to ensure every child a "Healthy Start, a Head Start, a Safe Start, a Moral Start" in life and a successful passage to adulthood with the help of caring families and communities. CDF seeks to alleviate child poverty through higher government spending. CDF monitors state and federal policies with regard to children and offers information and help to state and child advocates and to those who provide services to children. Some of the information provided includes statistics on children and families.

The CDF also advocates for affordable, safe, quality child care, early education, before- and after-school care, as well as the elimination of teen pregnancy. CDF also notes that parents need adequate wages and strong parenting skills. Neighborhoods and schools must be safe, protecting children from guns and school violence.

Over the years, CDF has supported programs and legislation that have expanded health care and education to millions of children, especially those from families with low incomes and resources.

See also Early Intervention

Chorionic Villus Sampling

This is a technique used to study genetic influences on the fetus. Chorionic villi are obtained by placing a needle through the abdomen and into the placenta, or by placing a catheter that is inserted into the vagina and cervix. The material extracted are cells that are identical to those of the fetus; when grown in the lab, they can provide information about the genetic status of the fetus. Chorionic villus sampling is slightly more risky than another procedure, amniocentesis, but in either case risk is relatively low.

See also Amniocentesis

Chromosomal Disorders
See Genetic Disorders

Circadian Rhythms
See Biological Rhythms

Circular Reaction

Circular reactions are learning mechanisms described by Jean Piaget in his theory of cognitive development. Babies are motivated to repeat actions, initially performed by chance, that they find pleasurable or interesting. These repetitions lead to distinctive ("circular," over and over again) patterns of behavior. Thumb-sucking is one example, as is opening and closing one's fist when first realizing that one controls that action.

A four-month-old sucking his fingers. (Elizabeth Crews)

Circumcision

Circumcision is the surgical removal of the foreskin from the penis. Performed for religious, health, and cultural reasons, the practice of circumcision is controversial because it is a painful procedure that many critics contend is of no medical benefit. The United States is the only country in the world that routinely circumcises most male infants for nonreligious reasons. Approximately 80 percent of the world's males are not circumcised. Studies of the effects of circumcision on the newborn indicate that it is related to elevated cortisol levels, high heart rate, intense crying, and behavioral distress. Some physicians advocate use of anesthesia during circumcision, but for the most part the operation is performed without painkillers. Evidence suggests that the effects of circumcision can be seen for up to a half-year after surgery.

See also Birth

References and further reading
Circumcision Resource Center (website 2001). http://www.circumcision.org/response.htm.
Gunnar, Megan, et al. 1985. "Coping with Aversive Stimulation in the Neonatal Period: Quiet Sleep and Plasma Cortisol Levels During Recovery from Circumcision." *Child Development* 56: 824–834.
Richards, Martin, Judy Bernal, and Yvonne Brackbill. 1976. "Early Behavioral Differences: Gender or Circumcision?" *Developmental Psychobiology* 9: 89–95.

Classical Conditioning

A set of procedures originally developed by the Nobel Prize–winning physiologist Ivan Pavlov. These procedures were developed to study the formation of stimulus-stimulus and stimulus-response associations, or contingencies, in the environment. Pavlov was especially interested in stimulus-stimulus connections formed at the incoming (or afferent) side of the reflex arc.

Cleft Lip and Palate

See Prematurity; Prenatal Development

Coaction

"Coaction" is Gilbert Gottlieb's term to describe the bidirectional nature of epigenetic processes. Gottlieb argues that ontogeny involves the probabilistic emergence of new structures and func-

tions at all levels from the molecular to the organismic. Characteristics emerge from both horizontal coactions and vertical coactions. Horizontal coactions involve reciprocal relationships from gene to gene, cell to cell, and organism to organism, whereas vertical coactions involve reciprocal relationships across levels (gene to cytoplasm, cell to tissue, and neural activity to behavior).

Working from a systems view of psychobiological development, Gottlieb proposes three functional organismic levels of analysis (genetic activity, neural activity, and behavior) and three levels of environmental analysis (physical, social, and cultural) to guide investigation of the complete reciprocity among genetic activity, structure, and function. Gottlieb's reciprocal interaction view of developmental process stands in contrast to the unidirectional view of canalization. His definition of epigenesis is organizational, focusing on the emergence of new levels of organization resulting from coactions among the parts of a system and coactions from one system to another, with special emphasis on organism-environment coactions.

See also Systems Theory

Cocaine Addiction

The short-term impacts of maternal cocaine on the fetus and newborn has been measured. Cocaine use increases risk for miscarriage and in late pregnancy can cause premature labor. Babies exposed prenatally are at risk of death, prematurity, major and minor malformations, poor self-regulation, and biobehavioral dysfunction. Cocaine exposure is related to placental complications, low birthweight, urinary-tract malformations, feeding and sleep difficulties, and sudden infant death syndrome. Newborns experiencing withdrawal are especially at risk for death. Although infants exposed prenatally to cocaine seem to have normal intelligence, they are at higher risk for having attention and behavioral problems, at the least, in the school setting. Barry Lester of Brown University has established a national database that incorporates the outcomes of all scientific studies of the effects of cocaine on infants and young children. Scanning all studies of cocaine effects will enable investigators to determine specific short- and long-term effects on prenatal exposure.

See also Alcoholism; Prenatal Development; Smoking

References and further reading
Lagasse, L. L., and Barry M. Lester. 2000. "Prenatal Cocaine Exposure and Child Outcome." In Hiram E. Fitzgerald, Barry M. Lester, and Barry Zuckerman, eds., *Children of Addiction: Health Care, Research, and Policy Issues.* New York: Routledge, Falmer, pp. 29–44.
Lester, Barry M., et al. 1998. "Cocaine Exposure and Children: The Meaning of Subtle Effects." *Science* 282: 633–634.

Cognitive Development: Piaget

Jean Piaget (1896–1980) was a Swiss biologist by training, but his theory of how children learn has had a lasting and profound influence on the field of psychology. Piaget described how thinking (cognition) develops and what a child's thinking is like: Children do not see the world in the same way as adults. He believed that we all learn to think in increasingly more complex ways—so that we can solve more difficult problems and better understand the world—through a process of active environmental exploration.

The idea that people are a driving force in their own learning process is called "constructivism." According to constructivism, we do not grow up according to some automatic and effortless biological plan. Biology ensures that the brain is ready to gather information, but it is experience with the world that provides the actual information from which we learn. This experience can be by directly manipulating objects (because the objects themselves mean nothing to us until we do something to them), or through social transmission (e.g., when interacting with others in a social setting). The basic point is that humans are active, curious, and inventive. Children especially are naturally interested in their environment and enjoy seeing the effects of their actions on people, objects, and events. These interactions, and their consequences, teach them about reality. Overall, Piaget described a "learning by doing" process of acquiring knowledge. More experience leads to advances in logic and sophistication in thought.

Key Concepts
Schemas are the specific cognitive structures of the mind. They are the way in which ideas about behavior and perceptions are organized at any given time, based on one's understanding of the world. Organization makes sure that everything that one knows about the world makes sense as a whole. The basic tendency of life is to organize. Schemas fit together so as to form an integrated and consistent way of thinking. Schemas and their organization are not permanent, however; they have to change as new information and experiences are encountered.

It is ideal for people to exist in a state of equilibrium where everything makes sense. New information can challenge what is already known (the schema) and disrupt this steady state, leading to disequilibrium. In order to reattain equilibrium again, the existing knowledge (the schema) and the new information from the environment must be made to fit together. The goal is a balance between mental structures and reality. Being able to repeatedly reconcile schemas with reality is known as "adaptation."

Assimilation and accommodation are the twin processes of adaptation and occur when new information from the environment enters into cognitive awareness. In assimilation, the new findings are absorbed and incorporated into the organization that was already in place. They become part of the previously established way of thinking about things. When it is inconsistent with existing schemas, the incoming information is modified so that it becomes consistent. There is no change in the schema itself. Accommodation involves a complementary yet opposite process. Again, experience with the environment leads to conclusions that do not fit with any existing schema. To solve this dilemma, the schemas themselves are revised. There is actually a change in how the world is seen, not in the information itself. This is often the case when new facts are undeniable and unalterable. To summarize, assimilation involves adding to available schemas, whereas accommodation involves modifying them.

Stage Theory
Development is not instantaneous, and it takes four levels to reach the height of reasoning possessed by most adults. Piaget called these levels (1) sensorimotor, (2) preoperational, (3) concrete operations, and (4) formal operations. Accord-

ing to Piaget, movement through these levels and their stages is always in a specific order. Stages cannot be skipped. Change is qualitative, meaning that higher levels involve actual transformations of mental structures (so it is not just "more" of what came before). Each stage builds upon the previous one and growth is cumulative, so it is impossible to go backward. Development thus proceeds in a predictable way. This progression is universal for all people regardless of culture, although there are individual differences in the ages at which each stage is mastered. Specifically, the speed at which children pass through each stage can vary.

Between stages there is a period of disequilibrium. New ways of thinking emerge to deal with these inconsistencies. The result is cognitive change and higher levels of reasoning, with schemas that are not only more complex but that better fit with observations about the world. For a while, equilibrium is restored—until the child approaches a transition to the next stage. Notably, assimilation and accommodation usually work together, day to day, but accommodation tends to prevail during times of rapid developmental change.

The first major level of Piaget's hierarchical model encompasses the sensorimotor period, so named because the infant "thinks" solely on the basis of sensations (sight, sound, touch, smell) and motor actions (reaching, grasping, pulling, tracking). It describes all of early infancy and can be subdivided into six stages. Each stage is characterized by a different type of interaction with the environment and the unique accomplishments that each enables.

Stage 1. From birth (birth to one month), behavior is mostly reflexive, uncoordi-

TABLE 1   **Stages of cognitive development and related changes in the affective and social domains (age periods in months)**

Cognitive development (Piaget)	Affective development (Sroufe)	Social development (Sander)
0–1: Use of reflexes Minimal generalization/ accommodation of inborn behaviors	0–1: Absolute stimulus barrier Built-in protection	0–3: Initial regulation Sleeping, feeding, quieting, arousal Beginning preferential responsiveness to caregiver
1–4: Primary circular reaction First acquired adaptations Anticipation based on visual cues Beginning coordination of schemes	1–3: Turning toward Orientation to external world Relative vulnerability to stimulation Exogenous (social) smile	
4–8: Secondary circular reaction Behavior directed toward external world Beginning goal orientation	3–6: Positive affect Content-mediated affect Pleasure as an excitory process 7–9: Active participation Joy at being a cause Failure of intended acts Differentiation of emotional reactions	4–6: Reciprocal exchange Mother and child coordinate feeding, caretaking activities Affective, vocal, and motor play 7–9: Initiative Early directed activity Experience of success or interference in achieving goals
8–12: Coordination of secondary schemes and application to to new situations Objectification of the world True intentionality Imitation of novel responses Beginning appreciation of causal relations	9–12: Attachment Affectively toned schemes Integration and coordination of emotional reactions	10–13: Focalization Mother's availability tested Exploration from secure base Reciprocity dependent on information
12–18: Tertiary circular reaction Pursuit of novelty Trial-and-error problem solving Physical causality spatialized and detached from child's actions	12–18: Practicing Mother the secure base for exploration Elation in mastery Affect as part of contact Control of emotional expression	14–20: Self-assertion Broadened initiative Success and gratification achieved apart from mother
18–24: Invention of new means through mental combination Symbolic representation Problem solving without overt action	18–36: Emergence of self-concept Sense of self as actor Sense of separateness	

Source: Adapted from L. A. Sroufe. 1979. "Socioemotional development," in *Handbook of Infant Development*, ed. J. D. Osofsky. New York: John Wiley & Sons, Inc., 476–477. With permission of John Wiley & Sons, Inc.

nated, and self-centered. Adaption to the environment takes the form of inherited and unlearned reactions to stimuli.

Stage 2. Motivation becomes important after the first month of life. The actions in which the infant engages most often are the ones that lead to consequences that the infant finds intriguing or rewarding in some way. After a behavior that takes place spontaneously leads to some form of positive reinforcement (pleasure), the

Children learn about the world they live in through interaction with people and objects, leading to more and more sophisticated thought processes. This twenty-two-month-old girl demonstrates the ability to use objects correctly (with the hairbrush) as well as an ability to play make believe; she has obviously reached stage six. (Laura Dwight/Corbis)

behavior is repeated and can be incorporated into a planned pattern, or action scheme. These repetitive cycles (circles) of events are called "circular reactions." In primary circular reactions (one to four months), reflexes are chained together to create more complex patterns. Behaviors involve and are directed toward the baby's own body. The infant's actions are centered on physical needs and bodily sensations. There is repetition of self-involved actions that bring pleasure to the child, and habits are formed. For example, thumb-sucking may begin when the child puts his hand in his mouth by chance but is continued because of the enjoyment it brings.

Stage 3. During the secondary circular phase (four to eight months) there is an interest in interacting with the environment. Attention becomes centered on objects beyond the infant's own body. There are intentional interactions with these external objects. For example, children begin playing with toys at this stage. A rudimentary understanding of cause and effect is achieved. The infant acts, others respond, and the infant repeats the action. Infants can track and anticipate movements and will look for moving objects at the point at which they are expected to cease moving or come to rest. As such, there exists a primitive object-location schema. However, search and retrieval is only for objects that are partially hidden from sight. Completely covered objects are not recognized.

Stage 4. With the coordination of primary and secondary reactions (eight to twelve months), schemes become more complex and are often combined to form routines. Cause and effect is better understood. This is in terms of means-ends:

Actions are directed toward the achievement of some goal. There is an unmistakable purpose to behavior. For example, one form of problem-solving requires that an obstacle be removed before another task can be performed. Suppose that an infant pushes aside a box to grab the toy behind it. The pushing of the box can be seen as the means of attaining the end (goal): playing with the toy. Another indication of this higher level of reasoning is that infants can find completely hidden objects. Understanding object permanence is definitely a significant milestone of cognitive development. Object permanence implies knowledge of the fact that objects in the environment continue to exist even when not being directly perceived. Children now appreciate the fact that objects have their own existence. This is compared to earlier stages (stages 1 and 2, for example) in which the unconscious rule of thumb was "out of sight, out of mind." Despite all of the dramatic advances in stage 4, there are still flaws in reasoning ability. Imagine that a toy is hidden either in location A or B while the child watches. When the object is hidden in A, the child easily finds it in repeated attempts. When the object is hidden in A but then moved to B in plain sight, the child still looks for it in A. This is known as the AB problem.

Stage 5. The AB problem is resolved in tertiary circular reactions (twelve–eighteen months), although switches in location that are "invisible" (not in plain sight) are still confusing for the developing child. Also, not until this age does behavior become truly exploratory. The toddler begins to think more creatively and engages in active experimentation. Again, the typical pattern is cyclical, as follows: The child acts, others respond, and the infant repeats the action. Now, however, this frequently occurs with variation or trial and error. There is an understanding that alternate actions can produce the same response; children look for new means to the same end.

Stage 6. Finally, there is a transition to more mature reasoning, which occurs between eighteen and twenty-four months. The child learns to internalize thoughts, imagine actions, and understand invisible displacements. Symbols are used to represent real objects and events, and the world is understood not just as an external thing but something that can be mentally represented. Actions can take place completely in one's mind. It is here that children first begin to play make-believe.

Between the ages of two and seven years, children enter the next level of thinking as defined by Piagetian theory. This is better known as the "preoperational period." Internal representations are more firmly established. Thinking is no longer dependent on what the child can see or hear at any given moment. Children can form images of objects in their minds, which are available for manipulation even when the object itself is not physically present. Children can now think "inside their heads" to solve problems and are no longer dependent on physical trial and error. Ideas can be conveyed through language or expressed as mental imagery. At this point, however, thinking is still based on intuition, not logic. Solutions to problems depend on superficial judgments about physical appearance. More important, children still cannot take the perspective of others. Reality is subjective and based on one's own point of view. This self-centeredness is known as "egocentrism."

The typical experimental procedure for demonstrating preoperational egocentrism involves a task known as the "three mountains problem." A tableau of three mountains of differing heights is presented to a child standing in one location. A doll is positioned at other locations, and the child is asked to choose which several photographs best represents what the doll would see from any given position. Most children at this stage select a picture that depicts the mountains as seen from their own perspective, not that of the doll.

Moving well beyond the infancy years, the final two levels of thinking are achieved during the concrete operations period (seven to eleven years) and the formal operations period (eleven years and older). During concrete operations, children are able to mentally reverse their actions. They also understand that when numbers or quantities of objects change in shape, nothing is lost. There is conservation of matter, irrespective of appearance. In formal operations, thinking becomes even more abstract. Alternate realities are considered, and many possibilities arise in solving problems. An adult level of reasoning is achieved.

Common Themes
As children proceed from one stage to the next, they develop a better and better understanding of causality—the connection between action and consequence. During the first two sensorimotor stages (reflexive and primary circular), infants are focused on themselves and their bodies. By secondary circular reactions (stage 3), there is interaction with and acting on the environment in order to repeat pleasurable responses. To a great extent, this is spontaneous. Stage 6, however, brings with it true recognition of cause and effect. Here

is a beginning of having real goals—using means to an end. Actions are planned. New actions are found which produce the same effect (stage 5). Of additional interest is how effects will change, when the action is varied in subtle and not-so-subtle ways. By the transition to preoperational thought, causes are not only understood but mentally tested and even predicted.

Also developing across stages are object concepts. According to Piaget, children learn by acting on objects. Knowledge is based on the interaction between self and object and is not just a property of the object alone. Children come to understand what the object is by manipulating it and creating a schema of it. First they realize that objects are separate from themselves (stage 3). At this point infants also recognize partially hidden objects, meaning that they are able to reconstruct the identity of an object (and know what it is) by just looking at part of it. Next there is the understanding that objects continue to exist on their own, even when they cannot be seen anymore (stage 4, object permanence). Object concepts become more sophisticated as the child moves through the stages and substages of development. By the preoperational period, children are capable of thinking about objects as just images in their head. An abstract concept is borne.

Overall, what has been learned is a sense of constancy, that objects are real things in and of themselves, independent of human perception and particular settings. Their existence is constant. Also constant are the object's most basic characteristics. Round balls do not suddenly become square. A doll with red hair will still have red hair even after it is hidden from sight. The preoperational child, however, is still easily swayed by appearance and perception and becomes fixated

on one detail to the neglect of others. For example, this child would still be unable to recognize that when water is poured from a tall but thin container into a short but wide container, the amount of water remains unchanged—it just looks different but isn't in any fundamental way. There is constancy in *what* something is (water is still water), but there isn't constancy regarding *how much.*

Various forms of imitation emerge at different points in cognitive development. Imitation involves copying someone else's behavior. During the first few months of life (stages 1–2), there is only pseudo-imitation. Soon infants are able to imitate other's behavior, but only while observing themselves doing so and paying attention to each movement that needs to be made (stage 3). In stage 4 imitation takes place purposefully, and the child no longer has to think about each and every movement. Success is only for behaviors that are familiar—that is, those that are already in the child's behavioral repertoire. By stage 5, even new behaviors, ones that have never been seen before, can be copied without much practice. Finally, there is delayed or deferred imitation—the ability to imitate behaviors some time after they have been observed. The fact that children can mimic a behavior previously seen implies that a symbolic representation of the event has been stored in memory (stage 6 and preoperational).

What most defines the Piagetian perspective as a common thread through all stages of development, however, is a belief in the inherent creativity and curiosity of children and adults. By their very nature, humans are constantly performing new actions, experimenting, and developing novel ideas in an attempt to transcend what they know already and to understand the environment that surrounds them. They are interested in and curious about what things are, how they work, and the way in which everything fits together. The creativity of children is observed in their games of make-believe and symbolic play—that is, in their use of the imagination. It is evident in the way that they devise alternate strategies in order to solve a problem, beyond those that have been tried previously and even beyond those that can be tested physically (to those that are tested mentally).

Implications

Piagetian theory has been used as a model for parenting and education. One message is that the focus should be on children's reasoning abilities and an acknowledgement that children do not think in the same way as adults. Piagetian theory implies that adults should facilitate a child's own exploration and not directly teach or impose information. Experience is important. Knowledge is a process and cannot be taught passively, by rote. Because children learn by acting on their environment and exploring the world, adults should encourage hands-on activities, spontaneity, self-initiation, and open creativity. The popularity of causality toys is one indication of the common-sense applicability of this approach. According to Piagetian theory, instruction should also be developmentally appropriate and congruent with the stage of each child. Although the stage sequence is invariant, the exact age at which each is achieved is not. Consequently, it is important for parents and educators to accept individual differences and work within them to tailor the learning curriculum. Ideally, problem-solving tasks are presented at a level that is just above that

which the child has already achieved, in order to encourage that "next step up"; this technique is called "scaffolding."

Summary

Piaget's theory of cognitive development is one of the most well known and important. Children are constantly modifying their cognitive structures and acquiring new skills. The mind continually builds mental schemas that allow for a better and better adaptive fit with experience. This is an active process, with a purposeful selecting and interpreting and reorganizing of mental structures so that information makes sense, and with a refining of the schemas so that they remain accurate. Over the various stages of development, schemas become increasingly more complex and better reflect reality as seen by adults. New problem-solving skills emerge. Acting on objects permits an understanding of these objects. These understandings eventually become mental representations. Overall, there is the gradual attainment of increasingly effective cognitive structures, or ways of thinking. In conclusion, it may be useful to picture children as young scientists—constructing better models of the world with more and more sophisticated logic, gained by experience and invention.

See also Piaget, Jean; Theories of Development

References and further reading
The Jean Piaget Society (website 2001). http://www.piaget.org.

Colic

Colic, characterized by consistent and inconsolable crying, is not a serious health threat to infants, but it is one of the most uncomfortable conditions for infants and adults. Colic usually appears only in the first six months of life. Not all infants experience colic, and scientists do not know exactly what causes colic. Colic responses seem to stem from different situations including allergies to formula or breast milk and gastrointestinal problems, such as irritable bowel syndrome, excess intestinal gas, or difficulty in absorbing food nutrients such as carbohydrates. Other infants with colic seem especially sensitive to stimulation from adults or from the environment, such as lights and sounds.

Color Perception
See Oculomotor

Colostrum
Colostrum is a sticky clear or yellowish liquid produced by the breasts before birth and for one to five days afterward. It is the first food a breastfeeding newborn receives. It is a unique compound of water, sugar, protein, fat-soluble vitamins, and minerals. It is the ideal first food for babies because it is easy to digest and contains disease-fighting antibodies. The main function of colostrum seems to be to protect the newborn against infection and to provide important nutrients.

See also Breastfeeding; Nutrition

Comforting Techniques
See Child Abuse and Neglect; Crying; Pacification

Communication
See American Sign Language; Language

Competence
See Basic Motives

Compliance
Compliance means the infant's or toddler's obedience to requests or commands. Compliance is first demonstrated between twelve and eighteen months of age when infants begin to recognize the parent's or caregiver's expectations. Infants at this age begin to comply to these expectations, although they need many reminders. Learning to comply is a process dependent on several prerequisite skills. First, infants and toddlers must recognize themselves as separate beings from the parent/caregiver with the ability to engage in unique actions. Second, infants must have the cognitive skills, particularly representational and memory skills, to remember a parent's or caregiver's expectation and direct his/her own actions in accordance with that expectation. These developmental skills emerge over time as cognitive skills become more mature. However, other developmental sequences influence infant/toddler compliance as well. For instance, consider toddlers who are eager to explore and assert their newfound autonomy as they strive for independence. One way to assert independence is to refuse to comply with the requests or commands of the parent/caregiver. However, parent/caregivers who recognize toddlers' need for autonomy structure opportunities in which toddlers can be independent, thereby reducing the likelihood that toddlers will not comply with specific requests when asked.

Child-development experts have identified four categories of motivation to comply with a rule or expectation. These four categories are amoral, adherence, identification, and internalization. Infants are born amoral. In other words, they do not have a sense of right or wrong to guide their behaviors. When a curious infant pulls the long hair of the parent/caregiver, the baby does not have the skills to consider how this might be hurtful to the other person or does not immediately have the skill to read the behavioral cues of the adult and interpret them. However, as infants mature they become more skilled at reading behavioral cues and using those cues to guide their own behaviors and adhere to rules. The second category of motivation is adherence. Toddlers adhere to, or comply with, a rule to avoid punishment or to gain a reward, such as praise from a beloved parent/caregiver. Toddlers and young children at the adherence level of thinking do not understand why a certain behavior is appropriate, such as not hitting; they just recognize that the behavior is expected. A more advanced category of compliance motivation is identification. Young children are using identification as a motivation when they comply in order to please or emulate a beloved adult, such as a parent/caregiver. They admire the parent/caregiver and want to act like that person. Therefore, they base their behavioral choices on how they think the adult might respond. The most advanced motivation to comply is internalization. It occurs when the older child or adolescent has developed an internal sense of right and wrong and uses this internal code to guide behavior and compliance to the code.

See also Discipline; Parenting

References and further reading
Kaler, Sandra R., and Claire B. Kopp. 1990. "Compliance and Comprehension in Very Young Toddlers." *Child Development* 61: 1997–2003.

Kostelnik, Marjorie J., et al. 1998. "Guiding Children's Social Development." Albany, NY: Delmar.

Compulsive Behaviors

Some babies and toddlers rock their cribs so hard, the crib makes a dent in the wall plaster. Some rock their own bodies back and forth compulsively. Some twirl their hair, suck their pajama sleeve, or even pull out hair. Some infants are particularly sensitive to stresses, such as moving to a new dwelling or starting out with a new child care provider. Such changes are so stressful for some that the baby uses compulsive body movements to bring down his tension. For example, some babies pull on their penis when a diaper is taken off, or they pat the vulva or penis rhythmically and gently before drifting off to sleep. Other infants with high levels of anxiety pull on their penis all day long in order to ease the tension they are feeling. When a parent or caregiver notices compulsive body behaviors that are prolonged and seem to be done almost desperately by the child, this is an important warning signal. Make sure to try to figure out what is making the child so tense. The next step is for adults to think creatively: How can schedules be changed, or reassurance provided, or more soothing, intimate, loving routines set in place to make the baby feel less tense? Leisurely body massage daily may reduce tensions. More snuggling in the lap, or more time being carried on a hip, are other ways to reassure the baby and decrease anxiety.

Another cause of compulsive body actions is when babies are understimulated. In the Foundling Home where René Spitz did his research years ago, many of the infants left in cribs with no toys or play partners often rocked from side to side. They stared at their fingers over and over as they twisted them into bizarre configurations. Sometimes a quiet, inactive infant is left sitting on the floor of a child-care center for long periods. Because he does not demand attention by crying, the child may compensate for lack of playing time with a caregiver by self-rocking forward and backward. The easiest way to decrease this compulsive rocking is to provide plenty of one-on-one attention and personalized interaction time. For the infant who exhibits trichitillomania (pulling out of hair), the child's pediatrician may be able to prescribe new drugs that can lesson this compulsion.

Conception

The beginning of pregnancy as marked when a sperm, contributed by a male, fertilizes an egg (ovum), contributed by the female. Theoretically, conception can occur any time during the month but is optimal during the time when the ovum is released and travels down the fallopian tube and into the uterus.

See also Prenatal Development

Conditioning

See Learning

Congenital Abnormalities

Congenital abnormalities are birth defects that occur because of problems during cell division or because of difficulties with the uterine environment. Typically they do not include genetic abnormalities that might also cause birth defects.

Conscience

Conscience is the internalization of rules (moral standards) of conduct (behavior).

See also Discipline; Parenting; Prosocial Behavior

Constancy

Constancy means that objects are real things in and of themselves that exist independent from our perceptions of them. They also are endowed with certain properties and characteristics that are inherent—part of what they are. For example, round balls will always be round, not square. When a round ball is squashed, it no longer is round and therefore is no longer a round ball. Its inherent roundness no longer is part of it. This concept is derived from Jean Piaget's theory of cognitive development. Infants are said to learn this idea of constancy by the end of the infancy years and to refine it within the preoperational period (age two to seven years).

Constructivism

This is the perspective that individuals play an active role in their own development. The meaning of self, others, objects, and events is derived from experience, and constructivists maintain that the organism plays an active and critical role in structuring and engaging the environment. In Jean Piaget's theory of cognitive development, constructivism is the most basic assumption made about human nature and the learning process.

Context Effects

From the moment of conception, all development occurs in an environment.

The environment and the events that take place in that environment provide the contexts within which biopsychosocial development occurs. Contexts that may have a direct or indirect effect on infant development include such factors as family income, social support, family density, single parenthood, urban or rural residence, and parents' education.

Contingency Awareness

Contingency awareness means becoming aware of the relationships among events in one's environment, or of the relationship between one's own behavior and the consequences of that behavior (i.e., the expectation that B must occur before A can, or the probability that A leads to the occurrence of B). John Watson, a psychologist at the University of California–Berkeley, argued that learning in infants consisted, in part, of becoming aware of the relationships between events. But from his perspective, learning was not specific to the events (mother's voice predicts her arrival with a bottle), but rather consisted of learning that A predicts B. That is, it was the idea that the relationships between events are either predictable or they are not. Watson was one of the first to suggest that infants were active learners, extrapolating broader cognitive rules than previously imaged by researchers.

See also Learning

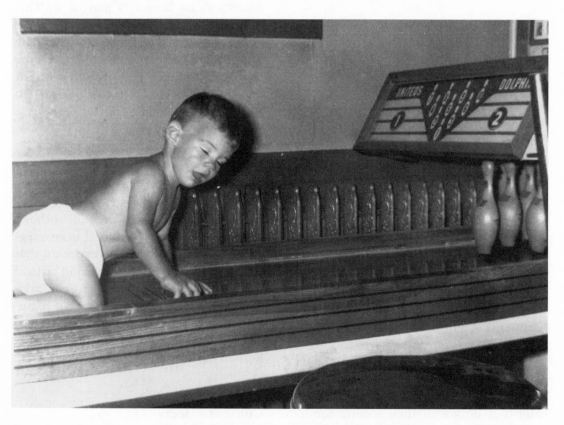

Learning takes place in extremely diverse settings, many of which have not been as intensively studied as they are in laboratory settings. (Courtesy of Hiram Fitzgerald)

Contingent

A relationship involving a dependency: To say that B is contingent upon A implies that A must occur before B can. In operant conditioning, receiving a reinforcer is said to be contingent upon the occurrence of an operant (the baby cries and is breastfed). In conjugate reinforcement, receiving a reinforcer is contingent both upon producing the operant (kicking produces a moving mobile) and upon the rate at which the operant occurs (the rate of the baby's kicks determines the amount of reinforcement received).

Contingent Responsiveness to Infant Cues

Another's response to an infant behavior that leads to a predictable sequence: Baby smiles, mother vocalizes, baby smiles, mother vocalizes, and so on. The adult responds to the infant's behavior in a prompt and predictable fashion.

Continuity

See Theories of Development

Continuum of Caregiving Casualty

A concept advanced by Arnold Sameroff to express the idea that developmental outcome is always the product of genotype, phenotype, and environtype (i.e., the environment within which infants are reared) and that biological risk alone is insufficient to account for development because it does not take into account the transactional relationship between the organism and the environment. Sameroff posed the continuum to counter the strong biological base for the continuum of reproductive casualty.

Continuum of Reproductive Casualty

The concept used to express the range of biological disability possible. The idea is that the degree of biological disability predicts the life-course outcomes for the individual. It is contrasted with the continuum of caregiving casualty. In reality, developmental outcomes are likely based on transactions between the biological presenting state characteristics of the individual and the various environmental contextual relationships the individual encounters over the life course.

Contraception

Contraception is the deliberate prevention of pregnancy. There are many methods, including hormonal contraction, the intrauterine device (IUD), surgical sterilization, the barrier method, spermicides, family planning, and abstinence. Hormonal contraceptives deliver the female sex hormones estrogen and progesterone into the body. These interfere with ovulation and affect the condition of the uterine lining to prevent the implantation of fertilized eggs. These hormones can be administered in pill form, through skin implants, or by injection and are available only by prescription. The IUD is a small plastic device inserted into the uterus that prevents pregnancy by either interfering with the ability of sperm to fertilize the egg, or by preventing a fertilized egg from implanting into the uterine wall. Methods of surgical sterilization are almost 100 percent effective in preventing pregnancy. These surgical procedures, tubal ligation for women and vasectomy for men, should be considered as permanent forms of birth control even though surgical techniques have been developed to reverse the original procedures. Barrier methods provide physical barriers that prevent the sperm from entering the uterus. Such methods include the male and female condoms, the diaphragm, and the cervical cap. Spermicides are chemicals inserted into the vagina that kill sperm. Natural family planning, or the rhythm method, relies on abstaining from sexual intercourse during the phase of the menstrual cycle where a women is most fertile (from five days before ovulation to two days after ovulation). Abstinence, or the avoidance of any sexual activity, is 100 percent effective as a contraceptive technique.

Cooing Turns
See Language

Coparenting
Coparenting means the interactions, feelings, and perceptions between parents (or parental figures) directed toward the mutual caregiving of their children. The conception of a coparenting relationship, as opposed to individual mother-child and father-child relationships, is relatively new. Most theory and research on family influences on child development have focused on the mother's role in parenting, with an occasional study examining the father's role. However, mothers and fathers do not interact with their children in isolation from each other; parents mutually affect and are affected by each other's attitudes, judgments, and behaviors toward their children. For example, when one parent chooses to let an infant play with the contents of a kitchen drawer, the other parent may have substantially different ideas regarding whether such behavior is safe and appropriate and

whether it should be allowed and encouraged. Parents must work through these sorts of issues on a daily basis, and the ways that parents behave toward each other during negotiations and their feelings about their mutual parenting represent the concept of coparenting.

From the perspective of family systems theory, a two-parent family with one child contains several subsystems: the marital relationship between the parents, the individual parent-child relationships between each parent and the child, and the coparenting relationship between the two parents. Each of these systems affects the others. For example, a disagreement between parents about whether to let the child cry himself to sleep or to comfort him might cause friction in the marital relationship, and a lack of consensus between parents regarding how to discipline the child for defying a parent can spill over into the relationship between the parent and child. Thus, coparenting is fundamentally an object of the family system, and changes in the coparenting relationship are likely to resonate across the family.

The coparenting partnership is initiated upon the transition to parenthood, when the first child is born (although couples who have intensively planned their pregnancy can begin negotiating the coparenting partnership even before the child arrives). Before the transition to parenthood, most couples have developed stable ways of interacting. In other words, for the most part they have agreed which partner will do which chores, how to allocate time and activities spent with friends and family, ways to ask for and show emotional support, and other issues that couples encounter in daily life. The period immediately after the transition to

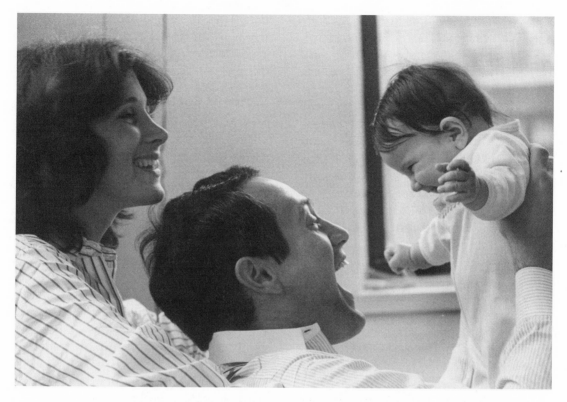

A mother and father interacting with their baby. (Shirley Zeiberg)

parenthood requires the couple to integrate an entirely new individual, whose unique personality cannot be anticipated, into the existing procedures that guide the family—and this will demand change and compromise. This process is made especially difficult because partners often have different expectations of how coparenting will proceed. Some couples plan that all tasks will be divided equally, including diaper changes, doctor's visits, feeding, and seeking day-care providers, whereas others expect that most caregiving responsibilities will fall to one parent, usually the mother. When partners have differing expectations, they need to renegotiate the family procedures. Otherwise,

a problematic coparenting relationship can easily result.

Definitions of Coparenting and the Division of Labor

Coparenting can be defined in several ways, which are described below.

The division of labor is the most concrete way to assess coparenting, as it describes which parent is responsible (or is perceived to be responsible) for each aspect of parenting and family life. Multiple methods of measuring the division of labor have been utilized. First, some researchers measure the absolute amount of time, or the number of hours, that each parent spends in caregiving activities.

Families that use child care are likely to spend fewer total hours in caregiving than families that do not use child care. Second, we can measure how much responsibility one parent has relative to how much responsibility the other parent has. This method does not give information about how much time parents spend in caregiving but rather describes who does what. A third way to measure the division of labor is to determine the degree of difference between partners in time spent, with the result that parents might spend similar or very different amounts of time in caregiving. These three approaches (absolute time, relative time, and discrepancies between partners) describe the ways that parents have overtly or implicitly negotiated caregiving roles in the family. The way that couples decide to divide labor characterizes particular types of coparenting partnerships, such as traditional (the mother does most of the caregiving) or egalitarian (parents divide caregiving more equally).

It is important to note that a satisfactory coparenting relationship does not necessarily mean that parents divide responsibility equally. If the mother is responsible for virtually all caregiving tasks, but is happy with the arrangement, and the father is content to relinquish responsibility, this too can be considered a satisfactory coparenting partnership. Two other approaches to measuring the division of caregiving relate to satisfaction with the functioning of the coparenting relationship. First, we can measure people's expectations before the child is born for how labor will be divided and see how well those expectations match with the way labor is actually divided after the child is born. Second, we can assess whether each parent perceives the division of caregiving as being

fair. That is, the critical factor is not whether one parent does the majority of the work but rather whether he/she feels the division is unanticipated and unfair. Perceptions of the fairness have major implications for the degree of conflict present in the couple's relationship.

The division of caregiving includes many different aspects of family work that tend to be allotted to mothers and fathers in distinct ways. Four dimensions of division of labor that have been discussed are direct care, managerial care, play, and emotional care. Direct care, which is used most frequently to describe caregiving labor, includes tasks that immediately affect the child's comfort and well-being; parents must decide who will feed, dress, and change the baby. Mothers tend to have primary responsibility for these tasks, especially during infancy, with fathers participating consistently less than mothers.

This marked division occurs immediately upon the transition to parenthood and is likely to result from a variety of factors. Social-role expectations suggest that women are better suited as caregivers while men should be breadwinners. Women can also breastfeed their babies, which places them in closer proximity to the child and makes them more likely to assume other maintenance functions as well. Mothers are also more likely to take family leave, usually until the child is a minimum of six to twelve weeks old, and can easily fall into taking most responsibility for caring for the child's needs even after returning to work. However, many parents do not expect the division of child care to be so unequal. In addition, whereas mothers typically do more direct care than they anticipated, both mothers and fathers report doing more than their partners credit them for. This sets up a

A single teenage mother at home with her mother and baby. (Shirley Zeiberg)

situation that has the potential for resentment and problems if the couple lacks the resources to negotiate a satisfactory compromise—or weather it out until better times arrive.

Because fathers do less direct caregiving than mothers, it has often been suggested that fathers do not parent well enough or often enough compared to mothers. However, it is unclear whether less direct caregiving on the part of fathers is related to child outcomes, and it may be that children are affected only when mothers become sufficiently unhappy with the division of caregiving to lead to strained relations in the coparenting partnership. Moreover, most research on the division of direct care has been conducted when children are infants, a period that requires more direct care than subsequent developmental periods. As children grow older and increasingly self-sufficient, the division of direct care can become less controversial.

In addition to direct maintenance tasks, parents must also determine how to divide managerial, organizational, or indirect care; these are more intermittent tasks that provide resources for the child or coordinate the child's overall activities. Managerial tasks include arranging child care, making health care appointments, updating immunizations, coordinating play dates, buying clothing, and directing children in self-management (e.g., cleaning room, brushing teeth). Almost exclusively, mothers are responsible for the managerial functions of the household. In addition, organization of the father's participation in caregiving tasks (asking the father to change diapers or feed the child, recruiting the father to take the child to the doctor) can also be considered a managerial responsibility assumed by mothers.

As children grow older, the level of managerial care is likely to remain relatively consistent, but the types of tasks change: older children need rides to and from school, activities, and friends' homes, homework assistance, and guidance in following household rules. Evidence suggests that even among older children mothers are more likely to have managerial responsibility, but much more research needs to be conducted, especially among parents of adolescents. Once again, however, if mothers resent this responsibility or fathers disagree with the choices made, the coparenting relationship is weakened.

A third aspect of the division of caregiving is play, and it is within the play domain that the greatest differences in the quality of mothers' and fathers' behavior emerges. Mothers play more with their children, but fathers spend proportionately more of their time with their children in play, so playing tends to be more associated with fathers. The quality of fathers' play also differs from that of mothers. Fathers tend toward physical, arousing play, involving large-limb movements, bouncing, lifting, outdoor play, and excursions, whereas mothers tend toward quieter play that involves objects, reading, and conventional games such as peek-a-boo.

Fathers' focus on physical play can contribute to child development in unique ways by promoting gross motor skills and spatial abilities. Additionally, when fathers stimulate children through roughhousing, children become highly aroused and are thereby forced to learn to calm themselves down. Alternatively, mothers' focus on quiet, instructive play suggests that they use reading or toy manipulation to encourage children's cognitive and fine motor abilities and to provide challenging learning experiences. The experiences of a child when playing with a father tend to be different. Maternal play is often embedded within ongoing caregiving activities—that is, mother tidies up, puts a load of laundry in, helps the child make a block tower, makes a snack, reads a book to the child, and so forth; playtime with mothers is more likely to be part of a continuous flow of activity. Playtime with father is more likely to occur as a special, uninterrupted activity, which may give paternal play a special quality.

The division of play also has implications for the coparenting relationship. On the one hand, fathers' tendency to roughhouse can cause some mothers to become concerned about their child's safety and introduce coparental conflict; on the other hand, mothers can find paternal play a welcome break from caregiving and see it as an opportunity for emotional engagement between father and child. Most of the research on parent-infant and family interaction uses structured tasks in which the parent attempts to teach the child about a toy or read the child a book. Because mothers are more likely to do these activities as part of quiet play, the findings from these studies can underestimate the role of fathers in family process.

A final dimension of the division of labor is emotional care: soothing, holding, and affection, asking the child about his/her day, and discussing the child's concerns. Through these interactions, parents teach children about emotions and how to manage anger and distress. Although little research exists on emotional care as a domain of the division of labor, evidence suggests that mothers are more likely to take on emotional work for the family. When mothers are present, fathers, even those who are primary caregivers, show less touching, holding, and physical affection to their infants than do mothers. When fathers do hold infants, they usually do so as a part of play. As a whole, these findings suggest that fathers may be less likely to do emotional work and that the quality of emotional involvement with children is sometimes different for mothers and fathers, although specifics are not clear. One possibility is that mothers can be responsible for socializing children to a wider range of emotions than fathers, who may be associated with more extreme and intense emotions such as joy and excitability (during play) and irritation and anger (when frustrated).

In general, the division of family work has two major implications for coparenting. First, the way responsibilities are divided between parents can be a driving force behind conflicts within the coparenting relationship; each parent's satisfaction with the division of labor for mundane tasks is likely to be associated with the quality of coparenting, whether hostile or cooperative. Second, the division of labor affects the *experience* of the coparenting dyad and the family system for the child. When fathers provide a substantial amount of caregiving, in whatever form, children are likely to perceive roles and relationships differently and to reap the benefits of having two parents attending to their physical and emotional welfare.

Coparenting Interactions
The coparenting relationship also includes ways that parents interact with each other when together with their infant. Three dimensions of coparenting behavior that have been identified are hostile/competitive, harmonious, and discrepant (in which one parent is noticeably less involved than the other parent). To assess the coparenting atmosphere, observers rate parents' behaviors; for example, parents can actively work together to teach the baby new tasks or to calm an irritable infant. Alternatively, they can try to undermine each other, compete for the baby's attention, and dismiss each other's attempts to join in the play.

Factors before the child's birth can indicate what the future holds for a couple's coparenting relationship. Fathers who feel that their own parents had a poor coparenting relationship are more likely to interact in a hostile-competitive way or to be disengaged from family play when their infants are aged six months. In addition, mothers who dislike having their judgments questioned also have husbands who tend to be more disengaged from the family. This suggests that when fathers have poor role models for coparenting, and when mothers have difficulty encouraging the father to participate in interacting with the infant, then the coparenting relationship is at risk for problems.

When couples also experience marital problems, poor coparenting can have effects on children, with different outcomes depending on the child's sex. One researcher found that parents of boys tended to be more hostile toward each other and to compete for the child's attention. However, parents of girls presented a pattern in which the mother was unusually involved with the child and the father was distant and uninvolved. This suggests that when the marriage is in trouble fathers might be more motivated to fight for involvement with the child when the child is a boy. Furthermore, parents who displayed hostile coparenting behaviors when their children were less than a year old had more aggressive children by the time they were preschoolers, whereas more discrepant parents had withdrawn, inhibited preschoolers.

Parenting Alliance

The prior definitions of coparenting have been centered around behaviors, but coparenting can also be defined in terms of feelings and perceptions. The aspect of the coparenting partnership that taps the subjective feelings of the parents is called the "parenting alliance," conceived as growing out of the already established marital relationship upon the transition to parenthood. Children present new parents with challenges that make vulnerable their self-esteem and sense of self in the parenting role. When parents have a well-functioning parenting alliance, they are able to provide support to one another to guard against these threats and maintain a sense of well-being as parents. To establish a successful parenting alliance, four criteria must be met: Each parent must be invested in the child; value the other parent's involvement; respect the other parent's judgments about parenting; and desire to communicate with the other about parenting issues. Thus, the parenting alliance represents perceptions of support, respect, and value for and by one's coparenting partner.

To assess feelings about the parenting alliance, each parent answers a questionnaire that includes questions such as "If my baby needs something important, I can rely on my spouse to provide it" and "My spouse likes to play with the baby but leaves the dirty work to me." On average, mothers report a lower parenting alliance than do fathers. That is, fathers are more likely to feel that mothers are committed to the coparenting effort, willing to make sacrifices for their partner's well-being, and willing to provide coparenting assistance. Because mothers do most of the caregiving, it is unsurprising that they tend to feel less satisfied with the state of the coparenting relationship. Fathers are more likely to feel that mothers lack respect for their parenting skills.

Research has examined the specific processes through which the parenting alliance might be associated with paternal involvement. Among mothers, all three factors predicted father involvement. Mothers who feel that the father is a good parent, perceive coparental child-rearing philosophies to be similar, and feel respected for their parenting have families with more involved fathers. For fathers, however, the critical factor in the level of involvement is whether they think their wife has confidence in them as a parent. Notably, the ways that parents actually behave together in the family triad are primarily related to *fathers'* feelings about the coparenting relationship. Fathers who feel unsupported and criticized come from families in which mothers and fathers showed discrepant degrees of engagement, with the father typically the less involved partner.

For both fathers and mothers, positive perceptions of the parenting alliance have been associated with higher perceptions of parenting competence, authoritative parenting styles, and lower levels of stress. Fathers' perceptions of the parenting alliance appear especially related to child outcomes, including paternal reports of attachment to the child and to children's positive functioning as rated by mothers, fathers, and teachers. In fact, some evidence suggests that fathers who experience a successful parenting alliance can have an *increased* vulnerability to stress; these fathers have been shown to report higher stress levels during a child's mild illness than fathers who are less satisfied with the parenting alliance. These fathers who report a stronger parenting alliance can be more involved fathers, whose lives are disrupted by child illness, both emotionally and because these fathers may be willing to take off work to care for the child.

Certain factors present before the child's birth indicate whether the early parenting alliance will be positive or problematic. The quality of the marriage before the birth is an especially good indicator of the subsequent parenting alliance. A couple that has established a warm, cooperative, and supportive prebirth relationship is far more likely to be able to work out differences later on. Although the transition to parenthood is, on average, related to decreases in marital satisfaction for new parents, many couples actually become more content with their spousal relationship after the transition to parenthood, and this is most likely to occur among happily married couples.

Higher socioeconomic status is also predictive of a more satisfactory parenting alliance. Highly educated couples may have more reasonable expectations for their partner's behaviors in coparenting, and educated fathers in particular tend to participate more in coparenting. In addition, greater financial security allows coparents more security, less stress, and can even provide funds to hire a baby-sitter so the parents can take breaks from caregiving, an option less available to financially strapped parents.

Individual beliefs, attitudes, and personality characteristics also affect the development of the coparenting relationship. For example, the expectations that mothers and fathers hold for life after the child's birth can affect how they cope with the reality of parenting. If parents are extremely motivated to have children, they may cope better, having fulfilled their dreams—or they may find that their expectations for a calm baby that they can rock and cuddle is not quite in line with the reality of an infant who is colicky, a fitful sleeper, and requires constant attention. Individuals whose expectations for the coparenting behavior of their partner are more realistic are less likely to encounter unpleasant surprises.

Flexibility, a lack of defensiveness, and an ability to be mature and empathic to other's frustrations and ideas are also important qualities in developing a cooperative parenting partnership. Moreover, fathers especially appear to be more satisfied and cooperative coparents when they have had good role models in their own parents. It may be that women are steered toward the parental role from early on but that fathers benefit particularly by being able to observe good coparents in action.

Finally, a positive parenting alliance is more likely to develop when parents hold similar beliefs regarding ways in which children should be raised. These may be issues pertaining to discipline, sleeping arrangements, or expression of affection. When major disagreements are found between parents' reports, the coparenting relationship is at risk. Moreover, couples who are unable to satisfactorily negotiate solutions to these differences are likely to reflect their differences through problematic coparenting practices.

The parenting alliance continues to be affected by changing relationships after the child's birth. Mothers are especially vulnerable to changes in the division of labor and are most disillusioned in the first months of infancy when they do the vast majority of work. However, as infants develop, fathers become more involved, both because many mothers return to work and because children become more active and engaging. As fathers grow more involved, mothers become increasingly satisfied with the coparenting relationship.

Coparenting the Changing Infant
Children change over time, and so do the demands of coparenting. The ways that parents are required to work together to meet the needs of an infant differ from the tasks they must accomplish with a toddler or adolescent. Predominantly, young infants require direct caregiving and maintenance, such as feeding, changing, and bathing. Parents must also regulate the emotional status of the infant by holding, rocking, and singing to him/her when overstimulated and fussy, and by playing with him/her when alert and interested. For coparents with an infant, these are the primary tasks about which they must coordinate and agree—and because direct tasks such as changing and feeding are frequent but not especially enjoyable, the division of labor tends to be the most controversial issue for parents of infants.

Other coparenting issues, such as sleeping arrangements and extended family, also arise with the birth of a new infant. Parents must agree about whether to pick up the baby or let him/her cry it

out, and whether the infant should sleep in a crib or a family bed, in the parents room or a separate room, and so forth. A new baby also tends to bring extended family such as grandparents and siblings into greater contact, which can sometimes cause conflict between parents. In addition, free time decreases, and it becomes more difficult to continue activities with friends.

As children grow into toddlerhood, they explore and investigate to a greater extent, and independence becomes an issue. With the arrival of the word "no" and the child's expression of his/her own demands, agreement about rules and limits becomes paramount in order to socialize the child while providing a safe context for exploration. This is likely to be a controversial time for many parents, particularly those who have different ideas about how permissive or restrictive one should be with children. Children and families are particularly vulnerable when one parent gives a child free rein while the other attempts to restrain him/her. In this case, one parent is vulnerable to becoming the bad guy.

Who Can Coparent?
Coparenting is not limited to married couples, or even to unmarried heterosexual couples. From a diverse perspective, any combination of people who come together in the service of a child can potentially be coparents. One notable example is the case of divorced parents; although they no longer have a marital relationship, in most cases they continue to have contact to discuss and coordinate issues for the good of their children. Research on children of divorced couples has revealed that when parents maintain good relations after divorce and do not

denigrate their former spouse or prompt their children to take sides, children do better emotionally, socially, and academically than children whose parents are hostile and place their children in the middle of the conflict.

Adolescent mothers frequently form coparenting relationships with their own mothers, so that both the biological mother and grandmother care for the child. Most research on this type of coparenting dyad focuses on the effects on the adolescent mother herself, and little is known about how children fare when they have access to what is in effect two mothers. Most likely, as in other coparenting partnerships, outcomes depend on the degree of agreement and the way that disagreements are negotiated between the teen and her mother about child-related issues. If the pair has markedly different ideas regarding the proper way to raise the child, the coparenting relationship will be poor and the child will be caught in the middle.

Gay and lesbian couples with children also form coparenting partnerships, although little is known about the ways in which gay couples coparent similarly or differently from other coparenting dyads. Single parents often coparent with the biological parent of the child, a boyfriend or girlfriend, or, sometimes, a sibling or friend who is willing to take partial responsibility for the child. In extreme cases, a social-service worker or juvenile-court representative can act as a coparent, although not on a full-time basis.

See also Parenting

References and further reading
Cowan, P. A., and J. P. McHale. 1996. "Coparenting in a Family Context: Emerging Achievements, Current Dilemmas, and Future Directions." In J. P. McHale and P. A. Cowan, eds., *Understanding How Family-Level Dynamics Affect Children's Development: Studies of Two-Parent Families*. San Francisco: Jossey-Bass, pp. 93–106.
Gable, S., J. Belsky, and K. Crnic. 1992. "Marriage, Parenting, and Child Development: Progress and Prospects." *Journal of Family Psychology* 5: 276–294.

Correlation

Correlation is the relationship between two events. Expressed numerically, a correlation refers to the degree to which two events deviate from a perfect relationship. Events can be perfectly positively correlated (1.00), perfectly negatively correlated (–1.00), or not related at all (0.0). In most instances, the degree of relationship falls somewhere between 1.00 and –1.00.

Cortisol

Cortisol is the main glucocorticoid hormone produced by the adrenal cortex. Nearly all of the cortisol in circulation is linked to protein. Cortisol is related to specific physiological activities, including increases in hepatic gluconeogenesis, hepatic glycogenolysis, and protein catabolism; inhibition of ACTH secretion; maintenance of blood pressure; and renal excretion. Serum cortisol solutions show circadian periodicity early in development, with peak fussy-period concentrations usually occurring during the daytime. Although many investigators are heavily studying the possible linkages between cortisol and HIV, the strongest linkages between cortisol and infant behavior are related to maternal stress.

When an individual experiences a stressful event, the adrenal glands produce elevated levels of cortisol. Increases in cortisol means that blood-sugar levels increase and readies the individual to confront stress or to avoid it—sometimes referred to as the "fight-or-flight response." In animals, exposure to high levels of cortisol over a prolonged period of time is related to shrinkage of the hippocampus, an important brain structure involved with attention and information-processing. Studies of soldiers diagnosed with post-traumatic stress disorder have demonstrated smaller hippocampus structures as well.

Studies of depressed mothers have demonstrated high levels of cortisol in both mothers and infants, particularly infants who are being breastfed. Thus, there is the possibility that exposure to chronically stressed mothers or fathers can lead to elevated cortisol levels in infants. Whether such elevated levels have an impact on the hippocampus or on attention and information-processing remains to be determined, but some evidence clearly points in that direction.

Cosleeping
See Family Bed

Crack Babies
See Alcoholism; Cocaine Addiction; Drugs; Prematurity; Prenatal Development

Crano-Facial Anomalies
See Genetic Disorders

Crawling
See Motor Development

Creativity
Creativity is hard to define and even harder to assess. A creative product should be something original and useful as judged by an appropriate audience. This usually requires a demonstration of divergent thinking or generating multiple answers to a problem. There is, at present, no good way to measure creativity. Creativity, however, plays a major role in the way that the infant and young child come to understand the world and how things work. For example, within Jean Piaget's theory of cognitive development, children are constantly trying out behaviors and observing the consequences of these actions. Devising new behavioral strategies and solving problems in novel ways requires creative thought. Creative thought, used as a means of experimentation, leads to learning.

See also Curiosity

Creeping
See Motor Development

Cri-Du-Chat
Cri-du-chat is a chromosomal disorder caused by a dysfunction in chromosome 5. Characteristics of the disorder include facial anomalies, mental retardation, small head and brain size, and a cry that subjectively sounds like a cat. This feature is so prominent that it became the basis for the disorder's name.

See also Crying

Critical Period
A time when the organization of a structure or behavior is most easily influenced

positively or negatively by environmental events.

See also Sensitive Period; Theories of
Development

Cross-Cultural Research

Cross-cultural research compares two or more cultures or cultural areas: race, ethnicity, beliefs, behaviors, and traditions. Such research is carried out when a person from one culture studies the characteristics of another or when two or more cultures are compared and contrasted. Culture plays an important role as an influence on the perceptions, behaviors, and development of infants and toddlers. Culture influences the expectations of developmental milestones, as well as practices regarding feeding, sleeping, toilet learning, discipline, and play. Studying the childrearing and child-care practices of other nations and ethnic groups is cross-cultural research applied to child development. Different peoples and societies have varying beliefs and behaviors regarding the definition of parenthood, the desired outcomes for raising children, expected childhood behaviors and developmental stages, childrearing routines, and child-care practices.

One's own culture informs the lens of perspective used to view another culture. If parameters for behavior are based on the researcher's own culture, the culture being observed may be seen in a negative light. However, if the viewer is objective in recording the beliefs and behaviors of the other culture, a favorable portrait may be obtained.

To begin objectively exploring the cultural characteristics of a group of people, one should value diversity, have an understanding of one's own cultural beliefs and practices, and be willing to remain objective and to adapt varying perspectives if necessary. They must have cultural competence. Most people believe that there is only one correct way to rear children and that all parents desire the same goal. That is not so. In the United States, the goal for most parents is to raise independent and self-sufficient offspring. The Puerto Rican culture places emphasis on respect for authority and contribution to the welfare of the nation. In Italy, the goals for children focus on the importance of family. Infants are included in all aspects of family life from birth. They are raised to become interdependent adults who readily contribute to the well-being of the family. Still, other cultures might prioritize other issues, such as spiritual development, as being primary to the optimal development of infants. How each cultural group views the expectations and process of childrearing is based on their deeply seated beliefs and traditions. Cross-cultural research has shown that there are few universals in regard to child development and childrearing practices.

Culture is both a descriptor and a process. As a descriptor, culture designates the characteristics of one's ethnicity, language, geographic location, religion, gender, and age. For example, a mother might list her cultural designations as African American, English-speaking, college graduate, Christian, twenty-three years old, female, married, and residing in a rural area of a midwestern state. Culture could also designate one's abilities and level of learning; for example, an infant would be expected to have fewer mobile and verbal abilities than a toddler and a preschooler. Cultures also overlap and subdivide. For example, an infant might be a member of a large family, a playgroup, and a child-care center. A toddler with cerebral palsy would be designated as a member of the disabled culture. As a process, culture determines the beliefs and common practices among groups. Therefore, any child born with a disability is viewed differently based on his/her cultural heritage and this culture's beliefs about disabilities and illnesses, their causes, treatments, and attitudes toward helpers. For example, African Americans can view a child born with a disability as divine punishment resulting from the sins of the parent. As a result, spiritual intervention may be sought as treatment for the disability, in addition to or even before medical treatment is considered. History also influences the formation of cultural practices. In the past, society encouraged the institutionalization or isolated care and education of children born with disabilities in the belief that this lessened the pain and stress of the parent. Because of the history of blacks in America, African Americans tend to be less willing to report conditions that might lead to the removal of children from the home. Instead, African Americans are more likely to practice inclusion, involving the child in the regular activities of peers and family and keeping the family together.

Culture also determines the definitions of roles, rules for behavior, occurrence of events, aspired goals, and measures of success. For example, U.S. hospitals typically circumcise all male infants within a few days of birth as a standard health precaution and procedure. Also, in the Jewish culture, male infants are circumcised, but as a religious act symbolizing the child's covenant with God. In some African cultures, both male and female youth may be circumcised at about age twelve, as a ceremonial

act designating their promotion to the status of an adult and their ability to marry and become parents. In contrast, circumcision of males or females is rare in other cultures, such as the Mexican culture.

The consideration of multicultural perspectives regarding child care has increased as the United States tries to meet the needs of all its citizens. Many are beginning to recognize that the United States is not a homogenous melting-pot where all cultures blend together. Rather, America is better described as a heterogeneous stew-pot, where each culture is recognized as a distinctly different ingredient bringing a contribution to the dish and enhancing its richness yet retaining its individual essence of being.

As more cultures enter America, consensus regarding the norms of child care and childrearing practices becomes even harder to define. What has been typically defined as setting the standards for U.S. child-care practices is based mostly on Euro-American cultural beliefs. Although these beliefs can resonate favorably with most white middle-class Americans, they rarely reflect the beliefs and traditions of ethnic minorities. The U.S. model of childrearing emphasizes individuality, independence, free exploration, and early stimulation of intellect and language. These values set the standard for measuring developmental growth. Thus, children are assessed by their achievement of milestones such as adapting to parent established schedules, ability to sleep alone and through the night, eat solids, walk unaided separate from parent, and acquire language skills. The majority of other world cultures do not share the same emphasis on autonomy and independence.

For other cultures, more emphasis is placed on developing and supporting social relationships, group membership, interdependence, and cooperation. Measurements of developmental milestones can be based more on observations of the strengths of social relationships young children have with others rather than focusing on individual accomplishments. As a result of the different emphasis for development, ethnic minority children often reach some of the white American milestones at later ages. One study of age expectations for milestone attainment noted that Anglo American children were expected to use a training cup by twelve months of age. In comparison, Puerto Rican children did not attain this goal until seventeen months, and Filipinos were about twenty-one months old before they used the training cup. However, when measuring for ages when children were toilet trained or toilet learned, Filipino children were twenty months, Puerto Rican children were twenty-nine months, and Anglo American children were more than thirty-one months.

Childrearing beliefs, practices, and desired outcomes reflect the ideals, social networks, and developmental expectations of the culture. They set the context or developmental niche for development. In Italy, where family involvement is important, infants may not have a set time for napping or sleeping. It is more important that they spend as much time as possible interacting with and becoming a vital part of the family. Therefore, they stay up until they fall asleep on their own. In comparison, most American infants have set times for napping and have a usual bedtime. In Italy, Japan, and Mayan cultures, infants sleep with their parents and/or other family members as a way of learning to harmonize with the group. Italian children may sleep with parents until age two. Japanese children usually sleep with

someone (parent, sibling, or extended family member) up to the age of fifteen. In America, infants are expected to sleep alone, in a separate bed and separate room, as a way of encouraging self-reliance. Anglo American mothers emphasize verbal communication and are known to talk directly to and often with their babies. In cultures where babies are carried on the backs of their mothers until actively mobile, about age two, more emphasis is placed on nonverbal communication. Social interaction is carried out through touch and body language. Less emphasis is placed on eye-to-eye contact or verbal communication. In some cultures, for example, the Gusii of Africa, direct eye contact, especially between adult and child, is an impropriety of social behavior. It shows lack of respect for the hierarchical positions of elders.

In addition to sleeping arrangements and communication, cultural context also influences feeding, response time to crying, what children are taught and expected to learn, how they learn, and who cares for children. Most cultures emphasize the role of the mother as the primary caregiver. Caregiving responsibilities can then extend to father, siblings, extended family, tribal members, and community. Beliefs about who is responsible for the care of children set the standards for child-care arrangements.

Cultures that emphasize the importance of family and extended family can be more prone to choose relative care (kin or informal care). It refers to the use of family members as primary caregivers in absence of the mother. In African nations where babies are carried on the mother's back while she works, when they become actively mobile they are left in the care of grandmothers or older siblings. Relative care is also found to be more prevalent among ethnic minority American cultures, as most place great importance on the extended family's role in the rearing of the child. Relative care is seen as an appropriate strategy for supporting family structure and networks. It is also believed to lessen the trauma of parental separation.

Another familial type of child care is communal care. This is usually seen in societies where the importance of community membership and sharing is emphasized. Israeli kibbutzim child care is probably the most notable commune-based program. Founded by Zionist pioneers as a way to promote economic survival, the kibbutz provides child care for all infants from six weeks of age on. New mothers are allowed maternity leave for up to six weeks, after which they are expected to return to working part-time, progressing toward full-time work by twelve weeks. At six weeks, infants are assigned to beds in the infant homes. The infant homes are designed to house two caregivers and six to eight infants. Infants spend the daylight hours with the caregivers and peers. They go home with parents at the end of the workday and return to the infant house the next morning.

Colombian child care is also a community effort based on need in the poorest of urban neighborhoods. Community mothers are selected from the neighborhoods to care for fifteen children in their homes. The national government pays them a small monthly stipend, provides initial caregiving training, and makes loans possible for upgrading homes so that they meet the minimum child-care standards. The parents of ten to fifteen of these group homes form an association to oversee the running of the homes in their community. Local schools and businesses also are partners with the association and provide technical support and training as needed.

Denmark also considers its national child-care program as community-based. Each municipality, or *kommune,* guarantees child-care placement of children at one year, regardless of economic status. Infants enter child care between six months and one year. There is a statutory-paid maternity leave for mothers, which extends from four weeks before birth until fourteen weeks after. This is followed by paid parental leave of ten weeks for one or both parents. Most Danish children stay in day care until they enter school at age seven. Fairly homogenous and politically socialist countries, Denmark, France, and Italy have nationally subsidized universal child-care programs and policies that benefit all children and families regardless of socioeconomic standing.

As a result of the multicultural, multiethnic, and multieconomic status of U.S. society, there is little consensus regarding child-care policies that meet the needs of all citizens. As a democracy, the United States allows states, local governments, and citizens to decide on the choice of care that best benefits the individual child and family. Child-care programs, regulations, subsidies, and quality differ dramatically from state to state. Types of child care range from in-home nannies to center-based care. Most child-care concerns are in regard to availability, affordability, and quality. State-regulated welfare reforms have created a need for more odd-hour care, as more parents in need of child care work second and third shifts and during weekends. There is also a drastic need for sick child care (substitute care for sick children), special-needs care for children with disabilities, and respite care for parents of children with special needs. Nationally, child-care issues also focus on paid family leave, child health insurance, federal subsidies, and quality control.

Cross-cultural research applied to child development helps to explain cultural contexts and how they influence beliefs and practices. It helps one to see that there is more than one acceptable road to take to becoming an adult. What one's road entails is based on his/her culture. Effective cross-cultural research of child development requires one to be aware of her own cultural beliefs and how they provide the lenses for viewing others; acknowledge and consider the cultural beliefs of the parents, community, and society in regard to childrearing and child care; and accept the road chosen by the culture as being best for the child within context of his/her family, community, and society.

See also Cultural Competence

References and further reading
Anderson, P. P., and Emily S. Fenichel. 1989. "Serving Culturally Diverse Families of Infants and Toddlers with Disabilities." *Zero to Three*. Washington, D.C.: Zero to Three.
Carlson, V. J., and R. L. Harwood. 1999/2000. "Understanding and Negotiating Cultural Differences Concerning Early Development Competence: The Six Raisin Solution." *Zero to Three* 20(3): 19–24.
Culturally and Linguistically Appropriate Services. Early Childhood Research Institute (website 2001). http://www.clas.uiuc.edu/.
Hoffman, Lois W. 1988. "Cross-cultural Differences in Childrearing Goals." In R. A. LeVine, P. M. Miller, and M. M. West, eds., *Parental Behavior in Diverse Societies: New Directions for Child Development*. San Francisco: Jossey-Bass, pp. 99–122.
Mann, Tammy L. 1999. "The Power of Providing Culturally Relevant Services." Paper presented at the conference for the Michigan Association for Infant Mental Health, Ann Arbor. Available on tape from the Michigan Association for Infant Mental Health.
Maternal and Child Health National Center for Cultural Competence (website 2001). http://www.dml. georgetown.edu/departments/pediatrics/gucdc/index.html.
Norton, D. G. 1990. "Understanding the Early Experience of Black Children in High Risk Environments: Culturally and Ecologically Relevant Research as a Guide to Support for Families." *Zero to Three* 10(4): 1–7.
Polk, C. 1994. "Therapeutic Work with African-American Families: Using Knowledge of the Culture." *Zero to Three* 15(2): 9–11.

Cross-Modal Transfer of Knowledge

Cross-modal transfer of knowledge involves using information from one sensory system to develop expectations about what kind of stimulation another sensory system would have experienced from that same object. So, for instance, toddlers who are blindfolded and given a circular toy to touch for a short time can later identify what the object they felt looks like in a two-dimensional picture even though they never actually visually explored the object.

See also Exploratory Behavior; Multi-modal Exploration; Perception

Cross-Sectional Research
See Research Methods

Cruising

Cruising is a locomotion skill in which the infant moves between pieces of furniture or other objects while holding onto them for support. Cruising emerges after the infant gains the skill to pull into a standing position but before the infant walks unassisted.

See also Motor Development

An eight-month-old boy excited at his cruising abilities. (Elizabeth Crews)

Crying

Crying is a rhythmic pattern of vocalization characterized by short bouts of breathy expiration, a long intake of air that sounds like a whistle, then a short rest before the cry begins again. Crying is a signal to caregivers designed to keep them close at hand and expressing a fundamental need of the infant: hunger, thirst, pain, discomfort, loneliness, and so on. The cry is thought to be biologically hard-wired in infants to elicit a response from caregivers. As such, crying becomes an adaptive response, ensuring the survival of the infant by keeping the caregiver nearby and ready to protect the infant as well as take care of all of the infant's needs. The human infant is extremely vulnerable. Unlike other mammals, they are immobile at birth (and for some time thereafter) and are unable to move out of the way of danger or search for food. They must rely completely on caregivers for survival and thus have developed the crying response to help ensure their survival. Physically, body systems such as heartbeat and lung intake, and the muscles of the larynx that modulate sound, are involved in the production of crying sounds. Mentally, crying involves the central nervous system and the autonomic control of internal state as perceived by the infant's brain. In a sense, the baby is conflicted by uncomfortable mental arousal (pain, hunger, etc.) and the automatic desire to inhibit that unpleasant arousal.

How Much Crying Is Normal?

The average Western infant cries twenty-two minutes per day in the first three weeks of life and thirty-four minutes per day until the end of the second month, when crying gradually decreases to fourteen minutes per day by twelve weeks of age. The amount any given baby cries varies greatly, and many babies cry much more than average. Crying seems to peak between six and eight weeks. Across all cultures, infants seem to cry more in the evening than any other time of day.

In many other non-Western cultures, infants cry much less and many virtually not at all. Researchers have speculated that this is due to cultural norms of caring in which infants are held constantly or placed in cloth slings around the parent's body, are breastfed on demand around the clock, sleep with their parents, and are immediately attended to when crying begins—usually by putting the infant to the breast. These cultural norms contrast sharply with Western caregiving, in which infants are generally scheduled for feedings, sleep away from their parents in cribs, are held much less, and are sometimes left to "cry it out."

Types of Cries
Crying immediately becomes a part of an infant's behavior—usually within half an hour after birth. In fact, crying is one of six identified behavior states. Infants cycle between the crying state and other behavioral states of being awake or asleep. Crying remains structurally constant between the second to the sixth month. At this point three kinds of cries emerge as a part of the baby's crying communication: angry, painful, and frustration cries. The angry cry occurs when a large volume of air is forced through the vocal cords. The painful cry comes suddenly and includes long periods of the baby holding its breath. The frustration cry is similar to the painful cry but also has a long whistle. By three months of age, baby's cries shift from expressive crying, when all cries sound the same regardless of what's going on with the baby, to more intentional communicative crying.

Sandy Jones, researcher, writer, and recognized authority on crying babies, has identified several types of crying, including the following:

- Hunger: Hunger cries are rhythmical. There may be a short, explosive cry followed by a pause for catching the breath, then another cry. The hunger cry quickly turns to a painful cry.
- Sleepiness: This cry is less rhythmical than hunger or pain cries, and is often just fussing.
- Thirst: The thirst cry is the same as the hunger cry.

- Stuffy nose: This cry occurs when the infant's nose is plugged, and the baby may wake up crying or stop nursing to cry.
- Air swallowing: This is also a painful cry.
- Wet diaper: This cry may just be fussing. Some babies rarely mind wet or soiled diapers, whereas others may cry every time they urinate or soil a diaper.
- Internal pain: This cry is characterized by its sudden onset. The first cry is loud, long, shrill, and urgent and is followed by a long pause as though the baby is holding its breath. Another scream follows, with a wide-open mouth and arched tongue. The baby's chin may quiver and the hand and feet may be drawn up or may cycle tensely.
- External pain: This cry is the same as for internal pain and typically starts suddenly and for no apparent reason. If a baby continues to cry with a pain cry, and the caregiver has checked all other possible causes for the crying, the following are possible reasons for a baby to cry in pain: circumcision, vaccination reaction, food allergy or intolerance, ear infection, or respiratory infection.
- Fever and illness: This cry is characterized by a whiny, nasal cry similar to a pain cry.
- Anger or frustration: While crying forcefully, the baby's face may have a snarled expression, and his/her hands may be tightly fisted. The baby may also arch his/her back and turn away from the caregiver.
- Tension release from overstimulation: The baby cries long and hard

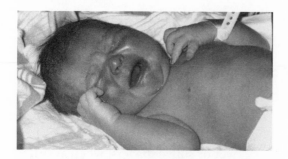

Early in the newborn period caregivers can distinguish the differences between hunger, anger, and pain cries. (Courtesy of Holly Brophy-Herb)

and is unresponsive to efforts to calm him/her. This type of cry usually comes in the evening.

- Bowel movement or urination: The baby may squirm, fuss, grunt, and bear down.
- Too cold: The baby may startle and cry when too cold, especially in the first few weeks after birth.
- Too hot: The baby may be irritable and whiny and may be flushed, sweaty, and breathing rapidly as well.
- Boredom or desire for attention: The baby's coos and gurgles may build up to protests and wails. Picking up the baby brings an instant halt to the crying.

Excessive or Unusual Crying

Some infants exhibit excessive or unusual crying. Colic is a condition characterized by such crying. A colicky baby, according to physicians and researchers, is one who is otherwise healthy but has intense periods of irritability, fussing or crying, lasting for a total of more than three hours a day and occurring on more than three days a week. The colic cry is often paired with the infant's arching of the back and extending or drawing in the legs. The long crying bouts usually begin within a few weeks of birth and last about three months. The colic cry may be strong and similar to a pain cry. Parents of colicky babies need a lot of support, as parenting a colicky baby is stressful. Parents of colicky infants can mistakenly blame themselves for their infant's colic, believing they are not skilled enough as parents. Parents misinformed about colic can blame their infants, believing that the infant is overreacting.

Sometimes serious medical conditions can affect crying behaviors. For instance, cri-du-chat, a chromosomal disorder, is characterized by an infant cry sounding like a cat. Parents become experts at deciphering the cries of their infants, often relying not only on the type of sound emitted but also on contextual cues. For example, parents pay attention to when the cry is vocalized, such as during the usual feeding time or naptime.

Responding to Babies' Cries

When parents respond quickly to their baby's cries, their infants cry less as compared to babies who do not receive immediate responses. Ignoring or delaying response results in more crying and an increased chance of the infant becoming clingy as a toddler. Also, the longer a parent takes to answer a baby's cries, the longer it takes to soothe the baby. The critical cutoff point for answering a baby's cry is a minute and a half. If a parent takes longer than that to answer, the amount of time required to quiet the baby increases by three, four, or in some cases fifty times. How and when parents respond to an infant's cries are dependent on other factors such as their own childhood experiences. Parents who were treated insensitively as infants sometimes have a more difficult time responding sensitively to their own infants. Cultural messages about crying also play a part in shaping how parents think about crying and how they respond to crying. In the United States, crying infant/toddlers are often told to "hush." Crying is often viewed as a negative or a disruptive behavior. However, crying is the primary mode of communication for infants and for many toddlers still struggling to learn oral language.

Constantly "shushing" a baby or ignoring the crying is somewhat like telling a conversation partner to be quiet or ignoring that person. Sometimes babies need to cry to discharge stress, express sadness or frustration, and so on. During these times, a sensitive parent/caregiver will provide emotional and physical support by affirming the infant's distress and holding the infant during the crying. The adult is not ignoring the infant or trying to distract the infant but rather providing a safe and nurturing space in which the baby can release strong emotions.

At other times, soothing strategies—designed to help the baby move from a crying behavioral state to a calm state—are appropriate. Every baby is different, and what will work for one baby may not work for another. In fact, what works for one baby may not work day to day. Infants and caregivers should experiment with the methods that work best. There are a variety of strategies for soothing crying babies, including the following:

- Sucking: Sucking can help a crying baby focus and tune out external signals to return to a calm state. A breast, bottle, pacifier, or finger can be used.
- Sounds: Certain sounds block out other stimuli so the baby can relax and fall asleep. The most effective are monotonous and droning, or rhythmical and repetitive. Examples include talking quietly and continuously, playing music, running the vacuum cleaner, dishwasher, or clothes dryer, white noise or recordings of womb noises, and so on.
- Motion: Motion acts as an inhibitor of minor discomforts, and rhythmical motion stimulates the baby's vestibular system. Walking with the baby, swinging up and down or side to side, a rocking chair, cradle, baby swing, soft baby sling/carrier, or a car ride can all be soothing.
- Visual Stimulation: Fascinating visual objects can be calming for baby (light and shadows, a mobile, wallpaper patterns, pictures, etc.). Baby should be held so that he/she can see (e.g., against caregiver's shoulder, semiupright in a baby seat, lying on his/her back, or propped up on his/her side).
- Immobilization and swaddling: Sometimes re-creating the closeness and security of the womb can be comforting. Holding baby tightly and closely, or swaddling the baby, helps to inhibit an overactive startle reflex and somewhat re-create the security of the womb.
- Wedging: Again, this helps to re-create a womblike atmosphere by putting the baby in a more confined area such as a bassinet or near the side of the crib, creating comforting boundaries.
- Touch: Simply holding the baby closely, with as much skin-to-skin contact as possible, can be comforting. Infant massage is also a very

soothing and relaxing technique for both caregiver and baby.

- Calm: Caregivers should try to remain calm themselves; babies seem to sense anxiety, which may further upset them. Sometimes caregivers need a break to relax and recharge, and fresh arms can have a calming effect on a baby.

Resources for Frustrated Parents
Even the most skilled and understanding parents are likely to become frustrated at some point in trying to support their crying infant. This is a normal reaction. When frustrated, parents need to take a break: Parents/caregivers should call a family member or friend to take over for a while. Medical and social professionals can be a resource as well, including the child's pediatrician, the local hospital, or local child abuse prevention services.

> **See also** Colic; Cri-du-chat; Emotion; Pacification; Temperament
>
> **References and further reading**
> Jones, S. 1992. *Crying Baby, Sleepless Nights.* Boston: Harvard Common Press.
> Small, M. 1998. *Our Babies, Ourselves: How Biology and Culture Shape the Way We Parent.* New York: Anchor Books.
> Southern Illinois University-Carbondale's Infant Cry Archive (website 2001). http://www.siu.edu/departments/coe/comdis/cryhome.html.

Cultural Competence

"Cultural competence" refers to the capacity, skills, and knowledge to respond to the unique needs of infants, toddlers, and families whose cultures are different from the dominant or mainstream society. It is also the ability to function effectively in the context of cultural differences. *Culture* includes race, ethnicity, beliefs, behaviors, language, and tradi-

tions. Culturally competent caregivers are able to respect and acknowledge cultural differences between self and the families served in regard to child-care beliefs and practices. The caregivers are able to adapt the care of children to integrate some of the practices from the home culture.

The Program for Infant/Toddler Caregivers notes that there are ten keys to culturally sensitive care. (1) Provide cultural consistency by harmonizing child care with what goes on at home. (2) Work toward representative staffing by employing staff who are of the same culture or speak the same language of the children being served. (3) Create small groups for manageability and ease of response to varying needs. (4) Use the home language of the children and families served. (5) Make environments relevant and reflective of the children and families served. (6) Uncover his/her own cultural beliefs and values to understand how they influence the type and way child care is provided. (7) Be open to the perspectives of others regarding childrearing; there is no one right way. (8) Seek out cultural and family information through reading and visiting with the family. (9) Clarify values by talking with the family and asking questions about concerns, practices and beliefs. (10) Negotiate cultural conflicts, be open to other points of view, and be willing to change as necessary.

> **See also** Caregiving; Parenting
>
> **References and further reading**
> Fitzgerald, Hiram E., et al. 1999. *Infancy and Culture: An International Review and Source Book.* New York: Falmer Press.
> Lynch, E. W., and M. J. Hanson, eds. 1992. *Developing Cross-cultural Competence: A Guide for Working with Young Children and Their Families.* Baltimore: Paul H. Brookes Publishing.

A eleven-month-old boy exploring by crawling through furniture. (Elizabeth Crews)

Curiosity

According to Jean Piaget, humans are motivated to actively investigate the world and the objects in it. Inherent in this learning process is the motivation to learn. From early in the sensorimotor period, there is this desire to interact with the environment in new and exciting ways. Children repeatedly engage in exploratory behaviors that will stimulate them physically and intellectually.

Custody

The determination by a judge, mediator, or parents regarding who will be a child's primary caregiver. The goal of custody is to protect and maintain the child's relationship with his/her parent. *Physical custody* describes where the child will live; *legal custody* describes who will make decisions regarding the child (e.g., schooling and medical care). A caregiver who is given sole custody will be the only person with whom the child lives and/or the only person who makes decisions regarding that child. *Joint custody* describes a situation in which the child resides with more than one caregiver and/or more than one caregiver makes important decisions regarding the child. There are multiple combinations of physical and legal custody that can be arranged depending on the best interests of the child.

See also Divorce

Cytomegolio Virus

This virus, known as CMV, exists everywhere and is a key cause of intrauterine infection in infants. Its prevalence accounts for about 2 percent of congenital CMV infection in the United States, or about 40,000 new cases per year. Transmission has been linked to mothers' low socioeconomic status, drug abuse, and sexual promiscuity. Symptomatic infants have a high mortality rate, ranging from 20 to 30 percent. Premature infants tend to be affected more than full-term infants.

Cytoplasm

The substance of a cell exclusive of the nucleus.

See also Neurobiology

D

Day Care

Day care is the care and supervision provided to young children during the day, usually while parents are at work. As more and more children are placed in child care during nontraditional times, the term is often interchanged with "child care" or "caregiving." It can also refer to the facilities used to provide care. Day-care facilities include family child-care homes, child-care centers, nursery schools, Head Start programs, before- and after-school programs, in-home care, and sick child care.

In-home day care is provided in the home of the child usually by a nanny or au pair. The child receives individualized care in a familiar setting by a live-in provider. In-home day care offers the most

Grandparents have special ways of communicating with infants and toddlers and can be extremely effective in child-care settings. (Courtesy of Nicole Davis)

convenience for families. However, it is also the most expensive. Family day care is provided in the home setting of the caregiver. The family day-care provider usually cares for three to six children based on age. If there is an adult assistant, the family child-care home may be licensed to care for up to twelve children. In some states, family day-care homes licensed for twelve children are considered group care facilities. Family day care provides a home setting atmosphere, individualized care in small groups, and flexible hours. The cost for families is usually based on a flat weekly or monthly rate. In some cases, a sliding scale determines rates based on the family's income and the number of children placed in care. Child-care centers are licensed to care for twelve or more children. Some centers can be as small as fifteen children, and others can be as large as 200 or more. The number of children allowed is based on the adult-to-child ratios, the number of child-care workers providing direct service to the children, and the amount of space available. Child-care centers are open predictable hours, and the program of care is more structured. The costs for center-based child care varies and depends on the sponsoring agency overseeing the center. Some employers provide space in the employment setting to house child-care facilities for the use of their employees. The fees for child care can be minimal and included as part of the wage deductions, or they might be comparable to other child-care settings in the area and subsidized by the employer. There are also religious-based child-care centers, nonprofit centers, and national child-care center chains.

See also Day-Care Workers; Family Day Care; Group Day Care

Day-Care Programs: Intergenerational

One innovative new program that has been increasing in popularity is the combination of child and adult day-care centers. Adult day centers come in a variety of models, but the social-model centers typically serve senior citizens who have slight to moderate cognitive or physical impairment levels. It also serves elders without impairment who would be bored and/or lonely at home during the day. Intergenerational programming in the day-care setting is considered in the literature to be an innovative direction for services that target older persons and children. Early estimates of the prevalence of intergenerational program models of adult and child day care reported less than 10 percent of adult day-care centers incorporated children, but the trend has been increasing. In addition, there is a trend in other services for the elderly, such as nursing homes and assisted living, to include infants and young children in activity programming.

Previous research in the area of intergenerational day care focuses on the benefits of putting adults and children together to minimize children's negative images of elderly persons, increase older clients' interaction with others, and to maximize efficiency in dependent care for employee caregivers. Companies such as Stride Rite and others have adopted policies and programs that combine the needs of employees who are elder caregivers with those who have young children.

Several investigators have described challenges and rewards of an intergenerational day-care program that are associated with a university setting. For example, in one program the location of the center in the higher education environment was considered optimal for training of staff members. They were able to utilize students from the child development program as well as those in gerontology. There were some concerns about whether staff members trained in early childhood education would be interested in older adults, and vice versa for those trained in gerontology. In addition, there were issues associated with how to plan the most effective program that would benefit both generations. Child development tasks were well known to early childhood staff members, but the more diverse needs and abilities of older clients must also be accommodated in the setting.

The research on the combination of adult and child day care is sparse and somewhat nonsystematic. It is not clear whether the intergenerational program works in positive or negative ways. Most concerns to date have been associated with whether participating children will develop unhealthy images of older persons, based on those clients with cognitive dementia or physical limitations.

Some research examines the effect of intergenerational programming on elderly clients in two adult day centers. One of these programs seemed beneficial to both generations (Center B), whereas the other one (Center E) varied in its success associated with the environment, behaviors, and activities between older clients and children. In Center B, activities were voluntary, only once per week, and clients were encouraged to assist children in various exercises and songs. In Center E, there were times when some of the older clients felt overstimulated by the presence of children, because they interacted with the children twice per day for thirty minutes each visit. In these interactions, the children were introduced into the front of the room and the older persons sat around the periphery. Clients in that center were

often treated as *status equals* with the children, which resulted in a potential loss of adult status for them. The environment of the senior room in the center was very child-oriented, with decor such as a giant leprechaun, Easter eggs, a 12-foot caterpillar made of paper plates, and other age-inappropriate decorations. In addition, there was no way for clients to retreat from the children, and some complained in interviews about the noise and inability to rest while the children were there. Intergenerational activities were mandatory and aimed at everyone in the room but were conducted only on the child's level. Staff members would sometimes treat older clients like children by calling them by nicknames (e.g., "honey bunny"), using high-pitched verbal intonations (baby-talk), telling clients to "behave," separating clients who interacted with one another, and administering child-oriented punishments (e.g., sending a client to a "time-out"). This practice of infantilization of older clients may lead to a lower level of adult self-identity and decrease adult-level social interaction among the seniors.

There were a couple of seniors in Center E that got a great deal of pleasure from interacting with the children. These clients were observed to be *child-oriented*, and they often initiated contact with the children. During an interview one client was asked if she enjoyed attending the center. She said,

Very much. Because I like the children. . . . They let you know you're still alive. I believe it helps us stay young. . . . The children seem to like me and I can walk into the room and ask 'Who's going to play ball with me today?' and six children will throw balls. . . . That is what I come for. . . .

It makes you feel like you are a real Grandma. I love the children and if they didn't bring the kids, I'd just as soon stay home, and I tell them so.

The success of this type of intergenerational day-care center seems to be associated with providing older clients with choice, autonomy, and an ability to separate themselves from the children if desired. It is important to identify seniors who are child-oriented and provide them with the ability to initiate behaviors with children. Center B was age-appropriate to seniors, because they were spoken to in an adult tone, given a choice in participation, had an adult environment, and had a role in assisting the children. Other successful intergenerational programs associated with nursing homes have been known to provide reading assistance and mentoring to older grade-school children, in addition to the interaction with younger children and infants. The success of future intergenerational programs involves simple training and education programs so that staff members who are familiar with one generation can become sensitized to the needs of the other.

See also Caregiving

References and further reading
Travis, S. S., A. J. Stremmel, and P. A. Duprey. 1993. "Child and Adult Day Care Professions Converging in the 1990s? Implications for Training and Research." *Educational Gerontology* 19: 283–293.
Watts, P. 1990. "A Giant Step for Stride Rite." *Executive Female* (July/August): 9.

Day-Care Workers

Day-care workers are the staff employed in day-care settings who are responsible for providing care and supervision to young children ages birth to three years. They may also be known as child-care providers, caregivers, caretakers, teachers, or educarers. Day-care workers who live in and provide care to the children living in the home are commonly known as nannies or au pairs. Day-care workers who use their own home to provide care to children are family care providers. Those who care for children related to them, for example, grandmothers or aunts, are known as relative care providers. Day-care workers typically work with children in small groups. Therefore, they need to have knowledge and experience in providing individualized care to young children in group settings, understand the ages and stages of infant/toddler development, be responsive to infants' cues, and be sociable with parents.

Licensed day-care workers are required to have a minimum of training on issues of safety, health, early childhood growth, and development. Care-center workers are required to be state-licensed or -regulated and receive ongoing supervision. Standards for licensing or regulation of day-care workers are determined by the state of residence. Family day-care workers must also receive mimumum specialized training to become licensed with the state and registered with the local child-care resource and referral agency. The only day-care workers not required to be licensed are relative care providers, as they are restricted to caring for related children only. However, some states will register relative care providers who receive federally subsidized monies and achieve a minimal amount of child-care training.

As child-care centers are professional organizations, the employed day-care workers have set hours for working and, sometimes, paid benefits, including sick

A caregiver soothing a two-year-old at a child-care center. (Elizabeth Crews)

leave and vacation time. Pay is based on the size of the child-care center and its financial base, level of education received, and seniority.

Family day-care workers are able to provide more individualized care to children in a family setting. In essence, they are small-business owners operating from their home. They have more flexible hours for working and few, if any, paid benefits. If the family day-care provider is sick, usually the parents are responsible for locating alternative care. If the regular child-care center provider is sick, a substitute provider is available. Family day-care providers are limited in the number of children they can provide for based on licensing restrictions and recommended adult-to-child ratios. In most states, fam-

ily day-care homes are initially licensed for six children. After one year, they may have the option to become licensed for twelve with the hiring of an assistant care provider. The recommended adult-to-child ratio for family child-care homes is four infants to one adult, or six children of varying ages (no more than three infants) to one adult. The ratios increase as the children get older.

One major issue for day-care workers has been the earning of a livable wage. The pay for family day-care workers is based on the income of the families served and subsidies from employers and/or local and federal governments. Some employers provide child-care subsidies as part of the wage package for employees. Federal subsidies are available to licensed family day-

TABLE 1 Characteristics of competent infant caregivers

Desired caregiver characteristics	Cues to desirable caregiver characteristics
I. Personality factors	
A. Child-centered	1. Attentive and loving to infants.
	2. Meets infants' needs before own.
B. Self-confident	1. Relaxed and anxiety free.
	2. Skilled in physical care of infants.
	3. Individualistic caregiving style.
C. Flexible	1. Uses different styles of caregiving to meet individual needs of infants.
	2. Spontaneous and open behavior.
	3. Permits increasing freedom of infant with development.
D. Sensitive	1. Understands infants' cues readily.
	2. Shows empathy for infants.
	3. Acts purposefully in interactions with infants
II. Attitudes and values	
A. Displays positive outlook on life	1. Expresses positive affect.
	2. No evidence of anger, unhappiness, or depression.
B. Enjoys infants	1. Affectionate to infants.
	2. Shows obvious pleasure in involvement with infants.
C. Values infants more than possessions or immaculate appearance	1. Dresses practically and appropriately.
	2. Places items not for infants' use out of reach.
	3. Reacts to infant destruction or messiness with equanimity.
	4. Takes risks with property in order to enhance infant development.
III. Behavior	
A. Interacts appropriately with infants	1. Frequent interactions with infants.
	2. Balances interaction with leaving infants alone.
	3. Optimum amounts of touching, holding, smiling, and looking.
	4. Responds consistently and without delay to infants; is always accessible.
	5. Speaks in positive tone of voice.
	6. Shows clearly that infants are loved and accepted.
B. Facilitates development	1. Does not punish infants.
	2. Plays with infants.
	3. Provides stimulation with toys and objects.
	4. Permits freedom to explore, including floor freedom.
	5. Cooperates with infant-initiated activities and explorations.
	6. Provides activities which stimulate achievement or goal orientation.
	7. Acts purposefully in an educational role to teach and facilitate learning and development.

Source: Reprinted from A. L. Jacobson. 1978. "Infant Day Care: Toward a More Human Environment." *Young Children*, Vol. 33, no. 5 (July 1978): 14–23. Copyright © 1978, National Association for the Education of Young Children, 1509 16th Street, N.W., Washington, D.C. 20036.

care workers, relative care providers, and qualified nonprofit child-care centers. Even with the subsidies, some day-care workers can make less than the federally mandated minimum hourly wage. As a result, the turnover rate for day-care providers is high, as most cannot afford to provide financially for their own families. April 27 is Worthy Wage Day, a national day of focus on the issue of livable wages for professional child-care providers. Making less than a livable wage greatly reduces the number of trained day-care workers, thereby reducing the number of available child-care slots and the ability of parents to work.

See also Caregivers, Training of

Deafness
See Audition; Fraiberg, Selma

Death
The death of an infant/toddler is an especially difficult experience for parents. Nearly a third of all women experience mental health problems, and an equal percentage of all parents experience marital difficulties following the death of an infant. Although parents will always live with the death of their infant/toddler, some investigators find that grief increases over time in mothers but decreases over time in fathers. Moreover, fathers seem to be affected more by the death of their sons than the death of their daughters, but mothers did not show such gender-specific effects. Although death rates are relatively low during the first three years of life, rates are deceiving. Thousands of children between the ages of birth to three die in the United States annually.

Delivery
See Birth

Denver Developmental Screening Test II
The Denver Developmental Screening Test (DDST II) is a screening tool for children from birth to age six. The DDST II is designed to identify children with developmental delays and to monitor children at risk for developmental problems. It is a revision of the original DDST, which was created in the 1960s. The DDST II has 125 items tapping four aspects of functioning: adaptive/fine motor, gross motor, language, and personal-social development. It is administered by trained medical or early intervention workers, includes both parental reports and observer ratings, and typically takes fifteen to twenty minutes to complete. Each item receives a rating of pass, fail, no opportunity to observe, or refusal to perform. Overall test performance is rated as normal, abnormal, questionable, or untestable. Standardized norms are available for a sample of 2,096 Colorado children stratified by age, race, socioeconomic class, and urban versus rural residence. Preacademic and academic skills are not tested. A Spanish-language version is available.

References and further reading
Frankenburg, Willaim K., and John B. Dodds. 1990. *Denver II*. Denver, CO: Denver Developmental Materials.

Dependent
Being dependent means one is reliant on someone else to have one's needs gratified. For example, an infant is dependent upon someone else for nourishment and emotional support. As self-initiated and

autonomous behavior emerges during development, the infant becomes increasingly independent and capable of self-gratification.

Depression

The first major description of depression in infancy was offered by René Spitz when he described anaclitic depression in infants as young as six months of age. Spitz's work with institutionalized infants helped to give structure to a new discipline: infant mental health. According to Spitz, anaclitic depression resulted from inadequate contact with affectionate, stimulating, loving caregivers. In 1983 another child psychiatrist, Justin Call, included anaclitic depression in his nosology as an attachment disorder. Depression as a clinical disorder is not the same as the postpartum, or baby, blues. Although the baby blues might be symptomatic of depression, there is no causal link because many women do not experience the baby blues after giving birth. A French child psychiatrist, Antoine Guedeney, has developed a clinical tool for assessing depression (sustained withdrawal reaction) in infants.

References and further reading
Guedeney, Antoine. 2000. "Infant Depression and Withdrawal: Clinical Assessment." In Joy D. Osofsky and Hiram E. Fitzgerald, eds., *WAIMH Handbook of Infant Mental Health, Vol. 4: Infant Mental Health in Groups at High Risk.* New York: Wiley, pp. 457–484.

Depth Perception

The perceptual experience of seeing a three-dimensional image that implies distance. Because the visual stimulation on the retina is only two-dimensional, infants must acquire a sense of how distant the observed object is from them in order to adapt well within the environment. Infants gradually develop more sophisticated interpretations of depth, ranging from use of kinetic depth cues involving their own bodily motions or those of objects, to binocular depth cues relying on the disparity in images seen in the two different eyes for cues about depth, to use of pictorial cues that rely on the features within the image itself to provide depth information about objects. Depth-perception skills show considerable improvement when infants become mobile and independently navigate through their environments, discovering the dangers associated with changes in depth such as stairs and drop-offs. Other sensory modalities also provide information that contribute to perceptions of object distance.

See also Perception; Size Perception; Time Perception; Visual Cliff

Development
See Theories of Development

Developmental Delay

"Developmental delay" refers to lags in some developmental phenomenon as judged against a normal standard. In many states, infant/toddlers who lag more than two standard deviations below the mean are defined as developmentally delayed and are eligible for special educational services.

See also Assessment; Individuals with Disabilities Education Act

Developmental Milestones: Cognitive, Motor, Social, and Language

Infant development is not the same for all children in all cultures. Each infant is unique, thereby creating her own personal developmental timetable. However, as we study infants, we have come to realize that many behaviors and activities follow a progressive sequence. We have been able to generalize that most children reach certain developmental milestones at certain ages. A *developmental milestone* is a behavior or activity that an infant engages in at a particular age. Some children advance beyond their peers at exhibiting a behavior; others are somewhat behind what is expected. The developmental milestone for any given age is the average behavior at that age. The infant's development is frequently assessed as part of her well-baby checkup at the pediatrician's or health care provider's office. A *well-baby checkup* is an assessment of the infant's general growth and development. During the appointment the infant is weighed, and her length and head circumference are measured. The infant's eating, defecating, and sleeping habits are discussed with her primary caregiver. The pediatrician or other health care professional assesses the infant's general health, as well as the infant's age at accomplishing certain developmental milestones. Most children are seen frequently during the first three years of life so that the pediatrician/health care provider can closely monitor development. Most infants are evaluated at two weeks, two months, four months, six months, nine months, twelve months, eighteen months, two years, two and a half years, and three years. These frequent visits allow the infant's health care provider to become familiar with the infant's own developmental path and to assess that the infant is progressing normally. If a developmental lag is observed, the frequency of the visits allows for reevaluation to take place a short period later. An infant can be reassessed at the next visit as either making progress or in need of further evaluation.

Developmental milestones are evaluated in different domains. A *domain of development* is the specific area of development under scrutiny; they include cognitive, motor, social, and language development. *Cognitive development* is the development of the intellectual processes of the infant; this includes awareness and memory. *Motor development* is the development of the coordination of the muscles. There are two types of motor development. Gross motor skills are the coordination of the large muscle groups like the arms, legs, back, and neck. Fine motor skills are the ability to coordinate hand-eye movements. *Social development* is the development of interactions between the infant and the significant people in her world. *Language development* is the developmental process of communicating with others.

The table shows the approximate age at which different developmental milestones occur, the average age at which the infant should achieve a specific behavior or activity. These developmental milestones reflect the development of an infant who lives in the United States, receives positive interaction with her primary caregiver, and lives in an enriched environment, where the living space stimulates the infant's growth and development by having a variety of things to look at, touch, and investigate. If an infant

TABLE 1   Developmental Milestones

Domain of Development	0–3 Months Old	4–6 Months Old	7–12 Months Old	12–24 Months Old	24–36 Months Old
Cognitive	Looks at objects Follows movement with eyes	Repeats enjoyable behaviors Taking in lots lots of information	Learns by using senses Learns by exploring and interacting with objects	Learns by trial and error Object Permanence (knows an object does not disappear when infant does not see it)	Begins to order and classify objects Egocentric view of self in world Has trouble understanding difference between make-believe and reality
Gross or Large Motor	Moves arms and legs Raises chest when on stomach	Sits supported Rolls from back back to front Reaches out to be picked up Sits alone	Stands with support Crawls Pulls self up Walks with help Walks alone	Can go from standing to sitting Runs Jumps Climbs	Tries to imitate actions of grown-ups Begins toilet training
Fine Motor	Reflexive squeezing of objects when placed in palm Holds hand in a fist Puts hand in mouth	Reaches for objects Pulls object to mouth Picks up objects to put in mouth	Transfers object from one hand to other hand Drops objects on purpose Feeds self finger food	Holds spoon Holds cup and drinks from cup Able to grasp most objects Opens drawers and cupboards	Feeds self Opens bottles and packages Can undress and dress self Can stack a small tower Scribbles/Draws
Social	Responds to being held Smiles Learning to trust that needs will be met	Recognizes familiar people Prefers people to objects	Prefers specific familiar person Upset when familiar person leaves Shy with strangers	Begins to leave caretaker's side to be on own for a moment Parallel Play (plays next to but not with another child)	Imitates adults— role playing Looks for parent's approval May play with others for short period of time
Language	Cries to make needs known Babbles Coos	Laughs and squeals Puts vowel and consonant sound together	Imitates sounds Responds to own name Uses single words that have meaning	Two word sentences	Large vocabulary Asks lots of questions Wants to know name of everything

Source: Julie Haddow, 2001

is not developing within these three criteria, it may be inappropriate to compare her to these developmental milestones.

See also Theories of Development

Developmental Models

Developmental models are ways of representing the causal influences on behavior, both as it occurs in the here and now (cross-sectional models) and over the life course (longitudinal models).

Developmentally Appropriate Curriculum

A developmentally appropriate curriculum (DAC) is an educational program that was developed according to principles of developmentally appropriate practice. For instance, DAC for infant/toddlers is a curriculum developed specifically for the developmental needs of infant/toddlers. A child-care center using DAC features the following: child-directed activities as opposed to adult-led activities; many sensory experiences; flexibility in the schedule so infant/toddlers can nap and eat according to their preferences; small groups of infant/toddlers to allow for one-on-one interactions with an adult; primary caregiving practices; and continuity of caregiving.

See also Developmentally Appropriate Practice

References and further reading

Bredekamp, S., and C. Copple. 1995. *Developmentally Appropriate Practices in Early Childhood Program.* Rev. ed. Washington, DC: National Association for the Education of Young Children.
Honig, A. S., and J. R. Lally. 1981. *Infant Caregiving: A Design for Training.* Syracuse: Syracuse University Press.

Lally, J. R., et al. 1995. *Caring for Infants and Toddlers in Groups.* Washington, DC: Zero to Three.

Developmentally Appropriate Practice

Research has determined that the care of children should be provided in a way that meets the physical, emotional, mental, and social needs of the child based on the child's age and stage of development. This is referred to as "developmentally appropriate." Programs with activities and goals suited to the level of ability, interests, and learning style of each child are considered to be developmentally appropriate programs.

Developmentally appropriate practices meet children where they are while supporting their emotional well-being, stimulating their senses, challenging their abilities, and encouraging learning and growth. For example, some caregivers and parents expect children to achieve toilet-training competencies by about eighteen months of age. Developmentally appropriate practices understand that toilet learning may occur at anytime between fifteen and thirty-six months of age. Each child's readiness for and success at toilet learning is based on the interaction of the child's physical, cognitive, and emotional stages of development. Physically, the child must be able to contract and release the sphincter muscle. Cognitively, he/she must be able to sense a bowel movement and to understand what the sensation means. Emotionally, the child must be interested in learning how to use the toilet. Unless these three things are in sync, toilet learning can be stressful. Thus, cues are taken from the child, emphasizing that developmentally appropriate activities are also child-directed rather than adult-directed. The environment supports the child's interests and facilitates exploration and engagement with materials and others. Activities that constrict movement, exploration, and expression are avoided. Developmentally appropriate programs promote responsive care, individual growth and development, self-identity, and self-confidence.

See also Developmentally Appropriate Curriculum

References and further reading
Bredekamp, Sue. 1987. *Developmentally Appropriate Practice in Early Childhood Programs Serving Children from Birth Through Age 8*. Washington, DC: National Association for the Education of Young Children.

Dichotic Listening

Dichotic listening is a method for assessing lateral specialization of the brain. A series of pairs of different sounds are played simultaneously through earphones, one to the left ear, one to the right, and the subject is asked to report the sounds heard. For verbal sounds (spoken letters and words), accuracy is usually better for sounds played to the right ear than to the left; for nonverbal sounds (music, animal cries), the left ear usually has the advantage. Because the auditory regions of each hemisphere receive more neural projections from the contralateral (opposite side) ear than from the ipsilateral (same-side) ear, the right-ear and left-ear advantages are assumed to reflect the specialization of the left and right hemispheres for linguistic and nonlinguistic sounds, respectively.

See also Lateralization

Differential Conditioning

"Differential conditioning" refers to situations where the learning must respond to one stimulus or event and not to another in order to solve a problem.

See also Learning

Differential Emotions Theory

This is a theory of emotional development, proposed by Carroll Izzard, in which the roles of different emotions during different developmental stages are emphasized. According to differential emotions theory, emotions play a key role in both social and cognitive attainment during various developmental stages throughout childhood by aiding in the organization of thought and subsequent behavior. As the child moves through a developmental stage, certain emotions can play a more important role at that particular time than other emotions. According to differential emotions theory, discrete emotions are organized into what Izzard calls "modules," which are highly organized and function independently of each other. Although discrete emotion theorists believe that facial expressions correspond to particular emotions, differential-emotions theorists specify that the emotional state can exist without facial expression. As infant/toddlers mature cognitively, these emotion systems become integrated, which allows for the existence of more sophisticated emotions such as anxiety, pride, and so on.

See also Emotion

Difficult Babies
See Temperament

Disabilities

See Genetic Disorders; Individuals with Disabilities Education Act

Discipline

Discipline is the process through which adults teach and children learn the guidelines for appropriate behaviors in various situations. Throughout history, discipline styles have been influenced by the scientific, philosophical, and societal beliefs and values of the time. Cultural values and family beliefs also shape discipline practices. Different styles of discipline influence children's development in different ways.

From a historical perspective, infancy was not considered a very influential time in the child's development. In fact, during the medieval period, young children were viewed as miniature adults. Little thought was given to infancy, toddlerhood, and early childhood as being unique periods in human development. Expectations of children were based on these beliefs. During the 1600s and 1700s, discipline practices were influenced strongly by the Reformation, in which the Puritan belief in original sin was emphasized. The idea of original sin purported that infants were born evil, stubborn, and sinful. A parent's role was to civilize the infant, to turn the child away from sin and evil, and emigrants from England to the United States brought these beliefs with them. Harsh discipline was characteristic of this period.

Philosophical changes during the 1700s and 1800s shaped new beliefs in discipline practice. John Locke, a British philosopher, was influential in shaping beliefs about young children. He described the young child as a "tabula rasa," that is, a blank slate. In other words, he believed that infants were born into the world without being good or bad. The parents' role was to shape the child's character, growth, and development through specific practices, such as instructing young children in proper behavior, exemplifying good behavior, and rewarding children's good behavior. Locke supported the idea of kindness and compassion toward children, and he did not believe in the use of harsh physical punishment.

During the eighteenth century, a more child-centered approach to discipline and childrearing continued under the influence of Jean Jacques Rousseau, a French philosopher. Unlike Locke, who believed that infants were born as blank slates, Rousseau referred to young children as "noble savages," born with an innate sense of right and wrong. He also believed that infants were born with an internal plan for growth and development, and so instruction and training from parents was not necessary and perhaps even harmful to the child. Rousseau emphasized the parents' role in being responsive to children's needs throughout the periods of childhood, infancy, childhood, late childhood, and adolescence.

The scientific study of childhood, which really began in the nineteenth century with Charles Darwin, marked the beginning of expert advice for parents. The early to mid-1800s saw a more relaxed attitude toward discipline. Interestingly, this shift coincided with some of the first laws designed to protect children, such as child labor laws.

During the twentieth century, parents relied on child-development experts for advice. Throughout the twentieth century, discipline attitudes varied, and parents often received conflicting advice

*A mother disciplining her children by
spanking them. Woodcut, 1889
(Bettmann/Corbis)*

about how to discipline children. During
the early part of the century, discipline
tended to be strict, and parents were
advised to keep infants on schedules, use
firm discipline, and refrain from over-
indulging infant/toddlers with too much
affection. Child-development research
was based on the work of theorists such
as Sigmund Freud, Erik Erikson, John
Watson, and Albert Bandura. For example, behaviorism was popularized by the
work of psychologist John Watson.
Behaviorists believed that a child's
actions could be shaped through environmental stimuli and reinforcement. This
movement was especially popular during
the 1930s and 1940s, and parents were
advised to train infant/toddlers to behave
in appropriate ways.

In the 1940s and 1950s, pediatrician
Benjamin Spock offered more permissive
parenting advice in a popular parenting
book published in 1946, *The Common
Sense of Baby and Child Care*, which
eventually sold more than 39 million
copies. Spock, influenced by Freud's
belief in the importance of childhood in
shaping adult personality, encouraged
parents to use common sense in caring
for their infant/toddlers. In the late 1960s
and 1970s, attachment research conducted by researchers such as John
Bowlby and Mary Ainsworth highlighted
the importance of the relationship
between infant and parent. In the late
twentieth century, distinctions were
made between the goals of discipline and
those of punishment. Discipline practices at this time reflected a belief in nurturing youngsters' emotional development in the early years.

Today, many child-development experts
believe the ultimate goal of discipline is for
the child to develop self-control and self-
regulation, that is, the ability to recognize
and control one's emotions and behaviors
in any given situation. Punishment, in
contrast, tends to be punitive and not
focused on skill development related to
behavioral control. The growth of self-control takes time and practice. How successful children are in developing self-control
depends largely on how they are disci-
plined. There are many approaches to discipline in childrearing, some approaches
more positive than others. Three main
approaches to discipline are *authoritative,
authoritarian,* and *permissive.*

Authoritative Discipline
Adults using an authoritative discipline
style have high behavioral expectations
for infant/toddlers, but expectations are

clearly communicated in a warm and nurturing manner. This style is also characterized by clear affection for the child, respect, and a democratic approach in which the child's ideas and opinions are heard and valued. The occurrence of inappropriate behavior is seen as an opportunity to teach the child more appropriate behavior and to facilitate an environment in which the child can learn from mistakes. Numerous strategies, designed to prevent negative behaviors and promote positive social behaviors, are characteristics of the authoritative approach.

In order to prevent inappropriate behavior from occurring, the adult engages in proactive behavior. That is, the adult structures the physical and emotional environments to be conductive to positive behaviors. Examples of proactive strategies in the physical environment would be moving objects inappropriate for a toddler's explorations out of reach. If the desirable object is out of the child's grasp, it cannot be broken. Temper tantrums, common during toddlerhood and throughout the early childhood years, are most likely to occur when the young child is under stress, overstimulated, or fatigued. In order to help prevent out-of-control behavior, the wise adult might reduce the amount of stimulation in the environment. For instance, the adult might provide some quiet time for book-reading with a toddler amid holiday visits to relatives. Proactive prevention is a very effective discipline strategy.

With infant/toddlers, the use of distraction and redirection of behavior can be useful discipline strategies. For example, an infant interested in pulling on the edge of the dining room tablecloth might be distracted with an interesting toy or redirected to a similar, but safer, activity, such as fingering interesting fabric squares.

Setting clear limits and modeling appropriate behaviors are additional strategies associated with authoritative discipline. Infant/toddlers find security in knowing what their limits are. Behavioral limits usually have to do with making sure the child and others are safe and healthy; protecting the rights of others; protecting property; and teaching children about appropriate social behaviors. Over time as the child matures, the child can take part in setting limits and reaching compromises about limits. This shared responsibility and, to some extent, shared decisionmaking is characteristic of the authoritative discipline style. In the early years, however, the adult sets most limits. Further, the adult should not only set appropriate limits but also model appropriate behaviors within these limits. For example, if the adult believes that using words such as "please" and "thank you" is a desirable social value and this in an expectation in the home, then the adult should use such words with and around the young child regularly. Using encouragement and positive reinforcement are additional ways to reinforce the importance and desirability of specific behaviors. Young children generally want to please adults and often repeat behaviors for which they receive encouragement or positive reinforcement. Although reinforcers can sometimes be effective, adults must remember that the goal of discipline is for the child to be intrinsically motivated, or motivated by internal factors, to act in a desirable manner rather than be motivated by extrinsic factors, such as the promise of reward.

One of the most effective strategies to help infant/toddlers develop intrinsic

Dr. Benjamin Spock with a baby, c. 1945. (Hulton/Archive Photos)

When misbehavior does occur, there should be a consequence for the action. The authoritative discipline style calls for the use of logical consequences. A logical consequence is linked to the offending behavior and is meant to help the child understand the effects of the behavior on another person. For example, if a toddler hits a sibling, a logical consequence would be to help the adult get an ice pack and hold it to the injured area. Over time, the child may join in making suggestions as to what a logical consequence for a behavior might be and how to make amends for that behavior.

The use of authoritative discipline appears to have very positive effects on young children. Children exposed to authoritative discipline tend to display positive social qualities and are often described as friendly, cooperative, empathic, responsible, self-controlled, and curious. They tend to be high achievers and set high goals for themselves.

Authoritarian Discipline
Adults who use authoritarian discipline value children's immediate obedience to rules and expectations. This style of discipline is characterized by high demands and high expectations of children, but, unlike the authoritative discipline style, it is marked by low communication between the adult and child and little physical or verbal affection. Authoritarian discipline focuses less on prevention of inappropriate behavior or the development of the child's understanding of why a behavior is inappropriate and what the consequences of the behavior on others might be. Instead, punishment is used as the primary method of discouraging inappropriate behavior.

One common type of punishment associated with the authoritarian disci-

motivation is the use of induction and reasoning. Induction and reasoning involve pointing out the effects of the child's behavior on others and providing explanations about why the behavior is inappropriate and what the appropriate behavior is. Over time, the goal of induction and reasoning is for the child to develop an understanding of why some behaviors are inappropriate, to develop empathy for others, and to develop skills to think carefully about the consequences of a behavior before undertaking it. Of course, explanations and reasoning with infant/toddlers must be short and simple. As the child becomes cognitively more mature, discussions about behavior can become more complex.

pline style is called "love withdrawal." Adults who use this strategy attempt to control the child's behavior by expressing anger paired with statements such as "I don't like you when you act like that." The message to the child is that the adult's love is available only when the child is obedient. Use of this technique is associated with high levels of anxiety and even fear of abandonment in children.

Other common types of punishment characteristic of authoritarian discipline include scolding and shaming. Use of these techniques can be damaging to the developing self-esteem of the infant/toddler. In these early years of life, young children are striving to develop a sense of themselves as autonomous and capable. Shaming can result in feelings of inadequacy and incompetence. Examples of shaming include the use of name-calling, such as calling the child "stupid" or "bad," and the use of physical gestures, such as glowering gazes or making faces at the child.

Corporal punishment, or spanking, is another form of authoritarian discipline. Most child-development experts agree that spanking should be avoided as a means of controlling behavior. Among parents, however, spanking remains a controversial topic. The main argument against spanking is that it sends the message that physical force is an acceptable way to force compliance. Many experts also believe that spanking sends contradictory messages to young children. For example, if a toddler is told not to hit a sibling, but then receives a spanking as punishment, the message is that hitting is acceptable after all. However, the use of corporal punishment is accepted in some cultures, and within these cultures the use of spanking is not viewed as harsh or abusive. Similarly, children raised within cultures that accept corporal punishment can respond differently to this discipline technique than children raised in a different cultural context. For example, there is some evidence that the use of physical punishment predicts childhood aggression and behavior problems in children of some ethnic groups but not in others. These findings do not suggest that corporal punishment is an effective discipline technique but rather that the effects of this type of punishment are mediated by cultural perceptions.

One of the pitfalls in relying on negative punishment techniques is that punishment does not facilitate the child's intrinsic motivation to engage in appropriate behavior. Instead, the child's motivation is external: the avoidance of punishment. Thus, compliance is based only on a desire not to be punished. This is called the "adherence level of compliance." Young children who are exposed only to these types of discipline techniques have a hard time understanding why particular behaviors are inappropriate or how these behaviors might cause injury to others; they may understand only that they will be punished if they engage in the behavior.

Children raised with authoritarian discipline develop much different behavioral profiles than children raised with authoritative discipline. Strict authoritarian discipline strategies are associated with aggressiveness, apprehension, fear, low self-control, unfriendliness, and hostility. These children may also be described as moody, suspicious, or withdrawn.

Permissive Discipline
Permissive discipline is characterized by high levels of warmth and affection but low expectations for children and unclear communication. In such a permissive

A caregiver using induction and reasoning with a group of one- and two-year-olds. (Elizabeth Crews)

environment, infant/toddlers find little security. Very young children are comforted by clear boundaries and consistent discipline practices. The permissive style of discipline allows few opportunities for young children to understand what behaviors are appropriate and inappropriate because the adult does not provide explanations. Also, the child's inappropriate behaviors are often ignored, which suggests to the child that those behaviors are acceptable. With a lack of consistency in discipline practice and no clear guidelines about expectations, the infant/toddler has little opportunity to develop a clear internalized understanding of appropriate behavior. Without clear behavioral guidelines and consequences for inappropriate behavior, the young child fails to develop self-control or any intrinsic motivation for engaging in positive behavior. Children raised with permissive discipline have difficulty negotiating the social world. They are often described as immature, withdrawn, aggressive, impulsive, and rebellious. They tend to have little self-control and are low achievers in school.

Influences on Discipline Styles
Discipline style is influenced by factors such as socioeconomic status, the child's gender and age, and family culture and ethnicity. Keeping these factors in mind is important when considering the many approaches to discipline and why families discipline their infant/toddlers in different ways.

Socioeconomic Status. Discipline practices seem to vary according to socioeconomic status. There is some evidence that parents with lower incomes use less positive discipline strategies with their children and may have higher demands for compliance. However, in some circumstances, the child's unquestioned obedience is necessary. For example, strong parental control and demands for immediate compliance would be an asset for a young child growing up in an unsafe neighborhood. Further, the use of corporal punishment seems to vary across socioeconomic groups. Although the differences are not dramatic, working-class parents tend to use more corporal punishment as compared to middle-class parents, who tend to use reasoning and inductive discipline strategies. Some of these differences in discipline practices may reflect differing values between lower and higher economic families. Lower-income families, employed in skilled and semiskilled manual occupations, tend to value characteristics such as obedience. Higher-income professionals, however, emphasize the importance of characteristics such as creativity and curiosity. The use of discipline techniques such as reasoning and inductive discipline foster the growth of these characteristics in young children, whereas techniques such as demands for immediate compliance foster the characteristics such as obedience. Another possible explanation for differences in discipline practices across socioeconomic groups may be the nature of life experiences for the parents. For example, lower-income parents are more likely to work in positions in which they answer to an authority figure, often without question. Creating a similar power structure in the home can seem familiar and natural. Higher-income parents are more likely to work in an environment in which they have some control over their choices and input into work practices and decisions. They likely value aspects of this type of environment, such as the ability to be independent and self-controlled; because these skills are valued, they teach them to their young children.

Culture and Ethnicity. Like many child-rearing practices, discipline is embedded within a cultural context, shaped by cultural values and beliefs. For example, some cultures value characteristics such as strong social skills, creativity, and curiosity. Some cultures value obedience, respect for authority, loyalty, and hard work. Other groups emphasize independence, self-reliance, and self-control.

Particular discipline techniques can be more effective than others in fostering specific characteristics, valued by a cultural group. From outside the cultural group, the discipline style may seem inappropriate. However, within the cultural context, it may be entirely appropriate and viewed as normal by families. For example, within the Chinese culture, an authoritarian approach to discipline, characterized by high demands and high control, is common; within the cultural context, this discipline style is associated with children's positive outcomes, such as school achievement. Within a white Anglo group, authoritarian discipline is often associate with negative child outcomes, such as aggressiveness. In African American families, corporal punishment is used more often to discipline children than it is in white families. However, within the African American community, the practice is viewed as appropriate and normal and is not associated with poor outcomes in children. In Hispanic and Asian/Pacific Islander families, discipline is firm, requiring respect and obedience in regard to authority figures, but the style is also characterized by maternal warmth and nurturance in particular. In these cultures, respect for authority and family loyalty are important values, and a more authoritarian approach to discipline fosters these values.

These examples illustrate the fact that the meaning, origins, and purposes of discipline styles are very different between cultures, and discipline styles have little to do with how much parents love and care for their children.

See also Aggression; Caregiving; Parenting

References and further reading
Baumrind, D. 1996. "The Discipline Controversy Revisited." *Family Relations* 45(4): 405.
Brody, G. H, and D. L. Flor. 1998. "Maternal Resources, Parenting Practices, and Child Competence in Rural, Single-Parent African-American Families." *Child Development* 69: 803–816.
Forehand, R. E., and B. McKinney. 1993. "Historical Overview of Child Discipline in the United States: Implications for Mental Health Clinicians and Researchers." *Journal of Child and Family Studies* 2(3): 221–228.
Luster, T., ed. 1993. *Parenting: An Ecological Perspective.* Hillsdale, NJ: Lawrence Erlbaum Associates.

Discrepancy Hypothesis
The prediction that moderately different stimulation will elicit more sustained attention than will nearly identical or completely different stimulation.

Distractibility
Distraction is a discipline strategy in which adults attempt to divert the child's attention from a negative behavior to a more desirable behavior. For example, if the child is beginning to kick a sibling during a car ride to day care, the parent might attempt to distract the child by pointing out interesting sites along the road or perhaps engaging the child in a sing-along as they ride in the car.

Distractibility also is a dimension of temperament that refers to the effectiveness of extraneous stimuli in drawing attention away from an ongoing behavior. Some children are more easily distracted from a task than others. Children who are easily distracted also tend to have short attention spans.

See also Discipline; Temperament

Divided Visual Field Method
A technique involving the rapid presentation of stimuli to the left or right visual fields of each eye. Because the left field of each eye projects directly to the right hemisphere, the right field to the left hemisphere, any differences in the speed or accuracy of the individual's response to the stimuli is taken as evidence that the stimuli are better processed by that hemisphere. For example, verbal targets (letters, words) are usually better recognized when projected to the right visual field, consistent with evidence that the left hemisphere is specialized for processing of verbal stimuli.

See also Lateralization

Divorce
Divorce is the legal termination of a marriage. The debate over divorce has troubled professionals and nonprofessionals for many decades, as many people are concerned about the consequences of

divorce for children. Currently, about 50 percent of children living in America will experience parental divorce. Individual and societal factors have been associated with divorce. The effects of divorce on children vary depending on the age of the child and how the parents handle the divorce. Some people believe that an infant is not affected by divorce; this is not true. Divorce during the period of infancy can impact all areas of infant development. The effect that divorce has on infants is related to factors such as whether or not the infant's basic needs are being met, living and custody agreements, as well as marital conflict and domestic violence. Parents can help infants cope with divorce by providing consistent daily routines, meeting the infant's basic physical and emotional needs, and limiting the fighting that often accompanies divorce.

Divorce Rates in Historical Context
Since the mid- to late 1800s, divorce rates have been on the rise. For example, during the 1860s only about 1 percent of marriages ended in divorce, and by the end of the World War II 2.4 percent of marriages ended in divorce. After that, divorce rates leveled off until the 1970s, when about fifteen of every 1,000 marriages ended in divorce. During the 1960s and 1970s, U.S. culture shifted its emphasis toward individualism, which led to exploration of different lifestyles and a change in the values surrounding premarital sexual relations, abortion, and cohabitation. As a result of this cultural shift, the possibility of having a child outside of marriage or leaving a marriage because one individual was unhappy became more acceptable. During the late 1970s and early 1980s, there was another peak in divorce statistics, when approxi-

mately 40–60 percent of marriages ended in divorce. The divorce rate decreased and leveled off in the late 1980s, when approximately half of all marriages ended in divorce. At the beginning of the twenty-first century, about half of the divorces in America occur before the seventh year of marriage.

Individual and Societal Factors
Divorce is the result of many intertwined individual and societal factors; it is not simply the result of a dissatisfying marriage. An individual's age at the time of marriage has been associated with divorce. For example, teenage marriages are more likely to end in divorce, while women who marry above the age of thirty are less likely to divorce. Another factor related to divorce appears to be the lengths of time the wife spends in school. Women who finish schooling, whether a high school diploma, a bachelor's degree, or an advanced college degree, tend to be less likely to divorce than women who drop out. Whether or not dropping out of school contributed to the divorce, or if the divorce led to people dropping out of school, are unknown. People who have been previously divorced are more likely to divorce a second time, and couples who are less traditional and live together before marriage are more likely to become divorced. Although having children does not prevent divorce, childless marriages are more likely to end in divorce possibly because of the strain that infertility places on a marriage.

Divorce rates increased after each major war and decreased during economic depressions and booms. In 1970, no-fault divorce laws were introduced. Before the introduction of no-fault divorce, parties had to prove that that one partner was responsible for the split; if fault was not proven, the divorce was not granted. During this time, many couples who wanted a divorce were forced to lie or commit acts such as adultery or abusive behavior. Although some scholars argue that the introduction of no-fault divorce laws is not a factor that is related to divorce rates, the incidence of divorce almost doubled between 1970 and 1975. Others have noted that during the 1960s and 1970s family values were being replaced with individualism, which also had an impact on divorce. Other societal factors that affected divorce rates were the increase in the availability of birth control and the legalization of abortion. Birth control and abortion allowed couples to have more control over how many children they had, making women less dependent on men to support a large family and allowing women to move into the workforce. Experts believe that women's moving into the workforce has been the most important societal contribution to divorce. For example, in 1940 only 15 percent of women worked outside the home; by 1989, 58 percent of women worked outside the home. The movement of women into the workforce has allowed for greater economic freedom and less dependence on males for economic support. As a result, women in the workforce may not need to stay married for their financial security.

Effects on Infants
Many people believe that infants are too young to remember their parents' divorce and as a result are not affected by the process. Infancy is a time of great developmental gains where children learn whether or not they live in a world that is predictable and trustworthy. This basic sense of trust is the foundation for feelings of self-worth and power later in life.

Infants learn that they can trust their caregivers when they receive predictable caregiving and their physical and emotional needs are being met. The economic consequences of divorce, the parents' psychological adjustment to the divorce, the amount of conflict between the infant's parents, and the custody agreement all affect infant development by interfering with the parents' ability to provide quality caregiving.

After divorce, the custodial parent, usually the mother, undergoes a significant decrease in economic stability. When parents divorce, the same income must cover the expenses of two households. One parent can be ordered to pay child support to help cover the expense of raising a child. Although child support is often court-ordered, it is not always paid, adding to financial strain on the custodial parent. In addition, emotional strain can accompany divorce. Infants are very susceptible to their parents' emotional states. During the process of divorce parents often feel emotions such as guilt, abandonment, anger, anxiety, and depression. When these emotions become intense, it is difficult for parents to be emotionally available for their infant or to provide an infant with sensitive and responsive caregiving. Because of these financial and emotional strains, infants might not have predictable housing, schedules, or caregivers.

Marital conflict and/or domestic violence before or after a divorce can play a greater role in negative child outcome than the divorce itself. Infants who witness violence by their parents are affected directly by the violent behavior as well as indirectly by the effect that the violent behavior has on the availability of his/her parent. Infants are traumatized when they witness a caregiver involved in violence.

Permanent brain changes, aggressive behavior, low self-esteem, fearfulness, and insecure attachment have all been associated with witnessing violence in infancy. When an infant's parents have a violent or extremely conflictual marriage, divorce can be a necessary and positive occurrence. In these cases, divorce can actually decrease the stress in the home and provide the infant with more sensitive and predictable caregiving.

Because infancy is a time of enormous regulatory, cognitive, emotional, communicative, and social development changes, the custody settlement is an important factor in the infant's adjustment. One of the most important developmental tasks in the first twelve months of life is the establishment of a secure attachment relationship with a caregiver. Attachment protects the infant from external dangers by promoting closeness to the caregiver; it also regulates a person's response to threats and anxiety. The development of a secure attachment requires consistent sensitive caregiving. Another important factor affecting the custody settlement is an infant's sense of time. Infant's cognitive limitations make it impossible to remember where one parent now lives, to remember how his/her schedule changes, or to hold a memory of his/her parent. Custody settlements for infants should meet their changing developmental needs and ensure a consistent, predictable schedule where basic needs can be met and attachment relationships can be developed.

Impacts on Infant Development

Infants are distressed by changes in stability in their lives. Infants are unable to verbally communicate their feelings. Developmental indications of distress in infants following a divorce are often seen in the areas of sleeping, eating, motor activity, language, toilet training, and emotional independence. Infants whose parents are divorcing may stop sleeping through the night, refuse to go to sleep, or have nightmares. Another developmental indication of distress is an infant's refusal to eat foods that were once enjoyed or only eating a few different kinds of foods. Some infants will go back to using a bottle or stop eating solid foods. Some of the greatest gains in infancy include motor activity. Distressed infants can give up their last developmental accomplishment in this area. For example, an infant that was walking might revert to crawling. Also, infants can stop feeding themselves and stop picking up and examining objects. During infancy, babies learn to use their words to make wants known. Infants who once used words to make their wants known can go back to crying or pointing. Toddlers who have begun using small sentences can revert to using single words. Toddlers who had achieved toilet learning can go back to wetting themselves. Infants struggling with divorce can also withhold stool. These are examples of regressive behaviors, which are associated with stress.

Signs of Emotional Distress in Infants

In addition to developmental signals as a result of divorce, there are also emotional signals of infant distress. These signals include emotional changes, anger, fearfulness, withdrawal, and listlessness. The first emotional sign of distress is emotional change. Infants' emotional responses appear more intense than what might be expected. Infants might not be able to wait as long before being fed or cry more intensely than usual for a bath. These intense emotional ups and downs are the result of the infant's frustration that could possibly result from parental discord or depression or change in the infant's daily routine. Anger is another sign of distress in infants. Anger can be the result of the infant's needs not being met over time or the schedules becoming unpredictable. Finally, withdrawal and listlessness are signs of a distressed infant. Loss of interest in a favorite toy and or unresponsiveness to smiles and attention from a parent/caregiver can be the infant's way of withdrawing from a chaotic environment. Although some loss of developmental accomplishment, emotional ups and downs, anger, and frustration are common to nondistressed infants, distressed infants can show multiple signs of distress at the same time and will exhibit these behaviors or a cluster of these behaviors consistently over a period of time. Infants who show distress for longer than one month may require the attention of a pediatrician or mental health practitioner skilled at working with infants.

See also Attachment; Custody; Domestic Violence; Marital Conflict

References and further reading
Administration for Children and Families, Department of Health and Human Services (website 2001). http://www. acf.dhhs.gov/programs/cse.
Behrman, R. E, and L. Sandham Quinn. 1994. "Children and Divorce: Overview and Analysis." *The Future of Children: Children and Divorce* 4: 4–14.
The David and Lucille Packard Foundation (website 2001). http://www. futureofchildren.org/cad/index.htm.
Furstenberg, F. F. 1994. "History and Current Status of Divorce in the United States." *The Future of Children: Children and Divorce* 4: 29–43.
Kalter, N. 1990. "The Divorce Experience for Infants and Toddlers." *Growing Up with Divorce: Helping Your Child Avoid Immediate and Later Emotional Problems.* New York: Ballentine.
———. 1990. "Helping Infants and Toddlers Cope." *Growing Up with Divorce: Helping Your Child Avoid Immediate and Later Emotional Problems.* New York: Ballentine.

Domestic Violence

A behavior that occurs in a dating or marital relationship that is physically, emotionally, sexually, or financially hurtful to one or both of the partners. Physical violence includes, but is not limited to, pushing, hitting, kicking, or burning that may or may not leave a mark. Emotional violence can include name-calling, put-downs, threats, or isolating one partner from friends and family. Sexual violence includes forcing a partner physically or verbally to participate in sexual acts, calling a partner sexually degrading names, or sexually harassing a partner. An example of financial violence is not allowing one partner to have money.

See also Child Abuse and Neglect; Divorce; Marital Conflict

References and further reading
The David and Lucille Packard Foundation (website 2001). http://www. futureofchildren.org/dvc/index.htm.
National Coalition Against Domestic Violence (website 2001). http://www. ncadv.org.

Dominant Gene

A gene that will be expressed in the phenotype of an organism whenever it is paired with a recessive gene or another dominant gene.

Doula

Doula is a Greek term meaning "woman's servant" and refers to a layperson professionally trained to provide emotional, physical, and informational support to mothers during childbirth and the postpartum period. Throughout history and in most every culture, women have cared for other women during childbirth. Artistic images, stories, and anecdotal records throughout the centuries have described the role of an experienced woman comforting and supporting the new mother as she births her child. Unlike the midwife, who is trained to provide medical care, the doula is concerned with the nonmedical aspects of birth. The doula's goal is to provide continuous support and to aid the laboring woman in achieving a satisfying birth experience, as defined by the woman.

Certification and Training
In the United States, doulas are trained and certified either by the International Childbirth Education Association or Doulas of North America; each have doula certification programs. Certification requirements include a background of work and education in the maternity field or observation of a series of childbirth classes, the completion of training courses or seminars, completion of reading assignments, successful completion of written exams, some type of practicum experience, and positive evaluation.

Services Provided
Doulas who provide support during childbirth are called "birth doulas"; those who provide support during the postpartum period, such as information on newborn care and breastfeeding support or emotional support for the new mother, are called "postpartum doulas." Typically, a doula meets with the expectant mother or parents prior to childbirth. During these prenatal visits, the doula and her client begin to build a trusting relationship, and birth plans and/or postpartum plans are discussed. Once labor begins,

the doula remains with the laboring mother constantly until the infant is born. During labor, the birth doula provides continuous emotional, physical, and informational support. Emotional support includes encouraging and praising the laboring mother. Examples of physical support include soothing the laboring mother with massages, holding, and hugging and assisting the mother with various labor positions appropriate for each stage of labor. Informational support includes assisting expectant mothers and parents in learning about various childbirth options and providing advice and information on comfort techniques such as breathing, positioning, and relaxation. Doulas can also enhance the communication between the laboring woman and the medical staff by helping communicate needs and wishes.

When the laboring mother has her partner present, the role of the doula is not to interfere but rather to provide as much or as little support as desired. Partners can feel overwhelmed with the power of the childbirth experience. Seeing their loved one in pain and feeling helpless to alleviate the pain can also be a difficult experience and hinder the support the partner is able to provide. A doula can reduce this pressure on the partner. With the doula's continuous support, the partner can participate in the birth at a certain comfort level while still supporting the laboring woman.

Doulas work independently or through hospitals or other medical agencies. Most doulas charge a flat fee for their services, which typically include at least one prenatal visit, support during childbirth (for birth doulas), and at least one postpartum visit (more for postpartum doulas). At times, doulas can offer their services on a sliding scale.

Effects of Doula Presence
In the United States, the first studies of the effects of doulas on the childbirth experience were conducted in the 1970s by John Kennell and Marshall Klaus. These researchers found that doulas had very positive influences on childbirth outcomes. Since then, other experts have found similar results. For example, women who are assisted by doulas often have shorter labors, report experiencing less pain during childbirth, describe their labor pain as being more manageable than women without a doula, and are more satisfied with their birth experiences. Also, mothers assisted by doulas have lower rates of cesarean and forceps deliveries, experience fewer complications during childbirth, have lower rates of epidural use, and are more likely to deliver without the use of pain medication. Postpartum doulas also provide valuable support as mothers and their partners transition to parenthood in the weeks following birth. Postpartum doulas typically provide emotional support, practical help with errands, assistance with the baby, and advice on various aspects of parenting.

See also Midwifery

References and further reading
Kennell, John H., et al. 1991. "Continuous Emotional Support During Labor in a U.S. Hospital: A Randomized Controlled Trial." *Journal of the American Medical Association* 265: 2197–2201.
Kennell, John H., and S. K. McGrath. 1993. "Labor Support by a Doula for Middle-Income Couples: The Effect on Cesarean Rates." *Pediatric Research* 32: 12A.
Landry, Sarah H., et al. 1998. "The Effects of Doula Support During Labor on Mother-Infant Interaction at 2 months." *Pediatric Research* 43(4): pt. 11, 13A.
Martin, S., et al. 1998. "The Effect of Doula Support During Labor on Mother-Infant Interaction at 2 Months." *Infant Behavior and Development* 21: 556.

Down Syndrome
See Genetic Disorders

Dreams
When infants can form mental images and symbolic representations (such as using a block to sit a doll on and grinning as she says "potty!" to the doll), usually somewhere after eighteen months, they are more likely to have dreams and by two years of age, even nightmares. By eighteen months some infants become afraid of the dark or afraid of a doctor giving shots, and disturbing dreams may arise. If a two-year-old is afraid of monsters seen on television or heard in a story, he may worry about possible monsters hiding in the closet or under the bed and may waken from a bad dream crying out about a monster. Sometimes a young toddler calls out words in sleep, indicating that the child is having a dream. By three years, an older toddler can tell a beloved grandpa who has just come back from a trip: "Grandpa, I dreamed about you!"

Dressing Infants and Toddlers
Parents and caregivers often have questions about how to dress a baby, particularly newborns. During cooler weather, a good rule of thumb is to dress a baby six months or younger in one extra layer than the adult is wearing. Young infants may become colder easier for several reasons. For one thing, they cannot yet shiver. When an adult is cold, he shivers, and this action warms the body. Young babies lose about 25 percent of body heat from the

head, and this is why placing a cap on young infants is important. Generally, layers of light clothes are more effective and less cumbersome than a very heavy piece of clothing. Mittens and scarves also play an important role in protecting babies' skin outdoors. When traveling in the car in cold weather, at least one layer of clothing, hats, and mittens can be removed to prevent overheating, assuming that the car is heated. For walking toddlers, shoes should be waterproof. Both infants and toddlers should have a snack before going outdoors for any length of time. Maintaining body heat takes energy, and a snack before outdoor play can bolster the body's ability to stay warm. Any wet clothing should be changed immediately. Of course, if the weather is very cold, indoor play is more appropriate. Most experts recommend keeping the indoor temperature between 68 and 72 degrees during the day, although the temperature may be turned down at night. For warmth at night, layers of light blankets or the use of blanket sleepers are preferable to the use of heavy blankets that may increase the incidence of sudden infant death syndrome.

In warm weather, both younger and older babies/toddlers can dress in the same manner as adults. Generally in warm weather, babies do not need extra clothing. A light sweater or long-sleeved shirt might be useful in the cooler evening or in an air-conditioned room. A key piece of clothing in the summer, however, is a lightweight sun hat that will protect the face and nose from sunburn. Similarly, parents and caregivers should keep children out of direct sunlight during peak hours when the sun is at its strongest. Babies, with their delicate skin, are especially sensitive to sunlight. If babies and toddlers will be in

direct sunlight, light, long-sleeved clothing may be appropriate; a doctor may recommend use of sunscreen lotion in babies six months and older. Parents and caregivers should be mindful that the sun's powerful rays pass through cloud cover. Sun protection is necessary on cloudy days. Exposure to direct sunlight can also interfere with some medications, including some antibiotics, so parents and caregivers should check with physicians about sun exposure.

Overheating tends to be a problem in summertime. If the baby is perspiring (sweating), she may be too warm. Making sure cars are well ventilated and cooled before loading a baby in a carseat is helpful. Likewise, open windows and ceiling fans can help to cool and circulate indoors. If portable box fans are used, they must be placed out of the child's reach. A tiny finger can easily be poked through the protective grate of a fan. Taking in additional fluids also helps baby stay hydrated. Many babies like to play or sleep in just a diaper. This is fine for the baby. If the air conditioner is running a night, a light sleeper and very light cover may be used.

Dressing a Baby
Once the correct clothes have been selected, the next task is to get the clothes on the baby. Parents of newborns may be worried about hurting the baby as they manipulate arms and legs into leg and arm openings. Likewise, parents of older babies and toddlers find helping a wiggling child into clothes is a challenge. Choosing the right kind of clothes can help in both cases. For instance, clothes with wide neck openings or snaps at the neck are easy to maneuver over heads. Check the type of snap used. Often, large, wide snaps are easier to fasten than smaller, thinner

snaps. Likewise, zip closures running down the front or side of the clothing can speed dressing. Stretchy fabrics that give are easier to maneuver onto a baby than more tightly woven fabrics.

Another trick, especially effective with older infants and toddlers, is to make dressing a social time. Allowing toddlers to choose some of their own clothing reduces battles over clothing and helps the child feel in charge. When she feels in charge, she is more likely to cooperate in the dressing process. Games like peek-a-boo as baby's head is emerging from the head opening are fun, and a game of "where is baby's hand?" can make a baby eager to plunge her arm though the sleeve and push her hand out. Allowing plenty of time for dressing also eases the process for everyone. Dressing babies and toddlers takes time and is much more enjoyable if it can be a leisurely process with time for conversation and games.

Key Pieces of Clothing
For newborns, key pieces of clothing include one-piece body suits, commonly called "onesies"; cap; booties or socks; and sleepers. Newborns often spend much of their time in one-piece sleepers and playsuits. Cotton undershirts are also useful and can provide a light layer of extra clothing. As babies grow, their dressing needs become much like that of older children. As with any child, easily washable clothing made of breathable, natural fabrics like cotton are most desirable. Mix and match clothing can build a wardrobe with relative ease. Parents and caregivers should be cautious to remove any small objects or strings from clothing that could be bitten or chewed off and cause a choking hazard. New clothing for babies and toddlers rarely feature strings (such as hood strings), as they pose a serious strangulation risk.

Shoes. Although shoe manufacturers and advertisers might say otherwise, infants really do not need to wear shoes until they begin to walk or cruise around from one piece of furniture to another. Even then, they only need shoes when walking outdoors or on some other surface from which their feet need protection. When indoors or on another safe surface, going shoeless is preferable. Being barefoot or in gripper sole socks allows the baby to use her feet and toes to grip the floor. This exercise helps to build her balance and coordination and strengthens the muscles in her feet; all things that will aid her walking.

When choosing shoes for little feet, experts suggest looking for the following characteristics:

- Shoes made from breathable fabrics like canvas or leather.
- Shoes with little or no arch support. Although this might sound unusual to the adult who looks for good arch support, the arches on young children do not develop until the child is ten or eleven years old. Therefore, a shoe with an arch can be uncomfortable for an infant/toddler.
- Shoes with a wide cut to allow plenty of room for toe space. Cramped shoes force toes together and can cause calluses, corns, and bunions.
- Shoes with a thin, flat leather sole (for first shoes especially). Rubber-soled shoes grip the ground so well that they can disrupt the unsteady balance of a new walker.

Once toddlers gain their confidence and their balance in walking, rubber-soled shoes are fine. Shoes with a heel (wedge or platform shoes) are best saved for the later years when balance and agility are better developed.

- Shoes with secure closures that cross over the top of the foot or high-back shoes that nestle the ankle. Velcro closures are secure and easy to fasten on wiggly feet. Shoes with laces should always be double-knotted to prevent tripping.
- New shoes rather than hand-me-down whenever possible. As many adults know, shoes mold to the wearer's foot. Hand-me-down shoes may not fit the child's foot as well as they should. The good news is that parents and caregivers need not spend a lot of money on new shoes. Off-brand shoes at discount stores can function as well as pricier brand-name shoes.

Knowing what to look for in a shoe is one thing; determining the correct fit and size is quite another task. Infant shoe sizes are usually called "prewalkers" and run sizes 1–4. Toddler shoes run in sizes 5 to 8, and then youth sizes begin. Toddlers grow very quickly, and that goes for the feet too. Toddlers may outgrow their shoes every three to four months. When fitting shoes, the following tips can be useful:

- Ask the salesperson to measure the length and width of both of the child's feet, and buy the size that fits the largest foot.
- Have the child try on shoes with the type of sock he normally

wears. Shoes fit differently with the thickness of the sock.
- Check the shoe for any irritating elements, such as tags or seams on the inside of the shoe that can rub against the child's foot.
- Ask the child to wiggle her toes and check to make sure the toe does not rub against the end of the shoe.
- Check to make sure the shoe is the correct width. If the shoe is too wide, it cannot provide adequate support to the foot when the child is walking.

See also Traveling with Infants

Drugs

After three decades of intense research, there is no question that drugs can compromise the fetal environment and negatively affect the fetus structurally and functionally. What remains to be determined, however, are issues related to dose effects, time of insult, and the impact of cross-drug effects, including over-the-counter as well as illicit drugs. Many investigators today are invested in research that examines the impact of polydrug use, including combinations of alcohol, nicotine, cocaine, and heroin, among others. Narcotics readily cross the placental barrier, with such drugs as barbiturates linked to fetal distress. Newborns can be born addicted to barbiturates, amphetamines, and heroin, and withdrawal from such addictions is characterized by hyperirritability, vomiting, trembling, rapid respiration, and hyperactivity. The more intense the addiction, the more severe the withdrawal symptoms.

For decades we have known that nicotine affects the fetus. Studies in the late 1930s at the Fels Research Institute demonstrated that smoking caused acceleration of fetal heart rate. Lester Sontag and his colleagues deprived heavy-smoking pregnant women of cigarettes and then offered them a chance to smoke. Even before the cigarette was lit, fetal heart rate accelerated. This suggested a direct link between the pregnant woman's emotion-hormonal response and fetal heart rate. Smoking has also been linked with prematurity and small-gestational-age infants.

Alcohol can have profound effects on the fetus, producing a condition known as fetal alcohol syndrome or contributing to what have been described as fetal alcohol effects. Conditions associated with fetal alcohol syndrome include prematurity, mental retardation, heart abnormalities, small head size, facial disorders, and behavior problems.

See also Alcohol Effects; Prenatal Development

Dyad

A social unit consisting of two persons (e.g., mother-infant, father-infant, or mother-father). In many areas of research the quality of the dyadic relationship is believed to be important for development of interpersonal relationships or to contribute to issues related to emergent psychopathology.

E

Early Deaths
See Death

Early Head Start
See Individuals with Disabilities Education Act

Early Intervention
Early intervention aims at improving a child's potential. Infants who come into the world with handicaps such as cerebral palsy generally benefit from special programs. Benefits include improved cognitive functioning, language abilities, motor skills, and social-emotional growth. Early intervention services for handicapped children are supported by many government agencies. Unfortunately, developmental delays are not as obvious or treatable among children born into poverty. In the United States today, one out of every four infants lives in poverty. Families with inadequate financial support often fail to provide the necessary cognitive and social experiences for children's optimal growth. Parental stress and social isolation place children at risk for physical abuse. Early childhood experts, working together with government officials, have developed various types of interventions that improve children's potential for growth.

Center-Based Early Intervention
In the 1820s and 1830s, infant schools flourished in cities such as New York, Boston, and Philadelphia. These schools attempted to rescue underprivileged children from conditions of poverty by teaching them moral values along with basic reading and writing skills. The infant-school movement capitalized on the Enlightenment theory that children were basically good and that education should be based on children's natural curiosity. Swiss educator Johann Pestalozzi publicized infant schools as social reform through early childhood education. He believed that a nurturing environment, coupled with opportunities for intellectual stimulation, would compensate for inadequacies experienced by poor immigrant children. Innovative educational methods encouraged children's activity and curiosity rather than having them sit still for long periods. Yet with opposition from the emerging medical community and the middle-class public, private benefactors withdrew their support from the infant-school movement.

In the late 1800s, benefactresses such as Jane Addams provided center-based care for poor children, but government support for early intervention did not arrive until the 1950s. In 1952, Jean Piaget published *The Origins of Intelligence in Children*, which introduced the idea that intelligence began to develop in the earliest months of life. Early intervention programs for at-risk families were supported by the Supreme Court desegregation case *Brown v. Board of Education,* which affirmed all children's rights to an adequate education. Around the same time, John Kennedy's presidency ushered in the war on poverty. National concerns led to the development and evaluation of programs that aimed at lifting children out of poverty through education. Early intervention programs such as Head Start attempted to encourage cognitive development of young children in poverty.

When Head Start began in 1965, little was known about early intervention. An influential book by J. McVicker Hunt, *Intelligence and Experience,* claimed that IQ could be raised as much as seventy points by enhancing early experiences. His theories gave credence to the ideas of the war on poverty under Kennedy and then Lyndon B. Johnson. Government leaders and early childhood professionals hoped to eradicate poverty and ignorance by changing young children's environments. At the inauguration of Project Head Start, President Johnson explained the benefits of early childhood education for disadvantaged children: "The project is designed to put them on an even footing with their classmates as they enter school." Some researchers, however, cautioned that one year of preschool would not eradicate the effects of a lifetime of poverty.

Head Start benefited from the inclusion of early childhood education experts in its earliest stages. Members of the planning committee were chosen on the basis of their creativity and leadership in the early childhood field, rather than on the basis of their political strengths. As a result, they included several innovative elements, many of which proved to be essential to intervention programs. In addition to academic programs, health care, immunization programs, social services, and nutritious meals helped meet the needs of at-risk children. The inclusion of parents as volunteers within Head Start paved the way for later parental involvement in the public school system. Training of these volunteers often led to employment for mothers of children in the program, providing a more stable economic base for the family.

Other influential early childhood programs in the 1960s attempted to change home and school environments. Many universities tested model programs for at-risk children and evaluated the effects of these programs. Perhaps the best-known is the Perry Preschool Project. A longitudinal follow-up of this intensive model program indicated that the government saved $7 on social programs for every $1 spent. Teenagers who were involved in this project as young children were less likely to engage in criminal activity or become pregnant. They were more likely to complete high school and be self-supporting. The Abcederian Project out of the University of North Carolina–Chapel Hill provided high-quality child care for children from six weeks through kindergarten in the late 1970s. When the children were twelve years old, those who had attended the program had higher IQ scores and were doing much better in school achievement. In reviewing these and other model programs, researchers have concluded that intensive, center-based programs do make a difference in the future of at-risk children.

History of Home Visitation
Home visitation began in the late nineteenth century as a charitable institution serving impoverished families. Charity

Organization Societies initiated the social-work profession, originally using volunteer home visitors. In the early 1900s, it became apparent that there were not enough ladies of leisure interested in charity work to fill this need. Paid social workers, such as Mary Richmond, transformed the friendly home visit into casework. Richmond described the superiority of the home visit as a means for understanding the family system. Home visiting provided the opportunity for observation of the interrelationships of family members within their home environment. She also noted that visitors needed to be sensitive to the cultural differences between themselves and their clients. Visitors who were condescending toward their clients were not very useful.

Social workers all but abandoned the home visit during the 1920s and 1930s as part of a push for professionalism within agencies. In the 1940s and 1950s, home visitors practiced through welfare agencies and agencies involved in delinquency prevention. Research conducted among at-risk families in the 1950s concluded that home visits for first-time mothers strengthened the professional relationship between the client and social worker. It also provided useful additional information that could not be obtained by meeting in an agency's office.

The Office of Education's 1966 report *Equality of Educational Opportunity* influenced the direction of early intervention. This report indicated that children's home life had more of an effect on school success than the quality of schools attended. Professors such as Ira Gordon determined to change the quality of the home environment through home-visiting programs. The Gordon Parent Education Project attempted to break the poverty cycle by using parent educators to teach mothers in disadvantaged families. Weekly visits introduced educational toys and activities for children under the age of three, based on Jean Piaget's theories of cognitive development. Compared to similar children who did not receive home visitation, children participating in the program excelled in intelligence and later school performance. Continued follow-up programs during the early years of school enhanced children's academic gains. More recent home-visiting programs for young children in at-risk families have shown success in improving children's potential. Home visitation is often preferable to center-based interventions for families with very young infants.

References and further reading
Slavin, R., N. L. Karweit, and B. A. Wasik. 1994. *Preventing Early School Failure.* Boston: Allyn and Bacon.

Early Language Milestone Screening Tests
See Assessment; Language

Eclampsia
See Prenatal Development

Edge Detection
Detecting edges involves the discrimination of contrasts between light and dark. Infants become more sensitive to subtle differences in these contrasts after the first several months of life.

See also Face Perception; Perception

Ego Development
According to Sigmund Freud's theory of psychosexual development, the ego is the

part of the personality that balances the demands of the id, which drives basic biological needs, and the superego, which serves as the conscience.

See also Emotion; Freud, Sigmund

Egocentrism

During infancy and early childhood, Jean Piaget asserted, children have difficulty perceiving the world as seen and experienced by other people. Reality is subjective and based on one's own point of view. This self-centeredness was termed "egocentrism." Egocentrism is an important part of Piaget's theory of cognitive development and characterizes what he originally called the early stage of the preoperational period (two to seven years of age). Several other investigators were dissatisfied with the discrepancy between Piaget's characterization of the preschool age child's cognitive abilities and so designed experiments that demonstrated that Piaget's tasks were partially responsible for how children responded to them. Notable among critiques of Piaget's theory in that regard, Rochel Gelman demonstrated that when one uses other tasks children between two and seven are not so egocentric as Piaget claimed.

See also Piaget, Jean

Embryo
See Prenatal Development

Emde, Robert N.

Robert Emde is an extremely influential child psychiatrist at the University of Colorado Center for Health Sciences whose work has significantly advanced understanding of early emotional development and self-regulation. Emde has served as president of nearly every key professional society that is concerned with child development, infant development, and infant mental health, and he has been a core member of several national studies of child development in the United States. He is also instrumental in maintaining the traditions of the Developmental Psychobiology Group at the Health Sciences Center, a group that historically is connected to the work of Adolph Meyer and René Spitz.

See also Basic Motives

Emotion

Emotions are feeling states, experienced by all infant/toddlers, that increase in complexity over time. The word "emotion" was derived from a Latin word meaning "to excite." Defining emotion can be complex, as any definition is likely to vary according to particular theoretical orientations. For instance, some scientists define emotion from a social and behavioral point of view; they think about behaviors associated with various emotions and ways in which the environment shapes the display of emotional behavior. Other scientists think about emotion from a physiological and neurological point of view; they are more interested in emotion as a neurological process, which reflects the activity of the brain and central nervous system.

Theories of Emotional Development
There are many theories describing how emotions develop. Some of the most well known theoretical perspectives include behaviorism and social-learning theory, psychoanalytic theory, discrete emotions

theory, and differential emotions theory. Ecological systems theory also provides a framework to explore how emotional development is shaped.

Behaviorism emphasizes the role of techniques such as conditioning and reinforcement in shaping emotion and emotional expressiveness. For instance, psychologist John Watson conducted a classic experiment in which he taught an eleven-month-old infant, Albert, to fear a white rat by exposing the infant to a loud, sharp sound, alarming to most any infant, each time the rat appeared. Initially, Albert was curious and reached to touch the rat. However, with the pairing of the sound and the rat, Albert soon began to fear the rat, crying and turning away from the rat as soon as it appeared. Watson called this *classical conditioning* and concluded that most emotional responses are learned through conditioning. Later, in the 1960s, *operant conditioning* was studied in relation to children's emotional development and expressiveness.

Operant conditioning uses strategies such as positive and negative reinforcement and punishment to shape behaviors. Scientists discovered that an infant's smiling, crying, and vocalizations could be shaped by the use of reinforcement or punishment. *Social-learning theory* highlights the importance of adult models in influencing infant/toddlers' emotional responses in various situations. Albert Bandura, a social-learning theorist, also believes cognition plays a role in how young children respond emotionally. For instance, Bandura's work suggests that as young children gain more sophisticated cognitive skills, they can attain a particular emotional state by thinking about a similar emotional situation they experienced or observed others experiencing.

Both behaviorism and social-learning theory emphasize the importance of the surrounding environment in shaping infant/toddlers' emotional experiences.

Psychoanalytic theories of emotional development suggest that our conscience and subconscious govern our emotional development. Sigmund Freud, the father of psychoanalytic theory, believed that there are three parts to one's personality: the id, the ego, and the superego. The id is that part of the personality concerned with basic physical needs and wants. The superego is that part of the personality concerned with cultural rules and moral values, and typically does not develop until the preschool years. The ego acts as a regulatory system, balancing the needs of the id with the concerns of the superego. The ego is also responsible for driving the infant to have needs met in the quickest manner. Freud believed that infants are primarily controlled by the id, that is, infants need their basic health, nutritional, and emotional needs met and can rarely delay gratification. Over time, older infants and toddlers can learn to delay gratification. For instance, the toddler who screamed to be fed as an infant can now wait a few minutes while someone prepares lunch, expressing his emotion with pouts, sighs, or even verbalizations.

Psychoanalytic theorist Erik Erikson outlined eight emotional conflicts to be resolved over the course of the life span. The first two tasks are related to the infancy period. According to Erikson, the first conflict that infants face is to attain a sense of basic trust versus developing a sense of mistrust. When infants' physical, social, and emotional needs are met, they come to perceive their world as being safe. When they are hungry, they know they will be fed. When they cry, they know they will be comforted, and so on. This sense of

A father and his newborn daughter.
(Courtesy of the Decker family)

trust enables the infant to explore the world and the people in it with confidence and the knowledge that she is safe and protected. An infant who perceives the world as being untrustworthy will have a much more difficult time connecting emotionally with parent/caregivers, unable to trust parents/caregivers to provide for basic needs. Erikson describes the second task in terms of an infant's autonomy. In order to resolve this task in the most positive manner, the infant must develop a sense of autonomy, or independence, versus developing feelings of shame and doubt. When the infant comes to perceive himself as autonomous and capable, he feels empowered to explore his surroundings with con-

fidence; such explorations facilitate all areas of his growth and well-being. Still, the infant who has doubts about his abilities will show much less initiative in exploring his world and interacting with the people in it.

According to *discrete emotion theory*, a specific set of core emotions is evident in the earliest weeks of life, including interest, fear, anger, sadness, joy, surprise, excitement, and disgust. Discrete emotion theorists believe that each emotion is separate and serves a specific purpose in the child's development. Each of the eight emotional states have distinct facial expressions, observable in infancy, that accompany the feeling. In turn, each facial expression serves a very specific function for the infant because it arouses a particular effect in the parents/caregivers. For instance, the facial expression depicting joy arouses a different response than that of anger. These specific facial expressions are also associated with a corresponding motivational state in the infant, that is, infants typically respond to certain emotions with actions unique to that emotion. Feeling joy is likely to motivate the infant to express joy not only through facial expression but also through body movements and vocalizations. In fact, scientists such as Joseph Campos and Linda Barrett believe that emotions are linked to clusters of related body movements, vocalizations, and behavioral goals rather than only being associated with a facial expression. From their perspective, emotion is expressed in a variety of ways. A happy infant, for instance, might express the emotion by squealing, wiggling, and smiling. Another infant might express happiness in similar but unique ways. As infant/toddlers age and mature cognitively they learn to express emotions in socially appropriate ways through social reinforcement and social learning or by watching adult models. In short, they learn to self-regulate, which means they develop the ability to recognize and manage their emotions to behave in a socially acceptable manner.

Other theoretical perspectives closely resemble discrete emotions theory. For instance, *differential emotion theory* suggests that specific emotions play an important role in development at specific times. Thus, some sets of emotions are more crucial to development than other sets of emotions throughout four key stages: infancy, toddlerhood through the preschool years, middle to late childhood, and adolescence. Differential emotion theorists view emotion as central to cognitive development and learning. According to differential emotion theory, discrete emotions are organized into what Carroll Izzard calls "modules," which are highly organized and function independently of each other. Although discrete emotion theorists believe that facial expressions correspond to particular emotions, differential emotion theorists specify that the emotional state can exist without facial expression. As infant/toddlers mature cognitively, these emotion systems become integrated, which allows for the existence of more sophisticated emotions such as anxiety, pride, and so on.

Whereas discrete emotion theorists emphasize eight discrete emotions, other scientists believe there are four core emotions at birth—joy, anger, sadness, and fear—that become more differentiated and specialized over the first three years of life. For instance, joy expands to include similar emotions such as happiness, contentment, satisfaction, pleasure, and pride. Taken together, the discrete emotion perspective and the differential emotion viewpoint represent a functionalist approach to emotional development. This means that emotions are viewed as purposeful and central to all aspects of development, including cognitive and social functioning. For instance, scientists have found that even in very young babies emotion appears to be associated with learning. First, emotions are evident when a task is mastered; the infant shows pleasure in mastering a task, such as shaking a rattle and producing noise. Also, the emotions felt during learning are remembered and influence the infant's approach to new tasks. Emotions are also powerful influences on social behavior, for infants and others. For example, even young infants learn to read and decode the emotional signals of others, and they use this information to regulate their own responses and behaviors. By three months of age, infants and mothers in face-to-face interactions have become quite skilled at responding to the cues of the other in specific ways. The infant's emotions also influence the behaviors of others. For instance, when an infant cries, the parent/caregiver responds with soothing words and touch.

Cognitive/constructivist theories of emotional development emphasize the parallel between emotional development and cognitive development. Theorists like Alan Sroufe believe that emotion develops as cognition becomes more advanced. For instance, in order to feel a sophisticated emotion like shame, young children must first have attained a sense of self as separate from others, be aware of social expectations, and understand that their actions have in some way violated those expectations.

As infant/toddlers experience emotion in themselves and observe the emotional behaviors of others, they learn to construct the social meanings of emotion. They learn what angry looks like, and they learn to express particular emotions in certain situations by watching adult models. Parent/caregivers can label emotions for them by making comments such as, "You're crying. You look sad." Practices such as this help infant/toddlers attach meaning and labels to their feelings. From the constructivist viewpoint, then, emotional development requires active learning in which infant/toddlers are continually experiencing emotion, expressing emotion in their daily experiences, and adapting emotional expression based on their experiences and observations of the environment and the people in it.

Finally, *ecological systems theory* provides a holistic framework to explore emotional development. A key principle of the ecological model of development holds that an infant influences and is influenced by the surrounding environment. Urie Bronfenbrenner developed the ecological model to conceptualize the complex relationships between the infant, family, and society. Bronfenbrenner described four levels in the infant's ecological environment: the microsystem, mesosystem, exosystem, and macrosystem. Each level represents a progressively larger environmental context. The microsystem refers the infant's connection to the most immediate environment, such as the family or child-care center; the mesosystem encompasses the relationships between key microsystem environments, such as interactions between the infant's family and the child-care center. The exosystem and the macrosystem are concerned with the relationships between social systems that do not contain the infant but influence the infant in some

way. The former includes settings such as the government and the economy that might not influence the infant directly yet shape the family in which the infant grows. The macrosystem encompasses larger cultural practices, values, and ideologies that shape all social systems. Either directly or indirectly, the social systems described in Bronfenbrenner's four environmental levels influence how infants develop emotionally, including how they come to understand and manage their emotions.

Milestones in Emotional Development
Scientist Alan Fogel describes emotional development in terms of growth in three related areas: emotional expression, emotional affect, and self-regulation. *Emotional expression* is concerned with how inner feeling states are expressed through facial expressions and behavioral expressions such as crying or vocalizing. *Affective development* refers to that part of emotional development in which inner emotional states are studied, whether or not they are expressed outwardly. As infants/toddlers mature, they experience more complex feeling states. Finally, *self-control*, or *self-regulation*, is the area of emotional development related to the infant's control and management of emotion. Each of the three areas of emotional development are characterized by different but related milestones in development. Milestones in emotional expression include the infant's growing abilities to express a variety of emotions and the acquisition of social display rules. Affective development is marked by the development of a sense of self and the ability to experience an ever-broadening range of emotions. Self-control is characterized by the acquisition of a variety of strategies to enhance self-regulation and by the

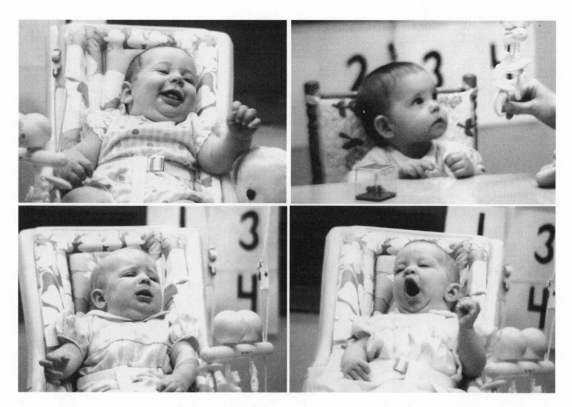

Babies show the same facial expressions of emotion states as adults do. These infants have expressions adults label as delight/happiness, sobriety/attentiveness, anguish/fretfulness, and boredom/fatigue. (Courtesy of Suzanne Siemering)

abilities to respond to the emotions in others while still managing one's own emotions.

Expressing Basic Emotions
Many scientists believe that core emotions (joy, anger, sadness, and fear) are evident during early infancy, peak in intensity at certain periods throughout infancy, and become differentiated over time. Joy first becomes evident at about six weeks; anger becomes evident at three to four months; sadness is first recognized and expressed at five to seven months; and fear is usually expressed for the first time around seven to nine months. These emotions are expressed through facial expressions, vocalizations, and body movements. The abilities to express emotion in different ways and to express a wider variety of emotion increases with age. Newborns, for example, display degrees of attention, arousal, and distress but cannot clearly express other emotions such as pleasure or happiness or sadness. By six to eight weeks, however, most infants begin to display social smiles, indicating their feelings of pleasure or happiness.

Also, according to many scientists, emotion and its expression are tied to cognition. Stanley Greenspan, a psychiatrist who has studied infants for many years, outlines the importance of language and cognitive skills in infants' abilities to communicate their ideas, wishes, and emotional ideas. For example, in order to feel anger, the infant must recognize from a cognitive perspective that he/she can cause things to happen and that anything or anyone blocking his/her attempts to create an action makes him/her feel angry. The emergence of negative emotions, such as anger, corresponds with emerging cause-and-effect understanding as outlined in Jean Piaget's stages of sensorimotor development.

Learning Social Display Rules. Over time, children learn to express emotion in appropriate manners as they come to understand social display rules. Social display rules govern how, when, and where emotions can be expressed and vary enormously by culture. Even in the earliest months of life, infants are aware of which emotions are encouraged and which are discouraged and under what circumstances. For instance, infants learn early on that the middle of the night is not the time to smile and seek social interaction with parents. Parents shape this behavior by making middle-of-the-night feeding or diapering encounters brief and boring. In American society, negative emotions, often expressed by crying, are discouraged, particularly in the presence of others. Think of how often a parent can be seen "shushing" a crying baby in the grocery store.

Emotional display rules reflect the values and practices of the community and culture in which infant/toddlers live. For instance, in one family a toddler might be encouraged to express anger and "fight back" when hit by another child, whereas another family might encourage the toddler to verbalize his feelings by saying, "Stop! No hit!" Parent/caregivers of tod-

dlers often verbalize social display rules as they talk about when and how to express particular emotions in various circumstances. Gradually, children learn that even though they may be feeling one emotion social display rules require that they express another feeling through their words and actions. This separation of emotional state from emotional expression takes time to develop but becomes ingrained in children's social understanding. For instance, a preschooler learns to smile and say "Thank you" for the sweater she received as a birthday present from Grandma when she really feels disappointed at not receiving the toy she wanted. Generally, social display rules require children to display positive emotional "masks" as opposed to negative emotional expressions. Social pressures, cultural expectations, and peer relationships all play a role in children's acquisition of social display rules.

Managing Emotion. The process of learning to handle emotions and adjust an emotional state so it is comfortable and not overwhelming is called *emotional self-regulation*. Psychiatrist Stanley Greenspan described self-regulation as being the first of six milestones in infant's emotional development. Learning to recognize and manage emotion is challenging for several reasons. First, infants need stimulation in their environments to learn and grow. Yet they must also learn to manage the environment so it is not too stimulating. Striking this balance takes time and practice. Second, the infant/toddler may be feeling several emotions at one time, and this can be confusing. For instance, the seven-month-old, in the grips of stranger anxiety, may feel anger, fear, and sadness as his parent walks out the door, leaving

him with his child-care provider. Infant/
toddlers rely on a variety of strategies to
help them manage emotion. Some of
these strategies are innate, meaning they
are present at birth, and other strategies
are learned. Even newborn infants possess
skill in self-comforting. Sucking on the
thumb, wrist, or hand is one effective way
the infant can calm himself and organize
behavior. Although the newborn is not
aware of any particular emotion in the
same way an older infant might be,
he/she is aware of basic comfort and discomfort. Sucking is one soothing strategy
that can help the infant transition from a
crying behavioral state to a state of quiet
behavior. For some infants steady rhythmical sounds, such as running water or
the constant hum of a hair dryer, can help
the infant sooth and organize behavior.
Other infants find staring at a light or
blank wall to be soothing. The sensitive
caregiver or parent will recognize the
most effective soothing strategies for
their infants and help them to use these
strategies when needed or engage in other
soothing behaviors such as rocking or
crooning to infants.

As infant/toddlers master language, it
can become an important skill in learning to manage emotion. The toddler who
can say "Me so mad!" at clean-up time
has found an appropriate way to express
his feelings. Similarly, the toddler who
croons to herself "Mommy back soon" as
she is left at child care feels more in control of her emotions. More mature motor
skills and mobility also help the
infant/toddler manage emotion. For
instance, after about four months of age,
the infant can consistently get her hand
to mouth, sucking to calm herself, but
still be able to engage the environment;
she might be feeling anxious because
there are strangers visiting in her home,

so she sucks her thumb but continues to
finger the blocks with which she was
playing. Similarly, the toddler who is
fearful of new people and things can walk
away from them and back to the safety of
the parent's arms.

Regulation and expression of emotion
may also be influenced by temperament.
Campos described temperament as differences in behavioral expressions of emotionality and emotional arousal. Alexander Thomas and Stella Chess identified
nine components of temperament style,
which includes the infant activity level,
rhythmicity, approach or withdrawal
style, adaptability, sensory threshold,
intensity of response, quality of mood,
distractibility, and persistence and attention span. Temperament plays a part in
how infant/toddlers express emotion. For
instance, some infants have very intense
responses to sensations such as pain or
hunger and may emit a piercing scream
when feeling these sensations. Other
infants may have less intense responses
and convey what they are feeling with
whimpers or less intense crying. Thomas
and Chess developed three styles of temperament based on the groupings of the
nine components of temperament. Infant/
toddlers with an "easy" or "flexible" temperament tend to display more positive
emotion, handle changes with less stress
than other children, adapt easily to new
situations, and so on. "Difficult" or
"feisty" and "slow-to-warm-up" or "fearful" infant/toddlers are more likely to display intense emotional reactions to environmental stimuli, changes in routines,
and so on. Thus, emotional regulation is
influenced by temperament. When par-
ent/caregivers come to understand individual temperament styles, they are better able to support the development of the
emotional self-regulation.

As noted earlier, parent/caregivers play an important role in helping infant/toddlers manage emotion. They help infant/toddlers manage emotion in several ways. Newborns have little capacity for excessive emotion stimulation. However, as infants mature neurologically, they are able to handle more stimulation. A three-month-old, for example, can easily engage the parent in "conversations" of cooing and smiling. The sensitive parent/caregiver adjusts the pace of the interaction to match the developmental level of the infant. By gradually upping the ante of the emotional interaction, the parent helps increase the infant's tolerance level for stimulation. As this tolerance level increases, infant/toddlers are better able to manage their emotions.

Parent/caregivers are also influenced by the emotional cues of the infant. For instance, when an infant cries, the caregiver comes to comfort the infant, and the infant's emotions are influenced by this comforting action. This interactive process is called *mutual regulation*. In the early months of life, mutual regulation is a very important part of the infant's emotional self-regulation. Over time, the infant's repertoire of self-regulation skills will grow, and the external regulation of the adult will be less necessary.

Infants organize and base their own behavioral responses according to the cues of the parent/caregiver. As infant/toddlers grow, they become experts at decoding the adult's facial expressions. In fact, by nine or ten months of age, infants decode facial cues and base their response on how they perceive the adult to be feeling. This is called *social referencing*. For example, when a new toy is presented to the older infant, she may look to her parent in deciding whether or not to approach the toy. If the parent looks fearful, the infant usually avoids the toy and turns away. However, if the parent looks happy, the infant will eagerly approach and explore the toy. Initially, infants recognize positive emotions illustrated in happy facial expressions earlier than they can decipher and take meaning from negative emotional expression, particularly if the expression is paired with a voice. Infants learn to decipher tone of voice before they learn to differentiate and take emotional meaning from facial expressions. Social referencing continues to be an important practice throughout childhood. Whereas infant/toddlers look to their parent/caregiver for behavioral cues, older children learn to look toward their peers as well.

Similar to social referencing is *affect sharing*. Alan Fogel explains that through affect sharing infants communicate and confirm their feelings with others. For instance, when an infant has figured out how to make the jack-in-the-box pop up by turning the handle, she smiles, giggles, and then looks to her parent for a confirmatory smile. Fogel explains that social referencing and affect sharing represent the infant's ability to delay an immediate reaction to an emotional situation and to assess alternative reactions. This ability to assess the situation is called *appraisal*. With social referencing, the infant uses appraisal to decide how to react to the emotional stimuli, and with affect sharing the infant responds spontaneously to the emotional arousal and then looks to the parent/caregiver for appraisal of that response.

Adults also help infant/toddlers regulate their emotional states by providing predictable, safe environments and by preparing infant/toddlers for changes in the environment. With the adult's careful preparation, emotional experiences such as going to child care, visiting relatives, or even changing routines at home can be less stressful and alarming to children. Talking about what will happen at child care; showing older infants and toddler pictures of Aunt Sue before visiting; reminding toddlers that there will not be time for the daily trip to the park today— all are strategies to help infant/toddlers handle their emotions in positive and comfortable ways.

Adults also play a key role in increasing infant/toddlers' repertoire of emotion-regulation skills by suggesting ways to manage emotion. For example, the parent who says, "You are SO excited about your birthday you're jumping on the chair! I'm worried you might fall. You can jump on the floor," has achieved two things. First, she has provided a word, "excited," to match the toddler's feeling; eventually he can verbalize his emotion. The more the parent labels and identifies emotions, the more quickly the child will learn to verbalize emotion. Second, she has shown him how he can safely express his enthusiasm by jumping on the floor. At other times, a parent/caregiver might suggest that toddlers talk about their emotions, draw a picture about how they are feeling, physically express an emotion, and so on, depending on the child's age and skills. Over time, children learn to use these and other strategies themselves without adult suggestions.

Achieving a Sense of Self

One of the most important milestones in emotional development is the infant's development of a *sense of self*. The sense of self, sometimes called the *self-concept*, refers to infants' perceptions of themselves. The sense of self is influential in personality development and the ways in which the infant experiences the world.

Therefore, the better the sense of self and the more infants view themselves as lovable, capable individuals, the more optimal emotional and personality development will be. Scientists believe the development of sense of self reflects three accomplishments: the development of self-awareness, the growth of self-recognition (recognizing one's image in photographs or in a mirror, which is called *self-mirror recognition*), and the achievement of self-definition. The success in mastering these tasks and achieving a healthy sense of self is influenced not only by cognitive development but also by infants' experiences. Interactions with parent/caregivers represent a significant component of infants' experiences in their surrounding environment. Generally, higher-quality interactions result in healthier emotional development. Stanley Greenspan described "emotional partnerships" between parent and infant as being vital to achieving a sense of self. He describes the emotional love affair between parent and infant, which peaks from about two to seven months of age, as a key experience in the formation of warm and loving relationships.

Over the first year of life, infants form attachments, which are emotional bonds with the parent/caregiver that endure over time. The quality of the attachment relationship is shaped by the sensitivity and responsiveness of the parent/caregiver. The infant also contributes to the attachment relationship by interacting with and responding to the parent/caregiver. Kathryn Barnard's model of parent-infant interaction depicts the parent's role in the interaction as responding sensitively to the infant's cues, responding to infant distress, and providing growth-fostering experiences. The infant's role in the interaction is to provide clear behavioral cues, such as smiling, vocalizing, or looking away from the parent, and to respond to the parent's interactive behaviors. Both parent and infant are needed to sustain the interaction.

Mary Ainsworth, a pioneer in the study of attachment, called this dance between the parent and the infant a "virtuous spiral." The positive cycle of the interaction is fueled by the parent and infant each responding contingently to the other; when the parent smiles, the baby responds in an appropriate manner. Likewise, when the baby initiates an interaction by cooing to the parent, the adult responds by imitating the sound or by some other action. As the turn-taking "dance" between parent and child continues, it builds in momentum, with each partner contributing to interaction, until a peak is reached and the dance ends or begins again. The momentum of the interaction is described as *entrainment*. These early dances between parent/caregiver and infant lay the foundation for later emotional growth.

Children with secure attachments to their parents may have an easier time dealing with emotion later on. For example, toddlers and preschoolers who were securely attached to their parents as infants show less frustration and more persistence in problem-solving tasks. The attachment relationship plays a key role in how infants organize their behaviors and display emotion. For instance, an eight-month-old infant will watch the parent's smiling face and smile or coo in response. However, if the parent disconnects emotionally and displays a dull, flat facial expression, devoid of emotion, the infant becomes disorganized and begins to look away from the parent, cry, and flail or jerk her arms and legs. Even as adults, individuals are influenced by the attachment relationship they experienced as infants. Adults who had securely attached relationships with their parents are more likely to perceive themselves as valuable and lovable and are more likely to foster secure attachment relationships with their own children.

Responding to the Emotions of Others. The roots of understanding and responding to others' emotional states and expressions start early, when infants begin to observe and detect differences in voice tones and facial expressions. By three months, infants can detect varying emotions expressed through voice tones, and by seven months they begin to match facial expressions and voice tones to ascertain the emotion being expressed. These skills form the foundation for learning to respond appropriately to others.

As with other areas of emotional development, infants/toddlers' abilities to respond to others is tied to cognitive growth and development. As cognitive skills, such as perspective taking, become more sophisticated, so too does emotional understanding. Glimpses of toddlers' and young children's emotional understanding is often displayed in comments they make. For example, one toddler might observe, "Ana cry. She sad." A slightly older child might be able to identify, "Ana want mommy. She sad." By the time children reach preschool age, they are skilled in understanding why a person might be feeling a certain way. As language emerges in the first two years of life, infant/toddlers acquire a vocabulary of feeling words, particularly if parent/caregivers have modeled the appropriate use of these words.

Infants/toddlers also learn how to respond to others by watching adult models and by recalling their own experiences. For instance, a toddler might gently hug a crying peer because he had observed the caregiver modeling this behavior or because he had received hugs previously to comfort him. These early actions are the beginning of more advanced expressions of empathy and altruistic behavior that will become evident throughout the preschool and elementary school years. *Empathy* refers to the ability to understand others' emotions and respond with similar feelings. In order to respond empathically, the child must be able to take the perspective of the other person and develop an appropriate response based on this perspective taking. Although infants/toddlers do not have the cognitive capacity to engage in complex perspective taking, they are capable of some empathic response. Imagine a group of infants in child care. One infant begins to cry and soon the other infants begin to cry as well. Martin Hoffman called this response "global empathy." Hoffman further described the efforts of toddlers with the term "egocentric empathy." An example of egocentric empathy is as follows: two toddlers, Sara and Keisha, are playing in the sandbox at the park while their mothers talk nearby. Keisha gets sand in her eye and begins to cry. Sara watches for a moment, gets up, and brings her mother, rather than Keisha's mother, over to comfort Keisha. In this example, Sara shows her egocentrism; Sara knows that she wants her mommy when she is hurt, so this must be the right solution for anyone else who is hurt as well. Toddlers, however, also show impressive sophistication in their empathic responses. For instance, Carolyn Zahn-Waxler and Marion Radke-Yarrow found that twenty-one-month-old infants would react to their mothers' simulated sadness by trying to distract their

mothers with toys, offering hugs and other physical comfort, and by asking other adults to help.

Skills in responding to others' emotions increase dramatically during the preschool years. For example, during the preschool years and beyond, feelings of empathy promote altruistic behavior. *Altruistic behavior* refers to actions that help others and are carried out with no expectation of reward.

Barriers to Healthy Emotional Development. Infant mental health disorders can disrupt healthy emotional development. Diagnosis of these disorders are usually made by psychiatrists, psychologists, or clinical social workers. Resources such as the *Diagnostic Classification: 0–3 Manual* outline several categories of disorders, such as communication disorders, affect disorders, and adjustment disorders. The disorders were developed for use specifically in the infant mental health field. Disorders can range from mild to severe. One example of a severe disorder is autism, a condition characterized by a devastating lack of social or emotional connection with others. Not always evident from birth, autistic characteristics can appear after the first year. In other cases, autistic characteristics are obvious in the early weeks of life. The exact causes of autism are unknown, but many scientists believe the condition is a result of some sort of neurological defect. Autistic infants/toddlers usually have little or no eye contact with parents/caregivers; avoid and turn away from affectionate touch; and seem to not experience positive emotion in their interactions with parents, caregivers, siblings, and peers. Because many autistic children have poor nonverbal and verbal skills, they have a difficult time communicating their feelings. They seem to be overstimulated easily and often respond by rocking, staring, or engaging in repetitive body movements. Scientists are not certain how autistic infant/toddlers experience emotion. Similarly, other communication disorders such as Asberger's syndrome and Rett's syndrome adversely influence the emotional development of infant/toddlers.

Affect disorders in infancy include mood disorders, such as depression in infancy; *anxiety disorders,* such as excessive separation anxiety, result in disruptions in early emotional development. Prompt and appropriate treatment can help to alleviate the damage caused by these disorders. Another category of disorders damaging to emotional development are *relationship disorders.* Parents who are either overinvolved with their infants (interferes with the infant's goals and desires; makes inappropriate demands; uses the infant to meet parent's own needs) or underinvolved (unresponsive to infant cues; fails to provide a safe environment; seems unaware of the infant's needs) undermine their infants' feelings of security and worthiness, hindering emotional development.

Abuse, neglect, and chronic unresponsive parenting can have heartbreaking effects on the emotional development of infant/toddlers. Persistent physical or emotional abuse and neglect and ongoing unresponsive parenting results in the infant's poor sense of self; the infant perceives herself as worthless and unlovable. The resulting insecure attachment relationship has profound implications for the child's emotional health and well-being. Infant/toddlers growing up in abusive, neglectful, and unresponsive homes tend to show severe antisocial behaviors later on, such as strong aggressiveness or a striking lack of concern for others and the inability to form close emotional relationships with others. Behaviors like these are often characterized as symptoms of attachment disorders.

Maternal depression, although less severe than abuse or neglect, is also very harmful to an infant's emotional development. Infants of chronically depressed mothers are most often described as fussy and withdrawn. During interactions, depressed mothers show little emotional expression and rarely respond to their infant's behavioral cues. Therefore, infants of depressed mothers have no models of appropriate emotional expression and are not likely to perceive themselves as capable of arousing emotional reactions, positive or negative, in those around them.

See also Attachment; Discipline; Facial Expressions; Parenting; Peer Relations; Smiling and Laughter

References and further reading
Berk, L. E. 1997. *Child Development.* 4th ed. Needham Heights, MA: Allyn and Bacon.
Greenspan, S. G. 1985. *First Feelings: Milestones in the Emotional Development of Your Baby and Child.* New York: Penguin.
Snow, C. W. 1998. *Infant Development.* 2nd ed. Upper Saddle River, NJ: Prentice Hall.

Emotion Regulation
See Basic Motives; Emotion

Emotionality
A dimension of temperament that refers to the tendency to be aroused easily and intensely and that is expressed and identified as distress.

See also Emotion; Temperament

Empathy

Empathy is the ability to understand how others feel and respond to them with similar emotions. Empathy develops over time, and the capacity for empathic responses is linked to children's cognitive abilities, as it requires some perspective-taking skills. Evidence of the individual's capacity for empathy is present in early infancy. For example, when one infant cries, other babies in the room can begin crying as well. Martin Hoffman called this "global empathy." As infant/toddlers develop self-awareness, they become better able to respond with rudimentary empathic actions. For instance, an eighteen-month-old toddler might offer his pacifier to another crying child or gently pat the child. As language skills increase, the child is able to verbally reflect upon another's emotional state as well as act to relieve the other's distress. For instance, the preschooler might say to a peer, "You're really sad that there aren't any blocks left. You can build with me." Empathic responses increase with the child's age as perspective-taking skills expand and the child becomes more sophisticated in evaluating how and why another is experiencing a particular emotion and what might be an appropriate empathic response.

Hoffman believes that the most advanced form of empathy is the ability to identify with and respond to those who live with chronic stressors such as poverty, sickness, and oppression.

Empathy and concern for others begins to be openly expressed during the toddler years. (Courtesy Timothy L. Ledesma)

The development of empathy is also influenced by parenting style. In general, authoritative parenting, in which strategies such as reasoning and induction are used, supports the development of empathy. This parenting style encourages children to reflect on the feelings of others, the consequences of their behaviors, and appropriate responses to others' behaviors. Also, parent/caregivers who model empathic behaviors are more likely to have children that demonstrate high empathy.

See also Emotion

Employed Mothers

An employed mother is one who works outside of the home on a part-time or full-time basis. The movement toward mothers in the workforce began during World War II. Since that time, the number of working mothers has increased, creating the need for infant child care. The 1950s were characterized by domesticity, and the majority of women stayed home to raise children as opposed to joining the workforce. The 1960s and 1970s marked a shift in roles in the home as issues such as women's rights and reproductive freedom emerged. Women's careers took on even more of a focus in the 1980s and 1990s as more and more began to delay childbearing while building careers. Between 1970 and 1996, the birthrate for women aged twenty to twenty-four decreased while birthrates increased among women aged twenty-five and older. In fact, during this period the birthrate for women in their thirties more than doubled.

Women's move into the workforce has raised several issues, such as balancing family and work responsibilities, family-leave policies, the increased need for infant child care, and employment policies and practices designed to support mothers. One of the most challenging tasks for employed mothers is balancing the heavy demands of parenting and work. In the first weeks and months of an infant's life, sleep deprivation, the transition to parenthood, anxiety over competing demands, and increasing financial responsibilities often leave mothers feeling overwhelmed. Single mothers in particular often feel overwhelmed and undersupported in trying to work and raise infants at the same time. Sole responsibility for managing finances, household tasks, and parenting duties fall to them in addition to work demands. Extended family members can offer some relief, although the influence and accessibility of extended family varies among cultures. In some cultures, such as the African American community, the extended family plays a valued role in supporting families with material, emotional, and financial support.

Even with the support of a partner or husband, the mother faces immense demands in several areas. For example, many married couples experience a decrease in marital happiness following the birth of a child. Moreover, even in households emphasizing equality of roles, women tend to take on more responsibility for infant care and childrearing, whether they work outside the home or not, whereas fathers tend to define their role as that of provider. When there is great variance in the division of responsibility, stress and dissatisfaction between the couple increases, often impacting the couple relationship, the parent-infant relationship, and even work performance. With such demands on employed mothers, the nature of the

A lawyer and mother picking up her three-year-old from child care. (Elizabeth Crews)

work environment and supports available to employed mothers play an important role in family life.

Maternity Leave
In 1993, the Family and Medical Leave Act (FMLA) was passed. This legislation allows employed mothers to take up to twelve weeks of unpaid leave following the birth of a child. Prior to 1993, no legislation existed to provide leave for families. At best, most employed mothers could take only up to six weeks to care for their infants at home. Although FMLA provides an opportunity for an extended leave from work, taking unpaid leave is not an option for many families,

especially for families headed by single mothers. As a result, many employed mothers take only a short leave, if any. Unfortunately, the stress of a baby's birth paired with short leaves from work can negatively influence the mother and her child. For instance, stress over a baby's birth and maternity leaves of six weeks or less have been associated with maternal depression and anxiety and less positive mother-infant interactions. Despite the resources available, the United States provides little support in the way of maternity leave for employed mothers as compared to many European countries. For example, most Western European countries provide up to twelve months of paid leave and allow both mothers and fathers to take leave from work. In Sweden, families may take up to fifteen months of paid leave. Such liberal leave policies are much more conducive not only to a healthy transition to parenting but also to a productive work environment once mothers return to employment outside the home.

Availability of Infant Care

The demands of balancing work and family are most intense for the mothers of infants/toddlers as compared to the mothers of older children. In fact, mothers of infants/toddlers miss far more workdays on average than mothers of older children, partly because infants/toddlers are so dependent on mothers and most in need of child care. When mothers do return to work, they are often faced with the challenge of finding quality child care for their infants. This task is daunting for several reasons. First, finding care is difficult. Approximately 6 million infant/toddlers spend at least some time each day in care by someone other than their parents. Many of these child-care arrangements are informal in nature, such as agreements between neighbors or extended family members. Although their number is growing, many child-care centers do not provide infant care. Many family child-care programs, in which an individual offers a child-care program in a private home, do provide infant care but can only serve one or two infants at a time. The demand for infant care has been intensified with revisions in welfare policies, requiring mothers to move off of welfare and into employment in a specified time after having a child. Most mothers moving out of welfare find minimum-wage positions. These positions often require mothers to work at night and on weekends without the benefit of a fixed schedule. Most child-care programs do not offer care on a flexible basis or care on nights and weekends.

Even after locating child care for infant/toddlers, mothers still report feeling stress in balancing work and family demands, and these demands can be more problematic according to the type of child-care arrangement. In general, mothers using nonfamilial child care, such as a child-care center or family child-care home, report more problems, such as being late to work and missing work, than mothers using in-home child care provided by a spouse, relative, or other caregiver. One explanation for this might be the flexibility of the child-care environment. For example, a sick infant might not be able to attend child care at a center child-care program due to the program's policy on illness, thus requiring the mother to miss work. Of course, illness for the infant in in-home child care is less likely to be associated with work absenteeism.

Another area of concern is the affordability of child care for employed mothers. Full-time child care can cost as much as $180–200 per week. Such financial burdens place additional stress on employed mothers. Finally, locating quality child care is challenging. According to national surveys, infant/toddler child care in the United States is of adequate quality at best. Lack of training of caregivers, low wages, high staff turnover, and inappropriate adult-to-child ratios contribute to the lack of quality child care. Placing infants in child care is often difficult for new mothers who feel guilt and sadness at having to leave their young infants, and this dissatisfaction is intensified when mothers are unhappy or concerned about the quality of care in which they place their infants/toddlers. These feelings can be a factor in employed mothers' satisfaction with employment, as well as in their job performance.

Family-Friendly Work Policies
In an effort to support employed mothers and increase satisfaction and productivity in the workplace, some employers provide flexibility in work environments and make resources available to employed mothers. One such resource is the provision of on-site child care. On-site child-care centers, sponsored by the employer and located at the place of employment, have several benefits for working mothers. First, the problem of finding child care is reduced. Convenience is a benefit too. Mothers just returning to work after birth may feel more at ease knowing their infants are close by, and they can report fewer problems related to balancing the demands of work and family. There is also evidence that on-site centers reduce absenteeism among employed mothers.

Other family-friendly work policies include alternative work arrangements, such as flexible work schedules, job sharing, part-time work, and telecommuting. Flexible work schedules allow the working mother to determine when and how long she will work, to a certain degree. One of the most important advantages is that flexible scheduling allows employed mothers to respond to unexpected situations, such as a sick infant who cannot go to child care. In other situations, flexible scheduling allows the working mother more time with her infant/toddler at particular times in the day. For example, an employed mother might choose to take a longer lunch break in order to nurse her infant and work longer in the evening to make up for the extra time taken, or she

might choose to come to work an hour earlier and leave an hour earlier. Another example of a flexible work schedule is the compressed week. In this arrangement, the employed mother works a full-time schedule in fewer than five days. Instead, she might work longer hours four days per week. The compressed schedule allows the employed mother to spend less time commuting to work and more time at home. However, it also means that she is working long days outside of the home, and this can add to fatigue. Flexible work hours offer different advantages in different situations. In general, flexible work schedules seem to be associated with lower rates of absenteeism among employed mothers, but there is little consistent evidence that this flexibility influences job satisfaction related to the work conditions.

In a job-sharing situation, two people share the same full-time position. This type of arrangement allows the employed mother to work on a part-time basis. Of course, salary and benefits, such as health insurance coverage, are negatively influenced. Telecommuting in a home office environment, in which the employee works at home for all or part of the week and communicates with the employer via technological means such as the Internet, tend to be popular with working mothers. Telecommuting allows the employees to have more control over their work environments and their home lives. Although telecommuting offers many advantages to employed mothers, it is stressful in other ways. For example, the lack of physical boundaries between home space and office space can present a challenge, particularly if young children are home with mothers when they are working, and the lack of boundaries as to when work hours begin and end may be associated with working too many hours. Nevertheless, employees using alternative work arrangements report greater job satisfaction and experience fewer conflicts related to balancing work and home roles, and employers report lower rates of absenteeism, lower incidence of staff turnover, and higher job productivity.

For family-friendly policies to work, however, the climate of the office must be supportive. Without widespread support of innovative employment policies, ill feelings among employees and lower-level managers become problematic. Moreover, even though the availability of adequate maternity leave and family-friendly policies can ease the burden on working mothers, many working mothers are at a disadvantage in the workplace. For example, surveys of companies featuring family-friendly policies indicated that those businesses had relatively poor records for promoting female employees. Further, many companies with females in high-ranking positions were not in favor of adopting family-friendly policies.

The availability of family-friendly policies also varies according to type of employment and the flexibility or rigidity of the job requirements. Some professions lend themselves to flexibility in the workplace more than others. For example, occupations in which there are set work shifts, such as law enforcement and emergency services, can have less flexibility in terms of strategies such as work hours and work from home, as compared to other professions.

See also Child Care: Choosing Quality; Parenting

References and further reading
Lilly, T. A., M. Pitt-Catsouphes, and B. K. Googins. 1997. *Work-Family Research: An Annotated Bibliography.* Westport, CN: Greenwood Press.
Neal, M. B., et al. 1993. *Balancing Work and Caregiving for Children, Adults, and Elders.* Newbury Park, CA: Sage.

Encouragement
Encouragement is a discipline strategy in which the adult tries to facilitate a certain desired behavior by offering physical or verbal praise and support.

See also Discipline

Endogenous Stimulation
Stimulation that arises from inside the body.

Engrossment
"Engrossment" is the term that Martin Greenberg and Norman Morris used to describe the reactions of fathers of first-born infants to the appearance and birth of their infant. Studying a sample of fathers in the United Kingdom, these investigators found that most fathers were positively moved by the birth of their infant regardless of whether they were present during the birth or not. The components of engrossment include:

- Visual awareness; fathers reported that they enjoyed looking at the newborn.
- Tactile awareness; fathers reported that touching and handling their newborn was pleasurable.
- Awareness of distinctive features; fathers were sensitive to their newborn's individual characteristics.
- Focus of attention on infant; fathers were drawn to their infant, especially to the face.

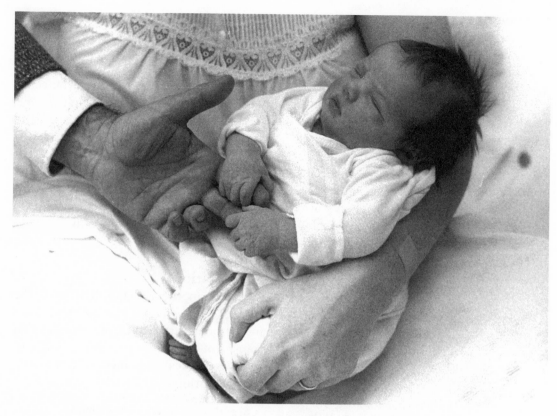

A father extends his hand to his newborn child. (Shirley Zeiberg)

- Feelings of elation; fathers described themselves as dazed, full of energy, feeling ten feet tall.
- Enhanced self-esteem; fathers took pride in their fatherhood.

Although the Greenberg-Morris study did not stimulate other researchers to investigate engrossment, their work was published at a time when there was generally strong interest in fathers and infants. That interest has continued to the present, and there are at least five large national studies of child development that include significant numbers of fathers as participants in research.

References and further reading
Greenberg, M., and N. Morris. 1974. Engrossment: The Newborn's Impact upon the Father. *American Journal of Orthopsychiatry* 44: 520–531.

Entrainment
Entrainment is a concept from ethological theory and refers to the regulation of a biological rhythm by an external stimulus.

Environments, Child Care
See Caregiving; Child Care: Choosing Quality; Family Day Care

Environtype

One of the leading spokespersons for the systems view in developmental psychology, Arnold J. Sameroff, defines "environtype" as the social factors that serve to organize development in much the same fashion as the genotype regulates physical development. Sameroff posits that social organization factors influence development through the family and culture. From this perspective, development of the individual must always be viewed as the transactional byproduct of the phenotype (the individual), the genotype (biological organizers), and the environtype (experiential organizers).

See also Genotype; Phenotype; Theories of Development

References and further reading
Sameroff, Arnold J. 1995. "General Systems Theories and Developmental Psychopathology." In Dante Cicchetti and Donald J. Cohen (eds), *Developmental Psychopathology, Vol. 1: Theory and Methods.* New York: Wiley, pp. 659–695.

Epidemiology

Epidemiology is the study of the distributions and causes of diseases and health problems. Epidemiologists track a wide variety of environmental and other factors related to infant mortality (death) and morbidity (disabilities) in an effort to isolate causal influences on development.

Epigenesis

Epigenesis is a principle of development asserting that organization is a constructive, emergent process in which each new level of organization represents a reorganization of prior levels that, in turn, generates new characteristics of the system. There are two main points of view about the process of epigenesis. Advocates of *deterministic epigenesis* argue that the determinants of epigenetic development are hard-wired in the genotype, with the environment playing a relatively minor role. According to the *probabilistic epigenesis* view, the developing organism is always a product of interaction with its environment; the outcomes of this interaction are not hard-wired in the genotype but rather emerge over the course of development.

Equilibration

In Piagetian theory, equilibration is the balance between assimilation and accommodation, the two inferred processes that transform the child's motor-action patterns (schemes) and mental representations of actions (schemas).

See also Cognitive Development

ERIC Clearinghouse

The ERIC Clearinghouse on Early Child and Elementary Education has many resources available pertaining to infant/toddler education and research. It reproduces talks and speeches given at conferences as well as published articles and chapters that are submitted to the Clearinghouse.

References and further reading
Materials are available from: ERIC Document Reproduction Services, P.O. Box 190, Arlington, VA 22210.

Erikson, Erik (1902–1994)

Whereas Sigmund Freud stressed the biological determinants of personality and the functions of id and superego, Erik Erikson stressed personality development in light of the individual's historical and cultural past. Building upon Freud's basic psychosexual theory of development, Erikson replaced Freud's emphasis on id and superego functions with an emphasis on the development of ego functions. For Erikson, personality is not fixed or final; it changes over the life course. The individual is always in a state of becoming. Erikson used the Freudian term "libidinal energy" to refer to the regulatory force that drives epigenetic development. He believed that personality organization occurs in a sequence of phases—his "eight ages of man." Each phase poses a conflict, the resolution of which structures the next phase and the next conflict. Each phase marks a turning point or choice point in the organization of personality. Central to infancy and early childhood is the infant's need to develop a sense of trust in its environment. This sense of trust prepares the individual to become an autonomous and self-initiated individual. Maier has captured the essence of Erikson's theory in his modification of Erikson's labels for each phase, the first four of which cover the age period typically included in the descriptor: infancy and early childhood.

Often a toddler's apprehension about being left alone is reflected by facial expressions that reveal a great deal about underlying emotional states. (Courtesy of Hiram E. Fitzgerald)

- Phase 1: Acquiring a sense of basic trust while overcoming a sense of basic mistrust; a realization of hope.
- Phase 2: Acquiring a sense of autonomy while combating a sense of doubt and shame; a realization of will.
- Phase 3: Acquiring a sense of initiative and overcoming a sense of guilt; a realization of purpose.
- Phase 4: Acquiring a sense of identity and fending off a sense of inferiority; a realization of competence.

Erikson's *Childhood and Society*, published in 1950, continues to be the best source for a description of his theory. His studies of the North Dakota Sioux and the Yurok of Oregon were significant as characterizations of Native American cultures; these studies, along with the work of René Spitz, brought sociocultural history into psychoanalytic theory and demonstrated the importance of theory-driven research to test the foundations of Freud's theory.

See also Freud, Sigmund

References and further reading
Erikson, E. 1950. *Childhood and Society.*
New York: Norton.

Erythroblastosis Fetalis

A blood disorder caused by the Rh factor. The name for this disorder derives from the Rhesus monkeys that were very much involved in the research that isolated the disorder. Each of us is either Rh-positive or Rh-negative. Roughly 85 percent of whites, 93 percent of African Americans, and almost all Asians are Rh-positive. So, these individuals have a red blood antigen (the Rh antigen) that produces no problem with the fetus when the fetus is also Rh positive. When the fetal Rh factor and the maternal Rh factor are incompatible, it produces problems. The Rh antigen is a complex of C, D, E, c, and e antigens; the D antigen is linked to the positive and negative classification. If the allele contains a D, the Rh designation is positive, but if the allele contains a d, the antigen is absent and the Rh designation is negative. When an Rh-negative woman has an Rh-positive fetus, antibodies pass through the placenta and cause destruction of red blood cells in the fetus. In contrast, when it goes in the other direction, the fetus will cause antigen sensitization in the maternal blood stream. If uncorrected, this will produce serious problems for the next pregnancy.

Rh incompatibility can be treated. For infants, the treatment involves blood transfusions that can be performed while the fetus is still in the uterus. For mothers, an immunization with Rh immunoglobulin within three days after delivery will prevent the formation of Rh antibodies. This removes danger for the next pregnancy, but if there is one, the whole procedure will have to be repeated if the blood incompatibility occurs again. If the RH incompatibility is not resolved, the fetus can be spontaneously aborted or can be stillborn.

Ethical Considerations

Developmental psychologists engaged in the study of children have *always* been especially aware of the ethics of research, perhaps because of the tender ages of their research participants. Guidelines for the ethics of research with human beings have been developed by the American Psychological Association, by that association's Division on Developmental Psychology, and by the Society for Research in Child Development. In general, the guidelines provide for the anonymity of individual subjects, the protection of subjects from physical and psychological harm, and the consent of children, parents, guardians, or those acting in loco parentis (teachers, school principals, and so on) to research participation, based on their informed opinion regarding the research. At the heart of all the specific ethical guidelines are the ideas that the research participant's rights supersede those of the experimenter, that the research participant must be protected from invasion of privacy, and that the experimenter is first and foremost responsible for the ethical conduct of the study.

In addition, the National Institutes of Health have guidelines for protecting the rights of all participants involved in all domains of research. All agencies (universities, hospitals, private clinics and centers, and businesses) that receive federal funds in support of their research with human beings must have an Institutional Review Board that oversees and approves informed consent statements and informational statements that are distributed to research participants. The role of the review board is to ensure that the participants involved in human research are as informed about the research and their rights.

Eugenics

The belief that one can improve some characteristic of the human race through selective breeding or planned mating. The ideas behind the eugenics movement were derived from a blending of the notion of survival of the fittest from evolutionary theory, with studies by Sir Francis Galton on the origins of genius. Galton's studies of genius led him to conclude that controlled mating would lead to enhanced mental capabilities for the species. Conversely, restricted breeding would over time eliminate individuals who scored low on measures of mental abilities used by Galton. Thus, eugenicists advocated restricted breeding for criminals, paupers, the mentally ill, and the mentally retarded.

The eugenics movement failed for a variety of reasons, not the least of which can be attributed to nineteenth-century knowledge about the genotype and its role in the genetic transmission of polygenetic characteristics and of its transactional relationship with experiential factors. During the twentieth century, the rise of behaviorism and environmentalism swayed scientists away from eugenics, as did political-social events such as the Nazis' use of eugenics to justify racial purification and extermination during World War II. Nevertheless, during the early part of the twentieth century, the ideas behind eugenics were used to justify sterilization and castration of drug addicts and individuals with various mental and/or physical disorders.

See also Behaviorial Genetics; Environtype

Event Memory
See Autobiographical Memory; Memory

Examining Behavior

Examining behavior occupies an important position in Jean Piaget's theory of cognitive development. It essentially describes the active process of exploration through which humans learn about objects in their environment. Just as an adult will pick up a new electronic device and examine it to learn more about what it is and how it works, infants are interested in novel stimuli and will also try to investigate. Often this requires reaching and grasping to bring an object into closer proximity. True examining behavior emerges during stage 3 of Piaget's sensorimotor period (four to eight months), although younger infants demonstrate an interest in examining their own bodies.

Exogenous Stimulation

Exogenous stimulation arises from outside the body and is contrasted with endogenous stimulation, which arises from within the body.

See also Pacification

Exploratory Behavior

Exploratory behavior allows infants access to information in their environments that was not previously available to them. It plays an important role in

A fifteen-month-old exploring the ins and outs of kitchen drawers. (Elizabeth Crews)

how children learn about their physical and social worlds and how to function effectively in them. From birth, infants actively explore their environments, using their different skills and abilities to understand the world. As they develop, infants acquire more skills as well as more effective techniques of exploration.

Early in life, exploratory behavior involves actions like orienting responses. Infants selectively attend to objects or events (i.e., stimuli) in their environment that are interesting. Often, they attend to objects or parts of objects that are different from the rest of the environment. Examples of things that display this kind of discontinuity might include sounds that are loud or unusual and visual con-

trasts. When babies orient to a stimulus, they prepare all their senses to pick up information about that object, and they begin to understand how it relates to the other stimuli they experience around the same time.

With development, babies begin locomotor exploration, moving their bodies to explore their environments. Infants expand their worlds by moving around within it. Babies can reach out to bring toys or other objects of interest nearer. A baby can also change the stimuli that he/she encounters by moving to an area where other objects, people, or events are present. Rolling, crawling, and walking allow children to explore physical objects and people and further understand interrelationships between objects, people, and events in their worlds.

Orienting responses as well as locomotor exploration involve the baby's movement or change in him/herself in order to learn more about the world. Another way that infants explore their environments is by investigating changes in objects or people as a result of their own actions on those objects or on some intervening object. Infants often bang, drop, and throw objects. By watching the effects of these kinds of actions using different objects, infants learn about the characteristics of those objects: hard, loud, heavy, rough, big. Infants also explore relationships between objects by manipulating one item (e.g., a button on the remote control) and watching to see what happens with another (e.g., the television turns on). Infants also explore social reactions to their actions. They can hold a doll up to be seen, or smear cake on their faces and watch how others respond.

Children use all three types of exploratory behaviors to attend to and understand the worlds in which they live. Often all three types are involved in the same interaction. Such exploratory behaviors are the backdrop for numerous social interactions that occur throughout the course of development. They promote the development of expectations about the relationships between objects, people, and events, and they continue to be important in increasingly sophisticated ways throughout life.

See also Orienting Response

References and further reading
Berlyne, Daniel E. 1960. *Conflict, Arousal, and Curiosity.* New York: McGraw-Hill.
Fogel, A. 1993. *Developing Through Relationships: Origins of Communication, Self, and Culture.* Chicago: University of Chicago Press.

Expressive Language

The ability to communicate through spoken or sign language.

Exteroceptors

The sense organs that are specialized to receive external environmental stimulation. For instance, the eye is the exteroceptor of the visual system because it receives light rays and changes them into the neural form needed by the brain.

See also Perception

Eye Contact

Eye contact involves the mutual gaze of two or more individuals toward each other. Research suggests that the perceptual capabilities of very young infants

A mother talking to her four-week-old. (Elizabeth Crews)

Although this may be a bit extreme, eye-to-eye contact plays an important role in regulating social interactions. (Courtesy of the Decker Family)

predispose them to initiate and reciprocate eye contact with their caregivers. Infants are initially attracted to edges of objects and areas with high levels of contrast between dark and light, such as the facial regions of the hairline and chin. Gradually, infants acquire improved ability to scan the internal features of objects and make finer discriminations of contrast. The presence of these high-contrast areas in faces attracts even young infants to attend to the faces of their caregivers. The infant's attention is reinforcing to caregivers and aids in establishing a foun-

dation for positive social relationships with these important individuals. Attention to the internal regions of faces also focuses the baby's attention on the mouth movements and facial expressions associated with later speech production and communication.

> *See also* Face Perception; Pattern Perception; Perception; Rules of Visual Search; Social Referencing

Eye-Hand Coordination
See Lateralization; Motor Development

F

Face Perception

Infants visually explore and perceive faces in similar ways to many other objects, however, they do show a clear preference for faces over other less complex stimuli. It is not clear whether this preference is exclusive to faces or is related to differences in contour density or brightness among these kinds of objects. When presented with a face, infants use eye movements to take in information about it. At birth, babies' scanning primarily focuses on the edges of objects and soon more closely examine the internal features of those objects. Young infants focus on the edges of the face with peak contrasts, including the hairline and chin. By two months infants scan a broader surface area and focus more extensively on the eyes and mouth in the face. By three

A baby studies his father's face. (Shirley Zeiberg)

months, babies have been shown to discriminate between photographs of their parents' faces and those of strangers.

See also Edge Detection; Pattern Perception; Perception

Facial Expressions

One of the earliest nonverbal forms of communication, facial expressions are used to express emotions. Human communication is intended to express emotions. Initially, the communication of emotions through facial expressions aids in the attachment process between caregiver and infant. They begin to understand each other by learning what cues mean, and they respond accordingly. The ability to bond is the foundation for early social and emotional development.

Some theorists believe that emotions, or affective feeling states, can be recognized early in infancy by means of facial expressions. Assumptions include that infants' facial expressions are true representations of their affective states. In addition, caregivers can appropriately differentiate between affective states and are able to appropriately respond. Over time and with more interactions with others, children begin to learn the behaviors that express emotions, and they increasingly gain control over facial expressions.

Infants begin to encode and decode facial expressions quite early. Infants are able to translate facial expressions into meaning. In addition, infants learn about facial expressions and are able to display their own intended expression by observing and imitating others. Therefore, the expressive styles of the caregivers may influence how the infant's facial behav-

iors. However, individual differences of facial expressiveness is apparent at birth.

Infants have many opportunities to express emotions and to respond to others' expressions. Infants take interest in others and observe the faces of others with great attention. Caregivers and infants are involved in much face-to-face play as they maintain eye contact and make playful faces at each other. This eye contact can signal attentiveness, threat, or affect. At first, face-to-face play is initiated by the caregiver in order to provoke a response from the infant. When the infant responds, the caregiver in turn responds with approval. This continuous feedback strengthens the infant's understanding of facial expressions and he/she eventually able to initiate this kind of play with others.

Many researchers believe that the earliest facial expressions are innate. Expressions such as fear and anger seem to be universal, as babies independent of their culture characterize the same expressive features. With socialization, however, children gain more voluntary control over their facial expressions, which can be modified. Paul Ekman's neurocultural model suggests that not all facial expressions are universal; some are culture-specific. Cultures vary in facial expressiveness because of different stimuli, emotional states, display rules, and behavioral consequences. In both preliterate and literate cultures, infants and adults are able to recognize the facial expressions of happiness, interest, surprise, sadness, fear, disgust, and anger. The common recognition and understanding that these cultures share make nonverbal communication possible.

An early sign of emotional recognition is at about three months of age when infants are able to discriminate between positive and negative emotions. As part of their development, infants learn to intentionally control their behaviors. One specific ability is for infants to modify their expression. However, infants must first develop consistent patterns of facial expressiveness and must be able to understand that specific facial expressions represent related emotional states.

There are several influences on infants' emotional development. The way that infants are socialized has an influence on how they identify and react to emotions. For example, some caregivers can directly comfort and console an upset child until the hurt feelings are less intense and the child proceeds with follow-up activities. Other caregivers can use reinforcement or verbal comments to help the child cope and manage his/her own emotions. Therefore, some children, when feeling upset, will expect and need direct intervention, whereas other children will try to help themselves. Other socialization influences include rules about expression. Some caregivers encourage children to openly express emotions as they are felt; other children learn to hide their emotions while trying to keep an overt stable emotional state.

Children also observe and model caregivers as they express emotions. Children learn how to overtly express emotions in particular situations. These observations help build a mental representation of emotional expressiveness. Emotional development and personality development may be related. In interaction with others, infants express emotions and receive responses from others that influence their development of personality characteristics. As children progress and develop, their emotional expressions help them direct behaviors and guide their understanding of social experiences. For example, express-

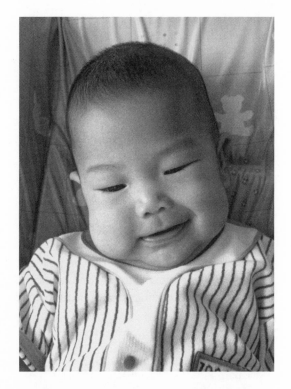

A happy baby at four-and-a-half months. (Elizabeth Crews)

ing anger when a toy of interest is removed can motivate and direct the child toward behaviors of regaining the toy.

Differential emotion theory suggests that each single emotion has a related unique motivational character. Facial expressiveness can play an important role in the survival of infants because it requests interaction with caregivers and is the basis for experiencing emotions. Facial expressiveness allows infants who have not yet learned to communicate verbally to get their messages across and develop relationships with others. Babies use facial expressions to communicate and relate to others.

Facial expressions are very important in our ways of communicating throughout life. Everyday we use facial expressions to imply feelings, meanings, and personalities of others. At birth, infants display facial expressions and respond to others' facial expressions with great interest. Through interaction, infants continue to learn the associations between facial expressions and emotions. And as children develop cognitively, and with increased socializing experiences, children are better able to regulate their own emotions. Through development, children learn a variety of ways to use emotions in relation to others. Children learn that single emotions, like happiness, have a variety of intensities, from merely happy to ecstatic. Simple facial expressions become more complex to incorporate different emotions.

See also Emotion

References and further reading
Ekman, P. 1993. "Facial Expression of Emotion." *American Psychologist* 48: 384–392.
Haslett, B., and W. Samter. 1997. *Children Communicating: The First Five Years.* Hillsdale, NJ: Lawrence Erlbaum Associates.
Izard, C. 1992. "Basic Emotions, Relations among Emotions, and Emotion-Cognition Relations." *Psychology Review* 99: 561–565.
Mascolo, M., and S. Griffin. 1998. *What Develops in Emotional Development?* New York: Plenum Press.

Fagan Test of Infant Intelligence
The Fagan Test is a tool that measures infant cognitive potential and is often used to identify children with cognitive delays. It is appropriate for infants aged six to twelve months. A trained administrator uses special equipment to present visually novel items, such as pictures of diverse faces, to the infant sitting on the parent's lap. The tester records the length of time that the infant fixates on the visual presentation. The test is used primarily in hospitals and is costly but appears to have the potential to be a good predictor of infant cognitive development.

See also Face Perception; Perception

References and further reading
Fagan, J. F., and P. Shepard. 1987. *Fagan Test of Infant Intelligence.* Cleveland: Infantest Corp.

Failure to Thrive
Failure to thrive (FTT) identifies infants and children who, without superficially evident cause, fail to gain weight and often lose weight. This problem occurs most often in infants but is also observed in later children. FTT has also been described as the failure of children to grow normally or as expected.

Signs and Symptoms
Children most affected by this condition are under five years old and usually are the age of three to six months. It also occurs commonly among institutionalized children, especially those who are mentally retarded. However, any child who fails to gain weight at a normal pace, sustains a loss in weight, seems much smaller than his/her peers, still has unfused skull bones by the second birthday, is chronically listless or irritable, uninterested in food and surroundings, or exhibits any change in growth patterns should be seen by a doctor.

In addition to the signs and symptoms noted above, children with FTT can evidence any of the following characteristics: physical skills that are slow to develop (e.g., turning over in bed, sitting, standing, walking); mental and social skills that are delayed (talking, social interaction skills, self-feeding, toilet training); slow progression in physical development (height, weight, head circumference); and wide variation in the rate and change in normal developmental functions.

FTT has both organic and nonorganic causes and often discussion of the disorder is separated into these two areas.

Organic FTT. Organic causal factors have been linked to about 20 percent of all cases of FTT. Organic causes include most of the serious diseases of childhood, including cancer, inflammatory bowel disease, juvenile arthritis, and cystic fibrosis. Physical examination may reveal a history of vomiting, diarrhea, gastroesophageal reflux, disturbed food utilization, gastrointestingal disorders including parasites, and endocrine, genetic, or other systemic disorders.

Nonorganic FTT. Nonorganic causes of FTT are thought to arise from psychological and social problems. Children may become emotionally deprived as a result of parental withdrawal, rejection, or hostility. Children from families with significant stress due to relationships characterized by violence, chronic illness, familial disruptions, and lack of support systems can also suffer from emotional deprivation.

Confusion in the home as well as economic conditions can affect the child's nutritional and living conditions. Lack of food and exposure to environmental conditions such as exposure to toxins, lead paint, crowding, or unsanitary living conditions may can result in FTT.

Increased Risk. Children who are malnourished, have chronic diseases such as kidney failure, have genetic disorders, live in economic and/or emotional poverty, are physically deformed, or who have inexperienced parents are at increased risk for FTT.

Treatment. When FTT is suspected, children typically should have a medical evaluation. The evaluation should track the child's physical development relative to normal standards and note the child's medical history and developmental status. Often blood tests, X-rays of wrists to assess bone age, and other factors will be assessed. Because FTT has multiple causes, an interdisciplinary team may be involved in the evaluation. Delayed growth due to nutritional factors can be resolved by a well-balanced diet and education of the parents. If severe, the child may be hospitalized in order to verify food intake and to perform complicated diagnostic procedures. If psychosocial factors are involved, treatment should include parent-child psychotherapy and/or changes in living conditions. In cases of emotional dysregulation, hospitalization coupled with counseling, parent education, and support from health care professionals may be necessary. In some cases the child may be placed temporarily in foster care or permanently removed from the home.

Outcomes. Although some children respond well to treatment, others have more difficulty. Some FTT children never return to normal standards of growth but maintain normal development although small for their age.

See also Theories of Development

References and further reading
Drotar, D. 1991. "The Family Context of Nonorganic Failure to Thrive." *American Journal of Orthopsychiatry* 61: 23–34.

Phelps, L. 1991. "Non-organic Failure to Thrive: Origins and Psychoeducational Implications." *School Psychology Review* 20: 417–427.

Familiarization

Familiarization is the process by which researchers introduce an object or stimulus to infants and allow them to explore it until it loses its novelty. Familiarization is the first stage of habituation. Infants are allowed to visually explore stimuli until after repeated exploration they display behavior and physiological responses that suggest that they have lost interest in the stimulus or have habituated to it. Following familiarization, researchers often present a new stimulus to see whether the babies will dishabituate to it or show renewed interest in the object because it is viewed as having some novel feature. Habituation is an extremely useful research technique to understand infant perception and has also been related to later measures of child intelligence.

See also Forced Choice Preferential Looking; Habituation; Perception;

Family Bed

"Family bed" (or "cosleeping") is the term used to describe the practice of families sleeping together in the same bed. The family bed is a common occurrence in many cultures throughout the world, including Japan, Sweden, Africa, and Mexico. The family bed is less common in the United States. If families do sleep together, they typically do so in the first few months after an infant is born. Most parents sleeping with their infants move their babies to cribs in a separate room within the first few months after birth.

Advocates of cosleeping cite many positive aspects of the family bed; critics highlight concerns they have with families sleeping together.

Pros and Cons of the Family Bed
The concept of the family bed is controversial. In fact, many parents avoid telling others about a decision to sleep with their baby for fear of criticism or ridicule. Advocates of the family bed believe that cosleeping not only makes middle-of-the-night feedings easier but also eliminates the anxiety and fear infant/toddlers can feel when sleeping alone. Supporters of the family bed believe it promotes emotional intimacy and helps parents become more physically and emotionally attuned to their infants. Many experts who oppose the family bed believe that cosleeping is too intimate and can contribute to occurrences of sexual abuse.

Proponents of the family bed believe cosleeping reduces infant sleep problems. Infants cycle between states of light sleep and deep sleep. When emerging from a state of deep sleep, infants often awaken, at least partially. Advocates of cosleeping believe that when the infant is vulnerable to waking, she will sense her parent's presence and drift back into sleep without waking. Likewise, the parent can sense her infant beginning to stir and comfort her baby without waking fully herself. Critics believe that learning to fall and stay asleep on one's own is a skill important to the infant's independence. They believe that if an infant begins sleeping with the parents, the child will become too dependent on the parent and never want to leave the family bed. Supporters of cosleeping say that infant/toddlers can seem more dependent in the short term and probably will not want to

Infant and father cosleeping. (Courtesy of Heather Lewis)

leave the family bed until sometime between the second and third year or later. However, they believe that children who cosleep can have greater trust and confidence, two characteristics related to later independent behavior.

Cosleeping is a normal practice for most mammals, and scientists supporting cosleeping say there is a sound biological basis for the practice. From an evolutionary perspective, cosleeping was essential because the defenseless infant could not be left alone, vulnerable to predators. Moreover, there is evidence that cosleeping helps infants regulate their typically irregular breathing patterns. In a sense, the constant rhythmic breathing of the parent "reminds" the infant to breathe. Some studies have reported reduced rates of sudden infant death syndrome among infants who sleep with their parents. Other studies, however, show the opposite effect.

Moreover, there are cases of infant death attributed to suffocation when a parent rolls over on a child or lies on a child. Advocates of cosleeping say that parents who sleep with their infants become highly attuned to and spatially aware of where the infant is sleeping. This spatial awareness, called the "proprioceptive sense," reduces the likelihood that an adult will roll over on the baby. They point out that parents who roll over or lie on their children while cosleeping often are under the influence of drugs or alcohol, which reduce their spatial perception. The fear of rolling over on the baby has historical roots as well. For instance, psychologist Sharon Heller reports that in the seventeenth century many poor families, unable to feed their children, were suspected of engaging in infanticide, the killing of infants, by "accidentally" rolling over on them in the night. In reality, even a new-born infant is well equipped with survival reflexes and would protest loudly if an adult did so.

There is a risk that infants sleeping in an adult bed could fall between the mattress and headboard or the mattress and wall and be suffocated or risk suffocation under heavy bedding. Advocates of cosleeping say that responsible adults take precautions to make cosleeping safe, such as making sure the mattress is pushed flush against a wall or putting the mattress on the floor and using light bedding. They argue that any sleeping arrangement, including the traditional crib, can present risks if certain safety measures are not followed. Finally, critics point out that the family bed can interfere with the parents' relationship, as the privacy of sleeping alone as a couple and engaging in sexual relations are reduced. Advocates of the family bed believe that parents can find creative ways for private time together without much difficulty.

See also Cross-Cultural Research; Cultural Competence; Massage; Parenting

References and further reading
Heller, S. 1997. *The Vital Touch*. New York: Henry Holt.
Sears, W., and M. Sears. 1993. *The Baby Book*. New York: Little, Brown.
Small, M. 1998. *Our Babies, Ourselves: How Biology and Culture Shape the Way We Parent*. New York: Anchor Books.

Family Composition

Family composition is the overall structure of the family. In the United States there is a cultural myth that the majority of families historically and in contemporary times consisted of the nuclear unit of biological mother, biological father, and their offspring. In fact, the diversity of family composition has been evident throughout human history. Families have enormous variability in composition. Some families may have stepparents, stepchildren, adopted children, multiple generations, and multiple parents in polygynous relationships. Some families are headed by a single parent, and some have parents who are in homosexual relationships. The diversity of families has been evident through human history, but regardless of the family composition, all issues related to parenting, parent-child relationship, discipline, prosocial development, and skill achievement are the same, although the emphases may vary from family to family.

Family Day Care

Family day care is child care provided to children in the home of the caregiver. The term is used to denote the family and home focus of the child-care setting. Family day-care homes are state-licensed for a total of six children. However, state licensing requirements limit the number of infants cared for by the provider to three. The 3:1 ratio is determined to be necessary to provide responsive, individualized, and safe care to children.

Family day care can be licensed or unlicensed, formal or informal. Trained child-care professionals who have knowledge of child development and issues of health, safety, and nutrition operate licensed family day-care homes. The child-care settings must meet standards of quality set by the state in order to become licensed. The curriculum of care is usually less structured and more flexible than what is common in larger group care settings. Family day-care providers provide formal or informal care. Formal care is licensed or registered by the state. Informal care is relative care, or child care provided by a relative. Relative care providers are not required to be licensed. However, many choose to become registered with the state in order to qualify for government subsidies.

Family day-care providers typically provide full-time care for infants and preschoolers while parents work. After-school and before-school care can also be provided to school-age children. The hours of operation are flexible to meet the needs of children whose parents work second or third shifts or weekends. Family day-care providers can also provide twenty-four-hour care for parents who are required to be away from home for extended periods.

Family day-care homes are most popular with parents because of their convenient location in the community, home setting and family atmosphere, flexible hours, ages of children served, and cost. Approximately 70 percent of infants in out-of-home care are reportedly placed in family day care. A large proportion of the parents who choose family day care are typically ethnic minorities. A number of studies also show that parents with higher incomes also choose family child care over center-based care for their infant/toddlers. As the children get older, they may be switched over to center-based care as preparation for formal schooling.

There are several problems in providing family child care. First, many providers often work alone and are isolated from adult contact. Second, the 3:1 ratio limit placed on providers caring for infants can hinder the caregivers' ability to make a living wage. Third, most federal subsidies are earmarked for child-care centers rather than family child-care providers. There are also complaints from family

day-care providers regarding the delay in receipt of subsidy monies from the government. Fourth, caregivers with formal training are not compensated by the income earned. As family child-care providers, most are barely able to earn a livable wage, and benefits are limited. Center-based child-care providers typically make more money and also receive benefits of sick leave and vacation time. Therefore, the more education and training a child-care professional has, the less likely she will decide to become a family child-care provider. This affects the rate of quality caregivers available to care for infants and young children.

See also Caregiving

Family Support Programs

Social services designed to facilitate parental and family development. Although family support programs have a variety of goals, they all focus on the important role that parents play in shaping children's lives. There are several family support programs, including Healthy Families America, Hawaii's Healthy Start, and Parents as Teachers. Family support programs strive to honor the racial, ethnic, cultural, and socioeconomic diversity of families and recognize family strengths as well as individual methods of coping. Other elements of family support programs include understanding and incorporating the developmental needs of infants, children, and adolescents and their families into service delivery systems; implementing policies that provide emotional and financial support to meet the needs of families; and designing service delivery systems that are accessible to families, culturally competent, and responsive to the need that the family identifies.

See also Family Systems; Home Visitation

Family Systems

The idea that family members function as a group or system and that anything affecting one family member has an effect on everyone else. The family systems approach to studying and working with families came about as a result of the emerging family therapy movement and a dissatisfaction with the existing theories that explained pathology as residing within the individual. The family systems framework has its roots in general systems theory, developed by Ludwig von Bertalanffy (1968), who believed that a system was any group of parts where a change in the behavior of one part led to a change in the behavior of all other parts. Before family systems theory, therapists were treating individuals for issues such as delinquency, substance use, and depression; for this group of therapists pathology was seen as residing within an individual. A group of therapists began treating the whole family of an individual struggling with these issues, but they had a difficult time finding explanations for how the family as a whole contributed to the individual's struggle with a particular issue. These therapists turned to systems theory for an explanation.

A family fits von Bertalanffy's definition of a system in that each person in a family has an important impact on the entire family. For example, when a couple has a baby, their lives change dramatically. The baby impacts their daily routine and financial stability and changes the nature of their relationship and their routine; their relationship in turn influences the infant. When a family member moves out of the household or dies there is also a shift. Every family member is affected in some way; roles and relationships are adjusted as a result of the change.

A family shares the features of all social systems in that it is seen as ongoing, open, goal-seeking, and self-regulating. Family systems can be described as "open," meaning that energy and information come into the family from their environment (input), and energy or information goes from the family system into the environment (output). For example, information flows into a family system through media such as television, radio, or printed material as well as through contact with other systems such as work or school. Many parents gain information about their infant's needs through information found in books or information that is given at routine well-child visits. This information (input) is used by parents as a means to understand and better care for their baby. Parents can pass this information on to others with infants or disregard information and ideas that they do not find useful (output).

A "closed" family system may not allow input from outside of their immediate family. For example, a family may have an opportunity for a family support person to help them learn about child development and discipline strategies. A closed family might not allow this person into their home or might not be accepting of the information that the family support person offers. Describing a family system as ongoing means that families are changing over time. Family systems are also described as goal-seeking and self-regulating. This means that families can identify and pursue goals; families

Older brother's affectionate first kiss. (Courtesy of Holly Brophy-Herb)

decide on a means to pursue goals, monitor the progress of goals, and correct deviations that have been made.

Families use self-regulation to make up for temporary changes in the environment and to resist change. Positive and negative feedback are mechanisms of self-regulation. Families can use input from another environment such as ideas to put their baby to sleep so that their sleep patterns are maintained. Positive feedback is designed to produce change and negative feedback aims to minimize change. When a family accepts a physician's advice regarding a nighttime routine for infants and the advice, when followed, allows the infant to fall asleep earlier, following the routine is considered positive feedback. An example of negative feedback could be when one of the caregivers in the family decides to return to work after some time off. The other caregiver may find him/herself with more household duties (a change in

homeostasis). As a result of this, the caregiver accustomed to having his/her partner home might begin to behave in a way to encourage the caregiver to return home (maintain homeostasis).

When a system is exposed to an internal or external stressor that is more permanent, the system tries to maintain balance or establishes a new homeostatic balance; this is called "self-organization." Families use self-organization during developmental changes, such as the birth of a new child or a divorce, as well as during nondevelopmental changes, such as a change in occupation or financial status. An example of a family moving toward a new homeostasis after the birth of a child is often seen when couples, who previously shared many domestic chores, move to a more traditional household. A husband who once shared cleaning and cooking responsibilities may move to the breadwinner role while the wife takes on more household responsibility while caring for the new child.

One concept of systems theory that applies to the family systems framework is wholeness and order. The basis of this principle is that an individual cannot be understood outside of his/her environment. A person using a family systems framework will try to understand patterns in the system in which the individual is a part. For example, one important developmental task for infants is to become attached to their primary caregiver. Understanding the attachment process requires one to look at not only the individual qualities of the infant and each parent but also the relationships between the infant and each parent and the relationship between the parents. To illustrate, one way that an infant becomes securely attached is through predictable, responsive caregiving. It is very important that a caregiver respond to an infant's needs. Some of the characteristics such as a fussy temperament or an illness that makes the infant difficult to comfort can affect responsive caregiving. Each parent has his/her own temperament along with beliefs about child-rearing that affect the attachment process. Working in a family systems framework requires still more information. A family systems perspective would also focus on how the marital relationship affects each parent's ability to respond to the infant and how each parent's relationship with the infant has an impact on the other parent's relationship with the infant.

A systems framework sees cause and effect as complex. Family systems theorists do not view cause-effect relationships as linear. Instead they describe a circular causality, a pattern of interaction between each person in the system. One example of circular causality is an infant's response to his/her mother. An infant smiles and coos at his/her mother's vocalizations and facial expressions; as a result the mother continues to vocalize to her infant, which increases her infant's smiles and coos, and the cycle continues with each person, mother and infant, contributing to it.

Another characteristic of a system is that it is made up of many smaller subsystems. Some subsystems that are found within a family include the spousal subsystem, the parenting subsystem, the sibling subsystem, and the parent-child subsystem. Individuals belong to multiple subsystems, and each subsystem has its own rules. Each subsystem has its own boundary, which serves to exclude others from the subsystem. There is also a boundary around the family system as a whole. A family system maintains a selectively permeable boundary between the system and its environment. A selectively permeable boundary means that only limited information can be exchanged between the system and the environment. For example, a family that is making choices about from whom to accept parenting information has selectively permeable boundaries. Without this boundary, the family can become overwhelmed with the large amount of information that it receives from people regarding parenting.

Boundaries are designed to keep unwanted outside elements from entering the family system and to maintain family loyalty. Boundaries can include the spatial territory of a family, such as their house, as well as the more symbolic territory such as family rituals and secrets. Some families have diffuse boundaries; these families may have an open-door policy for house guests, or they may feel comfortable talking about personal issues with people outside of the family, including strangers. Other families can have rigid boundaries; these families might have strict rules about keeping family secrets even among very close friends and might be unwilling to open their household to members outside their family. Individuals and families that have rigid boundaries are called "disengaged" individuals and families because they are relatively isolated and autonomous. Individuals and families with diffuse boundaries are called "enmeshed." Enmeshed families offer a great deal of mutual support, but it is at the expense of autonomy and independence. Individuals and families can also be characterized as having clear boundaries where there is a balance between autonomy and dependence.

Murray Bowen, a family therapist, focuses on triangles within relationships to explain interactions. A triangle can make up a spousal subsystem and an infant. A diffuse boundary could exist between the parent subsystem and the child, a rigid boundary between the mother-infant subsystem and the father subsystem. The result of this could leave the father feeling lonely and isolated and thereby pressure the infant to meet the emotional needs of the mother that are typically met by her husband. Triangles usually function to ease anxiety on the part of one family member. As a result of the anxiety, one family member turns to another family member or an outside person to ease the anxiety. In the previous example, the husband/father, as a result of feeling isolated, might turn to a coworker for support, which further isolates him from his family but temporarily relieves the anxiety associated with loneliness.

One result of family systems thinking has been the development of family sup-port programs. Family support programs take into account the idea that the family influences the individual and the individual influences the family. Furthermore, family support programs recognize that social support from outside the family has an impact on family functioning. Family support programs build on the idea that a family nurtures and supports a child and a community nurtures and supports the family. Family support programs include, but are not limited to, parenting groups where children are aloud to play with other children and parents meet other adults that are struggling with parenting issues; divorce adjustment groups for adults and children; and parent-infant programs where a support person advocates for and educates mothers.

See also Family Support Programs

References and further reading
Broderick, C. B. 1993. *Understanding Family Process: Basics of Family Systems Theory.* Newbury Park, CA: Sage.
Kagan, S. L., et al. 1987. *America's Family Support Programs: Perspectives and Prospects.* New Haven: Yale University Press.
Nichols, M. P., and R. C. Schwartz. 1995. *Family Therapy: Concepts and Methods.* 3rd ed. Boston: Allyn and Bacon.

Father

Once viewed as relatively unimportant in child development, fathers play a unique and important role. The role of the father has been influenced by several historic periods, culminating in the contemporary view of the father as a capable, nurturing parent and an important member of the family system. Fathers can be biologically related to the infant/toddler, or they can be emotionally tied to the child. Fathers who are not biologically related to the child but who are a consistent figures in infant/toddlers' lives are called "social fathers." Father involvement in a child's life is influenced by many factors such as cultural beliefs and family roles.

The word "father" often conjures up images of a man anxiously pacing the floor in a hospital maternity ward or fumbling with diapers. Yet fathers can be just as competent as mothers in caring for infant/toddlers. Just as there is no one type of mother, there is no one description of a father. Some fathers and mothers are uninvolved and absent from their children, either emotionally or physically, and others are not.

For many years, scientific studies of parenting virtually ignored fathers. Indeed, even theories of child development focused on the contributions of the mother to infant/toddler development. Fathers were not considered by theorists to be very important in the development of the child. For example, attachment theorists like John Bowlby first studied mothers and infants, believing mothers to be more significant figures in the attachment relationship.

Roles of Fathers
Michael Lamb, a researcher who studies fathers and their young children, outlined four historical periods that he believes have influenced the roles of fathers. During colonial times, the father's role was defined as that of disciplinarian. Fathers were also responsible for preparing their children, particularly sons, to make a living in a particular trade. Lamb identifies the Industrial Revolution as the next period influential to the fathering role. During this period,

factory work and similar employment drew men away from the home as fathers became the breadwinners; the mother's role was seen as that of caregiver. Scholars like Wade Horn believe that historical trends such as these were responsible for emerging views of fathers as being mere playmates and relatively unimportant figures in the lives of infant/toddlers.

The third influential period occurred in the 1940s. During this period, the father's role was defined as that of sex-role socializer. While mothers tended to interact in similar ways with their infant daughters and sons, fathers tended to treat their infant sons and daughters differently. Sex-role socialization continues in the modern day, reinforced by media stereotypes as well.

During contemporary times, the fourth influential period described by Lamb, the father came to be viewed as a nurturer, equally capable of becoming emotionally attached to infant/toddlers and providing nurturing care. Modern changes such as the movement of women into the workforce have created more opportunities for fathers to step up their involvement with infant/toddlers. Studies of father-infant interactions show that fathers are very competent in their roles as nurturers. Similarly, contemporary studies of fathers' interactions with their newborns show that fathers, like mothers, show extreme delight in their infants.

Father-Infant Interactions
Fathers interact differently with their infants than mothers do, although both fathers and mothers can be equally competent as caregivers. For instance, fathers tend to engage in more physical play with their infants/toddlers—bouncing babies on their knees or tickling them—as compared to mothers, who tend to

play more didactic and traditional games. Also, fathers spend more time interacting with their infants/toddlers in play rather than in caregiving activities, such as diaper changes. Mothers are more likely to carry out routine caregiving activities. Fathers, like mothers, can also influence the infant/toddler by managing and organizing the environment and activities within it. For example, fathers manage their children's activities by the way they organize the environment and the ways in which they allow their children to explore the environment.

Fathers' behaviors seem to be influenced by characteristics such as the father's age and education level. For example, older, educated fathers, those with at least a high school degree, tend to affectionately touch their infants more during play than younger, less-educated fathers. Some research also has shown that fathers engage in more sensitive interactions with their infants when they are residential fathers and live with their infants. This is not surprising because fathers who live with their babies are more likely to know their infants' behavioral cues and personalities. Whether or not a father is biologically related to the infant/toddler has little to do with how the fathering role is defined. Social fathers—men who are not biologically related to the children in their lives but are consistent figures in the children's lives—can be just as competent and love their children just as much as biological fathers. In fact, in many families the biological fathers plays a much more minor role in the young child's life than the social father.

Father Involvement
Michael Lamb describes three types of paternal involvement: interaction, avail-

A father playing with his eight-month-old baby. (Elizabeth Crews)

ability, and responsibility. *Interaction* refers to the father's direct involvement with the infant/toddler through play or caregiving. *Availability* refers to the father's potential to interact with the infant/toddler by being present. For example, residential fathers living with their infants have more access and opportunities to interact with their infants than nonresidential fathers. *Responsibility* has to do with the father's role in securing needed resources for his child: food, shelter, and clothing.

Different characteristics influence the three types of father involvement. For example, cultural influences shape interaction. In many cultures throughout the world, women tend to take the lead in childrearing. In patriarchal cultures in which a dominant male role as head of the family and family breadwinner is common, fathers are even less likely to engage in caregiving activities. However, in other cultures men and women share childrearing responsibilities more equally. In the contemporary mainstream culture in the United States, fathers are increasingly portrayed in movies as involved and committed to their children; magazines feature articles on fathers and father involvement; and a national organization to support the parenting rights of divorced fathers was created. Frank Furstenberg, who has conducted research on fathers, commented that today's father is at least as adept at changing diapers as tires.

A family's socioeconomic status is also a determinant of father involvement. Lower-income families are more likely to hold traditional views of the father as breadwinner and the mother as nurturer, which influences the amount of father-infant interaction. In addition, income level also impacts the father's abilities to secure resources for his children. Likewise, some studies have shown that when fathers perceive themselves as inadequate providers for their young children they have fewer positive interactions with their infants/toddlers. As the role of the involved father becomes prevalent, many fathers who have the financial resources to do so are taking advantage of the Family and Medical Leave Act and taking some time off after their babies are born. And the number of stay-at-home fathers who have left the workplace to raise their children has also increased.

Ross Parke, a longtime researcher on fathers, describes additional family factors that influence father involvement with infant/toddlers. According to Parke, mothers often act as "gatekeepers" between fathers and infants. For instance, the more competent the mother feels the father is as a caregiver, the more likely she is to encourage and facilitate interactions between father and infants. Similarly, mothers' positive assessments of fathers' interest in participating in child-care activities and their own attitudes about the value of father involvement are related to higher levels of father involvement. But mothers who doubt the father's interest in caregiving, mothers who place little value in the role of fathers, or those feel ambivalent about sharing the caregiving role with fathers are less likely to facilitate and support father-infant interactions.

For married couples, the quality of the marital relationship influences father involvement. Fathers in more satisfying marital relationships are more involved with their infants and are more competent in their interactions than fathers in less satisfying marriages. Whether or not both mother and father work outside the home is also a factor in fathers' involvement. In the United States and other Western countries, many studies indicate that fathers change their parenting behaviors, becoming more involved in child caregiving, when mothers are employed outside the home.

Despite the increase in involvement, mothers still tend to do more caregiving tasks than fathers. Workplace demands also impact father involvement. When fathers are highly committed to their work and toil long hours, they are less likely to be involved in direct interactions with their infant/toddlers and less available to them, although fathers with high work demands can have greater financial means to provide resources for their families.

See also Caregiving; Parenting

References and further reading
Booth, Alan, and Ann C. Crouter, eds.
1998. *Men in Families.* Mahway, NJ:
Lawrence Erlbaum Associates.
Department of Health and Human
Services Fatherhood Initiative.
http://www.fatherhood.hhs.gov/
Fitzgerald, Hiram, et al., eds. 1999.
"Fathers and Infants," Special Issue.
Infant Mental Health Journal 20(3):
213–221.
Horn, Wade. 2000. "Fathering Infants." In
Joy D. Osofsky and Hiram E. Fitzgerald,
eds., *WAIMH Handbook of Infant
Mental Health, Vol. 3: Parenting and
Child Care.* New York: Wiley, pp.
269–298.
Mackey, Wade C. 1996. *The American
Father: Biocultural and Developmental
Aspects.* New York: Plenum.
National Fatherhood Initiative (website
2001). http://www.fatherhood.org.
Parke, Ross. (1996). *Fatherhood.*
Cambridge: Harvard University Press.

Fear

Fear is one of the core emotions. Fear responses are more common among infants aged six months and older. Prior to this time, infants rely on their parent/caregiver to protect them from fearful situations and experiences. However,

*A one-year-old boy expressing fear.
(Elizabeth Crews)*

as infants become mobile, they are more likely to experience fear as they explore the environment. Over time, infants also begin to look to their parents/caregivers for cues as to how to respond to a particular situation. This is called "social referencing." If the parent looks fearful, the infant is likely to display a fear response as well. A fear response is characterized by raised and furrowed eyebrows, a retracted mouth, and intense eyes.

See also Emotion

Feedback

In human development, the meaning of feedback can be derived from cybernetics and engineering. The assumption is that systems attempt to maintain themselves in a steady state. Systems generate outputs, and when information from the output of a system is redirected to the system (feed back), the system must react. When the system receives too much feedback (positive feedback) the system overloads and becomes chaotic. For example, when a microphone receives too much feedback, the electronic system produces shrill and unpleasant noises that do not go away until the system readjusts and the positive feedback is eliminated. When the system receives negative feedback, it prompts the system to readjust, to absorb the information, and return to a steady state. Quite paradoxically, negative feedback is positive input for a system, whereas positive feedback is negative input for a system.

The other, more common meaning of feedback is the information that one provides another about that person's performance. When children are learning a task, the caregiver can provide information to the child at various stages of performance, making comments about how the child is progressing. In this case, providing feedback gives the child knowledge of performance and helps the child to understand whether the approach being taken is the correct one. In this sense feedback is akin to reinforcement.

See also Family Systems; Theories of Development

Feeding Problems
See Bottle-Feeding; Breastfeeding; Nutrition

Fertility Rates
Many countries either encourage or discourage reproduction, either intentionally or through family policy. European countries, because of their decreasing birthrate, tend to encourage women to have more children. Third World countries frequently discourage overpopulation by instituting family planning programs. Fertility policies of individual countries depend upon their particular demographic situation as well as the cultural orientation of the people.

The United States
The United States has had a birthrate below replacement level since 1972. The current birthrate of two children per adult female is still below replacement level, but large numbers of immigrants make it unlikely that the United States will be depopulated. The lack of U.S. reproductive policy in comparison with European encouragement of fertility, or pronatal policy, could be explained by the fact that the United States has a higher birthrate than Europe. In addition, the tradition of democracy discourages social

policies that actively interfere with the number of children per family.

The U.S. government does not sustain policies interfering with reproduction. In *Griswold v. Connecticut*, the U.S. Supreme Court asserted privacy rights for reproductive matters, and it has continued to uphold this decision. In general, U.S. policy allows individuals the right to control their own fertility and contraception, with some restrictions for late-term abortions. In 1942, the Supreme Court overturned an Oklahoma law that required sterilization of prisoners convicted of multiple sex offenses.

Yet it could be argued that we restrict these rights for the poor or for convicted criminals. In 1991, a Kansas legislator proposed that women on welfare be paid $500 to have Norplant, a long-acting contraceptive, implanted. In California a woman convicted of child abuse was ordered to use this contraceptive method as a condition of her probation.

Implicit discouragement of fertility for the poor in America is an attempt to reduce dependence on federal assistance. Conservative legislators argue that young people should delay childbearing until both parents are ready to assume the financial responsibility of raising their children. Many states have refused to pay additional sums of money to mothers who have a child while they are receiving welfare.

The health care system in the United States indirectly encourages fertility among families in poverty. Many states do not offer Medicaid to adults in poverty, although they do provide health services through Medicaid to the children. As a result, women living in poverty have to purchase their own contraceptive devices. The working poor, in most cases, do not have access to Medicaid or private insurance companies. Even if they do have private insurance, many companies do not pay for contraception, particularly those owned by Catholics. Refusal of private insurance companies to cover contraception is not based on economics; hospital births are much more expensive to cover than ongoing contraceptive medication. Such policies can limit the availability of contraception to those who can afford to pay the cost themselves. When families are unable to afford the cost of contraception, they may opt for cheaper and less reliable methods.

Europe

Whereas the United States neither encourages nor discourages fertility, European governments have a long history of pronatal policies, which encourage population growth. Family policy itself began as a result of demographic concerns in Western Europe. Family policies addressing the problems of low birthrate and low wages began in the late nineteenth and early twentieth centuries in France and Sweden. The first provision was an increase in pay by employers to household heads of large families who were in a lower income bracket. This initial practice developed into the universal family allowance.

In the last half of the twentieth century, European governments developed strong social policies to assist families with young children. Such policies also acted as an economic incentive for families to have children. In the 1950s, European governments began redistributing income from families without children to families with children. This policy continues today among all industrialized countries, except for the United States. Cash housing allowances for families with children were introduced in the 1960s. One decade

later, pronatalist policies addressed child care needs in Europe as women entered the workforce in larger numbers.

In spite of incentives to increase the birthrate, Europe continues to experience a decline in the number of children born. In Central Europe, the replacement rate has been remarkably low, reaching 1.3 in recent years. Rumania was a tragic exception to this rule. Until the overthrow of the communist government, abortion and contraception were banned in Rumania in an attempt to increase the birthrate. As a result of this policy, combined with a difficult economic situation, many children were malnourished or even placed in orphanages.

China

Communist China has alternately encouraged and discouraged population growth with surprising success in both instances. Before 1949, when China became a communist country, the high infant mortality and poor health conditions kept the population relatively low despite a high birthrate. Following the revolution, the crude birthrate remained very large, more than twenty per 1,000, but the life expectancy went from forty-seven to sixty-eight in the next thirty years. Also, infant mortality was cut in half. Although these demographic changes were occurring due to improved health standards, the government embarked on a strong pronatalist policy. There was a strict ban on abortion and sterilization as well as strong restrictions on contraception. After a dramatic increase in population size, the Chinese government began to manufacture contraceptives in 1955.

In 1970, due to a rising population, the stagnation of the economy became obvious. The Chinese Strategic Demographic Initiative was put into place. This policy was to become the most extreme antifertility system yet seen in the world. However, China's situation of exploding population growth, combined with limited space for agriculture, may have encouraged such measures. The total population exceeded 800 million at this time, well above the 583 million at the time of the revolution. Because of the rapidly increasing population size and no increase in production, leaders assumed that China was heading for a famine.

The new family policy involved later marriage, longer spacing between births, and fewer children. Financial incentives and "education," which borders on harassment, are used to enforce these measures. Although family planning use increased over the next seven years, the birthrate did not decline dramatically enough. Therefore, in 1979 China embarked on the one-child-per-couple plan. Job opportunities, health care, free schooling, and even a monthly cash stipend are given to those couples who agree to the one-child plan and maintain their contract. Severe penalties are imposed on those who have many births. Abortions and sterilizations are encouraged.

In the 1980s, this policy was modified to allow exceptions for rural populations, minorities, and other special cases. Later marriage also relaxed age limits by setting the minimum age for marriage at only twenty for women and twenty-two for men. Human rights violations include reports of forced sterilization, infanticide, and imprisonment of pregnant women by family planning workers. Reports of poor treatment and imprisonment of relatives of those in hiding in order to avoid abortion continue. Such actions are contrary to national policy; in fact, the Supreme People's Court specifically outlawed the taking of hostages by

government officials in 1990. Quite recently, China has allowed those families who have two sets of grandparents with only one child between them to have a second child. As the population declines, China has begun to make changes in order to ensure that there will be enough workers to support the aging population. China's success in its programs is due to two factors: the obvious economic situation caused by overpopulation, and the cultural tradition of obedience to government and society.

Although China officially allows families in rural areas to have more children, this policy has not been applied to Tibet. Family planning workers have used sterilization, sometimes of entire villages, as a political tool to gain land for China. Native Tibetans have dramatically decreased in number since the exile of the Dalai Lama in 1959. In 1960, the International Commission of Jurists ruled that China was guilty of religious genocide. Since that time, 130,000 Tibetans have followed the Dalai Lama into exile; 1.2 million Tibetans have died from war, famine, or imprisonment. The 6 million who remain are not allowed to own a picture of their religious leader. Possession of a picture of the Dalai Lama is punished by imprisonment.

Third World Countries

Undeveloped countries have shown a dramatic increase in family planning in the past few decades. The average number of children per female has dropped from just over six to just under four during this period. In the developing countries, about one-half of the women used birth control in 1990. Of course, there is still a large difference between undeveloped countries and the industrialized nations, where 70 percent use birth control.

TABLE 1   International Fertility Rates

Country	Total Population	Population Less than Age 5	Annual Birth Rate	Infant Mortality Rate per 1000	Fertility Rate per female
Australia	18,705,000	1,259,000	245,000	5	1.8
Belgium	10,152,000	549,000	105,000	6	1.6
Canada	30,857,000	1,810,000	343,000	6	1.6
China	1,266,838,000	19,821,000	97,793	33	1.8
Colombia	41,564,000	4,788,000	988,000	26	2.7
Denmark	5,282,000	324,000	63,000	4	1.7
France	55,886,000	3,572,000	711,000	5	1.7
Germany	82,178,000	3,857,000	736,000	5	1.3
India	998,056,000	114,976,000	24,489,000	70	3
Ireland	3,705,000	256,000	53,000	6	1.9
Israel	6,101,000	583,000	118,000	6	2.6
Italy	57,343,000	2,620,000	506,000	6	1.2
Japan	126,505,000	6,171,000	1,271,000	4	1.4
Malaysia	21,830,000	2,644,000	520,000	8	3
Mexico	97,365,000	11,202,000	2,324,000	27	2.6
Morocco	3,215,000	703,000	27,867	45	2.9
Nigeria	108,945,000	17,880,000	4,176,000	112	5
Norway	4,442,000	293,000	57,000	4	1.9
Philippines	74,454,000	9,800,000	2,064,000	47	3.4
Portugal	9,873,000	525,000	102,000	5	1.4
Russian Federation	147,196,000	7,006,000	1,434,000	18	1.4
Saudi Arabia	20,899,000	3,220,000	696,000	20	5.6
Spain	39,634,000	1,822,000	358,000	6	1.1
South Africa	39,900,000	4,909,000	1,055,000	54	3.1
Sudan	28,883,000	4,162,000	944,000	67	4.5
Sweden	8,892,000	478,000	86,000	3	1.6
Switzerland	7,344,000	414,000	79,000	3	1.5
Thailand	60,856,000	4,831,000	997,k000	26	1.7
United Kingdom	58,744,000	3,521,000	680,000	6	1.7
United States	276,218,k000	19,344,000	3,754,000	7	2
Venezuela	23,706,000	2,791,000	574,000	20	2.9
Viet Nam	78,705,000	8,454,000	1,654,000	31	2.5

Source: Constructed from assorted web pages compiling world demographic data.

In the 1950s and 1960s, change brought about a division between traditional cultural patterns and Western thought, marked by individuality and a desire for economic growth. Along with the cultural trends, there was a growing awareness of the problems associated with rapid population growth. While cultural changes were taking place in Third World countries, the United Nations identified fertility control as a basic human right. Paul Ehrlich published *The Population Bomb,* and developed countries poised themselves to provide financial assistance for family planning.

In 1951, India was the first developing country to promote population control through family planning. Pakistan, Korea, China, and Fiji also followed these policies within the next decade. Singapore began its program in 1965. Successful programs had the support of upper-class administrators who had training in the West. The best programs, such as those in Korea, Mexico, Colombia, Thailand, and Indonesia, used a variety of methods, including clinical services, outreach programs, evaluation, and training.

Initially the Third World countries felt that economic development had to go hand in hand with family planning. Research showed that a good family planning program could increase contraceptive use, regardless of socioeconomic change. However, the most successful programs did co-occur with steady economic development. Singapore had both a successful program and economic development. It now has policies in place that encourage population growth, similar to Western Europe. Singapore provides subsidized child-care services and free prenatal care for the first three children. Also, the third child gives all other children priority registration in public school. Tax relief and rebates increase with family size, especially for the third and fourth child. The government even gives an upgrade in housing for those who have a third child. As in China, successful interference with traditional family growth patterns led to a necessary reversal of government policy.

In summary, family policies that support or discourage population growth arise from various needs and goals. Many policies address concerns about child poverty or child welfare. Other policies are implemented in response to social change or labor-force requirements. Effective modern societies cannot ignore structural changes in the family or increasing child poverty. Family planning policies—within the context of each nation's values and traditions—often improves the quality of life for its citizens.

See also Birth

References and further reading
Bianchi, S., and D. Spain. 1996. "Women, Work, and Family in America." *Population Resource Bulletin* 51(3).
Demeny, P. 1986. "Pronatalist Policies in Low Fertility Countries: Patterns Performance and Prospects." *Population and Development Review* 12: 335–358.
Zigler, E. F., et al. 1996. *Children, Families, and Government: Preparing for the Twenty-first Century.* Cambridge, UK: Cambridge University Press.

Fertilization

Fertilization, or conception, is the process in which human sex cells (gametes: the male sperm and the female egg, or ovum) unite to form a single cell that develops into an adult organism. Fertilization begins when the sperm contacts the outer surface of the egg; it ends when the nucleus of the sperm fuses with that of the ovum. Fertilization is not instantaneous and may take up to several hours. Once this process is complete, the fertilized egg becomes a zygote. One interesting aspect of human sexuality is the extent to which nature has worked to provide optimal conditions for the union of sperm and ovum. For example, the release of the ovum from the ovary into the fallopian tube or ovulation occurs at relatively predictable times during the course of each menstrual cycle. Since the time between release of the ovum and its descent into the fallopian tube is roughly six hours and sperm cells live from twelve to thirty-six hours, impregnation could occur even if intercourse preceded ovulation.

The ovum is one of the largest cells in the human body. Some 200–500 million sperm are released with any one ejaculation of seminal fluid; several thousand will eventually cross the cervical barrier and literally seek out the ovum. Only one sperm cell must penetrate the ovum in order to complete conception. If fertilization does not occur, most of the uterine lining is discharged along with blood during menstruation. However, if fertilization does take place, usually in the fallopian tube, the ovum continues its three- to four-day journey down the fallopian tube toward the uterus and will eventually become embedded in the uterine lining.

Each gamete contains only half the genetic material of the original cell. During the sperm-egg fusion, the full amount of genetic material is attained: one-half contributed by the female, one-half by the male. Therefore, fertilization is necessary to produce a single cell that contains a full complement of genes. In humans, there are forty-six chromosomes, which carry genetic material, in each human body cell. The notable exceptions to this are the gametes, each with twenty-three chromosomes. As soon as fertilization is complete, the zygote that is formed has a complete set of forty-six chromosomes containing genetic information from both parents.

In-vitro fertilization is a medical procedure to assist couples conceive a child when they are experiencing difficulties in doing so naturally. One or more eggs are fertilized outside the body, and then the embryos are transferred into a woman's uterus. The process usually involves stimulation of the growth of multiple eggs by the daily injection of hormone medications; however, it is also possible to retrieve a single egg. The eggs can be recovered by two different methods. The more common method is sonographic egg recovery, which uses ultrasound. The other is laparoscopic, in which a small incision in the abdomen is made through which eggs are retrieved. Once the retrieval process is completed, the eggs are placed in a fluid with semen and left for approximately eighteen hours. The eggs that have been fertilized and are developing normally are then transferred to the woman's (or a surrogate's) uterus. Multiple embryos are typically implanted to increase the likelihood of pregnancy. Following the transfer of the embryos to the womb, progesterone injections can be administered daily to the recipient to assist implantation into the uterine wall. The probability of viable pregnancy is approximately 20 percent with one in-vitro cycle.

See also Birth

Fetal Alcohol Syndrome
See Alcoholism

Fetus
The fetus is the infant in the mother's womb. In a more technical sense, the term refers to the product of conception in humans from the ninth week of gestation until birth.

See also Prenatal Development

Field, Tiffany M.
More than anyone else, Tiffany Field has advanced our understanding of the role of touch in early human development. Founder of the Touch Institute at the University of Miami, Field's research has

focused heavily on the role of touch and massage on infant development as well as the impact of depression on both fathers' and mothers' relationships with their infants.

See also Depression; Massage; Touch

Fine Motor Skills

Fine motor skills are movements that require precision and dexterity, such as manipulative tasks. An example of this is the ability to pick up a piece of food and place it in the mouth. The skill of picking up an object moves from a less refined movement to a very refined action. Timing of development is rapid in the first year of life. In first attempts, infants use primarily the palm and fourth and fifth digit to grasp objects. However, somewhere between nine and fourteen

A baby picking up a toy. (Elizabeth Crews)

months, this action will change to grasping with the palm and middle finger and eventually the index finger and the thumb.

See also Lateralization; Motor Development

Folic Acid

Folic acid deficiencies are linked to malformations during prenatal development. There are two major causes of such deficiencies: diets that are deficient in folic acid, and medical problems that require treatment with anticonvulsant drugs. Folic acid deficiencies have been linked to the incidence of neural tube deficits such as spina bifida and hydrocephalus. There is evidence suggesting that administering vitamins containing folic acid supplements acts as a preventive measure against such malformations or that taking them after pregnancy reduces the risk for subsequent pregnancies. Green leafy vegetables provide a natural source of folic acid.

See also Genetic Disorders; Nutrition

Fontanels

Although the cranium (skull) becomes a hard protective shell for the brain, at birth it is soft, and its eight-bone structure can actually move. This feature helps the infant as it moves through the birth canal. The bones of the skull are connected by two structures: sutures and fontanels. The fontanels are sections of cartilage and are not closed at birth. Typically, the areas where they are not closed are referred to as "soft spots" and need to be protected. The back-skull fontanels close by about the third or fourth postnatal month, and the front fontanels close by about the eighteenth postnatal month. Sutures do not complete their development until late adolescence. Thus, there are ample reasons why children engaged in sports, riding tricycles, or riding bicycles need to wear helmets. Parents need to treat all head injuries during infancy and early childhood with special concern.

Forced Choice Preferential Looking

A research method used to examine infants' perceptual capabilities. Researchers familiarize babies to a stimulus until they habituate to it or lose interest in it. Then two stimuli are presented, one to the left and one to the right of the baby. Often one stimulus is the initial stimulus to which the infant was habituated, and the other stimulus is a slight variant of the original stimulus. Researchers carefully record the looking preferences of the infants to see if the infant shows a perceptual preference in his/her attention to the novel stimulus over that of the original stimulus. In other cases, researchers present two new stimuli during the forced choice phase in order to examine which of these two stimuli has the most similar features or characteristics to the originally presented object in the infant's perception.

Such work has helped establish information about infants' preferences.

See also Attention; Habituation; Perception; Perceptual Preference

Fovial Percept

The impression derived from sensory stimulation of light onto the foveal area of the retina. It produces the impression of an upside-down replication of the object upon which the eye is focused. The dense concentration of cones (spe-

cific neural cells to process bright light and color) in this permits extraction of information about features within the image and passes it on to the brain through the optic nerve.

See also Perception; Retina

Fragile X Syndrome
See Genetic Disorders

Fraiberg, Selma (1918–1981)

A psychiatric social worker, Selma Fraiberg established the Child Development Project at the University of Michigan in 1972. The project was designed to develop a home visitation intervention for mothers and their infants. Fraiberg emphasized the importance of interdisciplinary collaboration, and each of the three training groups that she supervised over the course of the program's existence reflected disciplinary diversity. Fraiberg's approach blended scientific training, psychoanalytic theory, and child development and was firm in its commitment to public policy aspects of early intervention. Graduates of her training program organized the first professional association for infant mental health in 1977 (the Michigan Association for Infant Mental Health).

Fraiberg's work with parents of blind infants is classic. She taught parents to use tactile and auditory stimulation to solicit, maintain, and enhance social behaviors and to express their relationship with their infants through nonvisual means. Her 1958 book, *The Magic Years*, sold more than 1 million copies and alerted the public to the importance of infancy and early childhood for subsequent development. As a scientist, clinician, and advocate,

Fraiberg stands as one of the founders of the infant mental health movement and of relationship-based family prevention programs.

Freud, Sigmund (1856–1939)

Sigmund Freud's theory of personality stimulated considerable controversy over such topics as the role of instincts in human behavior, the structure of the mind, the function of conscious and unconscious processes, the stage-sequencing of personality, and the various intricate relationships between parent and child that he thought determined the individual's personality. Freud's theory of personality development is a stage-sequence theory. Within each stage the individual must resolve a developmental conflict. If the conflict is not resolved, the

Sigmund Freud c. 1910. (Hulton/Archive)

individual can become fixated at a particular stage. Freud believed that certain adult personality types reflected such fixations.

Psychoanalytic theory divides the *oral stage* (roughly birth to two years) into two periods: *oral-passive* and *oral-sadistic*. During early infancy, libidinal energy (an innate motive force) is directed to the infant's mouth and upper digestive system. The mother becomes the primary gratification object in that she provides nourishment through breast or bottle. When weaning to cup begins, the infant is faced with a conflict, in that the primary source of gratification must be given up. Fixation during the oral stage may produce the *oral-passive character*, a person who is dependent and demanding, or the *oral-sadistic character*, a person who is sarcastic, independent, aggressive, and hostile.

The *anal stage* corresponds roughly to the toddler years of development. During this stage, libidinal energy is directed to the anal region, as the toddler begins to achieve self-control of bowel and bladder. Toilet-training practices provide the basis of conflict. Fixation at the anal stage produces either the *anal-retentive character* or the *anal-aggressive character*. Anal-retentive personalities are overly concerned with orderliness, are suspicious and rigid, and engage in a variety of obsessive-compulsive patterns of behavior. Anal-aggressive personalities go the other way—messiness, indifference to routine, and personal sloppiness are hallmarks.

The *phallic stage* roughly covers the years from three to five. During those years the source of libidinal energy shifts from the anal region to the genital region. The developmental conflict is one of making an identification with the appropriate same-sex adult. The conflict is often referred to as the *Oedipus complex* for boys and the *Electra complex* for girls. Initially, both boys and girls become attached to the mother. However, this attachment places the young male in direct rivalry with his more powerful father for his mother's attention. The young male develops *castration anxiety,* or the fear that his father will injure his penis if active competition for his mother is pursued. The conflict is resolved when the young male represses his sexual feelings toward his mother and his feelings of rivalry toward his father. Simultaneously, he identifies with his father, internalizing his father's behaviors, attitudes, and values.

Because the young female obviously does not have a penis she cannot fear castration, but the fact that she has no penis leads her to desire one. Because mother also has no penis, the young girl is caught between her desire for her mother's love and her desire for her father's penis. In either case, for boys and girls, resolution of the complex has two key results. First, it initiates and largely completes the process of identification with the same-sex parent. Second, it gives rise to the *superego,* which consists of the conscience and the ego ideal.

A major function of the superego is to restrict the free expression of id impulses. The id, present from birth, is the source of motivational energy. It operates according to the *pleasure principle,* that is, seeking immediate gratification. The ego acts as a mediator between the id and the superego. The ego operates according to the *reality principle.* Following the phallic stage, a period of latency sets in, which, after puberty, is replaced by the *genital stage* of mature sexuality. Freudian theory was the first major theory to attribute special importance to the early interactions between children and their parents. However, it did not place ade-

quate emphasis on ego functions or take adequate account of social and cultural influences on personality development. Efforts to blend the psychosexual stages of development into the social and cultural contexts are characteristic of neoanalytic theorists, among them Erik Erikson and Margaret Mahler.

See also Erikson, Erik; Mahler, Margaret

Freudian Defense Mechanisms of the Ego

Freud specified that when people are anxious and tense, they tend to use mental mechanisms of defense against their anxieties. Some of the defense mechanisms persons use to protect the ego are:

- rationalization ("I did not want that old toy anyway");
- sublimation (peering down a microscope in a laboratory instead of peeking at forbidden things);
- reaction formation (acting very sweet and overgenerous because selfish or aggressive feelings are too anxiety-provoking);
- splitting (Jekyll and Hyde characteristics);
- repression (wiping out of consciousness all memory of a naughty thought or deed);
- projection of evil (accusing another of having the "evil" thoughts you are ashamed of, or having done the forbidden actions you actually did);
- denial of reality (protesting innocence even though the evidence may be very obvious, such as scattered cookie crumbs and an empty cookie box);
- and escape to fantasy or nonrelevant topic.

Overpunishment can lead to young children's early use of these defense mechanisms.

Frontal Cortex

One of the four lobes of the brain, the frontal lobe constitutes the most anterior portion of the cerebral cortex. It is the largest lobe and, commensurate with its size, has many functions ranging from the programming, initiation, and inhibition of movements of the body and limbs to the control of certain aspects of emotion and memory.

See also Neurobiology

Full-Term Infant

An infant that is born after at least thirty-seven weeks of gestation.

Functional Lateralization

Functional lateralization means the asymmetries in the production or specialization of a behavior or function. It is most often used in reference to lateralization within the brain. Here, it is the specialization of a hemisphere for a certain task or procedure. For example, the left hemisphere is functionally lateralized for the processing (comprehension and production) of the verbal components of language. Likewise, the expression of emotion is functionally lateralized to the right hemisphere. Structural lateralization is not necessary for functional lateralization but often accompanies it. Functional asymmetry means the manifestation of behaviors or actions to one side of the body or space. The use of the right hand for writing is an example of functional lateralization.

See also Lateralization

G

Games

Parents initiate interpersonal games with very young babies. A parent, diapering a baby, calls out in a sing-song voice: "Who's my precious one? Who is my wonderful baby?" The baby learns early that by waving her legs, gurgling, and vocalizing, she is taking a turn in this interactive game. By five months, many babies are enjoying a game of "Ah-boom!" The parent lowers his forehead toward baby's forehead as he is sitting with baby on his lap. Gently papa bumps foreheads with baby. After many trials at this game, babies learn to anticipate the gesture just on hearing the initial words. They too bend their foreheads to meet the adult's forehead. Game-playing has begun.

By six to nine months, babies love peek-a-boo games. Parents not only play this game by lightly throwing a cloth diaper over baby's head and calling out: "Where's baby? Oh, there you are! Peek-a-boo!" as baby flings off the light diaper and crows with joy to see the familiar and beloved caregiver's face. Peek-a-boo may also be played as you enter baby's room and peek around the corner to see if baby in the crib is looking out to find your face. By creating variants on the game, you help babies learn to enjoy the game in a variety of settings and in a variety of formats.

Babies love the game of "So big!" Seat a baby on your lap and take her hands in yours. Then ask "How big is baby?" and answer "So big!" as you raise her hands way up in the air. Soon, in anticipation of your answer, baby herself will start raising her hands in the air.

These games teach basic communication skills to the infant. Baby learns turn-taking strategies. Baby learns to orient and attend to your verbal and physical cues and readies herself to respond appropriately in turn.

Some babies like tickling games, and some creeping babies like a chase game on the floor. However, be sure to watch for signs that baby is comfortable. Some adults continue a game of chasing or of tickling too long and babies will become distressed and cry. Be sure to watch for signs of emotional overload. Babies prefer games that are exciting but not too exciting.

Pat-a-cake is a game of clapping hands at midline that parents can do long before the baby can bring both hands to the body midline. By engaging baby gently in this game you help baby coordinate hands at midline and learn the rules of each chanted part of this game.

Babies like ball-rolling games. Sit with legs spread apart and touching baby's feet, which are also spread apart. Roll a ball back and forth to each other over this short space.

For some high-activity toddlers, games of running are a real pleasure. A toddler may even ask you to run. This simple game works best if you have a large space where you can pretend to run after the toddler around your living space and yet never seem to catch him.

A toddler loves the game where you put him on your shoulders and sing a marching song as you march around your living space. "We are marching to Pretoria" sings Grandpa, and the toddler crows with joy and even tries to repeat the words as you march along.

Young toddlers like to take turns in running into and out of a room and peeking through a door at a peer who is in the next room. Often toddlers will shriek with joyful pleasure as they take turns being the peeker and the one who is there to be peeked at in the next room.

Group circle games are difficult for toddlers because they have troubles coordinating so many actions together. In playing Ring Around a Rosy, toddlers have to continue to hold hands, continue to circle around, and to sing or try to sing the words. Often the hands will separate, and it is best for the adult to be part of the circle as you teach toddlers to play Ring around a Rosy together. Another variant on this circle game is:

> *Sally go round the sun,*
> *Sally go round the moon;*
> *Sally go round the chimney pots*
> *Every afternoon*
> *BOOM!*

Toddlers fall to floor and roll about at this last word.

After they have learned to go around in a circle with you holding hands, many toddlers will anticipate the BOOM part and throw themselves happily to the floor and roll about before you ever get to the last word.

When object permanence is firmly established, toddlers love to play a game where you come into a room and pretend that you cannot see them because they are playing at hiding, even though, perhaps, they are standing in your closet among your clothes and in full view. Be sure to say out loud "Where is my baby? I can't see her. I wonder where she has gone?" Pretend to look under the bed or near the closet. The toddler may be hiding in full view of you with a piece of clothing over her head. As you pretend to keep looking she crows and giggles. She has outwitted the adult, who is saying such loving and adoring words about her. As you continue to pretend to search and ask again "Where is my baby?" the toddler will call out "I'm hiding!" and will respond to the adult's happy "Oh, there you are, lovey!" by running into your arms for a hug.

Play with toys teaches babies about how to manipulate objects and what the baby can do to make interesting sounds or experiences by pushing, pressing, and turning parts of toys. Play with an engaged and loving caregiver is a priceless introduction to the world of interpersonal, intimate social coordination.

Playing gentle games with babies is a wonderful way to show them that caregiving ministrations are not the only way to interact. Games increase social pleasures and social skills for babies.

They are also a good introduction to pretend play. If you are reading a story about fish swimming in the water, babies can "pretend to swim" on the floor. They are not yet ready for the sophisticated roles of pretend play in the housekeeping corner, or with train tracks and toy trains running to the station. But you are helping them learn the rudiments of pretend play as they act out simple roles from stories you are reading.

See also Book-Reading; Songs and Sensory Development

Gametogenesis

The process that results in the production of sperm (spermatogenesis) and ova (oogenesis), the human reproductive cells.

Gay and Lesbian Parents

Understanding gay and lesbian parents and their families is facilitated by a family ecosystem perspective. A *system* is a set of two or more interrelated units constituting a whole that is different from and greater than the sum of its parts. A family is a system that as a whole is greater than the sum of its individual members. From a family ecosystem perspective, family is defined as being composed of individuals who may be related not only by blood, marriage, or adoption but also by sets of interdependent and independent individuals who share common goals, resources, and commitments to one another. This broadened definition of family was articulated strongly by pioneer family ecologists such as Bea Paolucci and Margaret Bubolz. For decades many gay men and lesbians have parented children despite the widespread notion that being gay or lesbian and being a parent was contradictory. Currently, and in increasing numbers, gay men and lesbians are becoming parents, many through use of reproductive technology such as artificial or donor insemination, and many through adoption, foster parenting, or surrogate parenthood. The open expression of parenthood by gays and lesbians in fact is a sociocultural and historical innovation in American society.

Diversity and Prevalence of Gay/Lesbian Parents

If gay and lesbian parenting is an example of diversity in parenthood, it is important to point out that there is diversity among gay and lesbian families as well. For example, roles may vary greatly from one gay family to another. The single-parent role, the coparenting role, and the stepparent role are just a few of the possible roles that exist in gay families just as they do in heterosexual families. Gay and lesbian families also have the same diversity in family structure (e.g., gay father, lesbian mother, gay father/lesbian mother, gay fathers/lesbian mother, gay father/lesbian mothers) that one finds in heterosexual families. Gay and lesbian families vary in socioeconomic status, employment, and parental education in much the same way as any other families do. Indeed, gay men and lesbians choose to have children for many of the same reasons expressed by other single persons or couples. They want to provide love, support, and guidance to children and share their lives and experiences with them as they navigate through life's challenges and joys.

It is hard to estimate the number of gay and lesbian parents in the United States because prejudice and discrimination prevent them from disclosing their parenthood. Most estimates suggest that approximately 10 percent of the population is gay or lesbian. Other investigators suggest that about 10 percent of gay men and 20 percent of lesbians are parents, and their children were conceived in originally heterosexual marriages. Based on these estimates, then, there are as many as 2 million gay fathers in the United States and up to 4 million children with gay fathers. This estimate jumps to 6–8 million children when lesbian mothers

268 Gay and Lesbian Parents

are included. Julie Schwartz Gottman, of the Seattle Professional Practice Institute, estimates that there are as many as 5 million lesbian mothers, with approximately 5,000–10,000 becoming mothers after coming out. Thus, the number of children of gay fathers and lesbian mothers in the United States most likely ranges from 6 million to 14 million.

What these estimates suggest is that there are more and more gay men and lesbians choosing parenthood after coming out, which Charlotte Patterson and her colleagues at the University of Virginia have termed the "gayby boom" and "lesbian baby boom." With these growing numbers comes an influx in the number of children with gay and lesbian parents. In contrast to past generations, currently a majority of Americans today report that they believe that gays and lesbians are equal to heterosexuals in their parenting abilities. Most research on gay parents has been conducted to dispel myths and misconceptions that are evident in mainstream culture. Because of this, only recently has the focus been the quality of parent-child relationships, rather than whether the parent is homosexual or heterosexual.

Legal and Political Context

Historically, the judicial system has not been family-friendly toward gay men and lesbians who want to become parents. On a national level, some states have laws stating that sexual orientation cannot be a determining factor in custody battles; however, other states presume that being gay or lesbian makes a man or woman unfit to parent. In court proceedings, mostly regarding custody, gay or lesbian parents are likely to lose. This is especially true in custody disputes for gay men. Moreover, courts have even forced gay men and lesbians to live apart from their partners or to sever contact with the gay and lesbian community just to have visitation or custody rights. It must also be noted that legal issues in general can be different for gay men and lesbians who have created their families intentionally versus those who became parents in heterosexual relationships or marriages. When a gay man or lesbian has a partner, he or she is usually denied adoptive rights, resulting in no legal relationship or rights for the children he or she has parented since birth or adoption. In general, relatives of the legal parent have more rights in court than the partner who has been in the parenting role and involved with the child.

There are two primary issues, the fitness of gay and lesbian parents, and the well-being of the child, that emerge in the courts of the judicial system. Within the judicial system there have been misconceptions about gay and lesbian parents, such as gay men and lesbians are mentally ill and are not fit to parent, lesbians are less maternal, and the gay lifestyle and community leave little time for gay men and lesbians to parent. Overall, there is no support from research studies for these assumptions, made by biased, value-driven courts. In fact, every psychiatric, psychological, and medical professional association has thrown out the stance that being homosexual is associated with mental illness. Moreover, there have not been any differences found between lesbian and heterosexual women regarding their approach to childrearing; neither have community factors been found to impact in a negative manner their ability to care for and raise children. In sum, then, there is no real foundation for stating that gay men and lesbian are unfit to parent based on their sexual orientation.

The second area of concern in the judicial system is fear of the impact on a child's sexual identity, personal and psychological development, and social and peer relationships. This fear stems from ignorance, prejudice, and the belief that having a gay or lesbian parent puts a child at higher risk for sexual abuse or that the child will be gay or lesbian themselves (as if this were negative). Again, there has been no research to support these fears, rooted in prejudice and ignorance. On the contrary, Charlotte Patterson has found that home environments provided by gay or lesbian parents are just as developmentally enriching and appropriate as those provided by heterosexual parents.

Gay Fathers and Lesbian Mothers
During the 1980s and 1990s, most interest in gay parenting came from concerns by the judicial system during custody proceedings of the fitness of gay and lesbian parents. However, since the mid-1990s other work has come from true interest in family and individual development within gay and lesbian families. There are two main areas that give us valuable information about the lives of gay and lesbian parents and the development of their families. The first area allows us to learn about gay men and lesbians who became parents in a heterosexual relationship or marriage, that is, before coming out. The second area informs us about gay men and lesbians who had already come out and then planned their families. A majority of what we know about gay and lesbian families comes from lesbian mothers because it is much easier for them to assume the parenting position. In addition, most of the earlier work compares and contrasts lesbian mothers and heterosexual mothers, whereas the most recent work focuses on individual differences within gay and lesbian families.

What do we know about gay men and lesbians who became parents in heterosexual relationships? The most widespread conclusion is that there are few differences and many more similarities than previously thought. For example, researchers have found no significant differences on self-concept, happiness, overall adjustment, or psychological state in a study that compared lesbian mothers to heterosexual mothers. Lesbians have the stigma of being overly masculine and less warm, which some feel is reason for lesbians not to be mothers. However, there is no support for these assumptions. In fact, research studies have shown that divorced lesbian mothers are more likely to live with a partner than divorced heterosexual mothers; lesbian mothers tend to be more economically sound and emotionally stable; they maintain more contact with the biological father; and they feel that their children benefit from having a lesbian mother. Their children are more tolerant of diversity.

Much less is known about gay men who became fathers in a heterosexual relationship. However, Jerry Bigner and R. Brooke Jacobsen at Colorado State University have found no differences for impetus to be a father when they compared gay fathers and heterosexual fathers. Moreover, contrary to the belief that gay fathers would promote more androgyny or be more permissive with their children, gay fathers tend to be more strict in discipline and encourage more sex-typed toy play; at the same time, they tend to be more responsive and display warmth, reasoning, and limit-setting—all very good characteristics of authoritative parenting, which is proposed to be the most effective parenting style.

Again, in the area of gay men and lesbians who chose to be parents after coming out, the majority of published literature is on lesbian mothers, with only a little information on gay fathers in gay planned families. In the late 1980s, interest formed in the area of lesbians who chose motherhood and their children. From this work, we have learned that the biological lesbian mother takes the primary caregiver role for her infant during the earliest months; however, the nonbiological lesbian partner's role increases over time, most notably after the first year. Other researchers have found that lesbian couples shared parenting tasks more equally than heterosexual couples and were more satisfied with the parenting arrangements. Similar findings have been found for gay men who have chosen fatherhood after coming out. For example, Daniel McPherson found gay fathers report even distribution in the areas of child-care tasks and household chores and are satisfied with the division of labor. They are also happy with their relationship, especially the cohesion and expression of affection. Overall, both gay men and lesbians who either became parents in a heterosexual relationship or chose to become parents after coming out are well adjusted in their parenting roles and fully capable of providing love, nurturance, and guidance in a developmentally appropriate manner for their children.

Children of Gay and Lesbian Parents

Charlotte Patterson and her colleagues have reported that systematic research on children of lesbians, and gay men to a lesser extent, who choose to become parents has been a relatively new phenomenon. Although we do know a little about children of lesbian mothers, unfortunately to date no research has been reported on the development of children with gay fathers.

Overall, there seems to be much similarity in development of children with gay or lesbian parents and children with heterosexual parents. Common fears and stereotypes about the development of children with gay and lesbian parents that are evident in parts of our society are not found or validated by any existing empirical research. This next section describes what we know about children of gay and lesbian parents.

Gender Development. Gender development has three main distinct aspects: gender identity, gender-role behavior, and sexual orientation. Gender identity is simply a person's identification as male or female. Gender-role behavior encompasses a person's behaviors, attitudes, activities, and the like that are regarded by one's particular culture as masculine, feminine, or a combination of the two. Sexual orientation refers to a person's attraction to sexual partners as homosexual, heterosexual, or bisexual.

Of the research that has examined the influence of parents' sexual orientation on children's gender identity and gender-role behavior, none have found any differences in their development. The third aspect of gender development, sexual orientation, has also been empirically examined. Overall, no differences were found, indicating that there is no greater chance of a child being homosexual just because his/her parent is homosexual. In summary, then, children of gay and lesbian parents usually develop a conventional gender identity and a typical heterosexual orientation.

Personal and Psychological Development.
The general conclusion by researchers on children's personal development is that there are no real differences between children of gay and lesbian parents and children of heterosexual parents.

Social and Peer Relationships. Studies in the area of peer relationships have consistently shown children of lesbian mothers have mostly same-sex peer groups; overall they have positive peer relationships within those groups. One would think children of gay and lesbian parents experience a greater amount of teasing; however, Fiona Tasker and Susan Golombok of the Clinical and Health Research Center, City University, London, conducted a study of adult children raised by divorced lesbian mothers and divorced heterosexual mothers that asked these adults to recall instances of teasing during childhood. They found that there were no differences in the amount of teasing by peers because of their mother's sexual orientation during childhood.

Other investigators have looked at child outcomes of gay fathers. The major findings were that a child's reaction to his/her father's homosexuality was age-dependent; the closeness that exists between the father-child promoted positive self-esteem for the child; and the child had a greater openness to alternative lifestyles.

There has also been some interest in the amount of contact that children of divorced lesbian mothers have with their biological father. Overall, children with lesbian mothers seem to have more contact with their father than children of divorced heterosexual mothers. Moreover, lesbian mothers acknowledge the need and importance of male involve-

ment in their child's social development, whereas this is less true of heterosexual mothers. This may be explained by fewer negative feelings by lesbian mothers toward their former male partner. More recently, Charlotte Patterson and her colleagues dispelled myths about children with lesbian mothers being isolated from their grandparents and relatives. They found children of lesbian mothers have contact on a regular basis with grandparents and other unrelated adults. Moreover, this social and family contact has been associated with fewer behavior problems and better well-being.

In conclusion, what we have learned about gay and lesbian families to date suggests children of gay and lesbian parents seem to develop normally, defined by conventional terms, in the areas of gender, emotional and psychosocial well-being, peer relationships, and other social relationships with adults of both genders. In addition, sexual orientation per se of the parent has not been supported as a meaningful indicator of successful child outcomes and development.

In summary, none of the existing research provides evidence that gay men and lesbians are unfit to raise children or that children of gay and lesbian families are in some way compromised in their development when compared to their peers. That is not to say that there is no variation among children of gay and lesbian families; however, there has not been proof that significant differences exist that have put children of gay and lesbian parents at a disadvantage. Moreover, several researchers have suggested significant positive outcomes for children with gay or lesbian parents. For instance, an open climate usually exists in these families, which allows for diverse paradigms to be formed in regard to sexuality, gender roles, peer and other social relationships, and egalitarianism within relationships.

Overall, then, the research to date suggests that family process or how the family interacts seems to play the more influential role in family development, rather than whether or not the parents are gay or lesbian. Moreover, everything we know about gay and lesbian families from research also suggests that gay men and lesbians are fully able to provide a positive and nurturing home environment for their children and that a parent's sexual orientation is not a good predictor of child outcomes. Finally, as the number of families headed by gay and lesbian parents continues to increase, the study of interactions among family members and the ways those members as well as the family as a whole deal with ecological influences will add to the knowledge base.

See also Caregiving; Parenting

References and further reading

Binger, J. J., and R. B. Jacobsen. 1989. "Parenting Behaviors of Homosexual and Heterosexual Fathers." In F. W. Bozett, ed., *Homosexuality and the Family.* New York: Harrington Park Press, pp. 173–186.

Gottman, J. S. 1990. "Children of Gay and Lesbian Parents." In F. W. Bozett and M. B. Sussman, eds., *Homosexuality and Family Relations.* New York: Harrington Park Press, pp.177–196.

LaRossa, W. R. Schumm, and S. K. Steinmetz, eds. 1993. *Sourcebook of Family Theories and Methods: A Contextual Approach.* New York: Plenum Press, pp. 419–448.

Paolucci, B., et al. 1977. *Family Decision Making: An Ecosystem Approach.* New York: Wiley.

Patterson, C. J. 1994. "Children of the Lesbian Baby Boom: Behavioral Adjustment, Self-Concepts, and Sex Role Identity." In B. Greene and G. Herek, eds., *Lesbian and Gay Psychology: Theory, Research, and Clinical Applications.* Thousand Oaks, CA: Sage Publications, pp. 156–175.

Savin-Williams, R. C., and K. G. Esterberg. 2000. "Lesbian, Gay, and Bisexual Families." In D. H. Demo et al., eds., *Handbook of Family Diversity.* New York: Oxford University Press, pp. 197–215.

Gaze Aversion
See Attachment

Gender Differences
See Sex Differences

Genetic Counseling
Screening couples to identify whether they are carriers of genetic conditions before they conceive a child. For example, individuals and couples with a family history of mental retardation, sickle-cell anemia, or other genetic anomaly can seek counseling to evaluate their own risks for conceiving a child with the condition.

Genetic Disorders
As the human genome continues to be revealed, more and more genetic disorders or anomalies are being discovered. Well over 2,000 such anomalies have been identified, about 60 percent of which are not fatal. There are two major causes of altered genes: mutation and faulty chromosome distribution during cell division. Mutations occur on the twenty-two autosomes or on the chromosomes that determine sex and are either transmitted at conception (when egg and sperm unite), or appear for the first time during cell division.

**FIGURE 1 Sex-linked transmission for hemophilia
(X = normal chromosone, X' = mutant chromosome)**

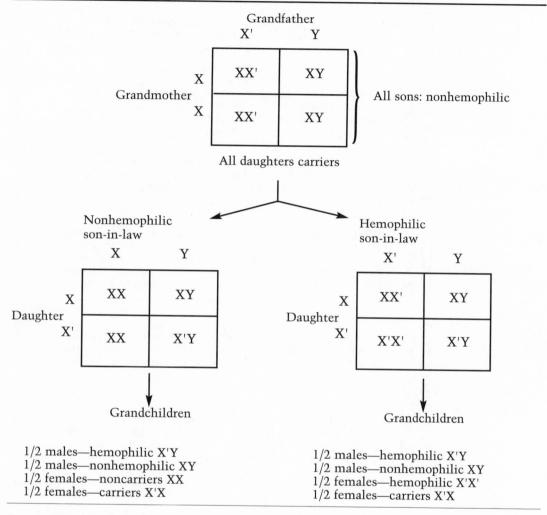

Source: Hiram E. Fitzgerald

Sex-Linked Chromosomal Disorders
Examples of sex-linked chromosomal disorders include hemophilia, color-blindness, Turner's syndrome, and Kleinfelter's syndrome. One of the interesting things about sex-linked chromosomal disorders is that they occur most frequently in males; that is, males are affected, whereas females are carriers.

Hemophilia provides an example of this sex-linked transmission. Hemophilia is a genetic disorder that interferes with coagulation of the blood and can express itself as early as the newborn period when males are circumcised. Because female carriers rarely mate with hemophiliacs, hemophilia occurs equally rarely among females.

FIGURE 2   Normal and major mutant gene inheritance (Mendelian inheritance).

Normal		Except for the XY, there is a pair of genes for each function, located at the same loci on sister chromosomes. One pair of normal genes is represented as dots on a homologous pair of chromosomes.
Dominant		A single mutant (changed) gene is dominant if it causes an evident abnormality. The chance of inheritance of the mutant gene (■) is the same as the chance of inheriting a particular chromosome of the pair: 50 per cent.
Heterozygous recessive		A single mutant gene is recessive (▶) if it causes no evident abnormality, the function being well covered by the normal partner gene (allele). Such an individual may be referred to as a heterozygous carrier.
Homozygous recessive		When both genes are a recessive mutant (▶), the abnormal effect is expressed. The parents are generally carriers, and their risk of having another affected offspring is the chance of receiving the mutant from one parent (50 per cent) times the chance from the other parent (50 per cent), or 25 per cent for each offspring.
X-linked recessive	X Y	An X-linked recessive will be expressed in the male because he has no normal partner gene. His daughters, receiving the X, will all be carriers, and his sons, receiving the Y, will all be normal.
	X X	An X-linked recessive will not show overt expression in the female because at least part of her "active" X's will contain the normal gene. The risk for affected sons and carrier daughters will each be 50 per cent.

Source: Reprinted from D. W. Smith, *Recognizable Patterns of Human Malformation,* 2d ed. (Philadelphia: W. B. Saunders, Co. © 1976). With permission of the publisher.

Occasionally XY and XX chromosome complements do not occur. In Turner's syndrome (XO) the female has only forty-five chromosomes; she is missing the X from her father. The absence of the paternal sex-determining chromosome results in an appearance that diminishes secondary sex characteristics and retards development of the ovaries. By giving estrogens during puberty, stimulation of secondary sex characteristics, including menstruation, is successful, but to date there is no solution for sterility that accompanies this disorder. Kleinfelter's syndrome (XXY, XXXY, etc.) affects males and alters physical appearance (underdeveloped genitals, enlarged breasts). The prevalence of this disorder is estimated to be about one in 700–900 live-born males and is correlated with an increase in maternal age. Physical development generally stays within normal ranges until puberty. Thus, as with Turner's syndrome, administration of hormones at puberty (androgen) stimulates the appearance of secondary sexual characteristics. It is important to note that for each of these disorders there is great variation from one individual to another in the extent to which the genetic anomaly is expressed in the phenotype. For example, individuals with Kleinfelter's syndrome can have mild mental retardation or can have above-average intellectual abilities.

Autosomal Disorders
Autosomal-dominant disorders require only one mutant gene in order to have an anomaly in the phenotype. Whether an autosomal disorder is expressed, however, depends on whether it is dominant or recessive. Autosomal-dominant disorders require only one mutual gene in order for the trait to be expressed. Examples of autosomal-dominant disorders include achondoroplastic dwarfism, retinoblastoma, and Huntington's chorea. The rate of autosomal-dominant disorders is correlated with an increase in paternal age.

Conversely, autosomal-recessive disorders require a mutant gene from each parent in order to be expressed in the phenotype. Examples of such disorders include phenylketonuria (PKU), sickle-cell anemia, and Tay-Sachs disease. Individuals with such disorders are said to be "homozygous" for the disorder. When only one autosomal-recessive gene is present, the individual is a carrier; that is, they are heterozygous (one dominant and one recessive) and the disorder is not expressed in the phenotype.

The individual with PKU lacks an enzyme necessary to convert phenylalanine (a protein found in milk) to tyrosine. As unconverted phenylalanine builds, it has a toxic effect on the central nervous system and leads to neurological problems including seizures, motor deficits, and mental retardation. Phenylalanine buildup is correlated with reduction in myelination in the brain and with reduced presence of the neurotransmitter domamine. Newborn infants in nearly every country of the world are tested for the presence of PKU by drawing blood from the foot for subsequent analysis. Only liver transplantation can cure PKU. There are treatments, however, that help to suppress the expression of the disorder in the phenotype. Treatment requires placing the infant on a diet that is low in phenylalanine, a diet that must be maintained more or less over the life course. Things like meats, dairy products, nuts, some grains, and eggs must be avoided. PKU is a very difficult disorder to treat, and even if early intervention prevents severe mental retardation the individual can still experience neuropsychological complications.

Autosomal disorders can occur more commonly among some ethnic groups than others. For example, PKU occurs more frequently among individuals of Northern European ancestry than among those of Asian ancestry, and it is rare among African Americans and Jews. However, Tay-Sachs disease has a high prevalence rate among Ashkenazi Jews, from Central to Eastern Europe, and sickle-cell anemia has a high prevalence rate among Africans and African Americans. Tay-Sachs disease is a disorder in lipid metabolism that expresses as early as four to six months after birth. Gradual mental and motor deterioration results in death, usually during the early elementary years.

In sickle-cell anemia, irregular-shaped red blood cells block small blood vessels, particularly the ones that supply the lungs and brain. Sickle-cell anemia is associated with swelling of the joints, pulmonary infections, lethargy, paralysis, and coma. About 50 percent of affected individuals die by the late teens. The prevalence rates are about one per 1,000 live births, and approximately 10 percent of African Americans are carriers. In one of the mysteries of nature's trade-offs, heterozygosity for the sickle-cell disorder provides protection again malaria. There is no cure for sickle-cell anemia, but treatment programs with diets rich in thiocyanate seem to help prevent death.

Polygenetic Disorders
Some chromosomal disorders are caused by differences in genes at many gene sites. As one might expect, phenotypic expression varies greatly for polygenetic traits. For example, height is a polygenetically influenced characteristic. So too are several physical anomalies, such as cleft palate and lip, spina bifida, and diabetes. Many physical malformations occur during embryonic development during the time when the individual's structures are forming. Meningomyelocele and anencephaly, two forms of spina bifida, most likely occur sometime between the nineteenth and twenty-eight day of prenatal development, because it is during this period that the neural folds begin to fuse and the neural tube closes. Anencephaly is a severe disorder that involves nearly complete loss of the cortex and leads to death very early in infancy. Meningomyelocele involves herniation of the spinal tissues and meninges, a malformation that can be treated surgically during early postnatal development, even during prenatal development. Although surgically

treated spina bifida children can have little or no intellectual problems, they often have some motor complications.

In all genetic disorders, regardless of the degree or type of complication, the quality of the caregiving environment is of critical importance for optimal development to occur. Arnold Sameroff refers to developmental outcomes as varying along a continuum of caregiving casualty to express the importance of environmental interventions for predicting final outcomes. This is well illustrated by chromosomal anomaly caused by faulty distribution during cell division, a disorder known as Down syndrome.

Faulty Chromosome Distribution
Two common causes of faulty chromosome distribution are nondisjunction and translocation. In *nondisjunction*, during the cell division that produces the sex-determining cells (meiotic cell division), the chromosomes fail to separate. As a result, one gamete (the sperm or the egg) contains two chromosomes rather than only one, whereas the other gamete has none. In *translocation*, part of one chromosome becomes attached to another chromosome. Other nongenetic chromosomal disorders occur when part of a chromosome is deleted during cell division, whereas at other times chromosomal parts can become inverted.

Down syndrome (trisomy 21) is the most prevalent chromosomal disorder. Individuals with Down syndrome have an extra chromosome, usually as a result of nondisjunction or translocation. When nondisjunction is involved, a gamete containing both members of the twenty-first pair of chromosomes joins a gamete that has the normal single chromosome producing an individual that has three of the twenty-first chromosomes. A small per-

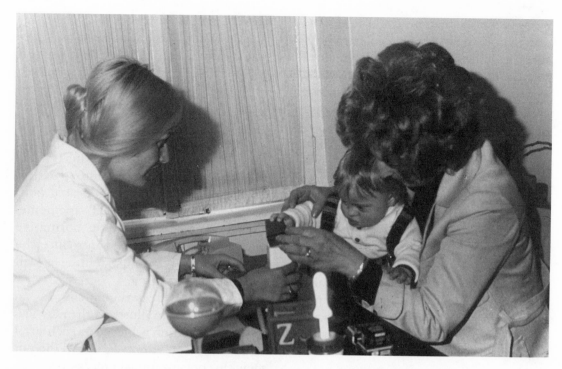

Photo of therapist working with mother and child with Down syndrome. (Courtesy of Hiram E. Fitzgerald)

centage of Down syndrome is due to translocation, and of these, nearly 70 percent are new translocations. The rest are transmitted by a carrier. When a carrier is involved, chromosome 21 hooks onto chromosome 14 during cell division. The carrier has the normal twenty-three pairs of chromosomes, but they are realigned. If the chromosome with the hooked 21 and the remaining free 21 are given to a mate who also provides a 21, then the offspring will have three 21s. Regardless of the error in cell division, individuals with three 21 chromosomes have trisomy 21.

The Down syndrome individual has a variety of distinguishing physical characteristics involving the appearance of the skull, face, tongue, eyes, hands, feet, and neck. Mental handicap is common and can be severe. They generally are of pleas-

ant disposition, and although smiling is common, laughter is not. However, it is important to note that the range of variation among Down syndrome individuals is very great in all of the characteristics that have been cited. Some Down syndrome individuals are able to live independent lives, some have written books, and some have had television careers.

See also Birth Defects; Prenatal Development

Genetic Epistemology

The original term that Jean Piaget used to describe his theory of cognitive development, "genetic epistemology" literally means the biology of knowledge. This descriptor is quite appropriate because

Piaget believed that he could apply the research methods of the biological sciences to understand the development of how the human being comes to know the world in which he/she lives. The meaning of "genetic" in the early part of the twentieth century was equivalent to "biology" (not to genes as we understand them today), and epistemology is the branch of philosophy that asks the question "How do we know?" (in the sense of how do we come to be aware of knowledge).

Genotype

The genotype is the basic genetic make-up of an individual, transmitted from parents to offspring at the time of conception. It provides a structure for biological organization of the individual.

> *See also* Behaviorial Genetics; Environtype

FIGURE 1   Genotypic Expression of Eye Color—
*BR*own eyes dominant; *BL*ue eyes recessive

Source: Hiram E. Fitzgerald

Gesell, Arnold (1880–1962)

Arnold Gesell was one of the most influential experts on child development during the first fifty years of the twentieth century. A strong maturation theorist, Gesell advocated direct observation of infant behavior, longitudinal research methods, the use of motion pictures to record infant behavior, and the translation of scientific studies into practical guidelines for parenting. Educated both in child development and medicine, Gesell generated the first normative growth charts and helped introduce the notion of readiness into parenting as well as education.

Gesell viewed development as an unfolding spiral to illustrate the new levels of organization achieved at each level of development. However, Gesell did not view this organizational process as driven by the environment, or even as unfolding epigenetically, but rather by a maturational process primarily predetermined by the genes. Among many developmental theorists, Gesell borrowed concepts from embryology in his theoretical characterization of postnatal development.

The principles, known as the principles of morphological development, were: individuating maturation, developmental direction, reciprocal interweaving, self-regulating fluctuation, and functional asymmetry.

The principle of individuating maturation recognized the uniqueness of individual development but held that the structural growth of the organism was regulated by internal biological processes, with little influence from environmental factors. The principle of developmental direction specified how structural differentiation of the individual occurred: cephalo-caudally (from head to foot) and proximo-distally (from center to periphery). The principle of reciprocal inter-weaving captures the notion of spiral-like development: Limb flexion is opposed to limb extension, and walking requires the two forces to integrate. The principle of self-regulating fluctuation captures the notion that development is basically driven by organizers that are internal to the organism. Examples of such processes include biorhythms that regulate the sleep-wake and nutritional-need systems. Finally, the development of lateralization of function (handedness, footedness) illustrates the principle of functional asymmetry. Gesell's work stood in sharp contrast to John Watson's behaviorist approach to development, and his influence on parenting and education in the final analysis was more substantial.

Gestation

The length of pregnancy in the mother is usually measured in completed weeks from the last menstrual period and is equivalent to the gestational age of her fetus or baby.

See also Conception; Fetus; Prenatal Development

Ghosts in the Nursery

The expression "ghosts in the nursery" was coined by Selma Fraiberg to refer to psychological issues that a mother has concerning her own relationship with her parents that can interfere with her ability to develop a strong, positive, loving relationship with her own children. Such problems can be unconscious or conscious, but in either case they have not been resolved and interfere with the mother's own relationship with her infant.

See also Fraiberg, Selma

Gibson, Eleanor
See Visual Cliff

Goodness of Fit

Goodness of fit is a concept used by temperament theorists to describe the quality of the match between the child temperament and the expectations of the surrounding environment, including the caregiving environment.

See also Temperament

Grandparents

For generations American kindergartners have sung, "Over the river and through the woods to grandmother's house we go, the horse knows the way to carry the sleigh over the fields of snow." This song captures the essence of the grandparent-adult/child-grandchild relationship: The horse needs little guidance because this is a well-traveled route; the generations are closely attached to one another, although they don't reside in the same home. There is a myth that young parents and their babies are isolated from the support of family and that the importance of family ties in the United States has weakened. Most babies won't live in an intergenerational home, but they will be supported by the love of extended family. American families prefer to live at an intimate distance. There is a desire for separate households in order to maintain the autonomy of each family; there also is the desire to remain an integral part of one another's lives. An intimate distance allows face-to-face interactions for important family celebrations and for stressful times requiring physical support. For some families this means living within a comfortable daily driving distance; for others it means the flexibility of

Top: Learning to cook the intergenerational way.
Bottom: Granddad and baby, who is babysitting whom? (Photos courtesy of Hiram E. Fitzgerald)

time and money to be able to travel to the others by air. The ways in which relationships are strengthened have changed over recent decades, yet the underlying bond of family love and support remains.

Help During the Transition to Parenthood

Expectant parents rely on their own parents as they prepare for the birth of a child. Modern transportation enables many babies to meet their grandparents if not in the first moments of life, then at least in the first few months. Expectant parents frequently need support in physical ways: caring for older children when labor begins, maintaining family routines during the mother's hospital stay, providing physical assistance when the baby is brought home. Grandparents do plan to help out, especially in unexpected circumstances or emergency situations. The adult children define the type of help that is needed and grandparents try to meet those needs. They might do laundry, wash dishes, and keep the household running smoothly. In U.S. society there is an informal norm that the maternal grandparents have a priority in providing physical support at the time of birth.

Often the plans of the paternal grandparents depend on the plans of the expectant mother and her own parents. Both sets of parents usually provide gifts, such as baby clothes or nursery furniture, to ease the financial burden on the new parents. Of even greater importance is the emotional support that the grandparents provide. Through their presence they provide reassurance. New parents are not receptive to intrusive suggestions regarding the care of the baby, but they do find support during the neonatal period by asking grandparents to provide information about specific situations.

Visiting Grandparents

It is not unusual for grandparents today to help with raising their young grandchildren. This means that aspects of the grandparent's home must be carefully reviewed with the safety of the grandchild in mind. Has a crib been carefully stored until the time it is needed? Have favorite toys been tucked away awaiting another infant in the household? Often, older baby equipment is brought out for temporary use during visits. It is important to check every item to make sure it meets current standards of safety, as requirements are more stringent today due to infant fatalities.

Once the grandchild begins to crawl, even more care must be taken to ensure a safe environment. One of the best ways to baby-proof a home is to get down to the baby's level and crawl; the safety needs of the children are paramount. Grandparents may also be less familiar with infant/toddler car seats, and so extra caution must be taken when transporting children. Care needs to be taken that the seat is fastened into the car correctly and that the baby is facing in the appropriate direction based on age. Taking the time to baby-proof the home and car will lead to safer and more enjoyable visits.

In-Between Visits

In the United States the birth of the first grandchild usually occurs when the grandparent is around fifty years old. Maintaining a strong relationship with a young grandchild is possible even with demanding work schedules or geographical distances. Scrapbooks can be created by the grandparent using photographs taken during visits together. Copying centers can laminate pages and bind them together so that chubby fingers can explore the pictures without damaging

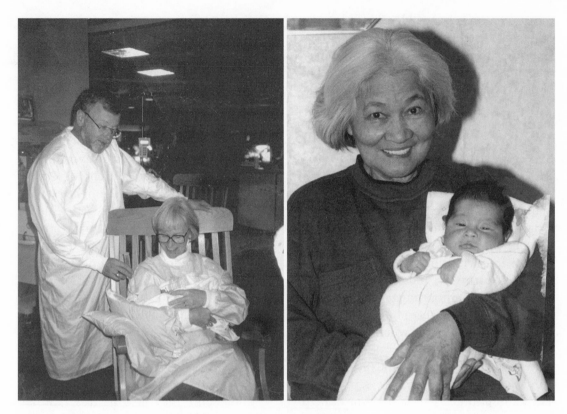

Left: Grandparents can provide emotional support for all members of the family from the beginning, even in the NICU unit with their twin grandchildren. (Courtesy of the Decker family)
Right: Grandmother and granddaughter enjoy a quiet moment. (Courtesy of Alice Sterling Honig)

the book. Grandparents can include their favorite activities, from infant games to bedtime stories read to a preschooler. Grandparents can search through their homes and libraries to find "oldies"— their own children's favorite books. By recording the story on a cassette tape the grandparent's voice becomes a part of daily life. Visits to the grandparent's home offer opportunities to read the now-familiar stories, sharing the pictures and then sharing stories of when the parents were little. This type of interaction strengthens the grandparent-grandchild relationship and also gives the child exposure to different perspectives. As the child grows older, the Internet offers opportunities for interaction. With parental assistance, many young children are learning how to stay connected through technology. By grade school, some are posting messages about their grandparents on family websites or sharing their own stories and ideas on personal webpages. Parents can keep grandparents up to date by taking pictures and videorecording. Video cameras capture highlights of the infant's development, and they keep grandparents posted on the latest activities.

When Stressful Events Occur: The Role of the Grandparents

When Adult Children Divorce. More than 100 years ago, U.S. President Teddy Roosevelt spoke of his concerns about the rise in divorce in the United States since the 1800s. Now, we consider the divorce rates of 1900 to be the "good old days" when marriages lasted. Adult children often turn to their own parents for support during the stressful transition from marriage to single parenting. When grandparents live nearby, their home can be a temporary residence for a parent in need of financial help and assistance with young children. When a noncustodial parent has custody on weekends the grandparents' home is often more spacious and child-friendly than the main residence. Immediately after the divorce the needs of the adult child can be great, and grandparents often provide increased assistance to help their own child weather the storm. In most cases, as the initial adjustments to divorce have been made, the adult child's needs are reduced and interactions with grandparents lessen due to the increased independence and stability of the adult child. When the mother is granted custody, maternal grandparents often find that the amount of interaction increases after a divorce. The paternal grandparents, in contrast, can find themselves seeing a young grandchild less often than they had anticipated. Is continued contact with grandparents in the best interests of the child after divorce? In most families this can be negotiated so that each generation's needs are considered. In some cases, however, conflict over the grandchild-grandparent relationship has led to court-ordered visitations and hotly debated legal cases.

Birth of a Baby with Special Needs. Even before pregnancy occurs, couples begin dreaming about having a baby. They have made commitments to one another and long for a child. The confirmation of a pregnancy fills them with the joy of anticipation as they begin to picture themselves holding a newborn. For some expectant parents, however, the picture of their future life becomes out of focus as they learn through prenatal testing and diagnosis that the unborn child has a birth defect. It is difficult to tell eager, expectant grandparents that the much-awaited grandchild has special needs. The parents can become confused about their own emotions, wondering how to reconceptualize their picture of family life in the future. Supportive grandparents can ease the situation by listening carefully to the concerns of the expectant parents and responding with sensitivity. In addition, it is important for family members to become familiar with the current status of medical treatment in regard to the grandchild's condition. The prognosis for a happy and fulfilling life for the grandchild is usually more likely than it was during the grandparent's own childrearing days.

One of the most common birth defects in the United States is spina bifida. This occurs early in pregnancy when the baby's neural tube is improperly formed. The severity of problems depends on the vertebrae involved; some children will be able to walk alone, others will need walkers and braces, and many will require wheelchairs to keep up with their friends at play. If grandparents live nearby, they can assist the new parents in several ways. Babies born with spina bifida require frequent surgery, and grandparents can care for siblings while the parents remain with the infant at the hospital. If the parents feel comfortable allowing the grandparents to attend appointments with physicians regarding the baby's health, then the grandparents can be aware of precautions in caring for the infant. This, in turn, can allow the parents needed respite to spend time together as a couple. Grandparents who live farther away can increase their telephone conversations to provide a sounding board for the new parents.

Grandparents can react with shock upon learning that their unborn grandchild has Down syndrome. They can recall a time when "Mongoloids" (an inappropriate word, based on the almond-shaped eyes of Down syndrome babies, used by Langdon Down in his nineteenth-century manuscript) were institutionalized at birth. But learning about others who have similar experiences is useful for parents and grandparents wondering what a baby's future might be like. The Internet has increased these opportunities for support beyond the immediate geographical area.

Sometimes a grandchild's condition is due to chance events, but other times it is directly related to parental behavior during the pregnancy. When women drink alcohol during pregnancy there is a possibility that fetal alcohol syndrome (FAS) or fetal alcohol effect (FAE; the same symptoms appear but the severity of symptoms is lessened) could occur. FAS is one of the leading causes of cognitive deficits in the United States. Physical birth defects also occur, including growth retardation, facial abnormalities, and behavioral problems. The diagnosis of FAS or FAE is difficult for most grandparents to deal with because it is a condition that is completely preventable if a mother abstains from alcohol during pregnancy. Thus, grandparents are con-

cerned about the well-being of the grandchild as well as angry at the adult child for behaving in a way that caused an irreversible effect on the baby. Because women who drink heavily have difficulty providing infant care under optimal circumstances, the situation becomes worse when caring for a baby with special needs. In situations such as this, grandparents can step in to raise grandchildren while the parents struggle with their own personal issues or addictions.

Grandparents Raising Grandchildren
Grandparents have been regarded as an emergency backup system for grandchildren under stress. When parents are unable to care for their children, middle-aged adults often find themselves raising children once again. In the 1990s the number of children raised by grandparents without any parental involvement grew dramatically, reaching well over 1 million by the end of the decade. In addition, another 2 million children lived in three-generation homes; in many of these households grandparents provided care on a frequent basis. Grandparents may long to help yet resent the intrusion into their own lives and dreams. Calming a toddler after a nightmare is not anticipated by older adults as they envision their empty nest. Why do grandparents end up raising a grandchild? There are several factors that lead to this need: Parents have died or are in prison; single teen mothers or drug-addicted parents are unable to cope with the child. But the underlying motivation in all these circumstances is that a beloved grandchild is in need.

Grandparents may not be familiar with current health practices in the care of infants and young children. Books for parents listed throughout this encyclopedia are useful for updating child-care skills. It can be comforting to learn that the behavior of a two-year-old granddaughter is commonly found among toddlers. Grandparents need answers to specific questions based on their life circumstances and their grandchild's needs. The questions may seem overwhelming to older parents whose later-life expectations were for travel and personal growth. Often grandparents have personal issues that haunt their thoughts; they may wonder if their parenting style led to substance abuse or other difficulties in their own children's lives. The presence of life-long friends can be helpful, but usually these friends have lifestyles that are not constrained by the needs of young children. The amount of time and number of activities engaged in with these friends can decrease. Embarrassment regarding the behavior of the adult child can also keep the grandparents from sharing details of their situation with friends. The grandparents might be grieving the loss of a dream; the expectation for a fulfilling family life for their own children has been shattered. It can be a relief to find another grandparent in similar circumstances to talk about feelings of loss and anger as well as concerns and delights in a preschooler's development.

Numerous support groups have emerged to help with the issues that these grandparents experience. Once again, the Internet has provided a connection so that grandparents have opportunities to interact with other adults who understand their life circumstances. Access to information from experts in psychology and law, human services, and medicine also is available. Caring for an infant/toddler is physically demanding for mothers and fathers in early adulthood. Providing this care, day in and day out, can be exhausting for older adults. Spouses need time to care for one another and to focus on their own relationship. Respite care to meet these needs is available in many areas of the United States.

One hundred years ago, most babies didn't enter the world with all four of their grandparents living. It was likely that at least one grandparent, usually a grandmother, would be alive when they completed adolescence, but few would have a grandparent living throughout their early adult years. In contrast, most babies born today have extended families that include all four grandparents, and chances are likely that grandchildren will be able to further this relationship well into their adults years.

See also Caregiving; Parenting

References and further reading
American Association of Retired Persons Grandparent Information Center (website 2001). http://www.aarp.org/confacts/programs/gic.html.
Bloom, B., and E. L. Seljeskob. 1988. "A Parent's Guide to Spina Bifida." University of Minnesota Guides to Birth and Childhood Disorders. Minneapolis: University of Minnesota Press.
Doucette-Dudman, D. 1996. *Raising Our Children's Children.* Minneapolis, MN: Fairview Press.
Down Syndrome Quarterly (website 2001). http://www.denison.edu/dsq/health96.html.
Generations United (website 2001). http://www.gu.org.
Grand Parent Again Site (website 2001). http://www.grandparentagain.com.
GrandsPlace (website 2001). http://www.grandsplace.com.
Kingsley, J. (contributor), M. Levitz, and A. Bricky. 1994. *Count Us in: Growing Up with Down Syndrome.* Orlando: Harcourt Brace.
Kornhaber, A. 1996. *Contemporary Grandparenting.* Thousand Oaks, CA: Sage.
National Resource Center for Respite and Crisis Care Services (website 2001). http://www.chtop.com.
Today's Grandparent (website 2001). http://www.todaysgrandparent.com.

UW Cooperative Extension Family Living Program on Grandparents (website 2001). http://www.uwex.edu/ces/gprg/qandas.html.

Grasping

Until the fourth month of age, an infant will reflexively grasp an object such as a rattle when it is placed in its hand. Asymmetries in grasping are characterized by the strength and endurance of hold on the object. On average, infants hold longer and more tightly in the right hand than in the left. The possible relation between this asymmetry and later handedness is unclear.

See also Lateralization; Motor Development

Grating Acuity

Grating acuity is a method used to determine the clarity with which infants can see images in their environment. Infants are shown a gray square and a striped square. The stripes are gradually moved closer and closer together until the infant can no longer differentiate between the gray and the striped patterns. The level of visual acuity is based on when infants stop showing the preference for the striped square. These estimates suggest that infants under two months of age see at 20 feet an image that is similar to what an unimpaired adult would see at 300 to 800 feet (20/300–20/800).

See also Perception

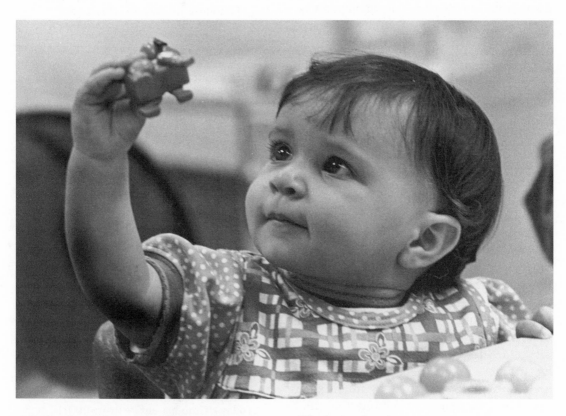

A baby shows fine motor skills in grasping a toy. (Shirley Zeiberg)

Grief Reactions
See Death

Gross Motor Skills

Gross motor skills are movements of the entire body or major segments of the body, as in locomotor activities. Gross motor skills progress from simple movements such as flinging arms and legs to more complex movements such as lifting the head while lying on the stomach and to even more complex motions such as kicking a ball forward. Motor development occurs rapidly in the first year. Newborns move various parts of their body while lying down and consequently gain muscle strength. The added muscle strength allows for more control over movements. When adequate control of arms legs and the head is acquired, complex combinations of motions allow for activities such as sitting up in the crib, rolling over, and standing momentarily while holding on to an object such as a chair. Motor development at around the second year of life is defined by refining the movements such as balancing, skipping, and jumping. Children will progress through stages of gross motor development at different times depending on genetic predisposition such as body type and activity level and environmental differences such as culture, and opportunities. Differences between cultures affect the rate at which a child develops gross motor skills.

Group Day Care

Group day care is child care provided to a small group of children. The size of the group is determined by adult-to-child ratios and the ages of the children and can range from as small as four infants to

A nine-month-old pulls himself up. (Elizabeth Crews)

as large as eight preschoolers. Other factors include room size and staffing patterns. Center-based child care is traditionally thought of as group day care. In some states, family day-care homes licensed for twelve are also considered group day care with mixed-age groupings. Technically, any care that involves more than two children and one caregiver may be termed group day care.

Group day care encourages socializing and relationship-building among young children. Group day care allows children to form attachments to other children and adults. This helps them to become socially competent individuals. Good care for infant/toddlers in groups must draw on two sources of knowledge: a grounding in infancy development and experience working with groups. It is important to recognize that the group context has the power to affect social emotional exchanges between child and caregiver. The relationship between the caregiver and each child is also influenced by the components of group care: the environment, peer group, the number of children in the group, and the temperamental mix of those children. Groups should be designed to provide intimacy and support for children to be cared for in responsive ways. The group size should provide a small adult-to-child ratio, allowing for primary caregiving assignments, continuity of care, and meeting the needs of the individual within the group context. The environment of the group setting should also be designed to ensure care that encourages cultural and familial continuity.

See also Caregiving

Growth
An increase in the size of the body as a whole of the size attained by specific parts of the body. Changes in size occur when one of three cellular processes are carried out. The first is an increase in cell number, or hyperplasia. Another is hypertrophy, or an increase in cell size. And finally, change in size occurs as a function of increase in intercellular substances, or accretion. Hyperplasia is a function of mitosis. Hypertrophy involves an increase in functional units within the cell, especially protein and substrates. This is evident in the muscular hypertrophy that occurs with regular resistance exercise.

Growth Hormone
The chemical somatotropin, which is essential for normal growth. Direct effects reflect the metabolic role of growth hormone on carbohydrate and fat metabolism.

Growth hormone enhances the mobilization of stored fat and conservation of carbohydrates. Indirect effects on somatic growth are mediated by the somatomedins. Somatomedins are growth-promoting substances produced in the liver in response to stimulation by growth hormone. Somatomedins stimulate protein synthesis and increase cell mitosis in many tissues of the body. Small amounts of growth hormone are present in the fetal pituitary gland by midgestation (1–3 milliunits per milligram of pituitary tissue). This amount significantly increases by the ninth month of pregnancy (5–25 milliunits per milligram of pituitary tissue). The growth hormone content of the pituitary increases progressively postnatally, reaching a maximum of about 85–95 milliunits per milligram between the ages of twelve to eighteen. The effects of growth hormone on growth are mediated through somatomedins, which are produced primarily in the liver. In this manner, growth hormone via somatomedins specifically affects the linear growth of bones (and, in turn, stature) and the accretion of various tissues.

Growth Spurts
Variation in the frequency and amplitude of growth-hormone pulses; both vary with age. During a growth spurt, physical growth is greatest due to a large amount of growth hormone for longer amount of time. Weight is a measure of mass. It is an important indicator of normal development from the time of conception to birth and beyond. During the period of gestation, weight increases linearly as a function of age. Birthweight can be affected by several factors: gender, socioeconomic status of mother, genotype, smoking during pregnancy, weight

gain during pregnancy, and others. Infants who weigh below 2,500 grams at birth are classified as having low birth-weight. Low-birth-weight infants are at greater risk for mortality than normal-birth-weight infants.

Height is the length of a person from head to foot. In infants, it most often refers to the distance from crown to heel. In general, boys are taller than girls. The average girl is shorter than the average boy until about age eleven. For the next two years or so she may be slightly taller than her twelve- and thirteen-year-old male peers. Around age fourteen the average male is once again taller than the average female. This illustrates sex differences in the maturation of boys and girls, which affects the time of the adolescent growth spurt.

See also Theories of Development

H

Habituation

Habituation is the response decrement that occurs when an organism experiences repeated presentations of the same stimulus. It occurs when infants effectively want to tune out a stimulus or object to which they have been repeatedly exposed. Evidence suggests that habituation can reveal important information about the cognitive functioning of the individual. Lack of habituation can indicate injury in the cortex. Habituation has been demonstrated at all age levels, from infants to adults, and to all sorts of stimuli, including auditory, visual, olfactory, tactile, and gustatory. The rate of habituation can provide information about the child's later intelligence.

See also Forced Choice Preferential Looking; Orienting Response; Perception

Hall, G. Stanley (1844–1924)

Frequently referred to as the "father of developmental psychology," Stanley Hall founded the first scientific journal in

TABLE 1   Procedures for demonstrating habituation

Procedures	Example
Phase 1: Habituation	
Procedure: Repeated presentations of stimulus A	Stimulus: 750-hertz pure tone—90 decibels
Observations:	Response: Heart rate deceleration
Initial trials: OR elicitation	
Later trials: Response decrement	
Phase 2: Dishabituation	
Procedure: Repeated presentations of stimulus B	Stimulus: 400-hertz pure tone—90 decibels
Observations:	Response: Heart rate deceleration
Initial trials: OR elicitation	
Later trials: Response decrement	
Phase 3: Rehabituation	
Procedure: Repeated presentations of stimulus A	Stimulus: 750-hertz pure tone—90 decibels
Observations:	Response: Heart rate deceleration
Initial trials: OR elicitation	
Later trials: Response decrement	

Source: From B. M. Lester, "The Consequences of Infantile Malnutrition," in *Developmental Psychology: Studies in Human Development,* rev. ed. H. E. Fitzgerald and J. P. McKinney (Homewood, Ill.: Dorsey Press, 1977).

developmental psychology, *Pedagogical Seminary* (1893), later renamed *The Journal of Genetic Psychology* (1927). He brought the questionnaire method to American psychology and, with his students, developed more than 100 questionnaires that covered a range of topics on childhood and old age.

Advancing the theory that ontogeny recapitulates phylogeny, Hall suggested that the development of the individual (ontogenesis) repeated the various phases in the evolution of the species (phylogenesis). He thought that the prenatal period reflected the aquatic phase of human evolution. Infancy (zero to four years) recapitulated the animal phase. Hall likened the newborn's involuntary grasp reflex to that of the nonhuman primate. Childhood (four to eight years) reflected humankind's hunting and fishing cultures. Youth (eight to twelve years) repeated the savage or primitive periods in cultural development, and Hall thought that at this age children were especially sensitive to drill, discipline, and training. Adolescence (twelve to twenty-five years) repeated the eighteenth century's idealism: revolt against the old, passion and emotionality, and commitment to goals. In late adolescence, the individual repeated the beginnings of present-day civilization.

Hall's recapitulation theory went beyond the implications of evolutionary theory in its view of adaptation as more or less completely governed by genetic factors rather than as a process involving organism-environment interaction. Nevertheless, his theory contributed to a strong maturational orientation among early development psychologists. Hall's advice to parents strongly reflected the maturation view. He advised parents to tolerate their children's socially unaccept-

able behavior, for, after all, these children were merely going through a stage.

Hand Preference

Hand preference is the preference to use a particular hand for a particular activity; also, the preference for use of a particular hand over most or all activities. It is related to but not synonymous with handedness.

See also Lateralization

Hand-Mouth Coordination

At about 3.5 to 4.5 months of age, most infants when visually fixated on an object reach slowly toward the object with the mouth and tongue working. The reach can be with one or both hands. When the object is captured it is brought to the mouth, but even before the object is grasped the lips and tongue begin to move or the mouth may simply open.

See also Lateralization; Motor Development

Haptic System

The haptic system (sense of touch) is one of the six sensory systems that extracts information from the environment and transfers it into a neural form used by the brain. This transformation allows, and indeed contributes, to the ability of the brain not only to sense the exact input that it received but also to perceive meaning associated with that sensation. Thus, the haptic system is crucial for being aware that stimulation is present in the environment, as well as for babies to perceive what types of mechanical pressure and contact with the skin represent an object or characteristic of an object and the implications of that object. The other sensory systems include the auditory, visual, olfactory, gustatory, and vestibular systems.

See also Massage; Perception; Touch

Harlow, Harry (1905–1981)

Harry Harlow was an experimental psychologist who studied learning phenomenon, usually with monkeys. According to folklore, John Bowlby, when visiting Harlow's laboratory, commented on the social behavior of the monkeys and suggested that they may be suffering from the consequences of being isolated from one another. Supposedly this launched new work, for which he became considerably more famous than his studies of learning. Whether the story is true or not, Harlow's work with social behavior of primates has become classic.

In one of the original studies, Harlow reared infant monkeys with two surrogate mothers available: a wooden-block mother covered in soft terry cloth, and a wire-mesh mother with an attached nursing bottle. Freudian theory had predicted that an infant becomes close to a mother because she feeds the baby. But the baby monkeys spent most of their time clinging to the terry-cloth monkey even though the wire-mesh mothers provided them with milk. Harlow concluded that infant primates go to their mothers for comfort as well as food.

See also Attachment

Health and Safety

In the early years of life, infants face a number of health and safety hazards. The development of vaccines has reduced the likelihood of infants contracting diseases once common in childhood, such as polio and diphtheria. Still, infants fall prey to many common illnesses. Safety issues are also a concern during infancy and toddlerhood. Accidents such as falls and scalding from hot water can seriously injure young children. In addition, unsafe environments, including exposed electrical plugs and cleaning products left within an infant's reach, are responsible for infant injuries and deaths each year.

Infant Mortality Rate

The infant mortality rate is the annual infant death rate. Mortality rates vary from state to state, with poor states often having higher infant mortality rates. Mortality rates vary by ethnic group and socioeconomic status. In the United States, high infant mortality rates are associated with infants born to poor families. Lack of prenatal care for pregnant mothers, lack of proper prenatal nutrition, lack of medical care for infants, no immunizations, poor infant nutrition, accidents rates, and disease rates are all factors associated with infant mortality.

Immunizations

Because infants have immature immune systems, they are more vulnerable to infection and illness than adults. Immunizations in infancy against communicable diseases are highly effective in protecting infants from disease. In the United States, the Advisory Committee on Immunization Practices, the American Academy of Pediatrics, and the American Academy of Family Physicians have approved an immunization schedule for infants and young children. Under this schedule infants and young children are immunized against polio, pertussis, measles, mumps, rubella, hepatitis, and certain types of influenza. In the year 2000, the varicella (chicken pox) vaccine was added to the list of required vaccines for infants entering group day care.

Vaccines are considered by physicians to be safe for infants. Although there is a risk of mild or severe reactions to vaccines, the benefits are thought to far outweigh the risks. Mild reactions to vaccines include low fever, redness and swelling around the injection site, fatigue, and general discomfort. Severe reactions, while very rare, are serious and may result in seizures, brain damage, or death. There is some discussion about possible connections between immunizations, particularly the measles, mumps, and rubella immunization, and the emergence of autism, a disorder that results in severe communicative difficulties and an inability to form emotional relationships with others. There is no conclusive information on any link between the two.

Common Newborn Conditions

Birth Injuries. As vaginally delivered newborns pass through the birth canal, they often sustain birth injuries, most of them not serious. Common injuries include a burst blood vessel in the eye (which heals within a few weeks), red marks, or scratches from a baby's fingernails pressed tightly against his body. If the baby was delivered with the use of forceps, bruises or scratches may be noticeable but usually heal within a few days. The collarbone may also be broken by the journey through the birth canal. Although this sounds serious, the broken bone tends to heal very quickly. The head, too, can appear conelike if the baby

was delivered vaginally. The head becomes compressed and molded while passing though the narrow birth canal. A baby's skull is designed for such a passage and is pliable enough to ensure passage through the birth canal. The head will take on a more normal shape within a week after birth.

Jaundice. Jaundice, or physiologic, is characterized by a yellowish or orange tint to a newborn's skin and occurs when there is an excess of a yellow-colored chemical called bilirubin in the blood. Bilirubin is produced during the normal breakdown of red blood cells and is processed through the liver and excreted. Newborns, however, have more red blood cells at birth than children or adults, so they have more bilirubin in their bodies. Their immature livers cannot adequately process the bilirubin, so the chemical builds up in the blood. The extra amounts of bilirubin in the blood are what cause color changes in the skin. The yellow/orange skin tone is first noticeable on the face, then on the chest and stomach, and then on the legs. Bilirubin levels usually rise for several consecutive days before they begin to drop. For most babies, bilirubin levels drop on their own without the use of medication when the baby is about a week old. Bilirubin levels are usually monitored by daily blood tests. Extremely high levels of bilirubin can lead to neurological damage, so close monitoring is necessary. If bilirubin levels are excessively high or if bilirubin levels do not begin to fall on their own, treatment is necessary. The most common treatment for jaundice is phototherapy. Phototherapy involves exposing the infant to a fluorescent light treatment for several days until the liver can process the extra bilirubin. The infant's eyes are covered to protect them from the light. Phototherapy treatment often takes place in a hospital. However, "biliblankets" provide portable phototherapy treatments that can be used at home under the supervision of a physician.

Jaundice babies often appear sleepy and sluggish and may not want to nurse or take a bottle. However, it is important that they take in nutrients. When the baby takes in food, the body will process and excrete the food in a bowel movement. Bilirubin is also excreted along with food waste in the bowel movement, which helps to lower bilirubin levels. The more the baby eats, the more waste, and therefore more bilirubin, are excreted. The bowel movements of a jaundice baby often appear yellowish or greenish in color. The color is caused by the excreted bilirubin in the stool. In general, bilirubin levels are higher in babies who are breast-feeding than in babies who are being bottle-fed. Some women have substances in their breastmilk that sometimes interfere with the processing of bilirubin. Most times, however, physicians will recommend that breastfeeding be continued, as frequent nursing during the newborn period is important in establishing the milk supply. Jaundice associated with breastfeeding usually corrects itself after a short period and does not usually present any great medical concerns.

A more serious and much more rare type of jaundice is pathologic jaundice. Bilirubin levels with pathologic jaundice are often much higher. Serious conditions such as an blockage in the liver, certain liver and blood diseases, and intrauterine and neonatal infections can cause pathologic jaundice. Because bilirubin levels are so high, the chemical can build up in the brain and result in a very serious condition, kernicterus. Left untreated, this condition can lead to brain damage or death. Pathologic jaundice is treated according to the cause of the disorder. Phototherapy, blood transfusions, and surgery are potential treatments.

Umbilical Cord Conditions. Parent/care-givers are sometimes a bit frightened by the look of the umbilical cord stump, left after the umbilical cord is cut after birth. The stump shrivels and falls off by itself a few weeks after birth. Until then, the stump should be kept clean by gently wiping the stump area with a cotton ball or swab soaked in rubbing alcohol. This cleaning procedure is not painful for the baby; it is much like cleaning any other part of the body. Lifting the stump up to clean underneath is important and prevents infection. An infection may be present if parents notice pus or red skin at the base of cord or if the baby cries with pain when the stump is touched.

Many infants are born with umbilical hernias. A hernia is a small hole in the abdominal wall. When there is pressure on the abdominal wall, such as when the baby is very full after eating or when the baby is crying hard, the tissue will push through the hole and make the umbilical cord or the navel (belly button), if the umbilical cord stump has fallen off, stick out. Generally, umbilical hernias heal themselves by about eighteen months of age. Surgery is a treatment option if the hernia does not heal on its own.

Skin Conditions. Newborn skin is often thought of as being smooth and flawless. Yet many skin conditions, normal in infancy, make the skin anything but smooth and flawless! Some infants experience newborn acne caused by elevated levels of mate glands (sebaceous glands). These areas of the body include the scale and creases in the skin such as the backs of the knees, wrists, ankles, neck, and behind the ears. The rash is not contagious and seems to appear when the oil glands are overactive. When the rash appears on the head only, it is called "cradle cap." Cradle cap is treated by using a mild shampoo to cleanse the hair and brushing the hair with a soft brush to remove the scales. Some parents use baby oil to soften the scales. Although this is not harmful, it is not necessarily effective and can cause the scales to build up on the scalp. If cradle cap is persistent, pediatricians will often recommend using a small amount of a dandruff shampoo to loosen the scales. They can then be brushed out with a soft hairbrush. Seborrheic dermatitis usually improves by itself and then disappears.

Other forms of eczema include atopic dermatitis and contact dermatitis. Atopic dermatitis can be more persistent and is often associated with a family history of allergy or eczema. Atopic dermatitis usually shows up between two and six months as an itchy, red rash with small bumps on the face or scalp. The rash can spread to other parts of the body, particularly to creases in the skin. Sometimes the skin condition will disappear over the first three years. However, it can persist through childhood and even adulthood and appear as round, slightly raised, scaly patches of skin. These dry skin patches can be very itchy. Pediatricians can treat the eczema with a nonprescription hydrocortisone cream. Occasionally, a stronger prescription steroid cream can be used. Contact dermatitis is a form of eczema that results from a skin reaction to some irritant, such as a laundry detergent or certain foods. Once the irritant is removed, the rash disappears.

In general, delicate baby skin should be treated gently. Unscented, mild lotions and creams can be used after a bath to moisturize skin. Infants are usually more comfortable in soft, natural, breathable fabrics, such as cotton. Using mild soaps and detergents and double-rinsing clothes when laundering can result in fewer skin irritations as well.

Thrush. Another common health condition is thrush, which is a yeast infection in the mouth. The infection is actually passed from the mother to the baby during the birth process. Yeast is a normal inhabitant of moist areas of the body, such as the mouth and vagina. Normally, bacteria and other microorganisms in the body prevent the yeast from overproducing. However, hormonal changes in pregnancy can disrupt this natural balance. When this happens, a yeast infection occurs. As the baby passes through the birth canal, he/she picks up the yeast infection. Thrush looks like small, white milk curds in the baby's mouth. Thrush is painful and can interrupt the baby's attempts to nurse at the breast or suck from a bottle. Fortunately, it is easily treatable with antifungal medications prescribed by a doctor. Sometimes older babies can develop thrush, particularly if they are taking antibiotics or other medications that can disrupt the balance of yeast and other microorganisms in the body.

Colic

All babies cry, but one with colic may cry for hours at a time. Colic, characterized by consistent and inconsolable crying, is not a serious health threat to infants, but it is one of the most uncomfortable conditions for infants, parents, and caregivers. Colic usually appears in the second or third week of life and can continue for several weeks or months. In most cases, colic seems to dissipate by three months of age and almost certainly by six months. Not all infants experience colic, and scientists do not know exactly what causes colic.

There are no specific treatments for colic, although some strategies seem to have success. One strategy is to change the baby's position. Other babies, however, want to be held in the same positions and become even more agitated if they are changed from one position to another. Studies also show that babies who are carried or worn on the parent's body in a sling or soft carrier for at least three hours per day cry less. This may or may not help with colic, but it is worth a try. Many parents report that infant massage, particularly strokes on the abdomen, reduce discomfort from colic. Trying to reduce the level of stimulation in the environment can help a sensitive colicky baby. For instance, turning the television off and dimming the lights can create a more peaceful environment to which the baby might respond.

Common Respiratory Illnesses in Infants and Toddlers

Colds. Illnesses such as colds, respiratory infections, and ear infections are common ailments of infant/toddlers. Colds are characterized by fever, general discomfort, and congestion. In older babies (at least six months of age) and young children, colds can usually be treated at home with rest and fluids. Congestion can be alleviated with a vaporizer or humidifier; adding moisture to the air helps loosen secretions in the chest and sinus cavities. A soft bulb syringe can be used to gently suction mucus out of the baby's nose, but such treatments can also be irritating to the infant's delicate nasal tissues. An alternative strategy is to put a few saline drops in each nostril and allow the baby to sneeze or cough to help clear the nasal passages. Very mild saline nose drops are available in most supermarkets.

Parent/caregivers are often concerned about fever. Unless it is high, fever is not necessarily a concern. In fact, fever is a sign that the body is actively fighting an infection. Some babies and young children tend to run fevers more than other children. A general rule of thumb is to consult the physician if a fever is above 100.2 degrees in a newborn, 101 degrees or greater in a three- to six-month-old. In older babies, it is usually a good idea to call the pediatrician if a fever persists for more than twenty-four hours. Certainly, if the child is running a high fever, becomes delirious, or has febrile convulsions, the baby should be seen by a doctor. Most times, doctors will want to know if the baby is eating, sleeping, and taking fluids. If the baby's appetite is okay and if his/her mood seems relatively normal during certain periods, the doctor can recommend treating the symptoms at home with acetaminophen or ibuprofen. Aspirin should not be used, as it is associated with Reye's syndrome, a rare but serious illness. Fever can also be controlled with lukewarm sponge baths or tepid water baths.

Taking a baby's temperature is often a daunting task for parents. Yet merely feeling the forehead is not an accurate measure of temperature. Parents have a number of choices: Mercury and digital thermometers can be used orally or rectally. Most experts believe that mercury thermometers are the most accurate.

Mercury thermometers are inexpensive. However, they are breakable, and they take two to three minutes, an eternity for a wiggly baby, to get an accurate reading. Some parents find reading the numbers on mercury thermometers to be difficult. Digital thermometers are very fast (one minute or less) and easy to read. They are more expensive than mercury thermometers. Rectal readings are far more accurate for young children, as a baby or toddler has trouble staying still and keeping an oral thermometer in the mouth or under the arm. Digital ear scan (tympanic) thermometers are common, but they are not very reliable for assessing an infant's temperature. Similarly, fever strips, or temperature-sensitive tapes, which are placed across the forehead, are not reliable either. Core body temperature varies slightly from one person to another, so it is a good idea to know the baby's baseline (normal) temperature. Similarly, temperature readings can vary slightly according to the type of thermometer used. It is a good idea to use one type of thermometer consistently.

Respiratory Syncytial Virus. A cold in an infant three months and younger can quickly become a serious illness, such as respiratory syncytial virus (RSV), a viral illness characterized by coldlike symptoms: coughing, wheezing, difficulty in breathing, and irritated and swollen membranes in the throat and nasal passages. If the baby is having trouble breathing or has very rapid breathing, hospitalization may be required.

Pneumonia. Pneumonia is a lung infection that often develops after a cold or respiratory infection. Pneumonia can result from either a bacterial or viral infection. The bacterial infection can be treated with antibiotics. Viral infections don't respond to antibiotics. Pneumonia is often characterized by difficulty in breathing. It may require hospitalization. Extra rest and fluids help ease the symptoms. A vaporizer or humidifier can also help loosen nasal and chest congestion.

Croup. Croup, an infection of the air passages in the chest cavity, is another common viral illness. When the air passages become swollen, hoarseness, labored breathing, and a barklike cough develop. With treatment, this illness is rarely serious.

Ear Infections
Ear infections are the most common infections among infants, toddlers, and young children. Known as otitis media, ear infections result from bacteria in the middle ear and often follow on the heels of a cold or other respiratory infection. Some ear infections, however, are caused by a virus. An infant's eustachian tubes, the tiny tubes connecting the middle ear with the back of the throat, are short and more horizontal than those of an older child. Because the eustachian tubes are short and horizontal rather than angled, bacteria from the nose and throat can easily back up into the ear and cause an ear infection. Likewise, because of the size and shape of the eustachian tubes, fluid does not always drain and can become trapped in the eustachian tube or in the middle ear. The fluid-filled environment becomes the perfect place for bacteria to grow, and an ear infection is born. Even when the infection is gone, fluid can still remain in the middle ear. This condition is called otitis media with effusion (OME). Infant/toddlers with OME may not have any symptoms but may experience a hearing loss until the fluid drains.

During an ear infection, the pressure of the fluid pressing against the ear drum and the pus from the infection cause pain. The symptoms of an ear infection include fluid discharge from the ear canal, earache, fever, and pain. The baby may pull at his ears, stick fingers into the ear, or cry during feedings because sucking· can cause uncomfortable pressure changes in the ear. Babies may also cry more at night, as lying down can cause discomfort. Sometimes, the pressure on the ear drum becomes so great that the ear drum bursts and the infected fluid, or pus, drains out of the ear through the ear canal. Once the ear drum bursts, the pain is actually alleviated. The burst ear drum normally heals on its own but should be checked by a pediatrician. Some babies and toddlers show no symptoms at all, except that they may not be responding to sounds as quickly, which may indicate a hearing loss.

Ear infections are most often treated with antibiotics. Home treatments to supplement antibiotics can include acetaminophen or ibuprofen to ease the pain. Warm compresses against the ear can also help. Some children have chronic ear infections. Often this happens when fluid never fully drains from the middle ear, providing a breeding ground for new bacteria once the old bacteria are killed by a round of antibiotics. This type of an ear infection is called serous otitis media. There are several concerns with chronic ear infections. Hearing loss can result; hearing can be temporarily diminished because of excess fluid in the ear, causing a delay in language development. Once full hearing is restored, language development typically progresses at a normal pace as well. Repeated antibiotics to treat constant ear infections can increase bacterial resistance to antibiotics. Some-

times when antibiotics are exposed to a medication time and time again, they become resistant to that medication at that dosage; stronger doses or perhaps even stronger medication are needed to kill the bacteria. Although rare, there are more serious complications, which include a mastoid infection (the infection moves into the bone), meningitis, bacteremia, pneumonia, brain abscess, or facial paralysis.

Children with chronic ear infections and/or chronic fluid in the ears may require a minor surgical procedure called a myringotomy. A myringotomy is usually considered if the child has had fluid in one ear for six months or in both ears for four months without improvement. In evaluating the need for a myringotomy, the pediatrician will often refer the child to an ear-nose-throat physician who will examine the ears, measure the amount of fluid using a tympanogram, and conduct a hearing test to evaluate any hearing damage. If recommended, the myringotomy usually requires an out-patient surgical setting and involves making a small incision in the ear drum to drain excess fluid. Most often, a small tube is inserted in the ear drum to provide a channel for continued drainage, thus reducing the likelihood of fluid buildup and ongoing infection. The ear tubes fall out by themselves about twelve months after the procedure. Although the procedure itself is quite simple and takes approximately fifteen minutes to complete, it does require a general anesthesia for infant/toddlers. Parent/caregivers should discuss the pros and cons of myringotomies and ear tubes with their doctors.

Some children seem more prone to ear infections than others. Risk factors include a family history of ear infection, exposure to a smoking environment, and exposure to a child-care environment where infections are spread easily. Protective factors seem to include breastfeeding for at least three months, feeding infant/toddlers in an upright positions, and, sometimes, low-dose preventive antibiotics for at-risk children during the winter, the prime season for ear infections. Also, the pneumococcal vaccine, which was available for public use in February 2000, seems to reduce the occurrence of ear infections for about 7 percent of infants; for those infants with chronic ear infections, the vaccine is associated with a 23 percent reduction in the incidence of multiple ear infections. The vaccine protects against seven types of the streptococcus pneumonia bacteria, which cause approximately 7 million ear infections each year. Fortunately, most infant/toddlers outgrown ear infections. As they grow, the eustachian tubes become longer and more angled, which promotes proper drainage of fluid.

Bronchiolitis
Another common illness in young children is bronchiolitis, a viral infection in the small bronchial tubes of the lungs. Symptoms include wheezing and difficulty in breathing. Often, bronchiolitis is brought on by an RSV infection. In young infants, bronchiolitis can be very serious and required hospitalization. Mild cases can be treated at home with saline nose drops and a vaporizer or humidifier to moisten the air, which eases congestion. In more severe cases, the pediatrician can also prescribe bronchodilating medications to help open the bronchial tubes. Babies with bronchiolitis can have a hard time nursing or taking a bottle, so parents must watch for signs of dehydration.

Gastrointestinal/Abdominal Illnesses
Diarrhea, characterized by a pattern of loose, watery bowel movements, is most often associated with a viral infection in the intestines. Other causes of diarrhea include bacteria, food allergies, food poisoning, and rotavirus infections. Sometimes infant/toddlers will suffer diarrhea as a side effect of taking antibiotics. On occasion, even other infections, like an ear infection, can cause diarrhea in some children. In the most common cases, a viral infection in the intestines causes temporary injury to the intestine, which prevents the normal absorption of nutrients, and diarrhea is the result of this malabsorption. The primary concern with diarrhea is dehydration, as the infant/toddler also looses fluid, minerals, and salt through bowel movements.

Mild or moderate diarrhea is usually treated by giving the infant/toddler increased amounts of liquids, including an electrolyte solution to replace lost minerals and fluids. If the infant/toddler is fever-free, is not showing any symptoms of dehydration, and is active, a normal diet is usually recommended. Electrolyte solutions can be purchased in grocery stores and are usually found in the aisle with baby foods and baby formula. They are available in various flavors and in a Popsicle form, which is often appealing to toddlers and young children.

If the child is vomiting and has mild diarrhea, the pediatrician may recommend that the infant/toddler be taken off solid foods for a brief period. As the diarrhea lessens, mild solid foods can be added gradually to the diet. Commercially available diarrhea medications are not effective for infants and, in fact, can do more harm than good. A pediatrician or nurse can assist parents in how to treat mild diarrhea. Severe dehydration can be life-threatening and often requires hospitalization so that fluids can be given intravenously. In most cases, diarrhea begins to dissipate after a few days. If the diarrhea persists, the infant/toddler can be suffering from a more serious illness and should be evaluated by a doctor.

Gastroesophageal Reflux

Infants, especially young infants, often spit up after nursing or taking a bottle. However, spitting up after most every feeding and even between feedings may be a sign of gastroesophageal reflux. Usually due to immaturity of the upper gastrointestinal tract, fluids and acids from the stomach back up into the esophagus and mouth. Most babies with gastroesophageal reflux outgrow the problem with no treatment.

With gastroesophageal reflux, infant/toddlers have no problem swallowing food. The food moves through the esophagus and into the stomach in a normal fashion. Once the stomach begins contracting and squeezing the food, however, the lower esophageal sphincter opens when it shouldn't. When this happens, the food and stomach acids can rise up into the esophagus (indigestion). Sometimes the fluids will spill out of the mouth.

Most cases of esophageal reflux dissipate by about twelve months of age, and many cases clear up even earlier. In rare cases, the condition persists into toddlerhood. There are treatments available to ease the symptoms of esophageal reflux. Common home treatments include position changes designed to lessen reflux symptoms. After feedings, certain positions can help to alleviate the symptoms of gastroesophageal reflux. For instance, lying down is a better position than sitting in an infant swing or infants seat. When sitting, infants cannot always hold themselves straight. When they slump down, pressure is increased on the stomach and may further irritate the reflux condition.

In some cases, physicians suggest the use of medications, which are grouped into several categories. Some medicines are designed to neutralize stomach acid; some decrease the production of acid; some decrease intestinal gas. Each medication can be successful in easing some of the symptoms of gastroesophageal reflux. Other medications are designed to improve the coordination in the upper intestinal tract, although such medications are not always effective in infants and may cause undesirable, sometimes serious, side effects. In very rare cases, surgery may be performed to improve the performance of the lower esophageal sphincter area. Although usually effective, there can be side effects from the surgery. Also, any surgery poses a potentially serious risk for the infant and should be considered carefully.

Although some parents believe that dietary changes can improve the reflux condition, there is really very little evidence to support this. Changes in formula or milk products are not thought to be related to any improvements in the reflux condition. Solid foods can be less likely than milk to back up into the esophagus, but this is only because solid food is heavier. Similarly, the amount of food is not thought to be related to gastroesophageal reflux. Some parents may be tempted to feed their infants smaller amounts more often. Although some babies will naturally have an eating pattern in which they eat small amounts frequently, changing the amount of food offered does not appear to be an effective treatment. In fact, infants who are left hungry by a small feeding can become agitated and upset, which can worsen the reflux condition.

Urinary Tract Infections

Urinary tract infections (UTIs) can be very common in young children, particularly girls. The urethra, the tube though which urine passes, is very short in female infants and toddlers; therefore, bacteria from feces can easily get into the bladder and cause infection. This is one reason why it is important to wipe from the vaginal area to the rectal area after diaper changes and toileting. The symptoms of UTIs include fever, abdominal pain, and pain when urinating. The child may cry out and resist toileting. There can also be blood in the urine and/or an unusual odor to the urine. UTIs require immediate medical treatment and usually clear up within a few days after antibiotic treatment. Consuming additional fluids is helpful. Some studies show that cranberry juice contains a substance that may help prevent UTIs by preventing bacteria from collecting in the bladder.

Other Skin Conditions in Infants and Toddlers

Impetigo is a contagious skin infection caused by bacteria, most often streptococcus or staphylococcus. Impetigo usually appears on the face, especially around the nose and mouth, and sometimes the ears. The infection usually causes fluid-filled or crusty blisters or sores to appear on the skin. The infection is treated with antibiotics and is contagious until the child has been on antibiotics for at least two days or until the infection disappears.

Fifth disease is a fairly harmless viral illness that results in a raised red rash on the cheeks, which spreads to other parts of the body within a few days. The rash usually disappears completely after about ten days. The child with fifth disease may also experience some coldlike symptoms, often just before the rash appears. Fifth disease is usually treated symptomatically. That is, the coldlike symptoms, including any aches, pains, and fever, can be treated with over-the-counter medication. Fifth disease is spread by physical contact.

Chicken pox is a very common viral disease in young children, although the varicella (chicken pox) vaccine is reducing the number of cases each year. The varicella vaccine is recommended for children who have not had the chicken pox virus. After the infant/toddler is exposed to the virus, there is an incubation period of ten to twenty-one days. The incubation period is the amount of time between the point of infection and the appearance of the rash. The chicken pox virus is most contagious one to two days before the rash appears and for twenty-four hours after the last batch of new blisters appear. This is usually a five- to seven-day period. The virus causes itchy, fluid-filled blisters to appear on the body. The first blisters often appear on the stomach or scalp and then spread to the face and limbs. In severe cases, the blisters appear inside the mouth and even on the inside of the body. As the virus runs its course, the blisters begin to form a crust, the fluid dries up, and the blisters heal. A slight fever and general fatigue can accompany the blisters. Fever and aches can be treated with over-the-counter medications such as acetaminophen. Oatmeal bath solutions, available in most drugstores and grocery stores, can ease itching. Although chicken pox usually doesn't present major health concerns, some children do experience several cases of the virus or complications. Hospitalization is usually required in these cases.

Hand-foot-and-mouth disease is a viral disease passed by mouth-to-mouth contact and is also passed via fecal matter. Handwashing after toileting can reduce the spread of the virus. The virus causes blisters or lesions to appear in the mouth and often on the hands and feet. The lesions usually last for about a week and then disappear. Fever usually accompanies the lesions, along with a loss of appetite and often a sore throat and mouth. The disease does not pose any serious medical risks. Fever and soreness can be treated with nonprescription medications.

Ringworm appears as a scaly, itchy round patch most often found on the scalp, chest, or face. Contrary to its name, ringworm is not caused by a worm but by a very contagious fungal infection. The infection is spread via skin contact. The patches form round circles with a raised, scaly border around the perimeter of the circle. Ringworm is treated with over-the-counter antifungal creams. If the ringworm is more persistent or has spread to multiple sites on the body, the doctor may prescribe a stronger medication.

Roseola is a common viral infection most often striking children under the age of two. The symptoms of roseola include a fever (usually 102–105 degrees and lasting three to five days), mild diarrhea, fatigue, coldlike symptoms, and slightly swollen eyelids. After the fever disappears, a pink raised area will emerge on the chest, spread to the arms and-neck and then fade after approximately twenty-four hours. The fever associated with roseola can be treated with over-the-counter medication.

Pink eye or conjunctivitis is an inflammation in the eye, usually caused by an infection. Pink eye causes the white of the eye to appear pink. Excessive tearing is also common. Pink eye is very contagious and should be treated right away. Contact with drainage from the eye can spread the infection to others. Careful handwashing is an important strategy to reduce the likelihood of spread of the infection.

Giving Medication to Infants and Toddlers

Infants and toddlers are not old enough to understand why it is important to take medication and in the proper amounts. However, a few helpful tips can help in administering medication to very young children. First, some liquid medications as well as medication in pill form (crushed) can be mixed with food, milk, or juice. The food or drink masks the appearance and taste of the medication, and the child takes the medication without knowing it. On the down side, the child misses the full dose of the medication if he doesn't finish the food or drink. If at all possible, giving medications when the infant/toddler is hungry is more likely to be a success than if the child is not hungry. A hungry child is more likely to take in anything that might be food. Chilling the medication is another strategy that makes the taste of the medicine less noticeable. Some medications can and should be refrigerated; others cannot be chilled.

Plastic medicine droppers and plastic syringes are effective tools for administering medication; they do not require the child to have the coordination to take liquids from a spoon. When using a dropper or syringe, the medication should be squirted gently toward the side of the mouth rather than toward the back of the mouth and throat. When squirted to the

TABLE 1 Examples of Antibiotic Medications Commonly Used with Infants or Young Children*

Medication	Some Possible Side Effects	Used to Treat
Analgesics		
Aspirin	Extensive	Pain (not to be used for fever due to any infection)
Codeine	Dizziness, Hyperactivity	Pain
Motrin® or Advil® (Ibuprofen)	Stomach problems	Pain, fever, inflammation
Tylenol®, and related products (Acetaminophen)	Minimal	Pain, fever
Ear Problems		
Cortisporin® otic solution	None	External ear infections
Vosol® (acetic acid solution)	None	External ear infections
Eye Problems		
Garamycin® solution 0.3% (Gentamicin)	Puffy eyes	Conjunctivitis
Ilotycin® ointment 0.5% (erythromycin)	Puffy eyes	Conjunctivitis
Sulamyd® solution 10% (sulfacetamide)	Puffy eyes	Conjunctivitis
Gastrointestinal Problems		
Antacids (Gelusil, Maalox, Tums, Rolaids, etc.)	Dizziness, constipation	Heartburn, stomach gas
Charcoal	Black stools	Counter ingestion of poison
Colace®	Diarrhea	Stool softener
Dulcolax®	Diarrhea	Laxative
Ipecac syrup	Lethargy, diarrhea, vomiting	Empty stomach by vomiting after ingestion of poison
Mineral Oil	Diarrhea	Stool softener
Senokot®	Diarrhea	Laxative
General Problems and Common Cold		
Actifed®	Irritability, sleep problems, drowsiness	Cold, upper respiratory infections

(continues)

TABLE 1 (continued)

Medication	Some Possible Side Effects	Used to Treat
Atarax® (hydroxyzline)	Drowsiness	Allergic reactions, itching, motion sickness, hay fever
Benadryl® (diphenhydramine elixir)	Drowsiness	Allergic reactions, itching, motion sickness, hay fever
Dimetapp®	Irritability, sleep problems drowsiness	Cold, upper respiratory infections
Robitussin®	Minimal	Cough
Rondec®	Irritability, sleep problems drowsiness	Cold, upper respiratory infections
Triaminic	Irritability, sleep problems drowsiness	Cold, upper respiratory infections
Multiple Problems		
Amoxicillin	Loose stools, skin rash, allergic reactions	Ear, sinus, urinary tract infections, gonorrhea
Augmentin	Skin rash allergic reactions	Alternative to amoxicillin
Biaxin®	Stomach upset	Infections
Dicloxacillin	Allergic reactions	Infections (e.g., skin impetigo) caused by staph germs
Gantrisin® (sulfisoxazole)	Allergy, skin rash	Urinary tract and ear infections
Ilsone®, E-mycin® (Erythromycin)	Nausea, vomiting, loose stools abdominal pain	Alternative to penicillin V, mycoplasma pneumonia, legionnaires' disease, impetigo
Keflex® (cephalexin)	Allergic reaction, loose stools	Alternative to amoxicillin for urinary tract infection
Lorabid®	Stomach upset, allergy	Skin infections
Pediazole® (erythromycin)	Allergy, skin rash, stomach upset	Alternative to amoxicillin for ear and sinus infections
Penicillin G	Soreness at injection site, allergic reaction	Strep throat, protection against rheumatic fever and bacterial endocarditis, gonorrhea
Penicillin V	Allergic reaction	Strep throat, protection against rheumatic fever and bacterial endocarditis, gonorrhea
Rifadin® (rifampin)	Red or orange coloration of urine	Prevent meningitis due to *Haemophilius influenzae B* and meningococcus

(continues)

TABLE 1   (continued)

Medication	Some Possible Side Effects	Used to Treat
Skin Problems		
Bacitracin ointment	Minimal	Skin infections
Butoxide (RID®)	Minimal	Lice
Kwell® (Hexagammabenzene)	May be toxic*	Lice
Silver sulfadiazine	Skin discoloration	Burns

* These are examples only. Parents should always consult a physician prior to using medications with their infants and toddlers to assure correct dosages and to minimize dangers of allergic reactions.

back of the mouth, a gag reflex often follows and the medicine is expelled. Also, only one swallowful at a time should be inserted into the mouth. Much more than one mouthful will cause the baby to spit out the medication. Sometimes putting the medication in a bottle nipple works well. The baby, accustomed to sucking, often responds well to this method.

A common mistake is to stop giving the drug when the child feels better or seems well. Many medications, such as antibiotics, must be finished completely in order to work. Antibiotics often take five to ten days to complete.

Sometimes it is necessary to hold an infant/toddler very securely when administering medication or when giving saline nosedrops or eyedrops. One effective strategy is to lay the child gently on his back. The adult then cradles the child's head between her upper arms with her forearm resting on the child's chest. One hand can hold the medication while the other holds the child's upper body still. The advantage to this hold is that the child can move his lower body

and legs and feels less trapped than being held down completely.

Preparing the child for a dose of medicine is helpful as well. Even talking to young infants and telling them what will happen next helps them to prepare and shows respect for infants' feelings. Toddlers and older children may want to role-play the scene by pretending to give medicine to a doll. Although role-playing can be very helpful, avoid using real medicine bottles. If the child plays with real medicine containers, she may believe they are toy objects.

Health Promotion
Many common health practices are effective in preventing illness and the spread of illness. One of the easiest and most effective health practices is handwashing. The most effective handwashing requires that hands be scrubbed together, washing the back and front of the hands and between the fingers. All together, this procedure takes less than a minute but is highly effective against the spread of germs. Handwashing should always occur before eating and after toileting,

sneezing, or coughing. Frequent hand-washing throughout the day is a good practice. Waterless disinfectants can be useful as well, particularly if there is no running water nearby.

Ensuring that infants receive adequate nutrition, enough fluids, and proper rest promotes well-being. When the body is depleted from lack of nutrition or lack of sleep, the immune system has a more difficult time fighting off infection, and illness occurs more frequently. Many scientists believe that physical well-being has a lot to do with emotional well-being. Also, there is scientific evidence that practices such as infant/child massage can boost the immune system and, therefore, increase the body's abilities to resist illness.

Allergies
An allergic reaction is really a reaction of the immune system to an allergen, a foreign substance. With each exposure to the allergen, the body produces an antibody designed to attack the foreign substance. Over time, the level of antibody builds. The more antibody that is present, the stronger the allergic reaction will be. Some allergies tend to run in families and may predispose some infants to allergic reactions. In fact, the American Academy of Allergy, Asthma, and Immunology states that a child with one parent with allergies has a 25 percent chance of developing an allergy. If both parents are allergic, there is a 65 percent chance that the child will development an allergy as well.

Some allergies disappear as the child's immune and digestive systems mature, usually by about five years of age. In other cases, however, allergies persist and reactions become more severe over time. For instance, allergies to seafood and nuts tend to persist throughout the life span. Common allergens include foods, pets, molds, dust, pollen, and irritants such as detergents and dyes. Certain elements in foods are likely to cause an allergic response in infants and are safer when introduced later. Allergic reactions can manifest themselves in many ways. Common symptoms include runny nose, itchy, watery eyes, nasal congestion, sneezing, rash, eczema, diarrhea, and vomiting. Serious allergic reactions requiring immediate medical attention include difficultly breathing, wheezing, disorientation, and loss of consciousness. In some cases, the allergy can become so severe that contact with the allergen will cause the body to go into anaphylactic shock, a condition in which the airways swell and close. Anaphylactic shock must be treated within minutes or it can be fatal. Many children with severe allergies carry "epi pens," through which a dose of epinephrine can be injected into the body to open airways. Generally, allergic reactions grow more severe over time. Infant/toddlers tend to have fairly mild reactions.

Generally, the response to a food allergen will occur immediately or within an hour. Children with very sensitive allergies need not even ingest the food. Carefully washing tables and hands are crucial safety procedures to protect children with severe allergies. Breastfeeding for at least 6 months and preferably a year is though to provide some protection against allergies. Breastmilk contains many elements that can enhance the baby's abilities to resist illness. Another preventive strategy is to delay the introduction of solid foods until six months, and then to introduce foods slowly, beginning with those most mild and least likely to cause a reaction in the infant. The more time the immune system has to mature, the less likely it is to cause an allergic response. This is why high-allergy foods such as peanut products and fish are best reserved for the older toddler.

Pet allergies are very common. The culprit is pet dander, or skin cells that have sloughed off and are contaminated with the pet's saliva or urine. Keeping pets outdoors is one way to combat pet allergies. Other household allergens include dust and molds. Dust mites, tiny microscopic creatures, are generally the cause of dust allergies. Dust mites can be found on everything from mattresses to furniture to stuffed toys. Some children are more sensitive to dust mites than others. Molds tend to grow in damp places, such as the bathroom and basement. Exhaust fans and dehumidifiers can help to reduce molds in the house. Disinfectants can also be effective against mold.

Pollen from plants causes sneezing, congestion, and itchy, watery eyes for many people. Pollen seems worse at certain times of the year. Keeping children away from pollen altogether is difficult. On days with especially high pollen counts, keeping children indoors may help. Keeping windows shut as well can reduce the amount of pollen that comes through the window into the house. Detergents and dyes can cause allergic reactions, often causing skin rashes and irritations. Using mild soaps and detergents and double-rinsing clothes when laundering are helpful strategies.

Trying to determine what is causing an allergic reaction can be challenging. This is the reason doctors recommend introducing only one new food at a time. If there is a sudden reaction, the parent can be fairly certain the new food is the cause.

With any allergy, removing the suspected agent and then observing the child to determine if the symptoms of the reaction disappear is useful. If the allergen cannot be identified by systematically eliminating certain substances one at a time and watching for improvement of symptoms, a doctor can conduct allergy tests. Although not common in infancy and toddlerhood, skin-testing and blood tests (RAST) can be conducted. Once the allergen is identified, parent/caregivers should guard against accidentally exposing the child to the substance. For example, many food allergens, such as peanut material, can be found in everything from granola bars to trail mix. Reading labels carefully is a must.

Serious Medical Conditions
Other conditions are much more serious and may even be life-threatening. For instance, meningitis is an inflammation of the brain and/or spinal cord. Meningitis can be fatal. Another brain disorder, encephalitis, causes inflammation of the brain and can cause neurological damage or death. SIDS and HIV/AIDS are examples of other fatal disorders.

Sudden infant death syndrome (SIDS), the leading cause of death of infants under one year of age, is a mysterious phenomenon in which a seemingly healthy infant dies suddenly. Infants appear to die in their sleep. Very little is known about SIDS, but scientists do know that SIDS victims are often firstborn children and that SIDS occurrences peak between two months and four months of age. SIDS appears to occur more frequently during the winter months, and more male infants than female infants die from SIDS. Other factors associated with SIDS include the following: exposure to tobacco smoke; sleeping on the stomach; preterm birth;

low birthweight; multiple births (twins, triplets, etc.); poor maternal prenatal care; infection and disease during pregnancy; closely spaced pregnancies; and economic disadvantage. Although these factors are associated with SIDS, they do not explain what causes SIDS. Scientists are exploring potential causes such as faulty genes, respiratory defects, prolonged pauses in breathing, cardiovascular and neurological impairments, body temperature regulation, and suffocation from breathing carbon-dioxide due to poor air circulation. However, no definite cause of SIDS has been identified. Doctors advise parent/caregivers to put infants to sleep on their backs. Once infants can roll by themselves, it is unlikely that they will stay sleeping on their backs all through the night. However, the risk of SIDS is greatest for young babies. SIDS rates decline as babies become older. Avoiding heavy bedding like blankets, pillows, and comforters is also thought to protect against SIDS. Doctors recommend dressing the baby in a warm sleeper instead of using heavy blankets to keep the baby warm.

Human immunodeficiency virus and the subsequent development of acquired immune deficiency syndrome (HIV/AIDS) are fatal to the infant. The HIV infection can be passed from the mother to the fetus during the prenatal period, through the birthing process, or through breast-feeding. If the mother is known to have HIV, she can take an antiviral medication, called AZT, which dramatically reduces the chance that her infant will become infected during the pregnancy.

HIV attacks and weakens the immune system, the body's mechanism for fighting infection. Therefore, HIV/AIDS infants are much more likely to become seriously ill from infections and bacteria that might be harmless to a healthy infant. Similarly,

their bodies cannot produce antibodies to fight off other life-threatening diseases such as measles.

Infants with HIV or AIDS are treated with a combination of medications designed to reduce the symptoms of the disease. Some infected infants may survive into their teenage years; many infected infants die of complications related to AIDS in their childhood years. Although there is hope that one day HIV/AIDS can become a chronic disease controlled by medication, there is no cure for HIV/AIDS at this time.

Health Practices
Good health practices can significantly reduce the development of many common illnesses. Handwashing is one of the most effective ways to reduce the transmission of germs and bacteria responsible for the development of colds and other respiratory infections as well as a number of bacterial infections. Sanitizing diaper-changing areas, paired with handwashing, can reduce the threat of diarrhea, a common health concern among infants. Proper handling of food, including infant formula, is important to child health and well-being. Other good health practices include sanitizing toys that may have been mouthed by infants, as well as spacing cribs far enough apart to reduce the spread of germs in day-care environments.

Safety
Accidental injuries are the number one cause of death in infants/toddlers. Yet simple safety practices can reduce the number of injuries and deaths. Infant/toddlers are curious. They taste, touch, smell, and play with most any object in their path. Parent/caregivers are often told to baby-proof their homes, examining every

part of the environment for unsafe features. Dropping down to hands and knees and really trying to see how the environment looks from the baby's perspective can be an effective strategy for identifying unsafe situations. Safety practices include the following:

- installing safety gates
- installing electric plug covers
- installing drawer latches
- padding sharp corners
- installing a safety gate around woodburning stoves, fireplaces, and radiators
- securing electrical cords to be inaccessible to baby
- removing any dangling cords
- removing all breakable items out of baby's reach
- removing all chemicals, cleaners, medications, and other personal products out of babies reach; parent/caregivers should also remember that seemingly harmless materials, such as toothpaste, mouthwash, shampoo, and hand lotion, can be harmful if swallowed by a young child and should be moved out of reach.
- setting the water temperature to 120 degrees or below
- covering the bathtub spout with a spout cover
- checking that stairway banisters are no more than 5 inches apart (baby could try to climb between the banister)
- placing skid pads underneath rugs
- purchasing toy chests that have mechanisms to keep them open in any position. This prevents the lid from falling on the child and/or the child being locked inside the chest

- constantly look for small objects that can be swallowed
- learning basic first aid and safety procedures
- installing window guards and making sure windows cannot open more than 6 inches to prevent baby from falling out
- securing bookshelves, chests, bureaus, and other furniture to the wall; a baby or toddler can pull the furniture over on himself when trying to climb on the furniture
- removing house plants out of the baby's reach

Unintended Injuries. Unintended injuries are a leading cause of death among infants and young children. Common unintended injuries resulting in death include burning or scalding, drowning, suffocation, poisoning, falls, and motor vehicle accidents. Burns or scalding can be caused by bathwater that is too hot. Toddlers can turn on a hot-water faucet out of curiosity or reach up to touch a hot pan on the stove. Burns can also result from electrical shocks caused by explorations of an electrical outlet.

Drowning, another serious safety concern, need not occur only in large bodies of water, such as a swimming pool. Infant/toddlers can drown in just a few inches of water in a bathtub, ice chest, or toilet. Babies should never be left near water, not even for a few moments. Some parent/caregivers mistakenly believe that infants are safe when sitting in a plastic bathseat. However, infants can slip out of the bathseats or become stuck. An adult should remain with the baby at all times. Rubber bathmats that suction to the floor of the bathtub help reduce slipping and sliding in the bathtub. Available in most any grocery store, bathmats are inexpensive and easy to use.

Suffocation can occur when a toddler is playing with a plastic bag and puts the bag over the face. Another common cause of suffocation is choking. Infant/toddlers can choke on food or vomit or objects they have mouthed and accidentally swallowed. Foods commonly associated with choking are nuts, popcorn, whole grapes, hard candy, and raw vegetables such as carrots. Toys with small or breakable parts that can be swallowed cause far too many unintentional chokings and suffocations each year. Generally, an object presents a choking hazard if it can fit through a toilet-paper tube. Parent/caregivers should learn appropriate first-aid procedures to care for a choking infant. Infants can also suffocate when they become tangled in cords such as drapery cords, clothing cords from jackets, or even the straps on a high chair. Cords should be placed out of reach; strings from clothing should be removed; straps on high chairs should be checked for safety risks.

Unintentional poisoning represents another serious hazard for infant/toddlers. A typical home contains countless poisonous substances such as medications, cleaning agents, insecticides, paints and other household items, and even plants. Mobile infant/toddlers are curious to explore their environments and eager to open drawers and cabinets. Such explorations unfortunately result in far too many poisonings. Parent/caregivers should have the number of the local poison control center posted by the phone. Treatment for poisoning depends on the material ingested. In determining treatment, poison control officials will want to know the type and amount of material ingested. Examples of treatments include inducing vomiting with syrup of ipecac to empty the stomach contents. This technique is generally not used with young infants, as they can choke on their own vomit more easily than older children. In some cases, inducing vomiting causes further harm. If the child has swallowed what are called "corrosive substances," such as bleach, vomiting the substance will burn the esophagus and mouth. In these cases, liquid charcoal is used to absorb the poison.

Falls result in serious or even fatal injuries for curious infant/toddlers. Infant/toddlers can easily fall from diaper-changing tables, high chairs, stairs, furniture, tables, shopping carts, and so on. Using safety equipment such as furniture bolts, safety belts in infant swings and chairs, and safety gates can prevent injuries from falls.

Fire Safety
Installing smoke detectors and carbon monoxide detectors in all levels of the home and in each bedroom is an important safety strategy. House fires can start quickly and spread in a short time throughout the house. Often, it is the thick, poisonous smoke from a fire that kills rather than the flames themselves. Batteries should be checked every six months at minimum. Families and caregivers should make and practice a fire evacuation plan and decide on a designated meeting place outside the home in the event of a fire evacuation. Most local fire departments also provide free reflective "tot finder" stickers. When placed on the window to a child's room, the reflective stickers help firefighters immediately locate children's bedrooms.

Carbon monoxide detectors can save lives as well. Carbon monoxide is a clear, odorless, tasteless gas. Carbon monoxide gas is released as fuel sources burn. With proper ventilation, the gas poses no threat. However, without proper ventilation of fumes from burning, fuel carbon monoxide gas can build up to lethal levels in the home. Inadequate ventilation from woodburning stoves, kerosene heaters, gas stoves, or other fuel sources can result in high carbon monoxide levels. Symptoms of carbon monoxide poisoning include headache and drowsiness.

CPR and First Aid

Most communities offer courses in CPR (cardiopulmonary resuscitation), mouth-to-mouth resuscitation, and basic first aid. Such courses can prepare parent/caregivers to handle emergency situations and potentially save their children's lives in the event of an emergency. CPR is used in the event that the child's heart has stopped beating and involves cycles of chest compressions paired with breaths into the child's mouth. CPR works by promoting circulation of oxygenated blood to the body. For children ages birth to eight years, the cycle is five chest compressions to one breath. If the child's heart is beating, but she is not breathing, rescue breathing is used. Rescue breathing involves breathing into the child's mouth. The chest should gently rise and fall with each breath. For children ages birth to eight, one breath is given every three seconds. Lack of breathing could be caused by a blocked airway. Choking is the most common cause of a blocked airway. Treatment of choking in infants up to age one year includes the use of back blows and chest compressions. Older children are treated with abdominal thrusts, called the Heimlich maneuver. If the child is unconscious, abdominal thrusts can be given while the child is lying on the floor or other hard surface. Abdominal thrusts work by forcing the air in the lungs up and out, hopefully pushing the foreign object out of the airway.

Automobile Safety. Finally, injury and death rates from motor vehicle collisions are a serious concern. The proper use of carseats for infant/toddlers can dramatically reduce the risk of injury or death should an accident occur. Unfortunately, many adults may be unaware that the safety seats are improperly installed. Similarly, adults must follow guidelines for the use of carseats according to the child's age and weight. Although car seats play a crucial role in protecting children in a car, there are other safety concerns as well.

The National Highway Traffic Safety Administration conducts safety tests on common automobiles. By performing crash tests in head-on and side-impact collisions, the organization rates car safety and makes recommendations on the safest cars. Likewise, independent organizations such as Consumer Reports test and rate cars each year.

Child Abuse and Neglect

Although many injuries and fatalities result from unintended injury, infants and toddler are seriously injured or killed each year due to intentional injury resulting from child abuse or neglect. Physically abused infant/toddlers are often punished in severe ways, including being beaten or shaken severely, which can result in broken limbs or brain damage, and being burned or poisoned. Accounts of abusive families often reveal that infant/toddlers are punished for behaviors such as crying or for toileting accidents. Neglect involves the failure of the adult to provide

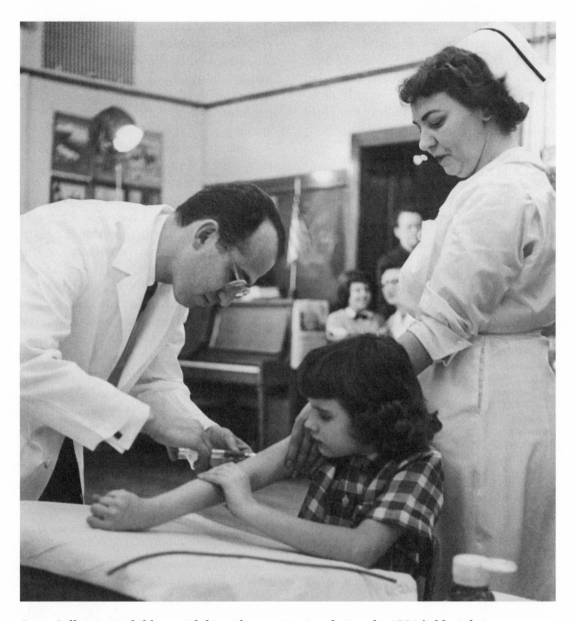

Jonas Salk injects children with his polio vaccination during the 1954 field trials in Pittsburgh. (Bettmann/Corbis)

for basic needs such as food, clothing, and shelter. Thus, neglected infant/toddlers can suffer from malnutrition and exposure to the elements. Neglected infants can develop a condition known as nonorganic failure to thrive, characterized by a lack of weight gain and a lack of physical growth. Emotional abuse is a third kind of abuse and neglect that poses a serious threat to the well-being of infant/toddlers. Emotional abuse is characterized by a lack of affection and the use of extreme

shaming and scolding of the child and other verbal means of destroying the child's sense of self and self-confidence. Emotionally abusive adults can also blame the infant/toddler for family problems, ignore the child, and keep the child isolated from social contact.

See also Birth; Birthmarks; Car Seats; Child Abuse and Neglect; Immunizations; Maternal Deprivation; Newborn Equipment and Material

References and further reading
American Academy of Pediatrics (website 2001). http://www.aap.org.
American Association of Poison Control Centers (website 2001). http://www.aapcc.org.
American Red Cross (website 2001). http://www.redcross.org.
Barber, M., M. B. Scott, and E. Greenberg. 2001. *The Parent's Guide to Food Allergies.* New York: Henry Holt.
Centers for Disease Control. 1996. "Sudden Infant Death Syndrome—United States, 1983–1994." *Morbidity and Mortality Weekly Report* 45: 859–861.
Shelov, S. 1994. *The American Academy of Pediatrics: Caring for Your Baby and Young Child.* Irvine, CA: National Pediatric Support Services.
Snow, C. W. 1998. *Infant Development.* 2nd ed. Upper Saddle River, NJ: Prentice Hall.

Hearing
See Audition; Perception

Hearing Education

The best way to approach educating children with hearing loss is not clear. Parents use a variety of different approaches or methods: oral or oral-aural; manual; and total communication.

In the oral or oral-aural approach, children receive input through speech reading (lipreading) and the amplification of sound. The children express themselves through speech. Some oral programs emphasize the use of residual hearing (auditory verbal), others stress the use of vision (auditory oral), and still others balance the two. All programs, however, prohibit the use of signs and finger spelling.

American sign language (AMESLAN) is a visual-gestural-spatial language in which placement, movement, and expression of the hands, face, and body are actually a part of the language. Its grammar and syntax are distinct from English. AMESLAN is the native language of the culturally deaf.

Total communication is a combination of the oral method plus the use of signs and finger spelling. The children receive input through speech reading, amplification, signs, and finger spelling, and they express themselves through speech, signs, and finger spelling. Traditionally, signs were used in coordination with speech, making necessary the use of manual codes in English (Sign Exact English) and not AMESLAN. There are a variety of manual codes of English.

Hearing Aids

A hearing aid is an electrical device that is used to amplify sound. Hearing-aid technology has advanced greatly over the years. The circuitry has been reduced dramatically in size for the development of tiny canal hearing aids. Hearing aids are designed individually with the person's hearing impairment in mind. Even with all the technology available, hearing aids do not restore hearing to normal. Individuals with conductive hearing losses (in the middle or outer ear) have better success with hearing aids than individuals with sensorineural (inner-ear) hearing loss. This is because the outer and middle ear functions to conduct the sound, whereas the inner ear functions to fine-tune the sound. Individuals with hearing loss can spend many thousands of dollars on hearing aids hoping to cure their hearing loss. Again, they are extremely helpful, but they never restore hearing. Often when a person purchases a hearing aid, he/she enters aural rehabilitation therapy that teaches the individual about ways to maximize communication cues (environmental manipulation and communication strategies).

Hearing aids are also designed for children. Battery doors are tamper-resistant, earmolds are soft and replaceable as the child grows, the aids and earmolds can be made in colors, retention devices are available to keep the aids from falling off, and the aids are made to be durable and small. Parents are taught the skills necessary to use, check, and clean the hearing aids. It is important that hearing aids be maintained so that the child receives the maximum benefit. Children are sometimes sent to school with batteries missing in their hearing aids, or aids not turned on and adjusted properly. Children need to rely on others to maintain their hearing aids for them. Some parents struggle with their children in the use and maintenance of the hearing aids. Other parents find that the children ask for their aids in the morning and then fight to take them off at night.

Cochlear Implant
A cochlear implant is a medical device that contains several main parts. The implant has a microphone that is mounted on a behind-the-ear hearing aid. It is attached through wires to an external speech processor worn on the waist. The speech processor converts acoustic information into an electric current that is sent through wires to an external magnet

that is attached in the mastoid bone behind the ear. The external magnet is held to the skin by a second magnet implanted under the skin. Electrical signals are transmitted across the skin by the magnet. An internal wire, attached to the internal magnet, passes through bone and tissues to the electrodes that are implanted into the inner ear (cochlea). The electrodes are electrically stimulated by the electrical signal patterned (generated in the external speech processor). The actual sounds that are heard are electrically stimulated. One postlingual deafened adult (deafness that occurred after language development) described the speech perception as "Mickey Mouse speech."

Many individuals have shown great success with cochlear implants. It is truly a miracle. Other individuals have had only limited success or have not been able to use the implant at all. Electrically produced acoustic stimulation is different from the normal acoustic stimulation, and thus hearing loss is never restored to normal. Furthermore, the surgeon might not be able to implant all the electrodes in the inner ear, the speech processors can break down, electrical stimulation of the facial nerve has been documented, and long-term effects of electrical stimulation for young children are still not known.

Individuals and families who consider cochlear implants are required to go through a candidacy evaluation. In the candidacy proceedings, family and educational support is documented. The distances to the hospital and the rehabilitation services are also considered. An individual most also be evaluated by an audiologist to determine that no useable hearing with hearing aids is available and that the auditory nerve can be stimulated.

The cost of implants possibly can be covered by insurance. The average cost of the evaluation, implant, and surgery is roughly $30,000. Additional billing is needed for maintenance and other rehabilitative services.

See also Auditory System

Heart Rate

The study of the nonverbal infant's response to environmental stimulation has been facilitated by the discovery that many physiological activities can be used as indicators of the infant's information-processing. Over the past thirty years, heart rate has become one of the most commonly used indicators. Heart rate occurs in two forms: tonic and phasic. *Tonic heart rate* refers to the level of heart rate over extended periods of time and varies with the biobehavioral state of the infant. A sleeping infant will have a slower tonic heart rate than an infant who is fully alert and awake.

Phasic heart rate refers to the response of the heart rate to specific stimulation in the environment. The phasic change in the heart rate can speed up (accelerate) or slow down (decelerate). Heart rate acceleration usually reflects a temporary arousal reaction. For example, one would expect a loud noise, such as a door slamming shut, to produce an acceleration of the infant's heart rate. However, once the noise ends we would expect the heart rate to return to its tonic level. Heart rate deceleration usually reflects the infant's attentional response to environmental stimulation, particularly to novel stimuli. The phasic heart rate response to novel stimulation typically would be something like a deceleration of about eight to ten beats, lasting for three to five seconds. Russian physiologist Yuri Solokov defined heart rate deceleration as one component of the orienting reflex, a reflex that mobilizes the organism to attend to environmental stimulation.

In addition to directional changes in heart rate, heart rate variability is frequently used as an indicator of attentional processing and emotional reactivity in infants. Respiratory sinus arrhythmia is a rhythmic change in heart rate that accompanies respiration. During respiration, the heart rate increases when the individual breaths in (inspires) and decreases when the individual breaths out (expires). Stephen Porges at the University of Maryland devised a method for extracting the variation associated with breathing from that associated with heart rate and argued that the variability in respiratory sinus arrhythmia serves as an indicator of tonic parasympathetic vagal tone. If so, this indicator provides evidence of the involvement of the vagus (the tenth cranial nerve) on heart rate activity. Porges's measure of vagal tone has been used extensively in studies of infant emotional responsivity with apparently good success.

See also Emotion; Neurobiology

Hemoglobin

Iron deficiency is the most common nutritional deficiency in the United States and most prevalent from age six months to three years. Hemoglobin (heme iron) is diagnosed when the level is less than 11 g/dl. Hemoglobin deficiency leads to irritability and lowered developmental scores in infants. A newborn baby has no tissue iron stores. Iron in human breastmilk is 49 percent bioavailable, but the trace of iron in cow's milk is not absorbed much. Thus, formula from cow's milk must be iron-fortified for infants. When hemoglobin scores are low, intramuscular repletion with iron leads to decreased solemnity and increased developmental scores for infants.

See also Behaviorial Genetics; Environ-type; Heritability

References and further reading
Honig, A. S., and F. A. Oski. 1984. "Solemnity as a Clinical Risk Index for Iron Deficient Infant." *International Journal of Biosocial Research* 2: 116–119.

Heredity Versus Environment
See Nature-Versus-Nurture Debate

Heritability
Heritability is a quantitative measure for behavior genetics. It is defined as the proportion of phenotypic variance that can be accounted for by genetic differences among individuals.

Heroin-Addicted Infants
See Alcoholism; Drugs

Herpes Simplex Virus
The herpes simplex virus is a DNA virus and is one of the most prevalent viruses in the human species. Cytomegalovirus (CMV) and herpes virus hominis (HVH) are both members of this viral family. Cytomegalovirus typically affects the woman's genitalia, breasts, urinary tract, and particularly the cervix. In most cases, women do not even know they are infected. When the infection is present on the cervix, the infant is exposed dur-

ing childbirth. The consequences to the infant are so severe, including high mortality rates, that cesarean delivery is advised. Short of death, CMV-infected infants have a high risk for mental retardation or congenital deafness. The incidence of CMV is about nine per 1,000 live births worldwide.

Herpes virus hominis usually affects the vagina or cervix and occurs at a lower rate than CMV. HVH occurs more frequently among young, sexually active, and/or poor women, although it can occur in women from any group at any age. Although the infection rate is low, the consequences of infection can be very severe. In fact, the range of infection impact is great and depends in part of the degree and timing of infection. Consequences range from death (rare) to developmental disabilities such as deafness, blindness, spasticity, seizures, and microcephaly. There are currently no cures for either CMV or HVH.

See also Acquired Immune Deficiency Syndrome; HIV

Hierarchical Organization
Comparative biopsychologist Heintz Werner asserted that the process of development consists of differentiation and progressive hierarchical organization. For example, a child may first learn to label all four-legged animals that bark as "doggie." For a time, the child generalizes the label to all four-legged animals. With time, the child begins to differentiate animals on the basis of the perceptual characteristics (size, sounds produced, locations, coloration) and learns to match appropriate labels to dogs, cats, and cows. When she learns that dogs, cats, and cows are all animals, her class concept

has become hierarchically organized, and she can begin to incorporate sheep, pigs, and goats into her concept of animal. Similarly, she will form class concepts for birds, fish, and plants. Thus, one of the impacts of hierarchical organization is that we become increasingly efficient in our ability to categorize the environment and to process information. Along with another comparative psychologist, T. C. Schneirla, Werner can be counted among the scholarly founders of contemporary systems views of development.

See also Theories of Development

High Amplitude Sucking Procedure

A procedure widely used in the study of infant speech perception. In this procedures, the infant sucks on a blind-nipple that is connected to a pressure transducer. Whenever the infant makes a high-amplitude (strong) suck, the suck elicits a reinforcing stimulus (usually a sound). As the sucking rate decreases (habituation), the infant is then either presented with a new stimulus or the old stimulus. If the infant receiving the novel auditory stimulus begins to suck strongly again, whereas the infant with the same old stimulus (familiar) does not, the investigator concludes that the infants discriminated the novel stimulus but not the familiar one.

Investigators have developed several variants of the HAS procedure that involve sucking interburst-intervals, visual stimulation rather than auditory, visual fixation, and headturning. All of these techniques have markedly advanced studies of the preverbal infant's ability to discriminate auditory stimuli and to demonstrate preferences for such auditory

stimuli as a mother's voice as early as the newborn period.

High-Risk Environments

These are environments that do not provide for optimal development of infant/toddlers. They are always to be assessed individually because broad-based indicators such as family income, parental education, community violence, parental substance abuse, and single parenthood do not always take into account the individual adaptive capabilities of parents and other caregivers. Nonetheless, there is little doubt that poverty, parental psychopathology, single parenthood, teen parenthood, parental education, and the like stress a family's ability to provide even a favorable environment to support optimal development.

Histogenesis

The formation and development of the tissues of the body.

History of Infant Care

Infant care is the care of an infant/toddler by a parent, family member, or nonrelative. The history of infant care in what is now the United States dates to colonial times. Yet the resources found to meet demands for infant care have repeated themselves over the years. Strategies such as foster care, group care, and in-home care have been repeated throughout the history of the country, influenced by the historical context of the time.

Child Care During Colonial Times

During the colonial period, childhood was short, with young children taking on adultlike responsibilities in the family as soon as they were physically strong enough to work. A Puritan work ethic drove families in this period. Children were seen as inherently evil, and idleness was sinfulness. This idea was not challenged until John Locke, an English philosopher, suggested that infants were not born as sinful but rather as "blank slates" (tabula rasa). Until this time, hard work and hard discipline were thought to be in the best interest of the child, as was an early approach to education.

Wealthy children as young as age three were sometimes expected to learn to read. Further, apprenticeships—training periods designed to train the child in a skill or craft—began early, sometimes as early as age five. Until that time, infants, toddlers, and young children were typically cared for in their homes. If families could not afford to care for young children or a woman was widowed or unmarried, local churches sponsored parish apprenticeships as a way to care for orphans or poor children. Historical records show that children, some as young as one year, were sent to parishes for care. This type of care foreshadowed the later emergence of orphanages in the United States. In other cases a poor mother might offer livestock or possessions to another family as payment to care for her child until she could allocate the necessary resources herself. This arrangement was an early form of foster care. Schools also played a role in caring for infant/toddlers. During the colonial period, it was fairly common for toddlers to accompany siblings to schools and play and sleep in the corner of the room.

Influences on Child Care during the 1700s and 1800s
Just as Locke's writings in the seventeenth century foreshadowed more modern views of infant/toddlers, the work of

Jean-Jacques Rousseau, a French philosopher of the Enlightenment period in the 1700s, also emphasized more respect and consideration for infants. Unlike Locke, Rousseau believed that infants were born not as blank slates but as individuals with some sense of innate morality and an ingrown plan for healthy development. Rousseau was one of the first philosophers or scientists to suggest that there are distinct periods of human growth: infancy, childhood, late childhood, and adolescence. Locke and Rousseau influenced the work of Johann Heinrich Pestalozzi, a Swiss educator whose ideas also shaped society's thinking about very young children. Pestalozzi was one of the first to suggest that young children learn through their senses and through play. Pestalozzi's emphasis on a child-centered approach to early education and care established the groundwork for developmentally appropriate practices.

However, despite emerging consensus that infants, toddlers, and young children might require specialized care, many children were put to work as soon as they were able. For instance, during the period of slavery, young slaves worked alongside adults in the fields, a trend later repeated during the Industrial Age. Infant/toddlers too young to work in the fields were often left in the care of slaves too old to work in the fields. Thus, an early form of group child care emerged.

The white children of slaveowners often were left in the care of older slave women. The roles of nannies and governesses, caregivers hired to care for infant/toddlers in their homes, would continue to play an important role in the provision of infant care through the twentieth century.

During the post–Civil War period, the country was swept into social reform.

During this time, society turned to very conservative views about the roles of women as mothers. This movement, called the fireside education movement, emphasized the importance of mothers in the home. Parent education was popular during this time, as mothers were thought of as the first teachers of infants, toddlers, and young children. Although the benefits of this movement were available to upper-class families, poor children and their families were left out.

The Influence of Immigrants on Child Care

The surge of immigrants into the United States in the 1800s and early 1900s influenced child care in several ways. The sheer number of immigrants moving into the country was staggering. Between 1880 and World War I, 17 million immigrants came to the United States, mostly moving into cities like New York and Chicago. Families with very young children had few options for child care. Often cut off from extended family members, mothers had no one to care for young children and so children often worked alongside their mothers as soon as they could. Older siblings took on much responsibility for child care of infants/toddlers. As one expert noted, older girls living in city tenements "didn't have dolls; they had the real thing." Families of the same ethnic origin often lived in neighborhoods and communities together, thus forming a type of extended family with some available support for child care.

One of the first organized efforts to provide child care occurred in Chicago in the late 1800s when Jane Addams founded the Hull-House. One of the first day nurseries, Hull-House offered care for infants as young as two weeks old while mothers worked. Meals were offered to children,

health screenings were conducted, and early parenting education information was even available. Shortly after Hull-House, similar programs were founded in other cities, such as New York and Boston. In many ways, these day nurseries were seen as alternatives to institutionalization of infant/toddlers, a positive way to keep families with very limited resources together.

Despite these efforts, many young children were orphaned or abandoned. The late 1800s saw an emergence of institutions designed to care for abandoned children. When they were established, orphanages were viewed as an ideal solution for young children with no one to care for them. After all, history tells us that infanticide or abandoning infants were common solutions for dealing with unwanted children, maimed children, or children whose parents could not afford to feed them. Orphanages were believed to provide children with a safe place to live, adequate food to eat, and perhaps even some minimal education. During the early twentieth century, there was an emerging sense that orphanages might not provide the best environment for infants, toddlers, and young children; perhaps infants needed more than just food and shelter. In fact, in some institutions the mortality rate among infants in the first year of life was nearly 100 percent.

Despite this early awareness, a more clear understanding of infant/toddlers' need for warmth and affection would not emerge until the 1950s, with René Spitz's groundbreaking research on the effects of institutionalization and custodial care on infant/toddlers. However, as people began to question the benefits of orphanages, foster care—in which children were sent to live with a family other than their own—was seen as a more desirable option for children. Foster care was not new to the United States. Early accounts of foster-care arrangements date back to the 1700s, and in the 1800s foster adoptions were arranged through the use of "orphan trains." Orphan trains were literally trainloads of young orphans that traveled across the country in search of families to adopt the children. Notices of coming orphan trains were posted in community churches throughout the country. Interested families greeted the trains and examined the children for possible adoption. Interestingly, these orphan trains were not unlike the "adoption parties" common today, in which prospective adoptive families interview and examine orphaned children at informal social events like picnics.

Foster care also became an important resource as the Great Depression gripped the nation in the early 1930s. By 1933, 12 million men and women were unemployed and living in poverty. As early as 1925, the Children's Aid Society's Foster Home Department was placing children in foster homes until their families could locate resources to care for them. The demand for care was enormous. For example, as the winter of 1931 approached, an estimated 630,000 homeless and dependent children needed some type of support from aid agencies. Unable to feed their infants, toddlers, and young children, many families felt they had to give up their children in order to ensure their childrens' survival. In an effort to create work for unemployed teachers, nurses, and others, President Franklin D. Roosevelt authorized the Works Progress Administration to create day nurseries. These nurseries marked the first governmental effort to fund child care for families in need.

The 1820s and 1830s saw a brief surge in popularity of what were called "infant schools" during the Industrial Revolution. As women came to work in the factories, infant schools provided care for children as young as eighteen months. The infant schools were first supported by local churches or social welfare agencies, and some infant schools were eventually subsumed by public school systems. Originally viewed as a resource for very poor families, infant schools eventually became more popular with more affluent families as the idea of child development, particularly the belief that the infant mind could be molded at an early age, become more widespread. Within a few short years, however, thinking about child development had shifted again, this time on the idea that direct educational training in infancy was undesirable and perhaps unhealthy. Infant schools began to fade and were replaced by custodial care (for the infants of very poor families) and private nursery schools (for the toddlers and young children of wealthy families). Custodial care provided for the basic physical needs of infants, whereas nursery schools provided a more educational focus for toddlers and young children.

Of course, child care was much less of an issue for wealthy families. Beginning in the mid- to late 1800s, hiring a British nanny was viewed as a sign of wealth and privilege. Nannies were hired to care solely for the young children and were charged with the responsibility of teaching "manners and morality" to the children. The employment of nannies was most common in the northern states. In the southern states, wealthy families typically employed maids who cared for the children while also tending to household duties. The use of nannies or other in-home caregivers continues today. During the late twentieth century, the use of au pairs, live-in nannies from foreign countries, became popular, particularly among upper-middle-class and more affluent families who could afford to hire them. Au pairs are typically young adults who receive some training in child care. Their host families in the United States pay room and board, and sometimes a stipend of some type, in exchange for child care.

Child Care in the Mid- to Late 1900s
With the U.S. entry into World War II in 1941, child care was influenced once again by the changing needs and demands of the population. Women became heavily involved in the war effort, going to work in factories producing supplies for the war. Approximately 1.5 million women with children under the age of ten entered the workforce, creating a high need for child care. In response to this need, the government passed the Lanham Act in 1944, which provided government funds to subsidize child care for working mothers. The Lanham Act marked the first time federal funds had been marked to support the administration of child care for all children, not just children in poverty. The Lanham Act child-care centers generally provided full day care for children ages two and older. By 1945 approximately 1.6 million children were enrolled in child-care centers and nursery schools; many other children received care from relatives during the day while their mothers worked. Although the emergence of federally funded child care was viewed positively by many, others felt great concern at the thought of mothers moving into the workforce and away from caring for their children in their own homes. Many people felt the mother's place was in the home caring for her children, not working outside the home, war or not, an interesting phenomenon, as infants had been placed in group care almost 100 years before in infant schools.

Despite the early historical context, public support for infant care was minimal at best. Although Lanham Act funds could be used to create group child care for infants under age two, government and laypeople alike believed that infants needed to be with their mothers. Nevertheless, some mothers of infants had to work outside the home, and their infants were placed in group child care. In answer to the concern of placing infants in large groups for care, some funds were used to create "foster family day care," very similar to family day-care settings today, in which small groups of infants receive care in a private home.

As the birthrate increased significantly after World War II and the baby-boom generation was born, many mothers returned to the home to care for their infants, toddlers, and young children. As work patterns began to change in the mid-twentieth century, the need for infant care began to emerge again. In the mid- to late twentieth century, common forms of child care for infants included child-care centers, which provided care for larger groups of infants/toddlers; family child care, which provided care for infants/toddlers in smaller, homelike environments; and in-home care provided by relatives, spouses, extrafamilial adults, live-in nannies, and au pairs. The late twentieth century also saw the first federal funding of Early Head Start, designed to provide early educational experiences for impoverished infants/toddlers in the first three years of life.

Head Start, a federally funded social program founded in the 1960s, was designed for preschool-aged children, and

Early Head Start was an expansion on the idea of getting at-risk children off to a head start in life. Evaluation research investigating the effectiveness of Early Head Start is ongoing. Other federal legislation relevant to child care was passed in the late twentieth century as well. In 1990, Child Care Development Block Grant legislation was passed, representing the most significant child-care legislation to be passed since the Lanham Act in 1944. The Child Care Development Block Grant provides federal funds to subsidize child care primarily for low-income families. Funds were also available for before- and after-school child-care programs for older children. In 1993 the Family and Medical Leave Act was passed, which allows mothers or fathers to take up to twelve weeks of unpaid leave after the birth or adoption of a child. This legislation was the first government act in the United States to guarantee parental leave to care for young children.

See also Day Care; Employed Mothers

References and further reading
Roopnarine, J., and J. E. Johnson. 2000. *Approaches to Early Childhood Education.* 3rd ed. Upper Saddle River, NJ: Merrill.
Youcha, G. 1995. *Minding the Children: Child Care in America from Colonial Times to Present.* New York: Scribner

HIV
Human immunodeficiency virus (HIV) and the subsequent development of acquired immune deficiency syndrome (AIDS) are fatal to the infant. The HIV infection can be passed from the mother to the fetus during the prenatal period, through the birthing process, or through breastfeeding. If the mother is known to have HIV, she can take an antiviral med-

ication, called AZT, which dramatically reduces the chance that her infant will become infected during the pregnancy.

HIV attacks and weakens the immune system, the body's mechanism for fighting infection. Therefore, HIV/AIDS infants are much more likely to become seriously ill from infections and bacteria that might be harmless to a healthy infant. Similarly, their bodies cannot produce antibodies to fight off other life-threatening diseases such as measles.

Infants with HIV or AIDS are treated with a combination of medications designed to reduce the symptoms of the disease. Some infected infants survive into their teenage years; many infected infants die of complications related to AIDS in their childhood years. Although there is hope that one day HIV/AIDS can be controlled by medication, there is no cure for HIV/AIDS at this time.

See also Acquired Immune Deficiency Syndrome

Hold-and-Operate Hand Skills
See Lateralization; Motor Development

Holophrase
A single word that represents a more complex linguistic utterance; a one-word sentence. When a toddler utters "Up!" he means "Pick me up!"

See also Language

Home Observation for Measurement of the Environment for Infants and Toddlers
A tool for assessing the quality of caregiving in the home, identifying risks for

developmental delay related to home factors, and providing information to help in planning appropriate interventions. It is used with children from birth to three years and measures adult interactions as well. Trained staff administer the measure in the home through a one-hour interview with the parent, as well as observations of parent-infant interactions. Staff complete a forty-five-item checklist that indicates the presence or absence of specific interactions and positive home environmental factors that are likely to contribute to healthy development.

There are six basic subscales: caregiver responsiveness, avoidance of restriction and punishment, organization of the environment, provision of appropriate play materials, involvement with the child, and opportunities for variety of daily stimulation. The HOME test has good reliability and validity and is a good predictor of whether development will be normal or delayed.

See also Assessment; Caldwell, Bettye
References and further reading
Caldwell, B., and R. Bradley. 1979/1984. *Home Observation for Measurement of the Environment.* Little Rock: University of Arkansas.

Home Stimulation
Home stimulation means day-to-day surroundings, activities, and caregiving that encourage and support healthy infant development. Home stimuli include surroundings that are safe and supportive of infant activities and development. Daily activities and routines are carried out in a caring matter, stimulating attachment, communication, movement, learning, and growth. Through touch and interaction with primary caregivers, infants are stimulated to grow physically and cogni-

tively. In some instances, specific home-stimulation activities or exercises can be suggested for premature infants or those with birth defects that impede normal development. Parent/caregivers might be instructed to massage the baby daily as a way to stimulate blood flow and muscle development and to promote attachment to the primary caregivers. Infant brain development research has noted that healthy home stimulation influences positive development and growth.

See also Attachment; Massage; Neurobiology; Parenting; Touch

Home Visiting
Intervention and remediation programs that choose home visitation as the primary program delivery system for services to infants and their families have been implemented since the early 1960s. Most of these services target families where living conditions increase chances that an infant will be at risk for developmental delays. From the early 1990s, the federally funded Early Head Start program has included some programs based exclusively on the home visitation model rather than center-based care for low-income families with children birth to thirty-six months of age.

The importance of early support for new parents is becoming more widely understood as an important societal goal. In the state of Missouri, the Parents as Teachers program offers home visiting to families of infants regardless of socioeconomic status, ethnicity, and parental age.

Historically, Ira Gordon's home visitation program in Gainesville, Florida, was one of the earliest programs to train paraprofessional home visitors to visit families. The staff taught mothers how to play Piagetian sensorimotor activities and games with their infants. During weekly home visits, paraprofessionals brought sample fact sheets describing each activity and how a parent could carry out each game.

In the 1970s, the Ypsilanti-Carnegie Infant Education Project also had as its main developmental objective a Piagetian-based curriculum designed to increase low-income mothers' awareness of, and ability to enhance, the cognitive growth of their infants.

In some of the earliest home visitation programs, home visitors focused their efforts on direct teaching of infants in high-risk, low-income families in order to promote infant sensorimotor and language competencies. A review of such efforts noted that enlisting parents as teachers of their infants was far more effective in ensuring early learning.

Home Visits: A Service Delivery Model to Special Populations
Special needs of families as well as infants have highlighted the appropriateness of the home visitation model to meet particular family needs.

Services for Mentally Ill Mothers. Maternal depression or other mental illness can result in disturbances of infant functioning by three months of age. Home visitation programs that meet the families on their own turf are well suited to providing the possibility of early screening and detection of risk factors. The home visitor is in a special position to make referrals to appropriate agencies where the at-risk infant can then receive timely preventive services.

Services for Infants with Disabilities. Some infants are born at risk for develop-

mental delays or manifest risks (such as deafness) some time after birth. Some disabilities, such as infant autism, may not become apparent until the second year of life. Maternal use of street drugs, such as cocaine or heroin, results in the birth of an infant who experiences withdrawal symptoms, including trembling, sleep disturbances, and difficulties with infant state (the baby may go from deep sleep to screaming cries but be unable to reach a calm alert state, the optimal time for attentiveness to mother-initiated teaching interactions).

Many outreach programs were set up to serve special populations that would otherwise be underserved. Parents with premature infants often need support in coping with the fragility of the infant's ability to handle stimulation. Families with infants born with disabilities and using medical equipment face complex logistical problems in transporting their infant to a program facility. Home visitation is an excellent method for service delivery, both for the parent stressed by the birth of an ill or atypical infant as well as the infant who requires direct provision of services.

The New York state department of health provides training for home visitors to serve at-risk infants and their families in a program entitled Training Together for Tots. Service providers, such as social workers, nurses, and educators, are given intensive training in how to carry out developmental screening and how to identify and refer at-risk infants for further services.

Training for the home visitors includes the use of specific case vignettes to help staff learn to recognize both risk and mitigating factors in the families they visit. Trainee group discussions of each vignette help providers to hone their diagnostic skills. This program uses KIDS (Kids Integrated Data System, a data-management tool) to assist staff in tracking the processes involved in providing the necessary services for at-risk infants and their families so that if the home visitor makes a definitive diagnosis of risk, then the baby can be enrolled in the state's early intervention program. If the home visitor determines initially that diagnosis of risk is not definitive, he/she carries out further screening during regular home visits to monitor the infant's status. Meanwhile, the home visitor provides easy-to-use strategies that can be used at home by parents in a developmental area (such as fine motor skills or language) where there is suspicion of possible delay.

Training for the home visitors includes introduction of several screening tools, such as the Denver Developmental Screening Test and the Ages and Stages Questionnaire (a parent-completed child-monitoring system available for use with parents of infant/toddlers). The screenings are part of a comprehensive health assessment to permit early identification of risk and potential developmental delays. The home visitor uses culturally sensitive screening as a potential means of teaching parents about the developmental needs and abilities of their infant, the sequential nature of development, and the need for differing types of stimulation and interaction at different stages of development. If a baby's score on a screening test is below the cut-off point, then the home visitor assists the parents in enrolling the infant in a program that provides special services.

Sponsored by the Ford Foundation, the Child Survival/Fair Start community-based program for low-income families has the goal of improving pregnancy outcomes, infant development, and health.

Another goal is to help families access local services such as the Women Infants and Children nutrition program, food stamps, and Medicaid. Local projects serve high-risk populations. Outreach work typically begins prior to the infant's birth. During home visits, the worker checks on parent follow-through for health care appointments, answers maternal questions, and helps the mother formulate strategies to solve problems she has brought up during the visit. The family worker is a local resident, and the emphasis is on creating a sustained relationship of reciprocity and intimacy with the mother. Workers chosen for training were typically well-respected older women who had reared their own children decades ago.

The caseload is increased gradually so that each home visitor has time to learn more about all the families served and time to help that family deal with crises. In addition, the outreach worker tries to help an isolated mother build a sense of belonging to a community.

Services for Chemical-Dependent Mothers. The National Center on Child Abuse and Neglect has funded randomized clinical trials to investigate the effectiveness of home visitation with sixty primarily African American single non-high-school-graduate women from low-income families. Biweekly home visits by a nurse began before delivery and continued until the child was eighteen months old. A trend was found suggesting more compliance with self-reported drug abstinence, primary health care appointments, and provision of developmental stimulation for the babies by the visited mothers. The intervention babies had marginally higher developmental scores at six months but not at later ages. Programs for parents with chemical dependence may require highly intensive work and greater provision of a wide array of enrichment services for the infants as well as the mothers. The Birth to Three project in the mid-1990s was a large-scale effort to enroll chemical-dependent women at highest risk who had not been able to seek prenatal care.

The home visitors were a multicultural group of female paraprofessionals with practical skills and experience in families with chemical dependency. Caseloads were small, and the focus was on working with the entire family to empower the mothers to identify and achieve their own goals as well as to work toward recovery and the best interests of their infants. Cross-site findings on 1,646 women indicated a 40 percent abstinence rate during program participation and a decrease in homelessness. Nearly 40 percent of the mothers took a parenting class. Higher birthweights for infants were associated with early or more prenatal care. However, many of the mothers still had abusive partners, and there was a high rate of birth defects in the infants born. Home visitation with families with massive needs involving partner abuse and chemical dependency may not provide enough intervention to improve infant developmental outcomes.

Services for Rural Families. Some home visitation programs have been initiated in order to provide assistance to rural parents, where distances are so great that families cannot travel to participate in services offered by a centrally located organization.

Services for Adolescent Mothers. The home visitation model is particularly suited to serve the needs of teenage mothers. Isolated socially after dropping out of school, teen mothers may not have the resources or knowledge base to seek out and travel to the site of services offered in centrally located agencies.

Home Visitation as an Initial Service Delivery Model. Some outreach programs were begun because the cultural mores of the family did not allow a mother to leave the home to participate in a group-based intervention service. For example, the Houston Child Development Center (a program of the Parent Child Development Center, or PCDC) served low-income Hispanic families beginning when the infant was twelve months old. The central goal of the PCDC models of the early 1980s was to provide center-based care for infants in low-income families. However, considerable trust-building during a year of home visits was necessary before husbands in the Houston PCDC program felt comfortable allowing the mother and baby to participate in enrichment in a group setting. For the Houston program, then, the home visitation model for providing services represented one phase of a piggy-back model of service delivery. Outreach to the home was the first service provision technique, and participation in a center facility was offered as the subsequent method of service delivery during the later toddler period.

Focus on a Variety of Goals. Home visitation models select different areas as a focus of their remedial efforts. Some models have broad-based goals; some are more focused. The central goal of the Child and Family Resource Programs (CFRP) at eleven sites in the United States in the late 1970s was to provide comprehensive family support. The common core of the CFRP model was a paraprofessional home visitation program with infants from birth to three years of age. Each site could also provide center-based social services.

Therapeutic Goals. Some programs are more therapeutically oriented. Their goal is to prevent infant emotional disturbance or the development of insecure attachments, as in the home visiting model Lieberman and Pawl have implemented with low-income Hispanic mothers in California. Home visitors in therapeutic programs are usually highly trained mental health professionals. They help the mother recognize and accept ambivalent or negative feelings she may have toward her infant, herself, others in the family, and even family members from the distant past. For example, if a mother had a bitterly resented sister who was the preferred sibling in the mother's family of origin, the newborn daughter may be ignored, receiving anger and hostility that stems from the mother's feelings about her sibling from her past. In therapeutic home-based programs, the worker tries gently to evoke the sad, jealous, or angry memories that are disturbing the ability of the mother to tune into the baby's needs. Workers provide ego strengths and "good parent" role-modeling to support and nurture gentler aspects of the distressed mother so that she can protect rather than threaten her child's well-being. The therapist works patiently over a long period to help the mother, besieged by disturbing anguished feelings, to "banish the ghosts in the nursery," as Selma Fraiberg so vividly identified this process.

A stressed parent may see the baby as "bad" because the parent had been treated as "bad" in her family of origin. The home visitor over time validates the par-

ent's grief and angry memories and helps her move toward a more realistic perception of the infant. The therapist frees the parent to attend to the actual baby rather than to act out rejections and frightening patterns from past relationships in the mother's life. As the therapist in home visits makes an alliance as a strong empathic and loving figure with the positive aspects of the mother, gradually the "ghosts" from the past that have hindered the mother from mobilizing her emotional resources to protect (rather than ignore or harm) the baby are banished. The therapeutic home visitation model has been particularly useful when potential risk for child abuse and neglect has been identified.

Prevention of Attachment Disorders. Van den Boom's home visiting program in Holland addressed the risks faced when infants with highly irritable temperaments were parented by low-income mothers. Mothers learned soothing and comforting techniques and how to attract the baby's attention and play gentle, interactive games. The home visitors helped the mothers tune into and respond to the infant's cues. This program produced remarkable results, so that a far greater percentage of the home-visited infants (in comparison with irritable control infants whose mothers did not receive home visitation) were assessed as securely attached to mother at the end of the first year.

The Ounce of Prevention Program. Set up to prevent child abuse and attachment disorders, the Ounce of Prevention Fund in Chicago represents an innovative program of joint funding between a state child welfare agency and a private philanthropist, Irving Harris. Geared toward prevention of parenting problems that could result in child abuse, this project provides a wide variety of services with an emphasis on community-based family support. Services include outreach to pregnant young mothers as well as high-quality infant care.

Home Visitation for Feeding Problems. Some home visitation programs have been implemented to assist mothers in learning more optimal feeding techniques with a failure-to-thrive infant. Mothers are given assistance in preparation of food, feeding positions, and creating a pleasurable atmosphere for the infant feeding situation. Home visitation nurses use the Nursing Child Assessment Satellite Training (NCAST) Teaching and Feeding Scales to assess mother-infant interactions in terms of the amount of responsive behavior exhibited by each member of the feeding dyad. NCAST scales target engagement and disengagement cues of both mother and baby. Some positive cues are: smiling, mutual gaze, reaching toward the caregiver, eye-widening, and facial brightening. If the parent is intrusive, this will be indexed by NCAST cues that specify infant gaze aversion and other physical signs of discomfort with the intensity or intrusiveness of the adult's behavior.

Prevention of Language Delays. Some programs focus more specifically on language games and picture book–sharing with tots. Home visitors introduce books for babies and for toddlers. The home visitors help parents learn techniques such as snuggling and sharing picture books and labeling events on each page. Parents learn how to arouse baby's interest in each colorful page and how to point to each picture. They learn how to make sounds appropriate to each animal to delight the infant. Parents learn how to embroider a story, or pare down a tale so that a baby just has to attend to the labeled pictures. Parents are shown how to help a toddler relate the story to the child's own experiences. For example, an oil-cloth picture book shows a toddler playing with a pail and shovel, getting all muddy, bathing in a nice warm bubble bath, and afterward being snuggled in a big fluffy towel. Parents are guided to relate the story to the toddler's own real-life bath experiences to enhance picture-book pleasure.

Other programs are more narrowly focused intervention to teach mothers reading strategies so that their children would be able to relate to story events on a cognitive level that reflected "distancing" from the three-dimensional world through verbal interaction focused on the pictorial two-dimensional book materials.

Home Visitation as Parent Education. Home visitors frequently concentrate on parenting education. They share knowledge about child development; they teach skills in managing behaviors. They introduce appropriate toy materials and games to play with infants at each stage of development.

The goal of the Missouri PAT program is to support parents as the child's first and most influential teacher. The Missouri legislature provides funds for each of the 543 school districts in the state to serve 40 percent of district families with infants from birth to thirty-six months. Regularly scheduled home visits are made by parent educators who are given extensive and ongoing training. The program includes periodic developmental screening of infant/toddlers.

The Mother-Child Home Program. Founded as the Verbal Interaction Project in low-income housing projects in Long Island, the Mother-Child Home Program (MCHP), which begins visitation at one year, has been widely replicated in the United States. Toy demonstrators are trained to develop a warm relationship with mother and child, demonstrate verbal stimulation techniques, and maximize mother participation. During the initial session, mother and visitor put together a special toy chest designed to store the eleven toys and twelve books provided annually as gifts that the toy demonstrator introduces as she and the toddler engage in play with a toy or book.

The program was designed so that twice weekly during half-hour home sessions, the toy demonstrator, using verbal interaction stimulus materials (such as a toy farm with a barn, farmer, and farm animals), demonstrates for the mother how to encourage a toddler to talk by asking him questions and by responding to the child's comments. The home visitor helps the mother to see herself as a mediator between the toy and the baby so that the baby is motivated toward pleasureful explorations and learning experiences with toys and play objects. Longitudinal follow-up into high school showed that more youths from the original group of visited families were succeeding in their lives compared with youths from control families.

Parent-Infant Interaction Model. The Parent-Infant Interaction Model in the UCLA Intervention program for preterm infants provided home visits between nine months (when a cumulative risk score indicated that the infant was eligible for the program) and two years of age. Intervention for the thirty ethnically diverse families was conceptualized as helping parents enjoy their infants in mutually pleasurable transactions. In case of staff illness, vacation time, or leaving the program, a pair of home visitors was assigned to work with each family.

Program goals were to strengthen parental sensitivity, responsiveness, and skills in the parent-infant system so that the parent experienced successes in her transactions with the baby. The parent was encouraged to gain confidence in herself as the primary change agent for the infant, so that the results of the home visitation program would be long-lasting. Home visitors tried to help the parent:

- Become a good observer of the baby's particular interests and skill level with toys, feeding, and play experiences.
- Read infant behavioral cues accurately.
- Respond to infant feelings, smiles, and signs of discomfort or distress.
- Acknowledge and vocalize back when the infant coos, babbles, and vocalizes.
- Identify activities where baby seems satisfied on his own and also identify games where the baby actively needs the parent's participation in order for the play to be enjoyable.
- Talk in a focused, attentive manner when the baby is looking at parent's face.
- Realize how much more an infant understands before producing words so that the parent gives satisfying feedback to early infant babbling and attempts at language.

- Initiate positive social interactions and social games and respond to baby's playful behaviors without being intrusive.

Program guidelines for home visitor attitudes and practices were set to encourage parental trust and to support open communication. Home visitors:

- Enable parents to remain in control rather than slide into overdependence on staff.
- Avoid the "authority-layman" gap by listening carefully to the parent and showing that her comments are valued in cooperative planning for the baby.
- Remain sensitive to parental primary needs and priorities yet walk a fine line so that parental crises could be attended to yet also help the parent to focus on the infant's needs.
- Become sensitive to parental strengths and positive parenting behaviors as a foundation for planning intervention content and strategies.
- Respect parental goals and priorities with the baby.
- Actively involve parents in planning so that they gain self-confidence from the partnership with the home visitor.
- Respect individual styles of parent-infant interaction.
- Talk specifically with a parent about why and how some of her behaviors and actions are helping the baby so that the parent gains insight rather than only the social reinforcement of the home visitor's praise.
- Provide an array of alternative possibilities in dealing with a situa-

tion, so that the parent does not feel discouraged or like a failure, and reassure the parent that not all ways may work for a particular baby.
- Listen empathetically to the frustrations a parent says she experiences in interacting with the baby.

The Parent Behavior Progression (PBP), the home visitor's assessment tool, is available in forms for parents of infants from birth to nine months and for parents of infants between nine and thirty-six months. PBP assesses the degree to which a parent behaves in mutually satisfying interactions with the infant. The PBP is divided into six levels.

At Level 1, the listed PBP behaviors index the degree to which the parent, on her own terms, enjoys being in the infant's company, caressing him, and playing with him. Level 2 assesses whether the parent is a sensitive observer of her infant, reads his behavioral cues accurately, and is responsive to them. Level 3 PBP behaviors assess whether the parent-infant transactions are mutually satisfying and provide opportunities for the development of secure attachment. Parents who have fully achieved Level 2 are more likely to receive positive feedback from interacting with baby and both have enhanced mutual pleasure. PBP Level 4 assesses whether the parent shows understanding of the kinds of activities, toys, and experiences that are just right for her infant's particular stage of development. The parent not only identifies but also plans such experiences. Level 5 parent behaviors index the initiation of new play activities and experiences for the infant based on principles that the parent has internalized from watching the home visitor model such transactions or internalized from lessons learned from her own and others' experiences. Level 6 behaviors indicate that at this stage the parent independently creates a wide range of activities and experiences that are interesting and appropriate for the infant, in new and familiar situations, and these created experiences are appropriate to the level of the baby's development and interesting to the baby.

The home visitor uses the six PBP levels, indexed by a series of descriptions of parent behaviors, to help her focus on the quality and kinds of parent-infant interactions. The PBP not only assesses how well the home visitor's intervention is succeeding but also hones the visitor's own clinical sensitivity in supporting positive behaviors in the parent's repertoire.

PBP positive parent behaviors serve as goals for the home visitor. Home visitors are asked to rate their intervention for each family as being either "successful," "partially successful," or "unsuccessful." Use of the PBP can quickly alert program staff to a crisis in the family, since stresses can result in a sudden decrease in PBP behaviors that the home visitor has checked on a given visit.

Home visitors use a variety of modes of intervention with parents. They listen empathetically, to communicate that they valued hearing the parent express her feelings. They observe the infant's play and the transactions between parent and child; they comment positively. Home visitor comments are concrete and specific. Home visitors also model for parents, give information, and gently suggest alternatives to ineffective parental interactions with baby. They motivate the parent to try a variety of new activities with the baby. Home visitors ask parents to make specific observations of the infant's play, language, and social behavior. They ask the parent to describe how she successfully handled a situation with the baby.

When the home visitor modeled a way of interacting with the baby by engaging the infant in play, the parent was able to see how the infant responded and decide whether she wanted to try that herself. Experimenting with different ways of working with the baby also provides the home visitor with insights as to optimal ways to engage that particular infant and capture his interest in an activity. This experimentation was particularly important for infants with disabilities or difficulties. By such experimentation, the worker avoided the pitfall of telling a parent that a certain game would work with that baby, when even the visitor herself had a difficult time while demonstrating.

Commenting positively on parental strength was frequent, as were encouraging words to prompt more parent initiatives. Home visitors took the initiative in choosing the most appropriate mode for working with each family. For example, families differed in how much they would profit from discussions, from modeling, or from having the home visitor comment positively as the parent herself worked with the baby.

Family Development Research Program
The Family Development Research Program (FDRP) for teenage mothers was an omnibus intervention program in the 1970s that provided home outreach beginning in the trimester before birth and continuing until the children graduated from the program at five years of age. A strong nutrition component as well as provision of high-quality, developmentally appropriate center care beginning when infants were six months old were other provisions of FDRP. The major premise was that parents are the

primary teachers and sustaining caregiving persons in a young child's life.

A cadre of paraprofessionals, called child development trainers (CDTs), was recruited and intensively trained to work with families of firstborn or second-born children of high-school-dropout low-income mothers. The goals for the CDTs were to support a rich quality of family interactions and increase family cohesiveness and an affectionate mother-child relationship. A learning game was taught to the parent during each weekly home visit. CDTs filled out checklists after each home visit describing the degree of parental participation and the responsiveness of the mother and infant to the modeled activities. The CDT acted as an adviser and confidant to the young parent, who often asked her for advice on personal relationships, finances, career changes, and education.

During each home visit the CDT:

- Taught families Piagetian sensorimotor games, such as finding a hidden object under a cloth, learning to stack or nest cups, and learning to use a tool, such as a string or stick, as a means to obtain a toy out of reach.
- Provided nutrition information and explanations for parents.
- Modeled rich turn-taking talk with very young infants and modeled labeling and responsive talk with toddlers.
- Introduced appropriate books for picture book–sharing with baby and carried with them a "book lending library" so that mothers could borrow a book to read to the infant.
- Offered positive encouragement and admiration to mothers who

tried to carry out a given activity during the home visit.
- Helped the mother to learn ways to modify games and activities (based on "matchmaking" between child's developmental level and task difficulty) so that the child was more likely to maintain interest and learn.
- Discussed sociable, positive ways to engage a baby and to encourage persistence in trying an activity.
- Suggested specific positive discipline techniques and explained developmental stages so that the mother could understand when a behavior was truly deliberately inappropriate or was stage-typical.
- Reframed behaviors parents deemed "bad."
- Utilized the friendly working relationships she continually developed with personnel in other service agencies to facilitate a family receiving services such as pediatric care, housing, and legal counseling.
- Encouraged family members to take an active role in finding and using neighborhood resources and learning environments such as public libraries and parks.
- Shared techniques for observing babies so that a parent could become more keenly sensitive to the baby's signals for needing comfort or for being optimally ready to focus on a learning task.
- Admired and supported parental efforts to devise their own appropriate learning activities and shared these creative ideas with other mothers in her weekly caseload.
- Worked with the family to help think of ways to embed curricular

games and sociable language-rich interactions within daily routines such as diapering, bathing, and feeding.

- Sustained young mothers' personal efforts to enroll for a general equivalency degree or enter job training.
- Offered the young mother who asked for help strategies for dealing with difficult personal issues or referred the mother to an appropriate resource.
- Provided specific role-playing practice in how to talk to school personnel and how to make and maintain contacts with public agencies.

The CDTs carried on considerable liaison work with the Children's Center teachers. The CDTs alerted teachers in the center to family crises and to home situations that were responsible for puzzling classroom behaviors. Weekly joint meetings of all FDRP staff facilitated these communications. Once a week, CDTs escorted parents and any sibling to the Children's Center for parent group meetings. At these meetings, parents could see films about infant development, have discussions about topics such as fire safety in an apartment, and make toys, furniture, and clothing, among other group activities.

CDT morale and skills were kept high by once-a-week all-day in-service training sessions. CDTs learned how to fill out the Weekly Home Visit Report and often discussed specific problems and strategies with supervisors. As advocates for the parents, CDT's were an especially valuable key to enhancing relationships between FDRP center staff and the parents. Home visitors can provide classroom teachers with valuable insights about each individual child and family. They serve a priceless role in motivating families to stay with a program when life problems seem severe and crises preoccupy a family.

Ten years after the youngsters had graduated from the FDRP program, outcome measures showed far less juvenile delinquency compared to a control group. Their parents reported the FDRP graduates as more prosocial, more close with family, and more likely to go on with schooling.

Choosing and Training Home Visitors
Some programs hire highly trained professionals, such as psychiatric social workers or masters-level child-development graduates. Other programs train paraprofessional workers. They may be high-school graduates who come from the same cultural background as the families served. These home visitors may be single mothers themselves, and they may have struggled with difficult economic circumstances in their own lives that make them particularly sensitive to the complex, stressed lives that some client families lead. Some programs employ trained nurses.

Home visitors are often chosen because they know the community they will serve and speak the language of the families they will visit. Regardless of initial level of education and training of home visitors, very complex skills will be required for effective home visitation work. Programs that have just sent home visitors out to check in on at-risk families have found that although the visitor and the parent might share a cup of coffee and talk together, no positive outcomes for child development were found when infants in control families were compared with infants in the families visited by poorly trained staff.

Planning and training for home visitation must help workers take into account parental needs as well as infant/toddler needs. As Bronfenbrenner has suggested in his theoretical ecological model, the child is embedded in the microsystem of the family, but other systems impact the transactions between parent and infant. The mother's relationship with the home visitor, for example, can affect how well a parent is able to accept and actively try out new ideas in positive behavior management, or new ways of talking with or feeding an infant.

Staff training for home visitors should be intensive before services are provided. Training must be ongoing during the time of delivery of services. Ongoing training permits teaching new activities and understandings of infant/toddler development, new techniques for reaching hard-to-reach families, and new ideas about how to help parents embed curricula in the course of daily activities in their busy lives.

Training meetings held on a regular basis give supervisors a chance to see how well data-collection is going. Some home visitors are unaccustomed to paperwork and find this aspect of their job uncomfortable. During scheduled meetings of home visitors with supervisory staff, workers have a chance to share the perplexities and joys of working in an outreach model and a chance to enhance their own growth. Training for outreach workers needs to include discussions of their own personal belief systems. If a home visitor is not sensitive to her own prejudices and discomforts, she may not be able to work empathically, for example, to help a pregnant teen with easy and positive talk about the importance of regular gynecological examinations during pregnancy or about the advantages of breastfeeding an infant.

Difficulties in Using the Home Visitation Model
Home visitation program staff do report frustrations and difficulties in delivery of services.

Attrition. Because some families are stressed and lead chaotic lives, they may simply not be at home during the scheduled visit. The mother can be dropped from program although assessed initially as urgently in need of services. Holly Brophy and Alice Honig reported that after three months of home visitation with high-risk teen mothers, with a special focus on fostering secure attachment and responsive interactions with infants, so few of the mothers could be located a half-year later that follow-up assessments of program efficacy were restricted to very few families.

Agency Collaboration. Unless home visitors network with a wide variety of social-service agencies and health care providers, they may not be able to meet the needs of families with particular crises that must be addressed before the family is ready to engage more actively in providing enrichment activities for the baby and providing positive warm responsiveness to the child's emotional needs.

Timing of Program Initiation. Sometimes a home visitation program does not start early enough. Secure or insecure infant attachment to a parent is built during the first year of life. Language richness is fostered through daily vocalizing and talking interactions between parent and baby. Starting home visitation during the toddler period rather than prior to birth or shortly after birth can increase the difficulty of truly engaging the parent in more appropriate interaction patterns than the ones the parent has already practiced since baby's birth. Alice Honig and Christine Morin, reporting on outcomes of the Syracuse Children's Consortium's twenty-four-month home visitation program with high-risk adolescent mothers, reveal that when home visitors began their work prior to the birth of the infant, then several years later the risk of social worker–confirmed child abuse or neglect was significantly lower. This prebirth program onset "protective" effect held even for those teen moms who dropped out after about seven home visits. Thus, the timing of initiation of home visitation with high-risk families to start prenatally may well ensure a higher probability of positive outcomes.

Personality. The fit between worker and parent may not be good because of cultural or language barriers or personal styles. Programs need to be aware that the chemistry between the parent and the home visitor needs to be considered in assigning, or perhaps reassigning, a caseload of families to an outreach worker.

Flexibility Is Crucial. If a home visitation program is too prescriptive and does not allow for flexibility in meeting all of the family's needs, then the worker keeps pushing a curriculum during visits when this is entirely inappropriate and family problems are overwhelming a parent. In the face of crises, as when a baby has a high fever, the mother has been violently

treated by her partner, or the family is facing eviction from housing, the home visitor must be very flexible. She/he needs to find internal and agency resources to provide individual, empathetic, perceptive, and effective support for the family through the crisis in order to be able to continue the home visitations. Home visitors who try to provide a narrowly focused program cannot meet the needs of the family. Other studies suggest that parent workers who served a variety of functions to help the parents in all sorts of ways were far more successful in finding parents at home and in completing home visits.

Lay workers in the Rural Alabama Pregnancy and Infant Health Program (RAPIH) became overwhelmed by the amount of technical information given to them during their intensive training. As a result, staff felt insecure and intimidated. The teenage, young, black, first-time pregnant women they visited felt they were being lectured. The young mothers perceived the lay visitors as too didactic and rigid in their manner. This experience led the RAPIH project to revise training efforts to emphasize the importance of building warm relationships with the young women as an adviser, model, and friend. RAPIH training also encouraged the lay workers to share their own personal histories. More sensitivity and emphasis in training lay workers added to the social dynamics of the household, where frequently grandmothers assumed responsibility for the infants of the unwed teen parent.

In Ira Gordon's pioneer Florida program, when the home visitors became discouraged (with parental lack of enthusiasm or motivation to work with the infants), they tended to work more directly themselves with the baby rather than try harder to focus on ways to engage the parent in responsive interactions with the infant. Supervisory staff must be alert to this issue. Helping home visitors to empower parents is crucial to ensure that the positive effects of the program are sustained in the long term. Yet home visitors sometimes need special emotional support themselves to keep going with their efforts to engage the parent as the baby's primary, loving, and responsive teacher. If a young mother has the television blaring during a home visit and breaks many appointments that she herself has agreed to, then the home visitor needs a highly trained supervisor to whom she can express concerns and ask for additional help with strategies. The Syracuse FDRP project provided such a staff person, someone the home visitor could call at home at any hour and with whom the CDT staff met weekly for sharing experiences, problems, and solutions.

Outreach to Fathers. Few home visitation programs focus on fathers. More ingenuity may be needed to engage fathers or father figures during home visits. In the FDRP program, one boyfriend was encouraged to get down on the floor and try the Piagetian activities with the baby. He became interested, whereas during previous visits he had played the role of amused bystander as home visitor and mother worked together with the infant.

Parent Literacy. Some parents are illiterate or are literate in a language other than English. These latter parents will appreciate receiving ideas for infancy games in their own language. When a parent cannot read, or reads at a low literacy level, then the home visitors may want to enlist artistic staff members to create line drawings of some of the activities to refresh a parent's memory during the week when she is trying to carry out the activity with an infant but cannot read the instruction pages that were left with her. Also, materials written at low literacy levels are helpful.

Power Relations. Parents are in charge of their own homes. If a home visitor has had prior experience in a center or classroom, he/she will have to rethink the power relationships in an outreach program. The home visitor has to be patient and accept a position of low power and immediate critical parental evaluation of his/her teaching style. Hopefully, as the home visitor and parent become closer, then the parent will be more accepting of the "power" of the home visitor as a skilled provider whose goal is to improve the social, emotional, language, and learning climate of the home for the infant and parent.

Frequency of Visits. Given the problems of some families and the medical and emotional difficulties of some children, some home visitation programs are too infrequent and do not extend over a long enough period to be effective. Needs assessments of the families to be served can help programs plan more effectively as well as to realistically schedule the frequency of visits. The CFRP staff averaged about three visits every four months. In contrast, the Syracuse FDRP home visitors made weekly visits to each adolescent parent. FDRP home visitors sometimes had to come back to a teen mother's apartment many days in a row in order to complete a weekly home visit. Cheerful dedication to their work is an important ingredient of success.

In Jamaica, aides took toys to homes and taught two concepts per home visit.

Infants between six and thirty months were recruited into one of three variations on frequency of visitation: monthly, twice monthly, and weekly visits. The infants' scores on the Griffiths Scale of Mental Development increased as the frequency of home visits increased. Indeed, the twice-monthly-visited infants were not much better than controls. Thus, program planning for intervention that truly ensures that infants and parents receive supports and service throughout the infant/toddler period requires not only special dedication and energetic implementation by staff but also weekly visitations.

Family Need and Cost/Benefit Ratios. Families with severe problems may not be reachable no matter how many efforts staff make to complete home visits. Cost-effectiveness requires that home visitation be carried out with families who can profit from services. The balance between inability to reach a family, and the case of families where stability and supports are already in place despite poverty or teen parenting, make choices difficult for program allocation of resources. For example, Sandra Scarr and Kathleen McCartney worked with the government of Bermuda to replicate Levenstein's MCHP with twice-monthly visits for two years. The program was implemented within an entire parish of 125 families, with random assignment to program and control groups. However, few demonstrable effects of program were found. The special situation in Bermuda is that almost all mothers are employed and almost all toddlers are in group programs by two years. All infants had a mean IQ of 100 (average) at the start of the study. Thus, the toddlers enrolled in visitation or control groups were not at great risk of developmental delays and received group care within the year.

Very different outcomes were found in a project carried out among impoverished families in the Gaza Strip. Project Care results with 268 children in the early 1990s revealed the potency of the home visiting model for families at high risk. Infants were recruited into the program in each of five infancy age windows and randomly assigned to intervention or control groups. After one year, regardless of the age of entry, intervention infants scored higher on the Battelle Developmental Profile. After two and three years they scored even higher, about two standard deviations above the controls. Home visitation seems to work more effectively when risk is greater but families are not overwhelmed by drug abuse and chaos.

Choice of Outcome Measures. Some home visitation programs do not conceptualize outcome measures well enough to reveal the efficacy of the program. For example, if a home visitor is working to promote language development in a language-delayed toddler, then program outcome measures should reflect that special goal rather than assess general cognitive attainment.

Outcome measures must be tailored to the actual interventions in order to assess the efficacy of the home visitation efforts in any community. Among the federally funded CFRP models, site-specific goals differed. Some emphasized provision of social services, whereas others focused on effective parenting and child-development behaviors.

Programs have to decide what cut-off point to use if a family is to be included in their data analyses of program efficacy. If a family was supposed to receive thirty

TABLE 1   Effective Home-Visiting Interventions

- Use a model appropriate to the population's level of risk
- Use a mental health relationship based approach with high-risk families
- Be clear about objectives and content and implement the core components of the model
- Use well-trained staff
- Support your staff through reflective supervision and agency policies
- Emphasize the home visitor's development of a trusting relationship
- Focus on both infant and parent
- Use a systematic process to enroll families during pregnancy or around the time of birth
- Visit frequently and long enough to accomplish objectives
- Be comprehensive in addressing situational stresses, social supports, psychological issues, and parental behaviors as needed by the family
- Link families to quality child care
- Be realistic about what can be accomplished

Source: Adapted from Tableman, B. 2000. "Effective Home Visiting for Very Young Children—3." Best Practice Briefs No. 20. East Lansing: Michigan State University, University Outreach Partnerships.

home visits and only twelve were completed, then can the family be considered as having "received" the home visitation program?

Objective measures are important. One program reported that the nurses who provided the visits felt discouraged that they had not changed parental habits of using physical punishment with infants. However, program parents were significantly more likely to exhibit positive scores on the Caldwell Home Inventory (which observes parental interactions and inputs with infants in a home setting) than control mothers.

Conclusion

The role of the home visitor can be a powerful catalyst for the provision of a supportive, loving climate in which a baby can thrive and learn. Whether a layperson or professionally trained, the home visitor needs extensive preservice training, ongoing in-service learning opportunities, sensitive support, and supervision. Families whose infants are

at risk for developmental delays need long-term engagement with the home visitor. Neither casual banter nor didacticism promote successful home visitation outcomes. Building a trusting long-term relationship with the parent is crucial for sustaining long-term positive outcomes. The home visitor who acts flexibly and with insight and compassion for the family and the community best serves as a change agent.

The predominant philosophy expressed in descriptions of home visitation programs is to create a working alliance with parents. Effective home visitors emphasize parent strengths and abilities. They show sensitivity to a family's cultural mores and beliefs. Home visitors view their overall role as helping parents gain competence in finding ways to solve the problems they have in interactions with their infant and in their family life. Toward this goal, staff provide parents with support, information, and encouragement.

The relationship between visitor and parent is the primary vehicle for change.

For change to occur, this relationship must be characterized by reciprocity and mutual trust. The home visitor shows persistent caring for the family. Optimally, the home visitor is a stable, predictable, positive presence in the family's life, despite situations of chaos. Effective home visitors are therefore good listeners. Generously, they share delight in the infant/toddler as well as affirm the priceless role of the parent. The effective outreach worker uses a wide variety of skills as well as child-development knowledge to meet family needs. Optimally, the home visitor empowers and supports the mother to become emotionally attuned to and responsively interactive with her infant. With this intensive long-term support, the mother will become a loving teacher of her infant, providing language-rich experiences that nurture the infant's adventures in learning.

See also Parenting

References and further reading
Fraiberg, S. 1980. "Ghosts in the Nursery: A Psychoanalytic Approach to the Problems of Impaired Mother-Infant Relationships." In L. Fraiberg, ed., *Clinical Studies in Infant Mental Health: The First Year of Life.* New York: Basic Books, pp. 1654–1696.
Honig, A. S. 1996. *Behavior Guidance for Infants and Toddlers.* Little Rock, AR: Southern Early Childhood Association.
Honig, A. S., and C. Morin. 2001. "When Should Programs for Teen Parents and Babies Begin? Longitudinal Evaluation of a Teen Parents and Babies Program." *Journal of Primary Prevention* 21(4): 447–454.
Klass, C. S. 1996. *Home Visiting: Promoting Healthy Parent and Child Development.* Baltimore: Paul H. Brookes Publishing.
Lally J. R., P. Mangione, and A. S. Honig. 1988. "The Syracuse University Family Development Research Program: Long-Range Impact of an Early Intervention with Low Income Children and Their Families." In D. Powell, ed., *Parent Education as Early Childhood Intervention: Emerging Directions in Theory, Research, and Practice.* Norwood, NJ: Ablex, pp. 79–104
Levenstein, P. 1989. *Messages from Home: The Mother-Child Home Program and the Prevention of School Disadvantage.* Columbus: Ohio State University Press.

Homeostasis
Coined by physiologist Walter B. Cannon, homeostasis is any process that changes an existing condition that in turn stimulates reactions that attempt to maintain the original condition. Biological homeostats are essential components of the nervous system's regulation of heart rate, body temperature, and blood pressure. Homeostatic mechanisms are important in providing information that we interpret as "being thirsty" so that we maintain water balance. Jean Piaget's concept of equilibration is an analog to homeostasis at a cognitive level, as it reflects the balance of assimilation and accommodation, two key change agents of mental structures.

Homology
In evolutionary theory, *homology* refers to structures that derive from the same ancestral genes. The more closely two species are related, the more likely it is that the species characteristics being compared are homologous. For example, the hormone prolactin plays an important role in offspring care in both birds and mammals. The presence and functional similarity of prolactin in these two classes suggests that it was involved in offspring care as long ago as the days of reptiles.

Hyperbilirubinemia
See Genetic Disorders; Jaundice

Hyperreactivity
See Attention Deficit Disorder

Hypertensive Disorders of Pregnancy
Sometimes called "toxemia of pregnancy," these disorders are classified as pre-eclampsia (if high blood pressure is accompanied by protein in the urine and/or swelling), and eclampsia (if convulsions and/or coma occur from shortly before until shortly after delivery).

Hypertonia
Excessive tone of the skeletal muscles. Subjectively, this means that the infant would provide strong resistance to passive stretching of a muscle. For example, a hypertonic newborn would provide strong resistance to attempts to bend her hand back toward the wrist, or to attempts to flex the legs.

See also Hypotonia

Hypotonia
Diminished tone of the skeletal muscles. Subjectively, this means that the infant would provide little resistance to passive stretching of the muscle. For example, a hypotonic newborn would provide little resistance to bending the hand back toward the wrist, or if pushing the bottom of the foot to flex the leg. In neurological examination, the examiner assesses the newborn's tonus actif (active movement of the muscles) and tonus passif (passive movements). Some newborns can have a degree of weakness and floppiness in the muscles as a result of the birth process and will recover as they regain strength (benign congenital hypotonicity).

See also Hypertonia

I

Identification

Identification means being like a model and adopting the values, attitudes, and beliefs of that model. Identification most commonly is discussed in relation to how boys and girls acquire the behaviors and attitudes expected of them within their cultural context. When cultures are closed and sex-role appropriate behavior is strictly defined, the boundaries between male and female roles are relatively clearly defined. In many cultures today, however, the boundaries defining appropriate behaviors for men and women are dynamic, and traditional views of sex-role appropriate behavior are constantly being challenged. It is less clear that toddlers and preschoolers perceive the world with the same degree of flexibility and equal opportunity. It is almost as if they must first link themselves to some fixed category, and then define the behaviors and activities that fit into their perception of that category. Michael Lewis refers to this as the "emergence of the categorical self" and suggests that it must take place before the more existential self can emerge.

From the psychoanalytic theoretical perspective, a key aspect of identification is that the young child internalizes values and attitudes and the consequences of internalization for behavior. Thus, if the child identifies with positive familial/cul-tural values regarding appropriate social standards of behavior, these serve a regulatory function by promoting a sense of guilt and a desired self referred to as the "ego ideal." If a toddler or preschooler violates a standard and receives admonishment from a loved one, it may elicit a sense of guilt and a violation of the ego ideal. A reinstatement of that relationship would serve to reinforce the internalized value. Identification, therefore, is a process felt to be implicitly linked to the development of prosocial behavior.

Imitation

Imitation involves observing and then copying someone else's behavior. Babies often imitate the actions of adults. For example, when her mother sticks out her tongue, a baby may attempt to mimic it. This is a major challenge to Jean Piaget's theory of cognitive development, because it represents an invisible imitation (a behavior the baby performs but cannot see). Presumably, imitation is not possible unless the individual has the ability to judge similarities and differences between his own behavior and that of the model. According to Piaget, the infant was not capable of imitating novel behaviors until stage 4 of the period of sensorimotor development, although stage 3 infants could imitate familiar behavior. The stage

Imitating the actions of one's older brother. (Courtesy of Hiram E. Fitzgerald)

4 infant also gained the ability to perform invisible imitations.

The work of Andrew Meltzoff and others, however, has demonstrated that even newborn infants are capable of invisible imitations, such as tongue-thrusting, mouth-opening, and finger movements. Because such behaviors have been observed reliably during the newborn period, they occur substantially earlier than Piaget had theorized. Whether the imitations observed by Meltzoff are a component of the newborn's adaptive behavior package that functions to build connections with caregivers is unclear. Moreover, it is not clear what developmental course such early imitations take. What is clear is that the human newborn engages in imitation-like behaviors immediately after birth.

Three-year-olds delight in imitating older children and adults. Preschool teachers take advantage of the three-year-olds' almost inherent interest in rhythm and repetition and use simple verse songs that almost inevitably have accompanying motor movements. When parents begin to act silly and march around the house or say silly things, the three-year-old is the first to join in the merrymaking. Dressing up in older siblings' clothing or stomping around the house in mother's or father's shoes are all examples of the extent to which direct imitations enter into young children's behavior. However, young children also imitate less desirable behaviors, including those of older individuals in their lives and those they observe in such media as television. For example, as early

*A father and son at a baseball game.
(Courtesy of Heather Lewis)*

as the preschool years some children already imitate the drinking behaviors of their alcoholic parents, and some act out aggressive behaviors they observe on television. Although these imitations tend to be most prominent immediately after observing a model, there is some evidence that prolonged exposure leads to the internalization of such model behavior in the form of mental representations, or schemas. So far as imitation is concerned, it is always well to bear in mind that children are watching and listening to their parents and siblings, and they are the first pathway for generation of and internalization of values, attitudes, beliefs, and behavior. Thus, imitation is closely connected to identification and the development of prosocial behavior.

Immunizations

Immunizations are the health care precautions provided children to help protect them from many dangerous contagious childhood diseases. They also protect the community from an outbreak of communicable diseases. Immunizations protect against hepatitis B, polio, measles, mumps, rubella (German measles), pertussis (whooping cough), diphtheria, tetanus (lockjaw), chicken pox, and spinal meningitis. Immunizations can also include screenings for environmental dangers such as lead poisoning. Children are most vulnerable to these diseases between birth and two years. Pediatricians suggest that they receive vaccinations and screenings from their health caregiver before the age of two years. Some of the vaccines also require subsequent follow-ups and booster shots at ages of four to six or eleven to twelve years. If doses are missed at the recommended ages, there are catch-up vaccines available for some of the diseases.

Proof of up-to-date immunizations is required for admittance to school. Licensed child-care facilities also require children to have immunizations before allowing them to attend. Many child-care providers keep records of the child's immunizations to make the parents aware of the need for recommended health care checkups and vaccines. As there may be some health complications that hinder receipt of the vaccine or occur as a side effect after receipt of the vaccine, only licensed health care providers should give immunizations. Vaccines can be provided in the form of

FIGURE 1 Recommended Childhood Immunization Schedule United States, January–December 2001

Vaccines[1] are listed under the routinely recommended ages. Bars indicate range of recommended ages for immunization. Any dose not given at the recommended age should be given as a "catch-up" immunization at any subsequent visit when indicated and feasible. Ovals indicate vaccines to be given if previously recommended doses were missed or given earlier than the recommended minimum age.

Age ▶ Vaccine ▼	Birth	1 mo	2 mos	4 mos	6 mos	12 mos	15 mos	18 mos	24 mos	4–6 yrs	11–12 yrs	14–18 yrs
Hepatitis B[2]	Hep B #1		Hep B #2			Hep B #3					Hep B[2]	
Diphtheria, Tetanus, Pertussis[3]			DTaP	DTaP	DTaP		DTaP[3]			DTaP	Td	
H. influenzae type b[4]			Hib	Hib	Hib	Hib						
Inactivated Polio[5]			IPV	IPV		IPV[5]				IPV[5]		
Pneumococcal Conjugate[6]			PCV	PCV	PCV	PCV						
Measles, Mumps, Rubella[7]						MMR				MMR[7]	MMR[7]	
Varicella[8]						Var					Var[8]	
Hepatitis A[9]										HepA-in selected areas[9]		

Approved by the Advisory Committee on Immunization Practices (ACIP), the American Academy of Pediatrics (AAP), and the American Academy of Family Physicians (AAFP).

1. This schedule indicates the recommended ages for routine administration of currently licensed childhood vaccines, as of 11/1/00, for children through 18 years of age. Additional vaccines may be licensed and recommended during the year. Licensed combination vaccines may be used whenever any components of the combination are indicated and its other components are not contraindicated. Providers should consult the manufacturers' package inserts for detailed recommendations.

2. **Infants born to HBsAg-negative mothers** should receive the 1st dose of hepatitis B (Hep B) vaccine by age 2 months. The 2nd dose should be at least one month after the 1st dose. The 3rd dose should be administered at least 4 months after the 1st dose and at least 2 months after the 2nd dose, but not before 6 months of age for infants.

Infants born to HBsAg-positive mothers should receive hepatitis B vaccine and 0.5 mL hepatitis B immune globulin (HBIG) within 12 hours of birth at separate sites. The 2nd dose is recommended at 1–2 months of age and the 3rd dose at 6 months of age.

Infants born to mothers whose HBsAg status is unknown should receive hepatitis B vaccine within 12 hours of birth. Maternal blood should be drawn at the time of delivery to determine the mother's HBsAg status; if the HBsAg test is positive, the infant should receive HBIG as soon as possible (no later than 1 week of age).

All children and adolescents who have not been immunized against hepatitis B should begin the series during any visit. Special efforts should be made to immunize children who were born in or whose parents were born in areas of the world with moderate or high endemicity of hepatitis B virus infection.

3. The 4th dose of DTaP (diphtheria and tetanus toxoids and acellular pertussis vaccine) may be administered as early as 12 months of age, provided 6 months have elapsed since the 3rd dose and the child is unlikely to return at age 15–18 months. Td (tetanus and diphtheria toxoids) is recommended at 11–12 years of age if at least 5 years have elapsed since the last dose of DTP, DTaP or DT. Subsequent routine Td boosters are recommended every 10 years.

4. Three *Haemophilus influenzae* type b (Hib) conjugate vaccines are licensed for infant use. If PRP-OMP (PedvaxHIB® or ComVax® [Merck]) is administered at 2 and 4 months of age, a dose at 6 months is not required. Because clinical studies in infants have demonstrated that using some combination products may induce a lower immune response to the Hib vaccine component, DTaP/Hib combination products should not be used for primary immunization in infants at 2, 4 or 6 months of age, unless FDA-approved for these ages.

5. An all-IPV schedule is recommended for routine childhood polio vaccination in the United States. All children should receive four doses of IPV at 2 months, 4 months, and 4–6 years of age. Oral polio vaccine (OPV) should be used only in selected circumstances. (See MMWR *Morb Mortal Wkly Rep* May 19, 2000/49(RR-5);1–22).

6. The heptavalent conjugate pneumococcal vaccine (PCV) is recommended for all children 2–23 months of age. It also is recommended for certain children 24–59 months of age. (See MMWR *Morb Mortal Wkly Rep* Oct. 6, 2000/49(RR-9);1–35).

7. The 2nd dose of measles, mumps, and rubella (MMR) vaccine is recommended routinely at 4–6 years of age but may be administered during any visit, provided at least 4 weeks have elapsed since receipt of the 1st dose and that both doses are administered beginning at or after 12 months of age. Those who have not previously received the second dose should complete the schedule by the 11–12 year old visit.

8. Varicella (Var) vaccine is recommended at any visit on or after the first birthday for susceptible children, i.e. those who lack a reliable history of chickenpox (as judged by a health care provider) and who have not been immunized. Susceptible persons 13 years of age or older should receive 2 doses, given at least 4 weeks apart.

9. Hepatitis A (Hep A) is shaded to indicate its recommended use in selected states and/or regions, and for certain high risk groups; consult your local public health authority. (See MMWR *Morb Mortal Wkly Rep* Oct. 1, 1999/48(RR-12); 1–37).

Source: American Academy of Pediatrics, www.aap.org.

shots or oral medications, by either a pediatrician or a licensed health provider.

See also Health and Safety

References and further reading
American Academy of Pediatrics (website 2001). http://www.aap.org.
Every Child by Two (website 2001). http://www.ecbt.org.
Healthy Mothers/Healthy Babies (website 2001). http://www.hmhb.org/Committees/IEAC/ieac.html.

Immunoglobins
See Nutrition

Imprinting
See Theories of Development

In Vitro Fertilization
See Fertilization

Inclusive Programs For Infants
Inclusive programs are designed to serve infants with special needs in natural environments alongside typically developing children. Inclusive programs can include child-care settings and parent-infant playgroups. During the 1970s and 1980s, this arrangement was known as "mainstreaming."

Inclusiveness
Inclusiveness describes the right of children with special needs to be included in environments in which typically developing children are present. The history of inclusion begins in the late 1960s when the Handicapped Children's Early Education Act was passed to promote educational interventions for children with special needs. Programs such as Early Head

Start and Head Start decrease the extent to which children will need special education services later in life. Early Head Start and Head Start are considered inclusive programs because they provide children with special needs and children at risk for special education services opportunities to interact with and to be educated alongside normally developing children. Early intervention services are one part of inclusion, in which the goal is to provide services to children with established medical conditions as well as children at risk for developmental delay and special education services. Another environment where inclusion takes place is in child care, where children with special needs are cared for in a natural environment with typically developing children. Because child care represents a natural environment for many children, it can be seen as one of the best locations in which to provide early intervention.

Early intervention services are designed to prevent further delay and therefore eliminate or reduce the need for special education services for some children. Developmental delays accumulate, that is, small delays in children under the age of three can lead to much greater concerns as the child ages. Thus, early intervention services can play an important role in the development of children with special needs. Children are eligible for early intervention services if they have a diagnosed physical or medical condition that is likely to result in a developmental delay or if they show a delay in physical, social-emotional, language, cognitive, or adaptive areas of development.

Early intervention practices that are included into child-care settings have the possibility of offering preventative services to all children. Including infant/toddlers with special needs into child-care programs that also serve typically developing children allows all children to participate in activities. Much of child care for infant/toddlers surrounds the tasks of daily living. An inclusive child-care setting allows children with disabilities to be incorporated into all activities such as eating and group play.

The idea of inclusion for infant/toddlers is relatively new. Passed in 1968, the Handicapped Children's Early Education Act advocated for the development of interventions within educational programs for children with disabilities. Seven years later, the Education for All Handicapped Children's Act was passed, requiring schools to provide an education to handicapped students that was free to families and appropriate for all children. In 1986, states were given funds to develop extensive early intervention systems (Part H of the Education for All Handicapped Children's Act) for infant/toddlers and were obligated to provide intervention services to all children aged three to five with disabilities if they were to receive federal preschool funds under the Education of the Handicapped Act Amendments. This amendment is now included in the Individuals with Disabilities Education Act Amendments of 1991.

The Part H amendments produced many important changes in the way that early intervention services were delivered to infants, toddlers, and their families. These changes included the role of the family; the requirement of coordinated services; and a person to assist the family in acquiring needed services. Under the new law families are seen as experts in knowing the needs of their children. Because of this belief, parents are involved as members of the intervention team. Children with special needs can work with a variety of professionals.

Some of the services offered to families include physical therapy, occupational therapy speech and language services, mental health services, nursing care, and respite care. Part H requires that the service providers for each family come together and discuss their roles and how they will help the family meet the goals that have been set for their child; this the Individualized Education Plan. In addition, Part H requires that the family designate a person who is responsible for assisting the family in acquiring all needed services; this person is the family service coordinator.

See also Inclusive Programs for Infants; Individuals with Disabilities Education Act

References and further reading
O'Brien, Marion. 1997. *Inclusive Child Care for Infants and Toddlers.* Baltimore, MD: Paul H. Brookes Publishing.

Individuals with Disabilities Education Act

One of the most comprehensive legislative acts serving people with special needs, the Individuals with Disabilities Education Act (IDEA) ensures that children with disabilities birth to age twenty-one have the appropriate educational elements necessary for "equality of opportunity, full participation, independent living, and economic self-sufficiency." Amended a total of five times since its inception in 1975, IDEA has made significant changes in the lives of children with special needs in a variety of settings and services. Although a strong civil rights statute, IDEA differs from other legislation concerning disabilities in that its main premise is in the improvement of the educational results for children. The Americans with Disabilities Act and the Rehabilitation Act of 1973 (specifically Section 504) are particularly designed to ensure that the educational, service, and employment rights of all individuals with disabilities, regardless of age, are upheld by institutions in the United States. School districts serving children three to twenty-one and agencies serving infant/toddlers are obligated under IDEA to provide children who may have special needs requiring adaptations and modifications for learning a free and appropriate education, regardless of the assistance needed.

In 1986, IDEA was amended to include mandated special education services for three- to five-year-old children. These amendments paved the way for a more in-depth collaborative effort between school districts and local agencies serving young children in each state and community. The 1997 amendment to IDEA provided even more impetus to the continued collaboration between differing community agencies, in that the requirements for serving infant/toddlers with disabilities were further defined.

The impact of this law is tremendous, in that it has provided funding for, and allowed for, the inclusion of children with disabilities in the general school setting in one way or another. Children with special needs now have opportunities for increased socialization, inclusive involvement in classrooms and community events, as well as further participation in sports and other extracurricular activities.

IDEA is divided into several subparts, including Part B and Part C. Part B organizes the legislation regarding the special education funding and services for children ages three to twenty-one. Part C serves the purpose of coordinating the early intervention funding and mandates, or requirements, for very young children (birth to three). It is designed with individual states in mind, in that each state is given discretion to design and implement a specific state plan to best serve infant/toddlers, including the eligibility criteria that infant/toddlers must meet to be served utilizing Part C funds. Parts B and C differ in many respects but are equally important parts of the framework that makes up IDEA.

The law is made up of six guiding principles that enable a school or other agency to design and provide educational services to students with disabilities. The first principle, a *free appropriate public education*, requires that local school districts provide an education that meets the standards of the state education agency, conforms with the individualized plan for a specific child, and includes those students who may have been suspended or expelled. All of this is to be done in the context of a second principle, the *least restrictive environment*, determined by the plan set for a specific child. This means that the environment for learning for a particular child can be different from another child. Regardless of the environment, the education is to be provided within the scope of the general curriculum chosen by the school district.

The third important principle *individualized education program* (for children three to twenty-one) and *individualized family service plan* (IFSP, for children birth to three). IDEA requires that an IFSP be written for each infant/toddler with a diagnosed disability or one at risk for developing delays due to health or emotional issues. This plan is to be a strength-based, comprehensive document with individual and family goals and objectives developed by a team of caregivers, teachers, related experts, and parents. This document should include a current level of performance, long- and short-term goals, and activities and strategies to meet those goals. It is to be reviewed at least annually and should be fluid enough that the document can be modified if necessary to better serve the child and family.

The next guiding principle is *parent involvement*, which defines "parents" and provides safeguards for the inclusion and full participation of the family. A "parent" is defined as a legal guardian but allows for a specified surrogate parent assigned to the child, if necessary. Parents are to be involved on several levels, according to the law. At the state level, they are to be represented on the State Interagency Coordinating Council, an advisory board made up of representatives from state agencies, the state legislature, program directors, personnel training programs, and, of course, parents of children with disabilities. At the local level, parents are to be involved in decisionmaking policies and curriculum choice. IDEA ensures that parents are seen and utilized as partners in their child's educational experience. Being a part of the decisionmaking procedures in their community agencies helps parents feel like an equal partner. Parents are also to be part of the development of their child's IFSP, including all stages and evaluative reviews of that document.

The final two principles are *procedural safeguards* and *appropriate evaluation*. Procedural safeguards were designed within the context of the law to protect the rights of parents and their children with disabilities. Appropriate evaluation includes those performance goals and indicators set by the state and local levels for children with disabilities. This principle ensures that parents are involved in both levels of decisions made in the context of ongoing evaluation of the child with special needs.

IDEA is a comprehensive law that allows for and encourages partnering between state and local agencies and schools to better serve children and families. One of the most enduring partnerships on the national, state, and local levels is that between agencies funded to serve children with disabilities under IDEA (e.g., school districts, early intervention providers) and Head Start. Part C, framing the early intervention services for infant/toddlers and their families, enjoys a compelling collaborative relationship with the Head Start community to best serve those young children with disabilities in an inclusive setting. *Inclusion* is a concept that allows for the full participation of individuals with disabilities in a variety of settings, including child care, family day care, Early Head Start centers, early intervention programs, school districts, and a host of other community agencies serving babies and their families. The impact of collaboration among these community agencies is remarkable in that it allows for the enrollment and participation of many more children in these different settings and programs, with a variety of providers.

Early Head Start, the federal child development program serving pregnant women and families with infant/toddlers, was established in 1994 with the reauthorization of the Head Start Act. Early Head Start is designed to provide early, continuous, intensive, and comprehensive child-development and support services to low-income families with children under three years of age. Early Head Start programs must ensure that at least 10 percent of the infant/toddlers served by the grant are individuals with disabilities. The definition of "infants and toddlers with disabilities," as it applies to an individual Early Head Start Program, is consistent with the definition for infant/toddlers of Part C of IDEA, which has been adopted by the state in which the Early Head Start Program is delivered.

Head Start and Early Head Start are administered by the Administration for Children and Families within the U.S. Department of Health and Human Services. Fiscal grants are awarded by the ten Health and Human Services Regional Offices and by the Head Start Bureau's American Indian Program and Migrant Program Branches to community public and private nonprofit organizations and agencies for the purpose of operating Head Start programs at the community level. Programs serve both rural and urban areas in all fifty states, the District of Columbia, Pacific Insular Areas, and the Trust Territories.

Now clearly recognized as the most successful of the War on Poverty programs, Head Start is a comprehensive early childhood program; its overall goal is to support the social competence of children. "Social competence" means everyday effectiveness in dealing with both the present environment and later responsibilities in school and life. At the time of its inception, Head Start's inclusion of children with disabilities was a unique notion and did much to lead the way for very young children to be included in preschool education.

To be eligible for Head Start or Early Head Start, a child or pregnant woman must be living in a family whose income is below the federal poverty line, although policies allow 10 percent of children enrolled to come from better-off families. Head Start and Early Head Start services are offered via a variety of locations and models. Settings for services include classrooms, family homes, and child-care settings, important options for all families, especially those rearing children with disabilities or developmental delays.

Head Start and Early Head Start Programs are guided by a set of rules, or *program performance standards,* and other policies that require the delivery of services to ensure comprehensive care including health, education, parent involvement, social services, and disability services. Although the provision of these services is required of a local community operating a Head Start or Early Head Start program, parents are seen, as in IDEA, as the principle influence on their child's development and are expected to be direct participants and decisionmakers in the program.

Collaboration between differing agencies in a community serving children and families is made possible by the development and implementation of *interagency agreements.* IDEA and the Head Start program performance standards require that state and local agencies form written agreements to ensure ongoing cooperation and coordination of services for children with disabilities. Although barriers can obstruct the process of developing interagency agreements, such as turfism, agency rigidity, fear of fiscal responsibility, and lack of understanding of involved agencies and of the process itself, there are breakthroughs being made at every level. State interagency agreements can provide a framework for local agreements and the coordination of services. A majority of states report the development of these state agreements, thereby paving the way for the advancement of local agreements between agencies, including early intervention and Head Start/Early Head Start.

The importance of local interagency agreements cannot be undermined in that they can form a framework to design and implement effective services for children with disabilities in any agency. An agreement serves to: clarify staff roles and responsibilities; establish procedures for resolving disputes between agencies; identify those with financial responsibility; provide resource-sharing; offer a means for joint staff support and development; provide a mechanism for recruitment and enrollment activities between agencies; develop effective screening and assessment procedures for the ongoing evaluation of children with disabilities; allow for the development of the IFSP for the young child with special needs; and provide strategies for transition into the next service that the child's development requires.

IDEA and the Head Start community have helped to guide and promote the efforts between agencies for several years, providing children with disabilities the support and assistance necessary for their continued growth and development. Staff is also supported in this effort, as they are given additional opportunities for training and professional development through the ongoing partnership between states, local agencies, and families in meeting the needs of infant/toddlers with disabilities or developmental delays.

See also Atypical Infant; Early Intervention

References and further reading

ADD Warehouse (website 2001). http://www.addwarehouse.com.
American Speech-Language-Hearing Association Helpline (website 2001). http://www.asha.org/.
Americans with Disabilities Act (website 2001). http://www.adainfo.org.
Coordinated Campaign for Learning Disabilities (website 2001). http://www.ldonline.org.
Council for Exceptional Children (website 2001). http://www.cec.sped.org.
National Center for Learning Disabilities (website 2001). http://www.ncld.org.
National Early Childhood Technical Assistance System (website 2001). http://www.nectas.unc.edu.
National Information Center for Children and Youth with Handicaps (website 2001). http://www.nichcy.org.
Through the Looking Glass (website 2001). http://www.lookingglass.org.

Infancy and Infant Care: Historical Overview

During the long history of human evolution, child care has primarily been the responsibility of families. Yet the farther back one goes in history, the more likely children were to be physically and sexually abused, terrorized, and abandoned. Child sacrifice was a common practice among some ancient civilizations. In ancient Rome, male babies from poor families were sometimes castrated in order to provide young boys for the brothels of Rome. An ancient Egyptian tablet fragment reports that an abandoned infant plucked from the town refuse heap, where such infants were routinely left, had been given to the care of a wet nurse. By the early fifteenth century, in an effort to curb infanticide, large cities in Europe established foundling homes to care for abandoned children.

Considering the huge task of providing good health care, it is perhaps understandable that the mortality rate was high. By the eighteenth century, one in every three or four infants in some European cities was a foundling. In some foundling hospitals, because of unhygienic practices and lack of personal caregiving, only 13 percent of the children lived until the age of six. Abandonment was not the only method by which families escaped obligation to care for infants themselves. Rich families traditionally made use of wet nurses and nannies to rear their children.

Cultural beliefs and values over the ages have shaped the rearing decisions of caregivers. In ancient Greece and Rome a father had absolute rights of life and death over his family. Thus, on a father's order, an infant could be exposed in open country to be torn apart by wild beasts. In some cultures, infants were abruptly sent away from parents very early in life. In ancient societies it was often the custom to send a high-born young male child to be reared and educated at the court of a royal person in alliance with one's own kingdom. Thus, Greek boys whose education may have begun under the tutelage of an educated slave might be sent at very young ages to live among strangers. In the New World, centuries before the Spanish conquest, kings of Mesoamerica sent their young sons to be educated at the royal court at Xochicalco.

Child Care Ideology
Across the centuries, families and cultures differed greatly in the value placed on infants. The essayist, Montaigne, wrote casually that the death of two or three of his children in infancy had not been a great loss. Conceptualization about the importance of early enrichment for infants and young children has also varied markedly. Over the centuries, theories of the importance of education for the young child have been particularly linked with varied philosophical movements, cultural biases, social-class status, demands of rapid industrialization, and religious affiliation.

Religious concepts of childhood sometimes revealed a lack of understanding of infant and toddler needs that is difficult to understand from today's perspective. In the early history of the United States, Puritan religious beliefs shaped the early conceptualization of the infant and child as inherently evil. From such philosophical views flowed rigorous childrearing methods that we today would label child abuse. Despite the beliefs in severe child management techniques even with infants and toddlers, there was also a strong belief that parents were religiously obligated to provide moral education. The belief that infants and young children were inherently evil was not challenged until John Locke, an English philosopher, suggested that infants were not born as sinful but rather as "blank slates" or "tabula rasa." Until this time, hard work and hard discipline were thought to be in the best interest of the child, as was an early approach to education. Wealthy children as young as age three were sometimes expected to learn to read. Apprenticeships in a particular craft or trade began early, sometimes as early as age five. Until that time, infants, toddlers, and young children were typically cared for in their homes. In some cases in which families could not afford to care for young children, local churches sponsored parish apprenticeships as a way to care for orphans or poor children. Historical records show that children, some as young as one year old, were sent to parishes for care. This type of care foreshadowed the later emergence of orphanages in the United States. In other cases, a poor mother might offer livestock or possessions to another family as payment to care for her child until she could allocate the necessary resources to care for the child herself. This arrangement was an early form of foster care. Schools also played a role in caring for infants and toddlers. During the colonial period, it was fairly common for toddlers to accompany siblings to schools and play and sleep in the corner of the room.

Just as Locke's writings in the seventeenth century foreshadowed more modern views of infants and toddlers, the work of Jean-Jacques Rousseau, a French philosopher of the Enlightenment period in the 1700s, also emphasized more respect and consideration for infants. Unlike Locke, Rousseau believed that infants were born not as blank slates but as individuals with some sense of innate morality and an ingrown plan for healthy development. Rousseau was one of the first philosophers or scientists to suggest that there are distinct periods of human growth: infancy, childhood, late childhood, and adolescence. Despite emerging thought that infants and toddlers and young children might require specialized care, different from older children and adults, many children were put to work as soon as they were able.

New ideas about young children were promoted in the United States in the early 1800s. Men and women like Bronson Alcott, Emerson, Henry David Thoreau, Elizabeth Peabody, and Margaret Fuller, leading scholars of the time, admired the child, or, rather, their image of the child, because it exhibited none of the greedy materialism or spineless conformity that characterized its elders. The secret of education was, therefore to protect the innocent child from corruption and allow its innate divinity to unfold.

Condescension toward childhood, so characteristic of Enlightenment thought, now gave way under the Romantic impulse, to reverence. During this period, children were sent off to the "common" schools, where discipline was strict and rigid. From the 1850s onward such schools were no longer considered

suitable for children of tender years. Many communities therefore began to exclude children under five years from school. However, one pioneer, Robert Owen, an English cotton mill industrialist, had been influenced by the Swiss educator Pestalozzi. Owen envisioned the transformation of society by proper child care practices, even for infants. He opened his "Institution Established for the Formation of Character" which specifically included infants from one year old. Owen wrote that:

> the children were trained and educated without punishment or any fear of it, and were while in school by far the happiest human beings I have ever seen. The infants and young children, besides being instructed by sensible signs—the things themselves or models or paintings—and by familiar conversation, were from two years and upwards daily taught dancing and singing.

The ideas of Froebel, a German educator (1782–1852), were centered on creating a loving community of persons in a cooperative rather than competitive classroom. He reasoned that positive social values would flow from the "plays" of childhood. He was the first to introduce humanistic ideas of early childhood education and the cultivation of tender dispositions in young children.

From the early- to mid-1800s, utopian visions provided a powerful impetus for new modes of child care and education. The goals of the reformers were much like the goals of early education today. This movement was short-lived; given the social mores of the times, funding for these innovative reforms was not forthcoming. By the mid-1800s a so-called

cult of domesticity arose, which emphasized the crucial role of mothers in influencing the moral and religious upbringing of their children. Mothers were to
provide good models for children and
establish bonds of trust and love. Rather
than physical punishment, withdrawal of
affection was to be used. Mothers in poor
families often had no access to these new
ideas about the importance of enlight-
ened maternal involvement.

The 1900s
During the 1900s, new philosophical
ideas supported the importance of early
education and care for infants, toddlers,
and young children and the seamless
interdependence of both domains in supporting the optimal development of very
young children. Ideals about early education and care, however, were complicated
by societal forces, such as the surge of
immigrants into the United States in the
1800s and early 1900s. The sheer number
of immigrants moving into the country
was staggering. Between 1880 and World
War I, 17 million immigrants came to the
United States, mostly moving into cities
like New York and Chicago. Families
with very young children had few options
for child care. Often cut off from extended
family members, mothers had no one to
care for young children, and so children
often worked alongside their mothers as
soon as they could. Older siblings took on
much responsibility for child care of
infants and toddlers. As one expert noted,
older girls living in city tenements "didn't
have dolls; they had the real thing." Families of the same ethnic origin often lived
in neighborhoods and communities
together, thus forming a type of extended
family with some available support for
child care. One of the first organized
efforts to provide child care occurred in

Chicago in the late 1800s when Jane
Addams founded the Hull-House. One of
the first "day nurseries," the Hull-House
offered care for infants as young as two
weeks old while mothers worked. Meals
were offered to children, health screenings were conducted, and early parenting
education information was even available. Shortly after Hull-House, similar
programs were founded in other cities,
such as New York and Boston. In many
ways, these day nurseries were seen as
alternatives to institutionalization of
infants and toddlers and were viewed as a
positive way to keep families with very
limited resources together.

In the United States, public nursery
schools began in 1919. Parents in Cambridge, Massachusetts, formed the first
documented parent cooperative nursery
in 1923. In England in 1929, Susan Isaacs
advanced public understanding about the
distinctive educational needs of young
children. In the 1960s in England, Lady
Plowden proposed British Infants schools
with an emphasis on meeting young children's developmental needs, primarily in
setting up educational environments. In
Italy early in the 1900s Maria Montessori
created special school environments to
meet the needs of poor children in Italy.
Montessori programs emphasized the
importance of sequenced and orderly use
of materials and stressed how crucial sensitive teacher observations were to
teacher success in setting up excellent
classroom learning situations. Toward
the end of the 1900s, the Reggio Emelia
schools in Italy provided a further model
for excellence in meeting the developmental needs of very young children
through carefully nurtured projects and
activities.

The flowering of model child-care programs early in the twentieth century

received impetus from child-development research at the Minnesota Institute
of Child Welfare, the Gesell Child Guidance Nursery at Yale (about 1920), the
Merrill-Palmer Institute in Detroit
(1920), Bank Street College (1919), and
the Iowa Child Welfare Research Station.
These important centers operated model
early child-care programs. Researchers
felt that their findings could be helpful
for parents, and in turn parents were willing to have their children studied or
observed. In 1923, the Laura Spelman
Rockefeller Memorial Foundation also
began support of child study and parent
education.

Innovative child-care programming also
grew from the theoretical ideas of Sigmund Freud and neopsychoanalysts, such
as Erikson, and of pediatricians, such as
Spock and Brazelton, that children need to
grow more in accordance with their own
developmental timetables and styles.
Such freedom, according to the psychoan-
alysts, would free libidinal energy for
work and positive family functioning
rather than using repressive measures that
would increase neuroses. Even Arnold
Gesell, a pediatrician who emphasized the
primacy of maturational over education
factors in infancy, wrote that the preschool period was the most important for
an individual and that it influenced all
subsequent development. By 1949, the
Committee on Mental Hygiene in the
American Academy of Pediatrics became
a Section of Mental Health, and, in 1960,
a Section on Child Development.

A naturalistic study by psychoanalyst
René Spitz in the early 1940s revealed
the power of tender loving care, or lack
thereof, to affect intellectual outcomes
for infants. And long-term research following infants in families over many
years led to expanded real-world knowledge about early development. Political
events during World War II also spurred
new efforts to provide early group care of
high quality for infants and young children. During World War II, the need for
women's employment grew urgent. Inadequate care and latchkey children fueled
passage in 1942 of the Lanham Act, providing funding for child-care centers. The
Lanham Act day-care centers marked the
beginning of a national policy shift to the
idea of governmental and societal responsibility for child care.

The twentieth century also witnessed
a vigorous proliferation in the variety of
nonfamilial child care modes: infant and
toddler play groups; child-care centers;
family day care; home visitation programs; university-based early education
programs for infants; and the Early Head
Start national program. The earliest federally supported child care programs in
the United States were nurseries established under President Franklin D. Roosevelt by the Federal Emergency Relief
Administration and Works Progress
Administration. They were justified as a
source of jobs for unemployed teachers
during the Great Depression and for reasons much like those that would be
offered thirty years later for founding the
Head Start program: Excellent early
childhood programs would improve educational outcomes and thus enhance life
opportunities for educationally disadvantaged children.

New child-care initiatives arose in the
1960s. These included Head Start for
preschoolers from poor families. Head
Start was founded in 1965 under the Economic Opportunity Act, Title VII of the
1965 Housing and Urban Development
Act, and the 1965 Model Cities Act. In

the 1970s, the middle class was given tax credits and deductions for childcare as a business expense. Federal support for Early Head Start services for infants and toddlers (birth to three years) was not initiated until the 1990s.

Under President Lyndon B. Johnson, funding was provided for a remarkable array of research/demonstration programs that established high-quality infant/toddler care as their main goal. Exemplary theory-based, research-informed childcare models and programs to enhance cognitive and positive social skills of young children were set in place by state agencies and unions. These early programs documented more optimal cognitive and socioemotional infant/toddler functioning.

During President Ronald Reagan's administration, drastic cuts in federal funding for child care were made. In 1990, President George Bush signed Public Law 101–508, the Federal Child Care Bill, which provided $2.5 billion of new federal child care, block grant funds, provisions to protect children in child care, money to help low-income families purchase child care, and tax relief for low-income working families purchasing child care. Under President Bill Clinton, more funds were earmarked for improving the quality and quantity of early care.

The quality of child care depends crucially on caregivers, their level of training, their stability of employment in a facility, the number of children assigned per adult, and the number of infants in a group. In the United States, ratios vary widely. Many states require little or no preparation for employment, and the boundaries are blurred for describing child-care personnel as teacher, nurturer, caregiver, nanny, nursery nurse, or educarer.

The history of child care in the last century reveals strong differences in beliefs about the appropriateness of governmental supports for ensuring quality group care or highly trained home visitation specialists who can promote positive parenting skills with infants and young children.

What will the history of infant care look like a century from now? Clinicians and researchers have learned a great deal about the developmental needs of infants and how to implement them in care by families or by others outside the home. Hopefully, this knowledge can be communicated to citizens with sufficient passion and conviction so that citizens will be galvanized to press their governmental representatives for adequate funding to provide an optimal rearing environment for every infant and young child, regardless of whether the infant is reared entirely at home or by loving and trained nonparental caregivers.

See also Caregiving; History of Infant Care; Infancy in Historical Context

References and further reading
Aries, P. 1962. *Centuries of Childhood: A Social History of Family Life.* New York: Random House.
Boswell, J. 1989. *The Kindness of Strangers: The Abandonment of Children in Western Europe from Late Antiquity to the Renaissance.* New York: Pantheon Books.
Caldwell, B. M., et al. 1970. "Infant Care and Attachment." *American Journal of Orthopsychiatry* 40: 397–412.
Cleverley, J., and D. C. Phillips. 1986. *Visions of Childhood: Influential Models from Locke to Spock.* New York: Teachers College Press.
De Mause, L. 1974. *The History of Childhood.* New York: Psychohistory Press.
Dewey, J. 1916. *Democracy and Education.* New York: McMillan.
Gesell, A. 1923. *The Preschool Child: From the Standpoint of Public Hygiene*

and Education. Boston: Houghton-Mifflin.

Greven, P. J., Jr. 1973. *Child-rearing Concepts, 1628–1861: Historical Sources.* Itasca, IL: F. E. Peacock.

Honig, A. S. 1979. *Parent Involvement in Early Childhood Education.* 2nd Ed. Washington, DC: National Association for the Education of Young Children.

———. 1990. "Infant/Toddler Education Issues: Practices, Problems, and Promises." In C. Seefeldt, ed., *Continuing Issues in Early Childhood Education.* Columbus, OH: Merrill, pp. 61–105.

———. 1992. "Historical Overview of Child Care." In B. Spodek and O. Saracho, eds., *Yearbook in Early Childhood Education,* Vol. 3. New York: Garland Press, pp. 9–30.

Kessen, W. 1965. *The Child.* New York: Wiley.

Lally, J. R., et al. 1988. "The Syracuse University Family Development Research Program: Long-Range Impact of an Early Intervention with Low Income Children and Their Families." In D. Powell, ed., *Parent Education as Early Childhood Intervention: Emerging Directions in Theory, Research, and Practice.* Norwood, NJ: Ablex Publishers, pp. 79–104.

McGraw, M. 1935. *Growth: A Study of Johnny and Jimmy.* New York: D. Appleton–Century.

Osborn, K. 1991. *Early Childhood Education in Historical Perspective.* Athens, GA: Daye Press.

Owen, R. 1971. *Life of Robert Owen, 1857–58.* Rpt. ed. London: Charles Knight.

Pence, A. R. 1980. *Preschool Programs of the Nineteenth Century: Towards a History of Preschool Child Care in America.* Unpublished doctoral dissertation, University of Oregon, Eugene.

Sears, R. 1975. *Your Ancients Revisited: A History of Child Development.* Chicago: University of Chicago Press.

Strickland, C. E. 1982. "Paths Not Taken: Seminal Models of Early Childhood Education in Jacksonian America." In B. Spodek, ed., *Handbook of Research Methods in Early Childhood Education.* New York: Free Press, pp. 321–340.

Infancy in Historical Context: The Early Twentieth Century

Caring for Babies and Young Children

For many years, *Ladies Home Journal* featured an advice column written by a physician from The Babies Hospital of New York. In 1910, Dr. Emelyn Lincoln Coolidge added an additional resource for the young mothers who read her column. Dr. Coolidge had noted the overwhelming helplessness that many mothers faced when the support provided during the newborn period was withdrawn. To help women feeling this isolation she began the Young Mother's Registry. As soon as they had given birth, mothers could add their baby to the registry at *Ladies Home Journal.* A form was then mailed to the mother, who submitted information about her baby. Dr. Coolidge sent specific advice regarding baby care and nursery hygiene based on the report of the mother. Each month the mother was required to update the information on her baby: weight gain, digestion, general health, and sleep patterns. Mothers were to note anything that seemed out of the ordinary and were instructed to ask about the details of infant care that concerned them. Frequent contact was permitted, but monthly contact was required to remain in the registry. It was hoped that this would be of benefit to many mothers, especially those in rural areas who did not have access to up-to-date infant-care information. Frequently asked questions were published each month in *Ladies Home Journal.* In every issue, Dr. Coolidge also provided Golden Rules for the Nursery. The following rules were among those listed throughout the 1910 issues of the magazine.

Maintain a Healthy Environment
* From the first day of the baby's life be regular in everything you do for him.
* Give the baby a tub bath every morning; the temperature should be 98 to 100 degrees Fahrenheit.
* Give the baby a sponge bath every day between 5 and 6 P.M., and put on fresh night clothing.
* Have plenty of fresh air in the nursery but keep the baby out of drafts.
* Keep the temperature of the nursery in the daytime at 68 degrees Fahrenheit. At night it may fall as low as 50 degrees.
* Take the baby outdoors at the age of four weeks in winter and two or three weeks in summer.
* Train the baby from his first day to go to sleep by himself without rocking, walking, patting, singing, or having a bright light in the room.
* Do not give the baby a quantity of toys: one at a time will be more enjoyed.

The Importance of Good Hygiene and Health Practices
* Be very careful to wash your hands after changing the baby.
* Do not allow people to kiss the baby, especially on the mouth.
* Keep the food on ice till feeding-time, then warm it and give it immediately.
* If any food is left in the bottle, throw it away.
* Never allow a baby to have water from cars or parks. When going away from home take enough pure water in a corked bottle for his use.
* Never give sugar-water to a baby; it often causes colic. Teach the baby to take unsweetened water instead.

Many of the concerns of 1910 are still being raised by today's mothers.

Nutrition and Health
Dr. Coolidge also provided her readers with detailed instructions regarding feeding an infant. Mothers would do well to heed much of her advice today, although some of it is obviously outdated. The overall message is to achieve a balanced diet for the mother and to following good breastfeeding and bottle-feeding practice for the infant.

Because dental decay during the early years of life was a worldwide concern in the late 1800s and the early 1900s, she provide advice here as well. The general message? "You can't begin too early." Today, the American Academy of Pediatric Dentistry recommends a dental check up every six months in order to clean the teeth and assess dental health. Throughout the early years of childhood the pediatric dentist looks to see if there is crowding in the mouth, if teeth are coming in crooked, or if the child has a bite problem. Early orthodontics are encouraged if there is malocclusion, as straight teeth are easier to care for, thus reducing the amount of tooth decay.

Expecting a Baby: Explaining the Facts of Life to Siblings
As a mother, physician, and author, Mary Wood-Allen (1841–1908) had a powerful impact on U.S. attitudes toward reproductive health. Her book *What a Young Woman Ought to Know* provided women with technical information regarding menstruation. Her book also stressed freedom from restrictions that were often placed on women. Shortly after Dr. Wood-Allen's death, her daughter, Rose Wood-Allen Chapman, continued the efforts

Advertisements encouraged mothers to select rubber nipples carefully. The "Near Nature Nipples" were marketed as being able to prevent colic as well as being easy for mothers to clean. The Hygeia Nursing Bottle Company reported that it had constructed a rubber nipple that was "Just Like Mother."

For Baby's Sake Send 5 cents (Ladies Home Journal)

Just Like Mother. (Ladies Home Journal)

That's Why Baby Likes the Hygeia Nursing Bottle

The rubber part is so like the human breast in size and shape that in weaning or when natural supply is low, baby will go from breast to the Hygeia bottle without noticing the difference. The Hygeia is without a neck or angle; needs no funnel to fill, nor brush to clean the interior which is wiped out like a tumbler. The rubber breast is yielding, yet not collapsible; seamless can be turned inside out to clean thoroughly. It has no crack or crevice where dirt can gather or germs can propagate. The Hygeia is used and endorsed by every children's hospital in the country, because it fills every requirement of a perfect, ideal sanitary nursing bottle. If your druggist don't keep the Hygeia, send us his name and 38c. and we will mail you a bottle at once.

Breast for Baby

Cell for Food

HYGEIA NURSING BOTTLE CO., Dept. P, Buffalo, N. Y.

begun by her mother and wrote a series of columns for the readers of *Ladies Home Journal* ("How Shall I Tell My Child?: A Little Monthly Talk as Mother with Mother"). It reflected insights from her experiences as a child raised under a counterculture approach to this topic and from her experience as a mother using this approach with her own children. Readers' questions were answered in the magazine or by letter.

How should a mother respond to a curious child about the birth of a sibling? Many readers had to be convinced that informing the child of the details of reproduction was necessary. Why should a child be told any of this information at all? Mothers would rely on their own childhood experiences and wonder why a child couldn't be kept in ignorance regarding human reproduction. After all, it had worked well for their parents!

If a mother doesn't tell a child, who will? As the intellect unfolds, children's curiosity leads them to new questions and to an understanding of more complex explanations. Even when mothers agreed that children should be told accurate information there were sometimes obstacles. Under optimal conditions, the details of reproduction begin as soon as children show interest and curiosity in the topic. Although many women dreaded explaining the father's role in reproduction, it was the mother's duty unless the father undertook the explanations. Mothers needed to instruct children from the child's earliest years through all the transitions of adolescence. Many women were quite hesitant to initiate conversations that might go beyond their own expertise.

Gender Roles in American Families

It is surprising for many contemporary Americans to learn that the issue of gender roles in family life has been publicly debated for more than 100 years. The nineteenth-century father often is perceived as a stern authoritarian whose main parenting role was to dole out discipline at the end of the day. Indeed, many tin-type photographs of these fathers present the image of an unsmiling man standing ramrod straight over his children. Often we forget that the family was told by early photographers to assume facial expressions that they would be able to maintain for the minutes required for film exposure. Family members who were standing were braced by metal rods to prevent swaying. Facial expressions and body language that were due to the procedures of early photography are sometimes interpreted as the intentional postures of an unbending cohort. Although many Americans maintained a preference for traditional gender roles, others suggested that a father had to go beyond being a breadwinner to be a successful parent.

At the turn of the last century, society was adjusting to the numbers of women who were completing higher educations and becoming influential in their fields. For example, the American Psychological Association elected Mary Whiton Calkins as its president in 1905. In 1908 the president of Harvard University used the term "exceptional women" to describe women who had entered the traditional world of men. But women were accomplishing more than participation in the labor force. They were gaining equality in social policies, the right to vote being the most obvious example. More important, they were gaining a semblance of independence in their romantic relations.

The turn-of-the-century writer Barnetta Brown advocated a more active paternal role:

The home built and furnished, the family clothed and fed,—is there not more to fatherhood than this? What a bleak, dreary sordid fatherhood it is that sees but little beyond finances, that even sometimes say, "I have given them a comfortable home. They have everything money can buy." No such fatherhood can be truly successful and satisfactory. The heights of fatherhood lie beyond the material and necessary as the material part is, and great as is the privilege to perform it for those he loves, a still greater privilege awaits the father who can make this part merely the background of his fatherhood.

Family Structure and Concerns Regarding Divorce

Theodore Roosevelt was troubled by the divorce rate in the United States during his presidency. He believed that the ease of the divorce process was creating a menace to the lives of children in the United States. For example, adultery was the only reason a divorce could be granted in the state of New York. Because adultery was difficult to prove, and socially undesirable when proven, residents of New York tended to prefer a quieter divorce in a state with few rigorous requirements. Nevada was a popular choice because, with only six months residence in the state, a plaintiff in Nevada could easily end a marriage with a New York spouse.

We can identify three different perspectives regarding divorce in the American family: the Catholic Church view that even if the state were to grant a divorce the individuals would remain married in the eyes of God and the Church until one spouse died; the Protestant view that divorce is a necessary evil if a spouse would be deprived of a life of marital happiness due to the wickedness of the marriage partner; and the new science of sociology view that anyone in an irksome marriage has the right to a quick and easy divorce since all citizens have the right to experience as much earthly happiness as possible. The second perspective gained favor, and the circumstances under which divorce would be granted were: adultery, bigamy, extreme cruelty, intentional desertion of spouse and family for over two years, habitual abuse of alcohol for over two years, and conviction of a major crime.

Societal reactions ranged from one end of the continuum—that the very foundation for the American family was crumbling—to the other end—that divorce was not easy enough. For example, turn-of-the-century feminists noted that women should not be forced to continue having the babies of indifferent husbands simply because the men desired physical satisfaction. Continuing in marriages of this nature surely would erode the foundation of families, as mothers, in emotional isolation and without support, struggled to care for children.

Life Expectancy and Raising of Children

When babies were born in the year 1900 the life expectancy in the United States was in the late forties for women and the midforties for men. This didn't mean that when they reached their thirties individuals usually had only another decade to live. Because life expectancy is a statistical definition it is sometimes misinterpreted. A life expectancy of forty-eight would mean that of all the female babies born in 1900, half of that group would have died by that age. Many of the deaths within the 1900 cohort occurred during infancy and childhood. The number of early fatalities was a serious concern to the nation.

Charles Eliot, president of Harvard University in the early 1900s, wrote that women who have four to six children have an advanced intellectual life when compared to the mothers of one or two children. He noted that in larger families it was inevitable that there would be diverse dispositions that would make life more interesting and intellectually challenging for the "trainer" (usually the mother). It is difficult to imagine the perspective that large families were encouraged in order to ensure that at least one or two children reached adulthood. When parents today have children it is with the expectation that the parents will attend the high school graduations of every one of their children. Death is thought of as early, not only if the child were to die, but if either of the parents died before the children were old enough to leave home. Looking back a century, what concerns were evident as seen in the advice and recommendations given to parents longing to keep their children safe and healthy?

Childhood Diseases

Parents throughout time have worried about the exposure of their children to disease. Childhood diseases often were spread through ignorance and carelessness. Parents sometimes had to care for their sick children using home remedies and the advice of neighbors. But changes in communication, as well as advances in the field of medicine, required a different approach. In 1910 there were about 13,000 deaths per year due to measles, 10,000 to whooping cough, and about 6,000 to scarlet fever; preventive measures had to be taken to reduce the spread of these illnesses. Inspection of schools as well as the strict isolation of sick children were important. Most important, it was up to the parents (especially the mother) to undertake preventive measures by checking children for problems, especially during neighborhood outbreaks, by consulting with physicians when appropriate, and by becoming better informed.

The Child's Physical World

In the early 1900s, if a home had two stories then the baby's room was placed in an upper room to provide purer air and a

Johnny Jump Up. (Courtesy of Timothy L. Ledesma)

The Taylor Nursery Baby Bed Company advertised that it had solved the problem of how to care for the newborn. The baby slept in a bed that resembles a modern hospital tray in that it could be swung over the mother's bed so that the baby was in reach all night. A washable safety net stretched over the top of the bed to make sure that the baby couldn't fall from this high perch! If the mother preferred the baby's bed to be beside her own, then the baby bed was adjustable. The company suggested that the baby's bed would be much less stuffy than an ordinary crib. In addition, it took up such little space that it could be used even in small city apartments. In-between babies, it could be folded to fit inside a trunk for easy storage.

FOSTER'S **IDEAL** CRIBS

No worry for mother if baby is left in an Ideal Accident-Proof Crib. High sliding sides, closely spaced spindles, woven wire springs, patented rail fastener (on our cribs only)—guaranteed not to break. Different styles and prices. Enamelled white or colors. Write for booklet, "A Mother's Invention," sent free with name of dealer who sells the cribs.

Foster Bros. Mfg. Co., 105 Broad Street, Utica, N. Y. 1404 N. 16th Street, St. Louis, Mo.

Foster's Cribs. (Ladies Home Journal)

quieter environment. At first the baby would share the mother's room, but even during the newborn period it was suggested that if possible a nursery for the baby be prepared.

The recommendations for the baby's nursery were ones that are common today when children show childhood allergies—a crib would be better than a dust-gathering bassinet and hardwood floors would be much better for the baby than would a carpet. Safety issues were also important to those purchasing cribs in the early 1900s, and some patented cribs offered special protections to prevent baby from getting out (consumers are yet to find an accident-proof crib). The crib industry did adopt voluntary

At times playpens are used as a temporary sleeping arrangement when the family travels. Vinyl pads on the bottom of the playpen need to be inspected before each use to make sure that there are no ripped areas from which the toddler could pull out pieces of the foam padding to ingest. Padded railings keep babies from harsh bumps to the head, but they may also be nibbled on by the babies and so they require inspection, also. The mesh siding of the playpen should be checked to make sure that there are no tears that a little finger could push through only to become entangled. Since babies have become trapped when the drop side of a folding playpen is down, it is important to make sure that the side is kept up when in use.

Babies in the early 1900s could be pacified by means of vestibular stimulation both indoors and outdoors if their parents were to purchase the Combined Baby Jumper and Rocking Chair. Similar to contemporary baby swings, it could be carried out into the yard so that the baby could be comfortable in the healthy air out of doors. In colder weather it kept baby happy inside the home, watching mother pursue her activities. Contemporary parents also know how much babies enjoy the calming rhythm of swings as they watch what is going on in the room. Modern swings often are battery powered and so the soothing motion may continue for quite some time. Usually the A-frame design is used in modern swings. A flat plastic base often helps stabilize modern swings that can accommodate weights up to about twenty-five pounds.

What is the best way to transport a baby when the parents are on the go? Parents in the 1900s still purchased the older style perambulators but also had the option to purchase "Go-Carts" that were more portable. This stroller could be folded for more convenient use. It was designed to withstand the weight of a six-year-old; in fact, it had been tested to tolerate up to 150 pounds! Despite the fact that the Go-Cart manufacturers purchased advertisements on a regular basis in *The Ladies' Home Journal,* an editorial in the 1905 volume presented a negative picture of this new style of stroller.

Combined Baby jumper. (Ladies Home Journal)

Easytake folding go-cart. (Ladies Home Journal)

Keeps the baby clean

free from cold and "out of mischief;" develops handsome, straight legs.

Glascock's Baby Walker

Indispensable when children are learning to walk. Strengthens and develops the legs symmetrically; prevents their growing crooked. In it the baby can sit, stand, jump or walk (springs supporting his weight). Leading physicians urge its use. **Ask your dealer for "Glascock's"** — the standard hygienic walker. If he hasn't it write us and you will be promptly supplied.

GLASCOCK BROS. MFG. CO., 627 West St., Muncie, Ind.

A Great Invention for Infants

Exercises and develops all muscles, overtaxes none. A "Hygienic Nurse" that keeps baby off the floor, safe, contented, and well.

Dr. Martin's Infant Exerciser

Teaches baby how to walk. Relieves mother from all "Baby-Cares." Prevents crooked legs and amuses baby by the hour. Endorsed by Physicians and Mothers everywhere. Your money back if you want it. Buy of your dealer if he has **Dr. Martin's Exerciser.**

Write to-day for illustrated Booklet, FREE.

DR. MARTIN'S INFANT EXERCISER CO., 70 Ingalls Building, Indianapolis, Ind.

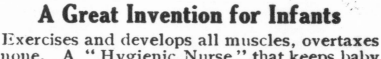

Top: *Glascock's Baby Walker. (Ladies Home Journal)*
Bottom: *Dr. Martin's Infant Exerciser. (Ladies Home Journal)*

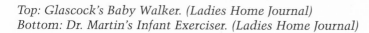

For more than 100 years, advertisers have stressed that "these days women are on the go!" and so convenient ways to travel alone with an infant have been marketed. In 1905, a mother could purchase the "Oriole Go-Basket," which she could attach to her side and thus carry her baby while shopping or visiting, easily able to travel on streetcars and in elevators. Wheels that were "invisible" when the basket was worn by the mother could be lowered so that the mother pushed the child along in the basket. When it was time for a meal the basket was then used as a high chair so that the baby could eat at the table. The Withrow Manufacturing Company advertised that its product was "scientifically correct" and was "endorsed by leading physicians." With a weight of seven pounds, a Go-Basket would be quite a bit heavier than modern baby carriers.

Oriole Go-Basket. (Ladies Home Journal)

standards, yet thousands and thousands of unsafe cribs remained tucked away in homes.

Despite our advances in manufacturing, there are still injuries and fatalities due to faulty baby equipment.

Clothing an infant in the early 1900s involved choosing an appropriate pattern and material. If expense didn't matter, then mothers were recommended to sew long cashmere wool coats for their infants. The coats were made extra large. When the child was old enough for a first short coat, the original baby coat would be cut down to serve this need. In this case, even when the financial aspect didn't matter, clothing was designed to give maximum wear for as long as possible. Many patterns recommended intricate embroidery designs to complete the baby's clothing. Magazines offered ideas and suggestions for home needleworkers to help them knit blankets, bonnets, booties, and wraps for their babies. Color pages were unusual in the 1910 volume of *Ladies' Home Journal,* but the page showing baby clothes was one of the few full-color displays. Bonnets and hats were made by mothers for everyday wear and for special occasions.

Bonnets and hats were made by mothers for everyday wear and for special occasions. When the pattern was described, the mothers were not only given detailed information about the material that should be used; they also were told the occasions for which the bonnet would be suitable! Lest the mother dress the child inappropriately, the bonnet descriptions included statements such as, "A prettily shaped bonnet which is suitable only for nice wear" or "a quaint little bonnet for everyday wear made of blue-and-white checked silk over a capenet foundation."

New products were available to change the way that babies were being diapered. Patterns for silk-rubber diaper protectors were sold so that the baby wouldn't soak through the diaper onto clothing. Families with higher incomes could purchase ready-made Stork Pants that were made from a rubberless, lightweight, waterproof fabric. Each pair of waterproof pants was 50 cents; for the same price a mother could purchase a diaper bag made of the same material in which she could carry the baby's supplies.

Toys, of course, were much different in the early nineteenth century. Between two and three years, the child was old enough to enjoy pretend play involving doll cradles and doll chairs, dollhouses with furniture, and rolling pins and biscuit boards. Picture books of animals, such as birds, cats, dogs, and cows were enjoyed by children of this age. Toy spades, rakes, and hoes, as well as stone blocks, provided outdoor creative fun. Building blocks provided hours of indoor

fun and creativity as a child approaches the third birthday. Fine motor skills were facilitated by providing the child with a wooden case with a small ruler and a pencil inside. Blunt scissors and a box of nonpoisonous watercolor paints were suggested ways to provide enjoyable activities for a young child.

Today, lead poisoning in children is associated with behavioral problems, learning disabilities, hearing problems, and stunted growth. In some of the paint chips from playground equipment, the levels of lead were high enough that a child ingesting a pain chip each day for two weeks to a month could have blood lead levels at or above the 10 microgram-per-deciliter amount considered dangerous for children, especially those six years old and younger. During the early nineteenth century lead-based paint was common, and the potential dangers to children were unknown.

Despite the significant differences that have occurred in the last 100 years—in communication and transportation, manufacturing and work conditions, family relationships and gender roles—there remains a core of similarity that rings true as each generation gives birth to the next: We long that our children attain a joy that fulfills their own lives and the generations to come.

See also Bottle-feeding; Car Seats; Causality Toys; Discipline; Dressing Infants and Toddlers; Employed Mothers; Father; Health and Safety; Parenting; Play

References and further reading
Smut, Robert. 1959. *Women and Work in America.* New York: Columbia University Press.
Walsh, Roger. 1999. *Essential Spirituality.* New York: John Wiley and Sons.
Wood-Allen, Mary. 1905. *What a Young Girl Ought to Know.* Philadelphia: Vir.

Infant Characteristics Questionnaire

The Infant Characteristics Questionnaire (ICQ) is a twenty-four-item measure designed to assess parents' perceptions of temperamental characteristics of the infant that make him/her difficult to care for. The four subscales are fussy/difficult, inadaptable, dull, and unpredictable. Internal reliability averages .72 on the ICQ. Versions of the ICQ exist for infants of different ages (six, thirteen, and twenty-four months) in order to account for developmental changes in children that affect perceptions of difficult behavior. The ICQ has shown longitudinal relations with preschool behavior problems.

See also Assessment

References and further reading
Bates, John E., C. B. Freeland, and M. L. Lounsbury. 1979. "Measurement of Infant Difficultness." *Child Development* 50: 794–803.

Infant Mental Health

Infant mental health is a multidisciplinary field that focuses on the social and emotional development of the infant and the infant's caregivers. Any condition that impacts the infant-family well-being is of concern to infant mental health specialists: premature birth, perinatal complications, inadequate prenatal care, infant mortality and morbidity, physical disability, mental retardation, poverty, supplemental child-care settings, parental psychopathology, parental stress, abusive parenting, parental drug addiction, and marital conflict.

The Maine Association for Infant Mental Health defines infant mental health "as the ability of infants to develop physically, cognitively, and socially in a manner which allows them to master the primary emotional tasks of early childhood

without serious disruption caused by harmful life events." Alicia Leiberman suggests that there are five principles that must be taken into account in infant mental health: (1) Infants are social beings who exist in relationships; (2) individual differences are an integral component of the infant's functioning; (3) environmental context can substantively influence individual functioning; (4) infant mental health practitioners attempt to understand the infant from within, not just by observable behavior; and (5) the practitioner's own feelings and behaviors have an impact on any intervention. Finally, Miguel Hoffman has argued that ethical issues related to development of infant/toddlers are fundamental aspects of infant mental health. Specifically, he draws attention to six types of poverty that are issues for infant mental health scientists, practitioners, and advocates: (1) poverty of subsistence (food and shelter); (2) poverty of protection (bad health systems, violence); (3) poverty of affection (exploitative relationships); (4) poverty of understanding (poor education); (5) poverty of participation (marginalization of women, children, and minorities); and (6) poverty of identity (due to forced migration, exile, or imposed foreign value).

References and further reading
Fitzgerald, Hiram E., and Lauren R. Barton. 2000. "Infant Mental Health: Origins and Emergence of an Interdisciplinary Field." In Joy D. Osofsky and Hiram E. Fitzgerald, eds., *WAIMH Handbook of Infant Mental Health, Vol. 1: Perspectives on Infant Mental Health*. New York: Wiley, pp. 1–36.

Infant Stimulation

Infant stimulation is the act of exposing the infant to environmental stimuli, such

Mother playing peek-a-boo with her delighted eight-month-old baby. (Elizabeth Crews)

as the sights, sounds, smells, and textures of the immediate environment. Infant stimulation plays a big role in infant learning, growth, and development. For instance, talking to an infant stimulates the infant's brain and aids in the development of language. Likewise, infant massage stimulates the brain and promotes neural development as well as emotional development. Yet too much stimulation can be overwhelming to the infant. When overstimulated, infants usually react either by crying and turning away from the stimulus or shutting out the stimulus by falling asleep.

Parent/caregivers also play a role in helping infants manage stimulation. Being aware of infants' behavioral cues helps adults know when infants are becoming overstimulated. Lowering voice tones or stopping talking, turning off the lights and television, and changing the infant's position are all ways to reduce the stimulation of the environment.

Infant Temperament Questionnaire—Revised

A measure of behavioral styles in four- to eight-month-old infants. Each of the ninety-five items is completed by the parent using a six-point scale that ranges from "almost never" to "almost always." The questionnaire takes fifteen to twenty minutes to complete and ten to fifteen minutes to score. The ten subscales are: activity level, rhythmicity, approach, intensity, adaptability, mood, attention span, persistence, distractibility, and threshold to stimulation. Summary scores can be used to classify the infant as difficult, easy, slow-to-warm up, or intermediate (does not fit into one of the other three subcategories). The questionnaire has been shown to be internally consistent and is related to later developmental milestones, cognitive abilities, and behavior problems. It is not recommended as a screening instrument for developmental problems but is useful for evaluating parental concerns about infant behavior styles or sleep problems that may require parents to modify their behaviors.

See also Assessment; Temperament
References and further reading
Carey, W. B., and S. C. McDevitt. 1978. "Revision of the Infant Temperament Questionnaire." *Pediatrics* 61: 735–738.

Infant-Parent Psychotherapy
Infant-parent psychotherapy is a mental health process that assists parents in understanding and nurturing their infant/ toddler within the context of early-developing parent-child relationships. Primary therapeutic tasks include the careful observation of an infant/toddler in interaction with a parent; the experience and exploration of feelings that threaten appropriate and affectionate parental response; questioning that offers a parent the opportunity to wonder, reflect, recall, and understand reactions; supportive listening; the clarification of thoughts and feelings a parent has; and empathic response.

The underlying therapeutic goal is to create a context in which a parent is able to explore the emotional connections between past and present experiences or relationships and to build a relationship with an infant/toddler that is free from

chronic ambivalence, pain, sorrow, anger, or distress. Crucial to the approach is the presence of the infant/toddler to provide a focus and an agenda for parent and therapist. Of equal importance is the therapist's attention and response to emotion as expressed either nonverbally (i.e., in the interaction between parent and infant) or in words. Believing that the developing relationship between parent and child is affected and shaped by present realities as well as past experiences, the infant mental health therapist is a careful observer in the moment and a thoughtful listener to the parent's dialogue. The infant-parent therapist uses what is seen and heard to assist parents in recovering and understanding thoughts about caregiving as well as feelings for the infant/toddler in their care.

Ann Arbor, Michigan, is the birthplace of infant-parent psychotherapy. Pioneers in the practice of infant-parent psychotherapy include Selma Fraiberg, Edna Adelson, and Vivian Shapiro. The original work of these three mental health therapists in the 1970s is described in *Clinical Studies in Infant Mental Health* (1980), edited by Selma Fraiberg. Dedicated to understanding the relationship of the past to present caregiving experiences, Fraiberg, Adelson, and Shapiro defined the practice of infant-parent psychotherapy within the context of a brand-new field: infant mental health. They integrated therapeutic approaches from the separate fields of psychology, social work, education, and psychiatry. They worked with children under the age of two years and their parents within a therapeutic environment that was nurturing and supportive. The intent was to interrupt the cycle of hurtful or neglectful care and to "free parents and their baby from old ghosts that have invaded the nursery." Understanding that each baby develops optimally within the context of at least one nurturing relationship, they offered a comprehensive model of service that would support early development, nurture parents, and reduce the risk of jeopardized relationships between parent and child.

As determined by these early infant mental health therapists, infant-parent psychotherapy was intertwined with other important strategies: concrete and emotional support, and the offering of developmental guidance. One, two, or all of these strategies were identified as appropriate to reduce the risk of emotional disorder or delay in infancy, to enhance parental sensitivity to the infant, and to encourage the development of a healthier attachment relationship in the infant's first years of life. The approach was unique in that the work required the referral of an infant under three years of age and a parent, often overwhelmed and ambivalent about the care of the baby. Of additional significance, the pioneering efforts were carried out by an interdisciplinary group of psychologists, social workers, nurses, and physicians who supported each other in offering support to vulnerable infants and their families. All were devoted to understanding the infant/toddler within the context of troubled parent-infant relationships.

Others contributed to the early development of the field of infant mental health and the practice of infant-parent psychotherapy. Many trained with Fraiberg and her colleagues at the Child Development Program in Ann Arbor in the 1970s. They continued infant mental health work with infants and families through direct services to families, training, consultation, and supervision. They estab-lished infant-parent programs in Michigan, Illinois, and California and provided training and careful supervision in the clinical practice of infant-parent psychotherapy. As the field has grown, others have helped to advance the practice of infant-parent psychotherapy, contributing to the understanding of early and intensive relationship-focused treatment to promote and support infant mental health.

Origins of Parent Psychotherapy
Early observations of children in institutions related the importance of early care to infant development and emotional health. John Bowlby's interest in caregiving and careseeking behaviors in the first year of life led to his development of *attachment theory*, confirming the importance of a young child's early relationship with at least one caregiver. Later work by Mary Ainsworth described the infant's early attachment relationship as *secure* or *insecure* and related those categories to specific maternal caregiving experiences. More recent work deepened the understanding of the adult's attachment classification and the intergenerational transmission of attachment from parent to child. Infant-parent psychotherapy addresses the importance of the *early developing attachment relationship* to an infant's optimal development and mental health by encouraging opportunities for parental reflection about the baby and about the self.

The Psychotherapeutic Process
There are multiple strategies embedded in this psychotherapeutic process. An infant-parent therapist works with an infant/toddler and parents together, often in their own home but also in an office or center-based setting. The presence of the infant is

clearly critical to the practice of infant-parent psychotherapy. The infant/toddler serves as an organizing force or energizing agent that shapes and fuels the psychotherapy. The parent's feelings in the presence of the infant/toddler can be intense and complex, offering the possibility of thoughtful exploration, the expression of emotions related to parenthood, and the containment of emotions related to infant/toddler care. The parent's perceptions and representations of the infant/toddler may be more available in the presence of the infant for therapeutic consideration and response. Aware that the infant/toddler evokes a myriad of thoughts and feelings, the infant-parent therapist observes and listens carefully, continuously aware of opportunities to experience and explore the ambivalent or conflicted feelings that threaten to interrupt the development of a positive and enduring relationship.

Clinical Issues
Major concerns in treatment include early trauma, unresolved loss, attachment relationships that were poor or unfulfilling, parental abandonment, extended or multiple separations from primary caregivers, broken or conflicted family relationships, maternal deprivation or intermittent care, and abuse or neglect leaving physical or emotional scars. These early experiences can gravely affect the parent's capacity to attend to or fall in love with the baby and alter the relationship as it develops in the infant's first years. Infant-parent psychotherapy offers the parent many opportunities to have and express emotions surrounding traumatic experiences, disappointing relationships, and unresolved losses, reducing the high risk of relationship dysfunction in the parent-infant pair.

Clinical Strategies
What unique strategies do therapists use in the practice of infant-parent psychotherapy? Most important, practitioners work with infant and parent together, in home or office settings. They observe infant and parent in interaction with one another, focusing on the details of the baby's development and affirming what the parent is experiencing in the presence of the child. They assess the dynamics of the developing relationship, signs of disturbance or dysfunction, and signs of strength. They share moments of intense emotion as expressed by the parent and young child to one another (e.g., joyfulness, helplessness, ambivalence, anger). They hold and contain feelings that are expressed as well as those for which there are few words.

Practitioners invite reflection and shared understanding of the baby and early parenthood. They listen to stories that parents tell about current struggles and past relationships, traumatic experiences, and unresolved losses. They offer empathetic support to parents and authentic, continuing responses in an effort to protect the infant from the parent's depression or rage. They offer their own relationships as a context for inquiry, discovery, healing, and change. In the process, parents recover their capacity for relationships with their children as they provide more optimal care.

Clinical Outcomes
What are the results of an infant-parent psychotherapeutic intervention? The relationship between parent and practitioner is crucial to the strength and success of the psychotherapeutic process in parent-infant treatment. Parents whose relationship histories are described as dismissing, preoccupied, or unresolved

(i.e., insecure) and are identified as insensitive or inconsistently responsive to their infants are at grave risk for repeating the cycle of relationship failure with the infants. Unsuccessful in entering into and maintaining successful relationships in the past, parents can feel anxious and uncertain about establishing relationships in the present.

The practitioner's interpersonal skills are important factors to successful relationship-building. How a therapist approaches the parent, the tone of voice used, and nonverbal gestures are critical to the process. As the parent experiences sensitive care and empathetic response, he/she grows increasingly trusting of the practitioner. The two enter into a therapeutic relationship that permits the parent to talk about the baby's care and development, early parenthood, and relationships past and present. Within this context of trust the parent and practitioner explore feelings that are crucial to the infant's mental health and thoughts that are related to the parent's capacity to provide appropriate care. This supportive relationship is a most crucial factor if change is to occur within an infant-parent psychotherapeutic service.

The Role of the Infant
The infant, small and dependent on a parent for protection and care, is nonetheless a powerful and essential player in infant-parent psychotherapy. The infant shows the practitioner what life is like in this particular household, what is going well for the family, as well as the risks. The therapist's observation of the infant within a caregiving environment is crucial to understanding emerging capacities as well as disturbances significant to the infant's early care. The infant's presence

also helps the therapist discover who cares for or plays with or responds to the baby.

The infant allows a story to be told. The way in which a parent handles the baby, gestures of care, playful interactions, or the absence of interaction suggest to the therapist what is going well but also what some of the conflicts, as yet unexpressed, might be. The infant-parent therapist pays careful attention to the behaviors and the nonverbal cues that carry complex messages about the baby, the parent, and the context of care.

The infant becomes the object of the transference in infant-parent psychotherapy. The therapist observes and listens carefully in order to reach an understanding of who the baby might represent to the parent (e.g., an abusive uncle, an abandoning mother, a sibling who required attention and care). The infant can also represent the parent as a small child. Faced with the neediness of a very small baby, the parent can feel all over again her own helplessness and reenact, quite unconsciously, neglectful or inconsistent or teasing patterns representative of her own early care. Alert to the struggle, the therapist wonders what other baby may have been neglected or hurt, abandoned or teased. The earlier traumas, and their defensive reactions, may never have been spoken about before. Within the context of the therapeutic relationship, aspects of early care can be more safely reexperienced, feelings attached to them expressed, and memories shared. By separating the past from the present, the therapist helps to protect a parent from repeating a hurtful cycle of care, awakening possibilities for different interactions with her own infant and providing a context for more positive care.

See also Parenting

References and further reading
Cramer, B. 1998. "Mother-Infant Psychotherapy: A Widening Scope in Technique." *Infant Mental Health Journal* 19(2).
Fraiberg, S., E. Adelson, and V. Shapiro. 1975. "Ghosts in the Nursery: A Psychoanalytic Approach to Impaired Infant-Mother Relationships." *Journal of the American Academy of Child Psychiatry* 14: 1387–1422.
Weatherston, D., and B. Tableman. 1989. *Infant Mental Health Services: Supporting Competencies/Reducing Risks.* Lansing: Michigan Department of Mental Health.

Infant-Toddler Developmental Assessment

A comprehensive tool for evaluating children from birth to age three, the Infant-Toddler Developmental Assessment (IDA) is designed to be conducted by a transdisciplinary team and to include parents as partners in all stages of the process. The IDA has six phases: referral and data-gathering before the interview; an initial parent interview to discuss parental concerns and the child's developmental history; a health review of information from parents and medical providers; play observation and assessment; integration of all the information; and intervention planning. A profile is generated that identifies the child's developmental level in eight domains: emotional development, interpersonal relationships, coping, gross motor, fine motor, relationships to inanimate objects, language/communication, and self-help. Evaluation studies and reports from practitioners indicate that IDA is an efficient, cost-effective, and comprehensive assessment tool.

See also Assessment

References and further reading
Provence, S., et al. 1995. *Infant-Toddler Developmental Assessment: IDA.* Chicago: Riverside.

Information-Processing

Investigators who take an information-processing approach to the study of cognitive functioning focus on the mechanisms that regulate coding of information, its storage into memory, and how it is applied.

See also Memory

Intelligence

Various definitions have been offered for the term "intelligence," including an innate capacity, specific abilities, a test score, and the effectiveness with which the individual adapts to his/her environment. More recently, investigators have proposed multiple types of intelligence. For example, Raymund B. Cattell and John Horn distinguished between fluid and crystallized intelligence. *Fluid intelligence* is relatively uninfluenced by experience, whereas *crystallized intelligence* is highly dependent upon experience. Fluid intelligence was proposed to be the substrate for both forms of intelligence because it derived from the *anlage,* or natural, predispositions of the organism. Basic spatial-perceptual processing and memory span are examples of fluid intelligence (the classic notion that memory is limited to seven plus or minus two bits of information).

With development, however, we acquired aids and concepts that enable us to expand the anlage. These experientially acquired helpers, for example, enable us to remember ten-digit telephone sequences by chunking the information

A two-and-a-half year-old working on a puzzle. (Elizabeth Crews)

into smaller memory units. Because crystallized intelligence flows from experience, one would predict that it should continue to grow over much of the life course, whereas fluid intelligence should show rapid early growth and then a leveling-off and decline as the anlage begins to decline. Evidence suggests that fluid intelligence peaks in the early twenties, whereas crystallized intelligence continues to increase until around the midsixties. More recently, Horn has proposed as many as forty primary abilities that compose intelligence. Horn is not the only investigator to propose multiple types of intellectual functioning. For example, Howard Gardner has described seven

dimensions of intelligence: linguistic, logical-mathematical, spatial, musical, bodily-kinesthetic, interpersonal, and intrapersonal. However, none of the traditions represented in the study of mental abilities or intelligence has addressed the infancy period as strongly as Jean Piaget. Individuals who attempt to blend Piaget's theory with information-processing approaches to the development of mental abilities, such as Robbie Case, have made substantive contributions in that regard and hold forth promise of delivering a more integrative understanding of the development of intelligence during the first three years of life.

See also Cognitive Development; Piaget, Jean

References and further reading
Case, Robbie. 1985. *Intellectual Development: Birth to Adulthood.* New York: Academic Press.
Sternberg, Robert J., and Cynthia A. Berg, eds. 1992. *Intellectual Development.* New York: Cambridge University Press.

Intensity of Reaction

A dimension of temperament that refers to the individual differences in intensity or energy level of response. Some infants laugh and cry with strong intensity, whereas others react mildly.

See also Temperament

Intentionality

See Piaget, Jean

Intergenerational Transmission of Insecure Attachment

See Attachment

Internal Models
See Attachment

International Society for Infant Studies
An international society of researchers who meet biennially to exchange information about their studies of infant development. The society is both international and interdisciplinary. The society sponsors the publication of its official journal, *Infancy*.

> **References and further reading**
> ISIS, the Institute for Children, Youth, and Families (website 2001). http://www.isisweb.org.

Interoceptors
Interoceptors are receptors specialized to respond to input from internal stimulation. For instance, the semicircular canals within the ear are interoceptors. They provide proprioceptive information to organisms by signaling movement in the fluid within the canals. This sensitivity to internal fluid changes provides reliable information about the body's orientation and movement to the organism. Other interoceptors respond to sensory information from internal organs, muscles, and blood vessels.

> **See also** Perception; Proprioceptive Information

Intersensory Equivalence
Intersensory equivalence is the condition in which information in one sensory modality is perceived to be the same as information in another modality. For example, an infant is shown visual stimuli and as a result of that experience is able to identify the same stimulus using touch.

Intervention Programs for At-Risk Infants
See Assessment; Early Intervention; Infant Mental Health

Intrasensory Equivalence
Intrasensory equivalence is the condition in which information in one sensory modality is perceived to be equivalent to the same information presented in an altered form.

Intuitive Parenting
See Parenting

Invariant
An *invariant* stage sequence is a sequence that always occurs in the same order, an implicit assumption in Jean Piaget's stage theory of cognitive development.